Amy, 27

Amy, 27

Amy Winehouse and the 27 Club

HOWARD SOUNES

VIKING

VIKING
an imprint of Penguin Canada

Published by the Penguin Group
Penguin Group (Canada), 90 Eglinton Avenue East, Suite 700, Toronto, Ontario, Canada M4P 2Y3

Penguin Group (USA) Inc., 375 Hudson Street, New York, New York 10014, U.S.A.
Penguin Books Ltd, 80 Strand, London WC2R 0RL, England
Penguin Ireland, 25 St Stephen's Green, Dublin 2, Ireland (a division of Penguin Books Ltd)
Penguin Group (Australia), 707 Collins Street, Melbourne, Victoria 3008, Australia
(a division of Pearson Australia Group Pty Ltd)
Penguin Books India Pvt Ltd, 11 Community Centre, Panchsheel Park, New Delhi – 110 017, India
Penguin Group (NZ), 67 Apollo Drive, Rosedale, Auckland 0632, New Zealand
(a division of Pearson New Zealand Ltd)
Penguin Books (South Africa) (Pty) Ltd, 24 Sturdee Avenue, Rosebank, Johannesburg 2196, South Africa

Penguin Books Ltd, Registered Offices: 80 Strand, London WC2R 0RL, England

Published in Viking Canada hardcover by Penguin Group (Canada), 2013. Simultaneously published in Great
Britain by Hodder & Stoughton, 338 Euston Road, London NW1 3BH.

1 2 3 4 5 6 7 8 9 10   (RRD)

Copyright © Howard Sounes, 2013

Manufactured in the U.S.A.

LIBRARY AND ARCHIVES CANADA CATALOGUING IN PUBLICATION

Sounes, Howard, 1965–, author
Amy, 27 / Howard Sounes.

ISBN 978-0-670-06696-4

1. Winehouse, Amy. 2. Singers—England--Biography.
I. Title.

ML420.W767S72 2013   782.42164092   C2013-902148-5

British Library Cataloguing in Publication data available

Visit the Penguin Canada website at **www.penguin.ca**

Special and corporate bulk purchase rates available; please see
www.penguin.ca/corporatesales or call 1-800-810-3104, ext. 2477.

'Now he's gone and joined that stupid club. I told him not to ...'

Kurt Cobain's mother

CONTENTS

Part One: LIFE

Part Two: DEATH

Part One

Life

Midway this way of life we're bound upon,
I woke to find myself in a dark wood,
Where the right road was wholly lost and gone.

Dante

EXIT, GATE 27

You departed from that busy gate, the so-called stupid one.
Eric Erlandson, *Letters to Kurt*

1

It was just after six p.m. on a summer's evening when Amy Winehouse's doctor visited the star at home in London. It was a routine house call, routine in as much as Amy's life had become so troubled in recent years, so precarious, that her doctor visited her at home almost as often as the postman delivered the mail.

Dr Cristina Romete saw at once that Amy had been drinking. She was tipsy and she smelt of booze. The doctor asked when Amy had started again, after two weeks of sobriety. Amy replied, shame-faced, that she didn't know. But her live-in bodyguard, Andrew Morris, said that she had begun on Wednesday. It was now Friday, 22 July 2011.

Doctor and patient proceeded to have a frank conversation, talking together in Amy's light and airy home in Camden Square. Dr Romete asked Amy *why* she had started drinking again. Amy's explanation was that she was 'bored'.

The doctor asked Amy whether she planned to stop drinking. Amy said she didn't know.

Dr Romete reminded Amy of how serious this was. Only two months ago she had warned Amy in writing, the letter copied to her father and her manager, that her habit of binge-drinking was putting her in 'immediate danger of death'. Amy assured her that she did not want to die. There were things she still wanted to do with her life. She didn't give the impression of being suicidal, though her behaviour was evidently reckless and self-destructive.

The doctor tried to persuade Amy to consider therapy, to deal with her alcoholism, as well as her underlying psychological problems. Amy shook her head. She had always resisted psychologists and psychiatrists, fearing that if she let such people into her mind, she would lose touch with the mercurial part of her brain that allowed her to create original work. Dr Romete knew this, and knew her patient to be a stubborn, yet intelligent woman, who always 'wanted to do things her own way'. In her most famous song, 'Rehab', Amy sang about when her family and colleagues first tried to get her into a rehabilitation clinic, to dry out, to which suggestion she gave an emphatic: 'no, no, no.' This simple but memorable repetition of words had become a catchphrase. It was also the story of her life.

After their talk, Dr Romete left the house. She would never see her patient alive again.

Amy had a history of substance abuse and self-destructive behaviour stretching back to when she was a teenager. The serious problems began, however, in 2006, when her album *Back to Black* was released. It won five Grammy awards. As Amy became a star she also became addicted to crack cocaine and heroin. Although she quit hard drugs in 2008, she did so by switching to alcohol. Amy was a small woman, five foot three inches tall and slightly built, but she drank like a sailor on shore leave, drinking herself into a coma in May, and into hospital as a result. Dr Romete wrote her a warning letter after this incident, but Amy didn't take it seriously. She joked that her doctor thought she might be dead soon. And she carried on binge-drinking, getting out of her mind before a show in Belgrade just five weeks previously. Between binges Amy had periods of self-realisation and guilt when she quit the bottle. But when the thirst returned she bought vodka at corner shops in Camden Town, stashing the booze in her room.

Amy was a Londoner who had lived her whole life – all 27 years and ten months, save vacations and tours – in north London. Her various homes from childhood until she died were within a few stops of each other on the London Underground. The Camden Square house was her grandest residence yet, a large Victorian property that had been gutted and refurbished to her taste. The décor was sparse and bright, with black floors and white walls, apart from the base- ment music room, which was red. The ground-floor kitchen was styled like an American diner. A vintage juke box had pride of place in the lounge. A gift from Amy's ex-husband, Blake Fielder-Civil, the juke box, like the marriage, had never worked properly.

Amy shared her home with friends and staff. Andrew Morris, her 'close protection officer', a huge young man of West Indian back- ground, slept in one of the guest rooms upstairs. During the four years he had worked for Amy, Andrew had grown close to the star, like brother and sister. 'She was a diamond person ... not a regular person,' he says fondly. 'She was the sort of person, if you met her once, you would never forget her. She was very honest. If she didn't like you, she'd tell you. If she loved you, she'd tell you.'

Amy's stylist, Naomi Parry, also stayed at the house on occasion, as did a friend named Tyler James, whom Amy had known since drama school. But Naomi and Tyler were away at the time. In fact, after Dr Romete left the house on Friday evening, Amy was home alone, save her minder and her cat, Anthony Jade.

Many of her friends were at a summer music festival. There were other friends whom Amy would once have called upon for company, but was estranged from at the end of her life. Amy was lovable, but demanding. She'd recently lost her temper with two of her band members, and had fallen out with several girlfriends over the years. The drinking didn't help. Lauren Franklin, who had known Amy at school and then drifted apart from her friend, had recently reconnected with her on Skype, and was shocked by the state Amy was in. 'She was terribly drunk,' she says, of the last time they spoke online. 'She had a bottle in her hand. I was, like, "What are you doing?"'

So, for one reason or another, Amy was on her own as the week came to an end. 'Basically, everyone was out,' says her friend Doug Charles-Ridler. 'She *hated* [being alone]. That's why everyone's feeling really guilty.'

Amy's father, Mitch Winehouse, a former London cabbie, was normally around, but he was in New York to perform his nightclub act. Mitch sang saloon-bar standards in the style of Tony Bennett. It was a semi-amateur career he'd revived on the back of Amy's success. He had visited his daughter at home on Thursday, just before his trip to the United States, and found her in an introspective mood, looking at family photographs.

Amy's mother, Janis, who was divorced from her father, had called in at lunchtime on Friday. Janis had multiple sclerosis, which made her seem older than her 56 years, but she was remarkably similar in looks and character to her famous daughter. Both exuded a charming mixture of intelligence, good humour and childlike innocence.

'I love you, Mummy,' Amy said, as Janis left the house.

Janis said that Amy seemed 'weary' at their final meeting, but that wasn't unusual. Her daughter kept rock 'n' roll hours, and she was on medication. For some time now Amy had been taking diazepam for anxiety and Librium to help her cope with alcohol withdrawal. And she had been drinking on top of her medication. Dr Romete had refused to prescribe any more drugs when she discovered that Amy had gone back on the bottle, but autopsy tests revealed traces of Librium in Amy's blood, along with high levels of alcohol.

Although everybody knew about Amy's drink problem, and she admitted to being an alcoholic, nobody seemed able to stop her drinking if and when she wanted to. Some of her nearest and dearest took the view that if Amy wanted 'a little drink' it was up to her because she could handle it. This was a dangerous delusion. 'Even I, to a degree, I must be guilty,' admits her boyfriend, Reg Traviss. '[I] said to her several times, I said, "Look, darling, if you want to have a drink, just have a drink. It's no problem. You can curb it."'

Reg and Amy had been dating for sixteen months, and they had talked about getting married. But Reg didn't live with Amy. He had his own flat in Marylebone and he was often busy with his work, writing and directing feature films. Reg rang Amy from his office in Holborn a little before eight on Friday evening to say he would be over later to see her, and suggesting that he bring a takeaway. 'She had had a drink … I could tell on the phone. She wasn't roaring drunk, but she was a bit tipsy.'

Amy decided not to wait for Reg. She told Andrew Morris that she fancied an Indian takeaway, just like they'd had the previous evening. They placed their order by phone, and when the food was delivered they took their meals up to their respective rooms.

Amy spent most of her time in her bedroom on the top floor of the house. The walls had been knocked through to create an interconnecting suite with a raised ceiling to give a spacious, loft-like feel. Amy's dressing room was at the back, with doors to her bedroom at the front of the house and an *en suite* bathroom in grey marble. Her windows overlooked the front yard, which was protected by a high wall and an iron gate with an intercom. Andrew was punctilious about keeping the gate locked and the house secure. In the past drug dealers and press photographers had swarmed around Amy like flies, and Amy had connived with the dealers to smuggle drugs past her bodyguards. There had been no trouble of that sort at the new house. A court order was in place, keeping the most troublesome *paparazzi* away, Amy was seemingly finished with drugs, and few fans knew her new address.

One fan had shown up during the week, however, an eighteen-year-old girl from Italy. After watching the house for a while she had tried to get into the garden. Andrew intercepted her. Amy asked Andrew to bring the girl to the front door where she gave her an autograph. It was the last she ever signed.

Beyond the gates, on the other side of the street, there was a small park, the green lung of Camden Square. Amy's neighbours were walking their dogs under the trees in the twilight. There were no fans or press outside tonight. Tomorrow there would be hundreds.

Amy flopped onto her bed. She wore a tracksuit for comfort, as she often did at home. She looked around for something to occupy her mind. Andrew Morris heard her upstairs, 'laughing, listening to music and watching TV'. There was terrible news on television from Norway where a fanatic named Anders Behring Breivik had set off a bomb earlier in the day, then gone on a shooting spree, killing dozens of people. This horror would dominate the news until Amy provided a rival sensation the following day.

Filled with nervous energy, Amy banged on a snare drum, part of a drum kit she had in the basement, and fiddled with her mobile phone and laptop. When she was alone, she would typically reach out to friends by text, Skype or Facebook, looking for distraction, desperate for company.

Just after ten o'clock she found some footage on YouTube of a man she used to date and ran downstairs to Andrew's room to tell him to come and look. They spent the next few hours together in her room, watching YouTube.

At around eleven thirty Reg Traviss switched off his computer at work and called Amy to say he was finally ready to come over, but she didn't answer her phone. This wasn't unusual. '[She] just misplaced her phone. Then she would forget where it was, or it would fall down the back of something. She used to do that a fair amount.' Yet Reg had a sense of foreboding. 'I was really alarmed by it.' Still, he stayed in his office, rather than going directly to Camden Square. 'In a weird way there was something preventing me from going there. That's something I can't really go into too much, because I don't want to sound silly. [But] it was like there was something saying, *Get over there. Just go over there.* And I couldn't. I just couldn't. I was literally rocking backwards and forwards going, *I'm going to go there now … No, I won't.* And this went on through the night. And I kept checking the phone. She hadn't called. It was just unreal.'

Around midnight Reg sent Amy a text message asking her to call him. 'What I didn't want to do was go over there if she was asleep. In which case what I would have done is go home first and wait until she'd wake up, which could be at one in the morning, and then go over, [which] we'd do quite a lot. But something was bothering me. And it was bothering me right there and then at the moment. I just sat [in my office] thinking, *What shall I do?* I thought, This is weird. I left a really long message. In the message I actually said, "If I don't hear back from you I'll probably just come over anyway" … That was a weird thing for me to say.' Reg had bought a book he knew Amy would be interested in: a history of Jewish London. He sat in his office and looked through it, hoping she would call. 'She didn't. And she didn't and she didn't. I just thought, this is really, really odd.'

Finally Reg walked into Soho where he had a late-night drink, still checking his phone in case Amy had rung. She hadn't. He hailed a cab. 'I said to the taxi driver, "Camden Square."' On the way to Amy's house he changed his mind and told the driver to take him to Marylebone. When the cab arrived at his flat, he felt he ought to go to Amy's after all. '[I] sat in the taxi outside and I said [to the driver], "You know what? Maybe take me to Camden Square." And he went, "Whatever you want." And I went, "Er, er, er. No, it's all right."' Reg paid the driver and went inside. 'I just can't explain how uneasy I was and how indecisive I was. It was *really*, really strange. It was just one of the weirdest fucking feelings I've had ever.'

Reg put on a DVD of an old TV series and sat watching an episode, still hoping that Amy might ring. For reasons he cannot explain he didn't think to ring the landline of Amy's house or to call Andrew Morris on his mobile. 'I wish I had ...'

Amy watched YouTube with Andrew until two thirty a.m., during which time she either didn't hear Reg's calls and texts or chose to ignore them. In her last few hours Amy looked at pictures of herself online. This was something she didn't do as a rule, but had been doing since her disastrous concert in Belgrade. Later Andrew said that looking at images of herself was the only unusual aspect of Amy's behaviour at the end, though nothing was ever quite normal with Amy. As he said, 'Amy was pretty normal – for Amy.'

By looking at herself online, and studying old family photographs, as she had been doing during the week, Amy revealed a sense of introspection and reflection, as if she was assessing her life. Jim Morrison of the Doors had behaved in a similar way the night before he died in 1971, aged 27.

Finally, Andrew left Amy to her own devices and went downstairs to his bedroom where he watched a film until sometime between three and four in the morning. Up until the point where he fell asleep he could still hear Amy moving about upstairs.

Amy may have dozed off for a while – she tended to catnap – but she was awake at three thirty and had evidently found her phone because she texted a friend, Kristian Marr. 'I'm gonna be here always xx BUT ARE YOU OK? XXX.' Interestingly, she didn't reply to Reg's texts.

Having drunk steadily all day and every day since Wednesday, Amy seemingly drank more when she was alone in her bedroom in the small hours of the morning. At some point she went into her bathroom and threw up in the toilet, possibly on purpose. Amy was a bulimic who drank and ate in binges, then made herself sick.

Finally she kicked off her shoes and lay on her bed, face down on the mattress with the duvet thrown back on a warm night. She was still dressed. Her laptop was open, and nearby were three empty bottles of Smirnoff vodka.

The sun rose shortly after five in London on Saturday, 23 July 2011. It was another glorious summer's day, the sort of day when one wants to be up and about. Andrew went to check on Amy at around ten. He called her name first and knocked at her bedroom door, opening it when she didn't answer. He saw Amy lying on her bed and assumed she was asleep. 'It wasn't unusual for her to sleep late in the morning.' So he left her.

Over in Marylebone, Reg Traviss rose late and went into Soho to get his hair cut and collect a suit from his tailor. He and Amy were due to attend a wedding on Sunday and he wanted to look his best.

Andrew Morris still hadn't heard any sounds from Amy's room by mid-afternoon, 'which seemed strange', so he went back upstairs.

He found Amy lying on the bed exactly as she had been hours before. 'I checked her pulse, but I couldn't find one.' Instinctively Andrew glanced around for evidence of drugs – Amy's old problem – but there was nothing of that sort, just the vodka bottles.

Andrew called an ambulance at three fifty-seven. He said on the phone that he thought his boss had had a heart attack. As he waited for assistance he saw Amy's friend, Tyler James, coming to the gate and let him into the house, telling him not to go upstairs. Minutes later an ambulance crew arrived. 'There was no pulse,' confirmed paramedic Andrew Cable. 'I noticed rigor mortis.' Amy must have been dead for several hours. She was declared so shortly after four o'clock.

Andrew made a round of desperate telephone calls: to Amy's doctor, to Reg Traviss, and to Amy's father in New York. The ambulance service summoned the police. Officers recovered three vodka bottles from Amy's room, two large bottles and a small one. All were empty. Amy may not have drained them all in her final hours, but the autopsy revealed that she had drunk a very large quantity of alcohol.

To appreciate how much alcohol Amy had consumed, drinkers appear tipsy with concentrations of 30–50 milligrams of alcohol per decilitre of blood; the drink-drive limit in the United Kingdom is 80 milligrams per decilitre; drinkers become uncoordinated at 50–150 milligrams; they become slurred, confused and unsteady on their feet at 150–250 milligrams; and they have difficulty in staying awake at 250–400 milligrams. Amy's blood alcohol level was 416 milligrams per decilitre of blood, with still higher readings in her urine and vitreous humour.* A pathologist explained at her inquest that this was a toxic level of alcohol associated with death: enough booze to depress Amy's central nervous system and bring about respiratory arrest, which is what, he said, had probably happened. The coroner recorded a verdict of misadventure, saying that Amy had died 'as a result of alcohol toxicity'.† In short, she drank herself to death.

By the time Reg Traviss arrived at Camden Square, the police had sealed off the house. He would next see his girlfriend in the morgue. The press had started to gather behind the police tape as the news broke:

Amy Winehouse – dead at 27.

2

Amy's life had been so chaotic in recent years that her death was not unexpected. Yet it came as a shock to those who knew her, and it was a major news story around the world.

* The jelly-like substance in the eyeballs.
† Unusually, there were two inquests into Amy Winehouse's death, as will be explained in due course. I refer here to the evidence at the second inquest, held in January 2013, though the verdict was the same as at the first.

The fact that Amy had died at 27 was seized upon by journalists as one of the piquant aspects of the case: she was the latest in a series of iconic music stars whose short, gaudy lives had ended at that particular age, a series of fatalities usually traced back to 1969 when Brian Jones of the Rolling Stones drowned in his swimming-pool. Jimi Hendrix choked to death in a London hotel the following year. Janis Joplin overdosed on heroin three weeks later in Hollywood. Jim Morrison was found dead in his bath in Paris in 1971. Kurt Cobain of Nirvana shot himself at home in Seattle in 1994. All were 27.

When Kurt Cobain died a reporter knocked at the home of his mother, Wendy O'Connor, who remarked ruefully: 'Now he's gone and joined that stupid club. I told him not to join that stupid club.' The term coined by Mrs O'Connor in her grief, encompassing all the stars who had died at 27, was widely quoted in reports of Amy's death seventeen years later. 'Tragic Amy joins rock's 27 Club,' read a typical headline in Britain's *Mail on Sunday*, while the *Washington Post* referred to 'rock 'n' roll's most dangerous number'. There were also references to the 'curse of the 27 Club'. With many of these stories – and in the chatter on television, radio and online – there was an inference that supernatural forces may have driven the musicians to their graves, with some commentators citing an astrological concept known as the Saturn Return as a malign influence; the less excitable said it was just a coincidence.

The 27 Club is, essentially, a media construct based on a coincidence. It is also a flippant, even vulgar term. Nevertheless the phrase is widely used and understood, and these deaths are intriguing. The question is: are there common factors, apart from coincidence, that help explain the death of Amy Winehouse and the five major rock stars who died before her at 27?

Before getting into the detail of these lives it is helpful to know whether the 27 Club deaths are statistically significant. The Big Six, as I shall call them, are not the only pop musicians to have died at 27. There are scores more. Over the years various lists have been published to support a theory that a disproportionately large number of artists have died at this age. To test the theory I compiled a list of 3,463 people who died between 1908 and 2012 having achieved notoriety in popular music. The first date marks the earliest notable 27 death I could find in the modern era, that of ragtime pianist Louis Chauvin (1881–1908); while 2012 is the year I began writing this book. I counted jazz as well as pop and rock musicians, also songwriters, record producers, managers, promoters and other people who achieved fame in the music business, or by connection to it, but excluded classical musicians, who would have enlarged the survey enormously. I tended to focus on Anglophone artists, but included non-English speakers who achieved renown. For simplicity I refer to all these people as musicians (or artists), although, as noted, some were not professional musicians.

The youngest person to die in my cohort of 3,463 artists was fifteen years old. The oldest was 105. It was not uncommon to find artists dying in their twenties, with 29 individuals dying at 25, for instance, and thirty at 26. Confounding my scepticism I found a sudden and dramatic increase to fifty deaths at age 27. The figures then fell back to 32 deaths at 28, 34 at 29 and so on, the numbers not exceeding fifty until middle age. From the early forties deaths rise with age, as one would expect, to a peak in the sixties, before falling again. This is best illustrated by a graph.

Graph Showing a Spike in Music Industry Deaths at 27

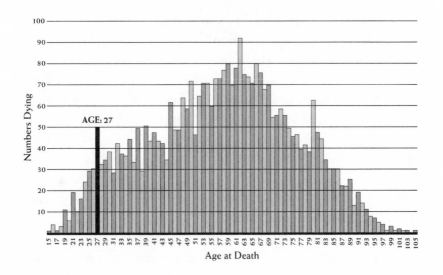

The figures, and the graph, seem to verify the theory that some-thing strange is happening with musicians at 27, but this may be a hasty conclusion. The graph also reveals other spikes: a smaller spike at 21, and substantial spikes at fifty and eighty. Nobody writes about the 80 Club, of course. The death of an octogenarian is no surprise.

It is also true that by looking for members of the 27 Club one is likely to find people who fit the theory. Because this survey was drawn from published sources it relies upon subjective decisions as to the choice of lives worth recording. The attention the 27 Club has received, especially since the advent of the Internet, means that almost every musician who dies at 27 is identified and inducted into the Club; if a musician of equal achievement (or lack of) dies at a different age their death may go unnoticed. As conscientious as I was, checking death certificates to eliminate mistakes, and discounting the most obscure artists who had died at 27, knowing they would pass without mention in normal circumstances, my survey is still probably skewed by what statisticians call the Texas Sharpshooter Fallacy. A Texan who is a bad shot blasts away at the side of his barn, then draws a target around some bullet holes that happen to cluster together, declaring himself to be a sharpshooter.

After Amy Winehouse's death an Australian academic, Professor Adrian Barnett, and colleagues, set out 'to test the 27 Club hypoth-esis that famous musicians are at an increased risk of death at age 27'. Instead of simply listing stars by age of death, as I and others have typically done, Professor Barnett and his associates compiled a list of all the musicians who achieved a number-one album in the United Kingdom between 1956 and 2007, including those still alive. The cohort amounted to 1,046 individuals, only a proportion of whom were 'at risk' at 27 in that they were successful at that age (many didn't achieve success until they were older). Of this lesser number only three had died at 27, a virtually identical rate to ages 25 and 32 in this survey. 'There was no peak in risk around age 27,' the statisticians concluded, adding that the 27 Club 'has been created by chance and cherry picking'.

There are shortcomings to the Australian research. The sample of musicians is narrow, excluding some of the most famous 27 Club artists because they didn't happen to have a number-one album in the UK between 1956 and 2007 (Hendrix, Joplin and the Doors didn't, surprisingly). Yet the survey does give an idea of the *risk* of death at 27, which most 27 Club lists don't, and the risk is apparently normal. This is borne out by a look at the hundreds of artists inducted into the Rock 'n' Roll Hall of Fame over the years, living and dead, only eight of whom have so far died at 27.*

Nevertheless, six of the biggest names in popular music died at that age, along with another 44 individuals (listed in the Appendix). The fact that a cluster of very big names died at 27, at the height of their fame, is what makes the 27 Club the phenomenon it is. While the fact that they all died at this particular age is undeniably coincidental, there are fascinating common factors that help explain why they all died young.

In the first place rock stars tend to die younger than the general population. In 2007 academics at Liverpool John Moores University made a survey of pop stars who had enjoyed success with an album rated as one of the all-time top 1,000 pop albums (based on a book by musicologist Colin Larkin). In the 25 years following initial success, those musicians were two to three times more likely to die than the general population. Drugs and alcohol were associated with more than a quarter of the deaths, which is crucial to understanding the 27 Club, but not the whole story.

Looking at my long-list of fifty artists who died at 27 only five (ten per cent) died of natural causes while drink and/or drugs played a part in eighteen deaths (36 per cent), nine of which were from straightforward drug overdoses. Amy Winehouse was one of four who drank themselves to death, while a combination of drink and drugs did for four more, including Brian Jones, Jimi Hendrix and, probably, Jim Morrison. Drugs were also significant in Kurt Cobain's death. Death was seemingly accidental in every case, except Cobain's. But some deaths are more accidental than others.

The most straightforward types of accident account for the second

* Dave Alexander of the Stooges, Jimi Hendrix, Robert Johnson, Brian Jones, Janis Joplin, Rudy Lewis of the Drifters, Ron 'Pigpen' McKernan of the Grateful Dead and Jim Morrison.

largest number of deaths, fifteen members of the 27 Club (thirty per cent), most of whom died in road accidents. Travel is part of the professional musician's life and travel is hazardous. It is likely that some of those fatalities were under the influence at the time; others were the victim of other drivers' carelessness, or bad luck. There are also less common accidents: two musicians – organist Wally Yohn and singer Maria Serrano Serrano – died in plane crashes, and Roger Lee Durham of Bloodstone was thrown from a horse. Eight 27s were murdered, a high proportion being gunshot homicides of African-Americans, such as Randy 'Stretch' Walker of Live Squad, whose tunes included 'Murderah', and the rapper Raymond 'Freaky Tah' Rodgers. The bluesman Robert Johnson was also probably murdered when he died at 27 in 1938, apparently poisoned by a cuckolded husband. The high proportion of homicides among black American stars is in line with evidence that young African-American males are more likely than their white and female contemporaries to be involved in such violent deaths.

Kurt Cobain is one of five Club suicides. He shot himself after taking a massive overdose of heroin. Even though the evidence that Cobain took his life is clear and strong, some refuse to believe it. Kurt's grandfather Leland Cobain argues in this book that his grandson was murdered as part of a conspiracy. Likewise friends and fans of Brian Jones say that he cannot have drowned by accident because he was too good a swimmer: he must have been held under the water. There are those who see hidden hands in the death of Jim Morrison, too. Throughout the story of the 27 Club there is reluctance on the part of family members, friends and fans to accept that such talented young people died in wretched and often banal circumstances. To suggest that they died because of their own foolishness is taken as an insult. It is even more egregious to suggest that they wanted to die.

Suicide is a taboo that offends and upsets people. It is widely denounced by religious leaders and has been treated as a criminal offence in many countries, including the United Kingdom where, until the Suicide Act of 1961, a Briton who attempted and failed to take their own life faced the additional misery of prison. Most people prefer to ignore this melancholy subject and look on the sunny side of life, devoting their energies to what Sigmund Freud called the 'pleasure principle'. Yet Freud observed that 'the death instinct' is a counter-force to the pleasure principle, with human beings prone to destructive instincts, including suicide, which is more prevalent than one might think. A million people take their lives each year, according to the World Health Organization, making it the world's fourteenth most common cause of death. The true figure may well be higher, because suicide is under-reported. Not all suicides leave notes to explain their intentions, and in the absence of clear evidence of the deceased's state of mind, the authorities tend to record verdicts of accidental death or misadventure.

Several of the artists on the 27 Club long-list who met apparently accidental, drug-related deaths may have intended to die. For example, the death certificate of Al Wilson, of Canned Heat, records that he died of an accidental drug overdose in 1970. But Wilson had a history of suicidal behaviour, including suicide attempts, and at least one band member believes that he meant to take his life. There are likewise those who believe that Pamela Courson overdosed deliberately in 1974 so that she would die at the same age as her boyfriend, Jim Morrison, though her death certificate records an accidental overdose. It is also true that people rarely gas themselves in cars by accident, as the German musician Helmut Köllen apparently did in 1977; neither, generally, do they plunge to their deaths from high buildings by mistake, as the Russian singer Sasha Bashlachev reportedly did in 1988.

In this book I argue that all six principal members of the 27 Club can be said to have killed themselves, though they didn't all do so as directly as Kurt Cobain when he shot himself. For the drug addict and the chronic alcoholic, the decision to be or not to be is drawn out over years, during which life becomes more tenuous to the point where death is likely, if not inevitable. Like all heroin users, Janis Joplin had several friends who died of overdoses. She had survived overdoses herself, knowing that she might not be so lucky next time. Yet she continued to use heroin until she overdosed and died. She may not have meant to die when she shot up for the last time, but if a drug addict or an alcoholic continues to indulge in negative behaviour in spite of the known risks they are, to some extent, 'the author of [their] own end', as Émile Durkheim wrote in his renowned study of suicide.

Durkheim noted that suicide is not a fixed concept. People define the word in different ways. In *On Suicide*, he concluded that the best definition is 'the term applied to any case of death resulting directly or indirectly from a positive or negative act, carried out by the victim himself, which he is aware would produce this result'. Amy Winehouse's decision to continue drinking after being warned by her doctor that this might result in death was a 'negative act', by Durkheim's definition, closely related to suicide, if not 'a fully realised' suicide, because Amy may not have meant to die at that moment. Indeed her doctor and the coroner at her inquest stressed that she did not seem suicidal. As with most of the 27 Club deaths (aside from Cobain's: he wrote a note), it is of course impossible to know what was in her mind at the end. This is the enigma of many sudden deaths. It is, however, plain that many of these artists, Amy included, were reckless and self-destructive over a period of years to the point of virtually throwing their lives away. And most were profoundly troubled in other ways.

Everybody knows that Brian Jones, Jimi Hendrix, Janis Joplin, Jim Morrison, Kurt Cobain and Amy Winehouse used drink and drugs to excess. They were notorious for it. Why they behaved like this, what it was about them as people that made them self-destructive, is what this book is about.

Apart from the headline coincidence of dying at the same age, the Big Six were all intelligent and talented people. Most were also psychologically flawed and, in many cases, they had personality disorders, bordering on mental illness. The roots and early shoots of such problems are often found in childhood. Despite appearing confident, many were dogged by low self-esteem. The business they went into is conducted at entry level in bars, where drink and drugs are part of the culture, and they developed bad habits when very young. All achieved fame in a giddy rush in their early twenties, getting high to celebrate success, conquer stage fright, beguile *longueurs* and overcome self-doubt. They tended to pair up with lovers who shared their frailties, while being surrounded by professional exploiters in a business that fetishises dissolute young rebels. Bored of past achievements, but unsure of their future, these fragile people got into the habit of getting high until they couldn't control themselves. With all six there is a sense that they were weary of life by the end – not all the time, perhaps: even the condemned man will joke with his jailer. But behind the brave talk they'd had enough.

That all these stars died at 27 is a coincidence. Living accelerated lives, they wore themselves out that fast. But behind the coincidence is a common narrative that helps explain why Jones, Hendrix, Joplin, Morrison, Cobain and Winehouse exited life through Departure Gate 27, what Kurt Cobain's friend Eric Erlandson describes as 'that busy gate, the so-called *stupid* one'. Comparing their stories illuminates their individual fates, and helps explain Amy's death in particular.

One

THE YOUNG DIONYSIANS

The god Dionysus or Bacchus is best known to us as a
personification of the vine and of the exhilaration produced
by the juice of the grape. His ecstatic worship, characterised
by wild dances, thrilling music, and tipsy excess, appears to
have originated among the rude tribes of Thrace, who were
notoriously addicted to drunkenness.
James George Frazer, *The Golden Bough*

1

Start at the beginning. If the 27s abused themselves because they
were unhappy, which we shall see is generally true, when did unhap-
piness begin? The poets answer the question with universal truths.
William Wordsworth wrote that 'the child is father of the man'.
Philip Larkin added that it's our parents who fuck us up. 'They may
not mean to, but they do.' The wisdom of these observations is borne
out in the lives of the six principal 27s.

Let's take them in order of demise, starting with Brian Jones.
Despite his talent and achievements, history has not been kind to
Brian. He founded the Rolling Stones. He was a key part of the
band's look and sound in the early years of its success, and precious
few bands have been more successful. Yet if Brian is remembered at
all, it is as a casualty of rock 'n' roll – a weak, foolish and unpleasant
person who could not cope with fame. He left the Stones by mutual

agreement in 1969, dying a few weeks later in a drowning incident that remains controversial. The Stones went on to greater success without him, as if to prove he was never that important. When his former band mates speak of Brian it is often with pity, even contempt. To Keith Richards, Brian was 'an asshole'. Yet there are those who remember him fondly.

Brian was born on 28 February 1942, the eldest child of Lewis and Louisa Jones, with two younger sisters, Barbara, four years his junior, and Pamela, who died in infancy. Dad was an engineer, an upright, church-going Welshman, who settled with his wife and family in Cheltenham, one of the most genteel towns in the west of England, where Brian attended Cheltenham Grammar School. As a result of this background, and that he was the best-spoken Rolling Stone – his voice had the self-consciously refined quality people of his background then typically adopted in public and on the telephone – he is often thought of as the most middle-class Stone. In fact, Mick Jagger was from a similar background.

Brian grew up in a semi-detached house at Hatherley Road, Cheltenham, where neighbours remember Mr and Mrs Jones as reserved. 'Mum and Dad were very private, they didn't chat to the neighbours or anything. If you saw them walking down the road they'd say good morning, or good afternoon, but that was about all,' recalls neighbour Marlene Cole. Brian later complained that his parents were overly strict, and didn't give him enough love.

Several of the 27s showed signs of mood or personality disorders from an early age, conditions that border on mental illness. Brian was one. '[Brian] was bipolar,' asserts Linda Lawrence, who had a child with Brian in the 1960s, later marrying the singer Donovan Leitch.* The term 'bipolar disorder' has come to replace 'manic-depression', though the older term is helpfully self-descriptive. Generally, the sufferer experiences mood swings, from mania, where they become over-excited, to depression. Creative people are often bipolar, and the disorder is found in many members of the 27 Club. 'The parents thought he was just a bad child,' says Linda. 'He was

---

* For clarity Linda Lawrence is referred to throughout by her maiden name.

a sick human being that needed comfort and love.' Brian also suffered from asthma. Linda says that a return visit to Cheltenham in adult life was so stressful to Brian that it would trigger an attack.

In common with all the principal 27s, Brian was intelligent. He also had a marked musical talent, which was not true of them all. His was a musical home, with Dad playing the organ and Mum giving piano lessons to local children. Unlike many rock musicians, Brian learned to read and write music, and he played a variety of instruments to a high standard, including the piano, clarinet, saxophone and guitar. 'He could pick up any instrument, particularly stringed instruments, and find his way around them,' recalls Peter 'Buck' Jones (no relation), who played with Brian in a local band. 'He just lived for music.'

Unfortunately, Brian's taste in music created conflict with his parents. As a teenager, he developed a passion for the blues, teaching himself slide guitar and harmonica in emulation of his American heroes. '[Brian's father] thought it was the Devil's music,' says his friend Richard Hattrell. As Brian became more interested in the blues, he started to neglect his school work, which caused further friction. 'Up to a certain point Brian was a perfectly normal, contented little boy, who behaved well and was well liked,' Lewis Jones said of his son. 'Then there came this peculiar change in his early teens ... He seemed to have firstly a mild rebellion against authority, which unfortunately became stronger as he grew older. It was a rebellion against parental authority, and it was certainly a rebellion against school authority.'

Sex was a factor. Brian was a handsome lad, with a mop of blond hair, athletic enough to work as a lifeguard at Cheltenham Lido during his summer holidays. He had an eye for girls, especially young girls, whom he could impress, and they liked him. It was not only his appearance: Brian had a sensitivity that endeared him to the opposite sex, though girlfriends soon discovered that he was jealous, violent, promiscuous and irresponsible.

While studying for his A levels, Brian dated a fourteen-year-old schoolgirl, who became pregnant with their child, to the consternation of their families. Arrangements were made for the baby to be adopted while the lovers finished their education. As soon as Brian completed his exams, he was packed off to London to train as an optometrist. He lasted two weeks in the capital before returning home. His parents next sent him to live with a family in Germany. He soon returned to Cheltenham where he took a series of unskilled jobs that fell short of his parents' expectations, working briefly in a record shop, a factory, as a bus conductor and as a coalman. In the evenings Brian haunted local jazz clubs and dance halls, getting onstage to play guitar whenever he could. '[He] was not terribly likeable, because he was constantly wanting to play with people who may not have wanted to play with him,' remembers Declan Connolly, who ran one club. 'He was [a] bit pushy.'

A fling with a married woman resulted in Brian's second illegitimate baby while he was still a teenager. As with the first, he played no part in the child's upbringing. Then he met Pat Andrews, a fifteen-year-old sales assistant at Boots in Cheltenham, on a blind date at the Aztec Coffee Bar. 'I walked into this room and there was this angel [with] beautiful golden hair,' recalls Pat, who fell in love. 'He was so charming, well-spoken, so articulate and knowledgeable.' Pat got the impression that Mrs Jones didn't think her good enough for her son, and that Brian wasn't loved at home, not like Pat loved him. 'I think Brian was looking for love,' she says. 'The one thing [Brian] wanted was for his father – more so than his mother – to say, "Brian, I'm proud of you. Well done."' From their point of view, of course, Mr and Mrs Jones were doing their best to raise respectable children, and Brian wouldn't conform. He had squandered his education and showed no interest in establishing a conventional career, wasting time on what his parents considered dead-end jobs and vulgar music. Worst of all, their teenage son had already fathered two illegitimate children by two women, and now he was knocking about with another silly girl. It wouldn't be long before Pat was pregnant, too.

Brian's conflict with his parents reached breaking point at Christmas 1960. After work on 22 December, he brought Pat home to Hatherley Road, planning to go out later to celebrate her sixteenth birthday. The teenagers found the house empty, the lights off, and Brian's suitcase in the drive. His parents had thrown him out.

2

Brian Jones's childhood problems pale in comparison to those of Jimi Hendrix, whose family was poor and dysfunctional. Jimi – named Johnny Allen Hendrix at birth – was born in Seattle, in the state of Washington, on 27 November 1942. Like many African-Americans, his racial history was complex, his ancestors including African slaves, white slave owners and Cherokee Indians. His father, Al, had grown up in Vancouver, before moving to Seattle, sometimes named the Emerald City for its verdancy, derived from abundant rainfall. At a time when much of America was segregated, Seattle had a reputation as a relatively integrated city.

Just before he was drafted for the Second World War, Al Hendrix had a relationship with a teenager named Lucille Jeter, which resulted in her becoming pregnant. Al and Lucille married in haste before Al went away. He didn't see his son until he came back to Seattle after the war, by which time Jimi was three years old. The marriage was fractious. Al suspected Lucille had been unfaithful to him and threatened to divorce her, but they stayed together for a further six years. During this time, Lucille gave birth to five more children: Leon, Joe, Kathy, Pamela and Alfred. The last four were born with health problems, probably linked to poverty, and were given up for foster care. In later life, Al denied that he was their father. The only child he seemed to want to claim as his own was the one who became famous.

Al and Lucille eventually divorced in 1951 when Jimi was nine, around the same age as Kurt Cobain and Amy Winehouse when their parents broke up. It is established that parental break-up can be a traumatic event in the life of a child, with consequences for their behaviour and mental health. Al and Lucille still saw something of each other, but increasingly Al lived alone with his eldest sons, Jimi and Leon, calling on relations, neighbours and friends to help raise the boys. The male Hendrix family moved frequently, living in cheap apartments and shack houses, mostly in the Central District of Seattle, where Jimi received his schooling and made friends, having dirt-bomb fights, acting out scenes from *Flash Gordon* and playing cowboys and Indians. 'Jimi is part Cherokee, so we wanted him to be the Indian,' remembers elementary-school buddy Sammy Drain.

Friends came to know a shy boy with artistic talent, a passion for music and an eccentric wardrobe. In adult life, Jimi was renowned for his individual clothing. He started dressing unconventionally by necessity, wearing cast-offs because his father didn't have the money to clothe his sons properly, though he did find the money to drink. Al worked as a gardener, and after a hard day mowing lawns, he relaxed with alcohol. 'His daddy drank a lot ... he was a lush,' says Sammy Drain. 'He was a drunk ... a wine drunk,' says another friend, Pernell Alexander. 'His dad would never buy [Jimi] anything.' A third friend recalls that Jimi's father also had a bad temper: 'I was scared of Mr Hendrix,' says Anthony Atherton, who met Jimi at Washington Junior High and stayed friends with him into adult life. 'After he'd get home from work, he was pretty tired, and he had a pretty short fuse, and alcohol didn't do him any justice.'

Jimi's friends tended not to visit Jimi at home because of his father's drinking and temper, and when they did call round they rarely saw Jimi's mother. A drinker herself, Lucille Hendrix collapsed in an alley behind a bar and died of a ruptured spleen in 1958, when Jimi was fifteen. Al did not attend the funeral. Neither did his sons. 'We both wanted to go,' Leon told Hendrix biographer Charles R. Cross, 'but Dad wouldn't let us.'

Jimi's interest in music started young, and became his obsession. Initially he pretended to play guitar on a broomstick, mimicking guitar sounds. 'He was just going around the darn streets playing on this broomstick,' chuckles Atherton. 'People thought he was crazy.' At the time Al and the boys were living in a boarding-house, whose landlord had a battered acoustic guitar for sale. When Al refused to buy the guitar for Jimi, a family friend gave him the money. The instrument was a wreck, with only one string, but Jimi coaxed music out of it, playing left-handed. Al tried to make his son use his right hand, with the result that Jimi learned both ways.

Whatever his shortcomings as a father, Al bought Jimi his first electric guitar when he was sixteen, a right-handed instrument that he restrung. Jimi took his guitar everywhere, carrying it in a bag because he didn't own a case. Neither did he have an amplifier. He went to Pernell Alexander's house to plug in and play. Jimi's obsession with music brought him into conflict with his father who wanted him to help with his gardening work. Jimi wasn't much interested in gardening, and feared his father would confiscate his guitar as a punishment. He asked friends to look after it. '[He] was afraid his father would destroy it,' says Anthony Atherton, who formed a jazz combo with Jimi and Pernell, the Velvetones. Unlike his friends, Jimi's musical passion was for what the boys called 'rotgut blues', the Delta blues of Robert Johnson and others, the same music that had caught Brian Jones's ear half a world away in Cheltenham, England. Jimi learned guitar licks from a local musician named Randy 'Butch' Snipes, whom friends also credit with teaching him such stage tricks as playing his guitar behind his back and with his teeth. As with Brian Jones, the guitar had come to dominate and define Jimi's young life. 'He always said he was going to be the world's greatest guitar player, and no one ever really took him seriously,' says Anthony Atherton. 'But he did.'

Jimi dropped out of Garfield High School in 1960, at a time when he was increasingly at loggerheads with his father. Anthony Atherton says Jimi decided to join the military to get away from the old man: 'He just couldn't tolerate his father any longer.' The boys went to the USAF recruiting centre in Seattle, hoping to sign up for pilot training, but failed the physical. 'They said the G-force of flying a plane would be a little too much [for us],' says Atherton, who later concluded that racism was probably the real reason they were rejected.

Shortly after this, in May 1961, Jimi was arrested for stealing a car and jailed overnight. No sooner had he got out than he stole a second car. The judge agreed to a suspended sentence on the proviso that Jimi enrol in the military. He signed up for the 101st Airborne. If they wouldn't let him fly planes, he would learn how to parachute out of them. So it was that Jimi Hendrix left his unhappy home in Seattle.

3

In many ways, Janis Joplin is the 27 Club member most like Amy Winehouse. Apart from the fact that both were female stars in a male-dominated industry, they were highly intelligent, articulate, quick-witted, well-read women with a lust for life; they loved to sing, joke, have sex and get high; they were also outspoken and flamboyant, with a unique sense of style. Yet Janis and Amy were profoundly insecure.

Born on 19 January 1943, Janis was the first child of Dorothy and Seth Joplin. She had two younger siblings, Laura and Michael. The family lived in Port Arthur, Texas, an oil town twenty miles inland from the Gulf of Mexico. Seth Joplin worked for Texaco. In her biography of her sister, *Love, Janis*, Laura Joplin describes a happy, stable, middle-class home, in which 'Janis was a bright, precocious child with a winning smile'. But Janis's adolescence was blighted by severe acne and, despite her cleverness and wit, she was ranked down the scale of teen popularity in Port Arthur because of her complexion, plain face and inelegant figure, which hurt. In interviews Janis gave the impression that her childhood had been a humiliation, complaining to the chat-show host Dick Cavett: 'They laughed me out of class, out of town, and out of the state, man.' She may have been self-dramatising: in her book, Laura Joplin recalls that Janis had many friends at high school, including a nice-looking boyfriend. This may be so. But it is Janis's perception that is important and, as with other 27s, she seemed to have had a distorted vision of herself, as if seeing herself in a fairground mirror.

On the surface Janis's background was conservative and predictable, which is true of Amy Winehouse's, though there were hidden tensions. Neither girl was raised in the epicentre of a great city, nor had parents of particular achievement, ambition or sophistication, though there was a modest degree of creative flair in both families. By background, Janis might have been expected to become a housewife and mother, sharing the values of her parents. Yet she made herself extraordinary, becoming a Bohemian who lived without regard for convention, moreover a white girl who sang the blues with as much heart as Bessie Smith.

Janis found inspiration for the person she became in literature as well as music. 'Janis always said, "I'm a beatnik,"' notes her friend and road manager John Byrne Cooke. Jack Kerouac's *On the Road*, published when Janis was fourteen, had a powerful influence on her, as it did on many contemporaries who went on to be music stars. Janis was enthused by the lust for life Kerouac captures in his novel, and his romantic vision of America, 'all that raw land that rolls in one unbelievable huge bulge over to the West Coast, and all that road going, all the people dreaming in the immensity of it …'

Beatnik themes of travel, exploration and experience were also part of the folk-music revival of the late 1950s/early 1960s, and Janis was a folk singer before she became a rock vocalist. It was from singing a song made famous by Odetta that Janis discovered she had a voice. Like all the great singers, Janis sounded as if she meant what she sang. Singing was not so much a performance as an expression of her inner self.

She began to seek out and embrace all kinds of experiences, including drunkenness. The characters Janis read about in novels typically drank (apart from the beats, she was taken with F. Scott Fitzgerald); and most of the adults she knew drank. Indeed, there may have been a problem in the Joplin family. Musician Sam Andrew, who was close to Janis throughout her career, came to understand that Seth Joplin was an alcoholic, though he managed to conceal and control it. 'Janis's father was a drinker. There may be some connection – maybe it was chemical.'

Janis's increasingly rebellious lifestyle led to run-ins with the police, which is typical of the 27s. The first incident came when she was on a double date with some boys who threw fire crackers from their car. Not long after this, she went on a joy ride to New Orleans with older boys and was stopped by police. Because of Janis's age, the young men she was with were technically in breach of the Mann Act, which prohibits taking underage girls across state lines. Janis was sent home in disgrace. But she had caught the travel bug. A dissipated trip to Houston followed. '[I] took a lot of pills, drank huge quantities of wine and flipped out,' she wrote of the adventure, adding that she was sent home and 'put in the hospital'. Janis's anxious parents also sent her to a counsellor, one of several mental-health experts Janis would consult over the next few years.

After graduating from high school, Janis enrolled at college in Beaumont, Texas, dropping out after one semester to take a clerical job. When she tired of it, she went to work in Los Angeles where she fell in with some 'big-league junkies'. By 1962 she was back in Texas, at the University of Texas at Austin, majoring in art. Janis sang with a student folk group, the Waller Creek Boys. She dated a member of the band, and fell pregnant, but lost the child. Her sex life had become promiscuous and varied, with lesbian as well as male lovers, and she was experimenting with drugs as well as drink in the beatnik spirit of wanting to imbibe experience. Janis became one of the biggest personalities on campus, a larger-than-life character who revelled in attention. Yet, paradoxically, she was easily hurt. Some friends say Janis laughed when her fellow students nominated her for the annual Ugly Man competition. Others say she cried.

Janis decided she'd had enough of Austin, and Texas. She wanted to explore America. 'I figured it out,' she said. 'Got to get outa Texas ... Soon as I get outa Texas everything's gonna be OK.' In January 1962 she dropped out of university and hitch-hiked to San Francisco, the destination of Kerouac's characters in *On the Road* as they race across the continent in search of kicks, and themselves.

4

Uniquely among the 27s, words were more important than music to Jim Morrison. The intellectual of the Big Six, Jim was a voracious reader who aspired to be a poet before he became the front man of the Doors. He was trying to return to the life of a writer when he died.

James Douglas Morrison was born in Melbourne, Florida, on 8 December 1943, making him slightly younger than Jones, Hendrix and Joplin, though their careers overlapped. His parents were Steve and Clara Morrison, and he had two younger siblings, Anne and Andy. Steve Morrison was a naval pilot who rose through the ranks to become the captain of an aircraft carrier when Jim was in college, ultimately achieving the exalted rank of rear admiral. When Jim was young, though, his father was, of course, more junior, and the family lived relatively modestly, moving frequently as Dad was posted to various bases. 'We didn't have any set home,' says Andy Morrison, who quashes speculation that this itinerant life made Jim wayward. On the contrary, he says the Morrison kids enjoyed travelling. 'It never bothered us. It teaches you to be outgoing.'

With the words of Wordsworth and Larkin in mind, Jim's relationship with his parents is particularly interesting. Jim wrote and sang about wanting to kill his father and have sex with his mother in the Oedipal section of 'The End'. Even if this was purely a work of the imagination, the biographical background is striking. Jim severed contact with his family when he was on the brink of fame, telling his publicist that his parents were dead. When it emerged that both parents were alive, and they wanted to see their son, Jim snubbed them. In a 1969 interview, he explained that he originally told people his parents were dead 'as some kind of joke', but he confirmed that he had no contact with them. His younger brother – whom he still saw – suggests that Jim may have been embarrassed, as a rock star at the time of the Vietnam War, to have a father of high rank in the military. Even so, it is remarkable that Jim declined to receive his mother when she came backstage at a Doors show, and refused to take her calls. Jim's former manager, Asher Dann, believes Jim hated his parents. Evidently something had gone wrong in his childhood.

The Morrison children were brought up to be as tough and self-sufficient as their parents. Andy Morrison describes their navy mom as a no-nonsense woman with 'a hard streak'. If one of the children was in a bad mood and sulked, the whole family would turn on them, 'like a pack of dogs', teasing them mercilessly. 'It helped you for life in the future, anyway, it toughed you up.' Andy recalls Dad as 'real easy-going', so long as the children abided by his rules, but concedes that Admiral Morrison may have been stricter with his first-born – and, indeed, Jim later complained about the discipline.

At the same time he was the apple of his father's eye, according to his brother, who notes that after Jim died Steve Morrison would make the touching subconscious error of addressing him as 'Jim'.

Along with the fact that Jim was raised in an atmosphere of military discipline and high expectations, it is surely significant that his father was away at sea for up to nine months of the year. This meant that Jim became 'the little man around the house', as Andy Morrison observes. 'So he and my mother – I'm not getting into the song "The End" or anything. There was nothing sexual, *as far as I know* – but they had a different kind of relationship.' Jim and his mother had the domestic arguments of a couple. 'I didn't know you wrestled with your mother,' observes Andy, of one fight he witnessed.

Although the Morrisons moved frequently, they lived within a community of naval families, Steve and Clara socialising with fellow officers and their wives. At boozy weekend house parties, Steve Morrison restricted himself to two gins and tonic. But Clara drank to excess. 'She drank too much when he was at sea,' says Andy, emphasising that this became most noticeable after his father had made admiral. 'She'd have the captain's wife and the commander's wife [over to the house]. All the girls in the unit were like a bunch of hens, and they'd get together at night. I'd come home at one in the morning and they're still sitting around in the living room drinking. When Dad got home, he put a stop to that.' Like their mother, Jim and Andy were heavy drinkers in adult life.

The family considered Jim a borderline genius. He read widely, interested in history, philosophy, literary fiction and poetry, including the work of Baudelaire, Rimbaud and the beat writers. Like Janis Joplin, Jim saw his yearning for experience expressed in *On the Road*, and affected a beatnik look and habits as a teenager, wearing shabby clothes and acquiring bongo drums, which he played in his basement den. He also took piano lessons briefly, but never learned to play an instrument with proficiency. Words were what excited Jim, writing rather than singing them. 'I never did any singing,' he told *Rolling Stone*, looking back on his youth. 'I never even conceived it. I thought I was going to be a writer or a sociologist, maybe write plays.' Anne expected her brother to become a poet 'and be poor all his life'.

As an example of his intellectual interests, she notes that when he graduated from high school in 1961 he asked his parents for the complete works of Friedrich Nietzsche as a reward, which says something about the sort of boy he was and offers a key to understanding the performer he became.

As a young man, Jim was enthused by *The Birth of Tragedy*, published when Nietzsche was 27, an exploration of Greek tragedy via the idea that there were two primal forces in Greek art: the Apollonians, who, like the god Apollo, were orderly and rational; and the Dionysians, who, like Dionysus (also known as Bacchus), were transgressive. Nietzsche suggested that great art was created in the conflict between those forces, which are archetypes. In mythology, Dionysus is the son of Zeus, the product of a liaison with a mortal. Zeus's jealous wife persecuted Dionysus, causing him to wander the world accompanied by frenzied worshipping women known as Maenads. Dionysus is the god of wine. He is sometimes depicted as a handsome young man, but also as an older bearded man with a drink, and is associated with both drunkenness and licentiousness. The relevance to the rock star Jim Morrison is striking. The Doors' female fans were modern Maenads.

Jim became fascinated with the Dionysian archetype, as described by Nietzsche, who wrote that Dionysian excess was a path to wisdom. Intoxicated with the idea, Jim became a Dionysian rock star: wild, drunken, sexually free and transgressive. He often referred to Dionysus in conversation, and is described in Dionysian terms by his band mates. In fact, all six principal 27s could be said to have lived Dionysian lives. But Jim Morrison was the only one who intellectualised his debauchery.

After leaving school Jim enrolled at St Petersburg Junior College in Florida, transferring to Florida State University where he studied philosophy and theatre history and acted in student productions. He was arrested for the first time in 1963, for being drunk and disorderly, a tentative start to the Dionysian life. That year Steve Morrison became captain of the USS *Bon Homme Richard*. Jim spoke of the shock of seeing his father in command of that mighty vessel. 'That was another pivotal point in his life when Jim went out on [the] aircraft carrier and realised his father could launch these planes, some of which were carrying really nasty weapons,' says Vince Treanor, the Doors' road manager. 'Jim said he couldn't conceive that one man could have that much power, and life and death decision over hundreds, if not thousands of people, and I think it was one of the things that put Jim into rebellion against the establishment.'

Still, Jim's parents tried to accommodate their precocious son. They supported his decision to leave Florida State and enrol in film school at the University of California, Los Angeles (UCLA). Steve Morrison reasoned that if Jim was serious about getting into the movie industry, as he said, this was the place to go.

Jim came into his own at UCLA. 'When he got to LA, all of sudden he was out in the open, he was free,' says Vince Treanor. 'That was when he began to realise there was an open horizon out there.' Jim made significant new friends at UCLA, including two film students of French background, Alain Ronay and Agnès Varda, both of whom would play a part in the drama of his death in Paris. Most importantly, he met Ray Manzarek. A tall, bespectacled film student of Polish immigrant stock, Manzarek was four years older than Jim, and had already served a year and a half in the US Army. Like Jim, Ray was an intellectual. He was also an accomplished keyboard player, a blues aficionado who played in a surf band, Rick and the Ravens. The students would go to clubs to see the Ravens perform. One night Jim got up with them and sang 'Louie, Louie'.

Also hanging around campus was the poet Michael C. Ford, who recalls sitting with Jim in film classes given by Josef von Sternberg at the end of his illustrious career. While von Sternberg held forth on directing *The Blue Angel*, Jim composed poetry. Ford was impressed by what he wrote. 'I would read things that to me were astonishing … I thought it had a brilliance about it.' Jim had been a drinker since high school, but it was at UCLA that he started using marijuana and LSD to 'super-charge his lyric writing,' says Ford. 'I think he was hooked on the whole idea of trying everything, [even] become addicted to it. That's romantic, too.' In this frame of mind, and under the influence, Jim became an increasingly wild Dionysian character. He also changed in appearance, losing his youthful pudginess, allowing his hair to grow long and curly, taking on the idealised appearance of a Greek god.

Upon leaving UCLA in the spring of 1965, aged 21, Jim seemed unsure of what he wanted to do with his life, other than that he didn't want to be drafted for the Vietnam War. He was registered for the draft, classified 1-A (qualified for service) in January 1962, then granted student deferment until the summer of 1965. Selective Services were about to contact him again, with every chance that Jim would be packed off to war. Meanwhile, he talked about going to New York to pursue his film career, but he ended up doing very little. He hung around Venice Beach, sleeping at a friend's house, sunbathing and getting high.

One day Ray Manzarek bumped into Jim on the beach and asked what he had been doing since college. 'I've been writing some songs,' Jim replied, according to Ray's memory of the pivotal conversation of their lives. That Jim spoke of song lyrics, rather than poems, may have been due to Bob Dylan's recent success in marrying poetry to popular song.

'You know what, sing me a song,' Ray urged. 'Let me hear what you've been writing.'

Jim recited 'Moonlight Drive', which begins:

> *Let's swim to the moon*
> *Let's climb through the tide*

Ray imagined music behind the sinuous, poetic words, the best lyrics he'd ever heard. 'Man, we got to get a band together,' he said. 'We're gonna make a million dollars!'

5

The fifth principal character in the story of the 27 Club was born on 20 February 1967, a month before the Doors released their début album, making Jim Morrison famous. The Rolling Stones were established. The Jimi Hendrix Experience had been launched successfully in Britain, and were about to break in America, as was Janis Joplin with Big Brother and the Holding Company. We shall catch up with all these stories in due course.

While the sixties started to swing, Kurt Cobain was born and raised in Aberdeen, Washington, a logging town a hundred miles south-west of Seattle, a journey that takes the traveller through a wet, green landscape mostly given over to forest, the gaps between the trees accommodating farms, hamlets, factories, trailer parks and cheap motels. Finally the road enters the port of Aberdeen, on the eastern shore of Grays Harbor, on the Pacific Ocean. Aberdeen is an unpretentious working-class place, rough around the edges, especially since the logging industry went into decline. In Kurt's youth Aberdeen was busier, well supplied with bars and whorehouses for the entertainment of the men who worked on the docks and in the saw mills. Such is the perversity of life that a sensitive, artistic boy was born into a place he decried as a 'redneck logger town'.

Kurt was the eldest child of Don and Wendy Cobain (*née* Fradenburg), teenage sweethearts from Aberdeen High. Wendy fell pregnant shortly after she graduated, giving birth to Kurt when she was nineteen. A second child, Kimberley, followed when Kurt was three. There was a history of odd behaviour and violent death in the extended family. On his mother's side, Kurt's great-grandfather died in a mental hospital of a self-inflicted stab wound. His daughter, Kurt's Grandma Fradenburg, subsequently became a recluse. On his father's side, Kurt's great-grandfather, Art Cobain, a county sheriff, died in bizarre circumstances. Reaching for a cigarette he dislodged his pistol, which fell to the ground, went off and shot him dead. Two of Sheriff Cobain's sons, Burle and Kenny, chose suicide by gunshot. Kurt decided there were 'suicide genes' in the family.

Kurt's father worked as a mechanic, later in a saw mill. When Kurt was two the family moved to a small wood-frame house on East 1st Street in a part of Aberdeen known as Felony Flats, over-looked by the more prosperous citizens on Think of Me Hill (named after a sign for a brand of cigars). Largely because of Kurt's comments in interviews, Aberdeen has acquired a bad reputation. It was certainly provincial, conservative and stratified when he grew up there, but everybody knew each other; there were plentiful jobs when Kurt was a boy; and it was a safe place for children, with space to play, trees to climb and rivers to explore. Sitting on the bank of the Wishkah river under the Young Street Bridge, at the end of his road, Kurt might have imagined himself in *The Adventures of Tom Sawyer*. It was an ideal place to make a camp. Later, when Kurt found that he wasn't welcome at home, he camped for real under the bridge, inspiring the song 'Something in the Way'.

Kurt was a hyperactive child, treated with Ritalin when he was seven. Later he developed mood swings. He decided he was manic-depressive (bipolar). He was also an artistic rather than a sporty boy, which seems to have been a disappointment to his father, with whom he had a poor relationship. 'Don was kind of mean to him. [He] would go by and flip his [finger] on his head. I said, "What did you do that for?"' recalls Kurt's uncle, Chuck Fradenburg. Don said he wanted to discipline Kurt. 'Poor little guy, he [didn't] know what's going on. He was probably five or six years old at the time. And I saw [Don] do other kind of verbal abuse to him – tell him he's dumb, he's stupid.'

The major trauma of Kurt's young life came shortly after his ninth birthday, in 1976, when Wendy Cobain announced that she wanted a divorce. Don tried to persuade his wife that they should stay together, but Wendy was determined. 'There was a lot of arguing, that's what Kurt didn't like. He didn't understand,' says Uncle Chuck. Don moved out of the family home, though he continued to have hope for the marriage. 'Donny, for a long time there, he thought he was going to get her back,' says his father, Leland Cobain. But it wasn't to be. The Cobains divorced, with Wendy retaining custody of the children. Kurt scrawled on his bedroom wall: 'I hate Mom, I hate Dad. Dad hates Mom, Mom hates Dad.' In later life he harked back to the divorce as the point at which his life had gone wrong; he blamed not only his parents, but a generation of adults who pursued personal happiness over the welfare of their children – at a time when the divorce rate rose dramatically in the United States. 'Every parent made the same mistake … my story is exactly the same as ninety per cent of everyone my age,' Kurt said. 'All these kids my age found themselves asking the same question at the same time – why the fuck are my parents getting divorced?'*

Divorce had a calamitous effect on Kurt, as it did on other members of the 27 Club. 'It just destroyed his life. He changed completely. I think he was ashamed. And he became very inward,' his mother has said. Marriage break-ups are one of the primary causes of psychiatric disorders in children, and Kurt started to show signs of being disturbed. He began to complain of stomach pain, which unhappy children often do to win sympathy and time off school (truancy and absenteeism are common in disturbed children). Kurt continued to complain of stomach pain into adulthood, ultimately using it as an excuse to use heroin.

His anxiety increased when his father remarried. Don's new wife had children of her own, and she and Don had another son in 1979, making Kurt feel even more marginalised, 'something in the way', as he sang expressively in the song of that title. 'He [Dad] got married and after that I was one of the last things of importance on his list,' Kurt complained. 'He just gave up [on me].' Kurt was sent to stay with relatives, including Wendy's brother Chuck and his wife. Chuck played drums in a rock band and helped Kurt develop an interest in music, buying him an electric guitar and arranging for him to have lessons. '[His] main goal was to play "Stairway to Heaven", which he denied later on,' says Warren Mason, who taught Kurt guitar and gave him advice on songwriting. 'I have to say he is one of the last people I would ever have predicted would make it, because he was so laid back. He just didn't show any drive ...' In his intro-verted way, however, Kurt became as obsessive about the guitar as Brian Jones and Jimi Hendrix. Like Hendrix, he played left-handed.

A school photo of Kurt at this time shows a fresh-faced boy with a broad smile. He looks like a member of the Brady Bunch, yet he felt like a misfit, becoming, in his words, 'fully withdrawn' by his

* The divorce rate more than doubled in the USA between 1965 and 1975. This was partly because of changes to the law, which made divorce easier, but was also the result of the ideas of the women's-liberation movement rippling out through America, with women like Wendy Cobain wanting freedom from unfulfilling marriages.

early teens. His mother was so worried that she sent him to a
psychiatrist. Kurt began to develop odd and disturbing obsessions,
significantly with death and suicide, which became a lifelong preoccupation. He got it into his head that Great Uncle Burle had killed
himself 'over the death of Jim Morrison'. Although there was no
connection, this shows that Kurt was already aware of the rock stars
who had died at 27. He couldn't have failed to know something
about Jimi Hendrix, the biggest rock star ever to come from
Washington state. Kurt's preoccupation with suicide increased and
became personal. At fifteen, he made a home movie titled 'Kurt
Commits Bloody Suicide'. This was more than a joke: it was a fixa-
tion, and a warning. Textbooks say that the children of divorced
parents are at greater risk of suicide. Kurt bore that out.

The unhappy teenager continued to be passed around the family,
living for a while with his grandparents, Iris and Leland Cobain, in
their stationary trailer at Montesano, a short drive from Aberdeen.
Kurt adored Iris, who shared his interest in art and music. 'He liked
his grandmother better than he did his own mother,' asserts Leland.
'He was [also] pissed at his dad, because his dad got married again.'

Kurt moved from his grandparents to stay with Uncle Jim Cobain.
Then he moved back to his mother's, transferring to Aberdeen High,
a short walk from home. It was Kurt's bad luck to be placed in a
class with a group of athletic boys whose parents had more money
than Kurt's, and who formed a clique with the pretty girls, a clique
from which Kurt felt excluded. 'The boys weren't necessarily as handsome [as Kurt], but they were preppy, they wore the polo shirts and
the nice sweaters and their hair was always done. They got all the
attention,' says classmate Penny Lloyd, who was part of the in-crowd.
She found Kurt to be painfully shy: 'He would barely look at me or
talk to me.' Ostracised and introverted, Kurt found expression in
music and art. His art teacher, Bob Hunter, recalls Kurt making
'incredible drawings', including an excellent caricature of President
Reagan, and cartoon Smurfs trying to kill each other.

Around this time Kurt's enthusiasm for classic rock gave way to
punk, a form of music practised by a local band, the Melvins, who
went on to fame. Kurt became acquainted with members of the

nascent group, who were slightly older than him, and started to hang around the Aberdeen home of the drummer. Concurrently, he began to experiment with drugs, which became, with music, the dominant force in his life. Drug use was depressingly common among Kurt's generation in Aberdeen, Kurt being one of a number of local boys who became heroin addicts, sometimes with fatal consequences. Drug use began as a laugh. Kurt and his friends would crawl under the Young Street Bridge to smoke dope in private, while cars rumbled overhead, including hearses on their way to the cemetery. It wasn't long before Kurt was coming into school stoned. 'When he was high, it was obvious,' says Bob Hunter. 'We'd take a walk to the door. I didn't feel it was doing a lot of good to refer him to counsellors, so [I'd say], "See you tomorrow."'

Wendy Cobain remarried in 1984, to a man named O'Connor, whom Kurt disliked as much as his stepmother. He despised both parents. In a letter to his father in later life, he wrote: 'I've never taken sides with you or my mother because while I was growing up I had equal contempt for you both.' Arguments at home led Wendy to ask Kurt to leave, after which he stayed with friends and relatives, sleeping on sofas, even in a car. The following year he dropped out of school, before graduation, and moved into an apartment with a friend. He went back to school briefly, to work as a janitor. That summer he was fined for spraying graffiti on the SeaFirst Bank downtown: 'HOMO SEX RULES'. Kurt had few sexual relationships, and those that are known about were heterosexual, but he empathised with gay people as fellow outsiders and used this as a way of taunting the conservative citizens of Aberdeen.

Unable to pay his rent, Kurt was kicked out of his apartment and found himself virtually homeless. It was at this juncture that he returned to the riverbank under the Young Street Bridge, later giving the impression in interviews that he had lived under the bridge. He may have slept there on one or two nights, but it is unlikely to have been much longer, still less likely that he sustained himself by fishing in the river, as he suggested.

Before things became truly desperate, Kurt was rescued by two school friends, brothers Steve and Eric Shillinger, whose father,

Lamont, taught English at Aberdeen High. 'One evening Steve and Eric came home and said, "Our friend Kurt got into a fight [at home] and they kicked him out of the house. Could he stay with us for a few days?"' recalls Lamont Shillinger. He and his wife agreed to give Kurt the use of their hide-away bed. 'He lived with us for about a year.' Even though the Shillinger home is a short walk from Wendy O'Connor's house in Aberdeen, Lamont Shillinger says he had no contact with Kurt's family while Kurt stayed with them. 'We never heard one word from his mom, dad, grandpa, anything.'

Such was Kurt Cobain's start in life. As with many of the 27s, it was a rocky beginning. But history shows that artistic people are often born in adversity and thrive on pain. In a sense we should thank the parents of the 27s, inadequate as many were, for creating an environment conducive to artists. If Mummy and Daddy had provided happier homes, their sons and daughters might have passed into anonymity. They might still be alive, but who would have heard of the optometrist Brian Jones, assuming he had followed the career his parents envisaged? Who would have known Jimi Hendrix, landscape gardener, or care about Janis Joplin, Port Arthur housewife; who would read the sociologist Jim Morrison, or given a damn about school janitor Kurt Cobain? As for Amy Winehouse, she worked briefly as a reporter before she went into show business, and might have been in journalism still, had her background and character been different.

Two

DADDY'S GIRL

There was a little girl
Who had a little curl
Right in the middle of her forehead,
When she was good
She was very, very good,
But when she was bad she was horrid.
Henry Wadsworth Longfellow

1

Although her family were Reform Jews, who did not observe all the traditions of the faith strictly, Amy Winehouse's Jewish background was a vital part of her identity. She often spoke of her Jewishness, sometimes introducing herself by saying: 'My name is Amy Winehouse – that's a Jewish name.'

The family is Russian-Jewish. Amy's great-great-grandfather, born in Minsk, was named Wienhaus. He was among the hundreds of thousands of Jews who fled persecution at the end of the nineteenth century, immigrating to Britain while other Russian Jews, such as Bob Dylan's ancestors the Zimmermans, fled to America. The family name was seemingly anglicised to Winehouse upon arrival in England in 1890; at which time the first name of Amy's great-great-grandfather was registered as Harris, which also sounds anglicised. As a result Winehouse is a highly unusual, if not unique, family name with the hundred or so Winehouses in the United Kingdom descended from Harris and his family.

Like many immigrants, the Winehouses settled in Spitalfields, a cheap, crowded area of east London, Harris arriving two years after Jack the Ripper had terrorised the neighbourhood. Harris was a tailor, a typical Jewish trade, probably working from home on a pedal-operated Singer sewing machine. His son Ben (Amy's great-grandfather) served in the British Army in the First World War, after which he established a hairdressing business on Commercial Street, Ben's Toilet Saloon, in which his son, Alex (Amy's grandfather), also worked. Family legend has it that Alex cut the hair of some of the East End's notorious gangsters. Alex was an extrovert, 'full of laughter and comedy,' says Amy's cousin Jonathan Winehouse. The Winehouses are typically friendly, gregarious and wilful, quick to joke and sing. Alex married Cynthia Gordon, Amy's beloved grandmother, whose name and image Amy had tattooed on her arm. In her youth, Cynthia dated the jazz saxophonist and club owner Ronnie Scott. Another show-business connection was made when cousin Neville Winehouse married Frankie Vaughan's sister.

Amy's father, Mitchell, was born in 1950 to Alex and Cynthia Winehouse in Stoke Newington, the family moving soon afterwards to Stepney in the East End. Mitch grew into a heavy-set young man with curly dark hair who wore a moustache in early adulthood. In character he was and remains chatty and ebullient, full of jokes, a natural show-off who loved to sing at family gatherings in the style of his heroes, Tony Bennett and Frank Sinatra. Amy's success would change Mitch's life beyond imagination. His daughter's celebrity was an entrée to showbiz, putting Mitch in a position where he could meet and get to know Tony Bennett and record his own album.

In 1976, when Mitch was 25 and working in a casino, he married a 21-year-old pharmacist named Janis Seaton, who had been born in the United States, but had grown up in the Jewish community of east London. Janis is a tiny, twinkly woman, the image of her daughter, as many comment. She cheerfully agrees: 'Whenever I see Amy appearing on TV ... I think, Hang on, that's me!'

When the Winehouses had made a little money they moved from the inner city to the suburbs. Mitch's parents relocated to Southgate, in the north London Borough of Enfield, one of the dormitory suburbs that spread around the capital in the 1930s. It was a pleasant, affordable place in which to raise a family, with convenient high-street shops, parks and schools, and within commuting distance of work by Underground. Southgate is anonymous and slightly dull, yet many 27s came from such places. This was where Mitch completed his education. His father died young, but Cynthia continued to live locally, and when Mitch and Janis married they set up home near his mother and started their own family.

A son, Alex, was born in 1979, at which time Mitch was driving a black taxi cab, another traditional occupation for working-class Jewish Londoners. The Winehouses bought a semi-detached house on Osidge Lane, where they were living when Amy Jade Winehouse was launched upon the ocean of life at Chase Farm Hospital, on 14 September 1983, completing the family.

Amy was an attractive, clever and curious child with a tendency to get into trouble. 'She was mischievous, bold and daring,' Mitch writes in his book, *Amy, My Daughter*, going on to document the times Amy scared her parents by getting lost or choking. When Amy saw the fuss her parents made of her brother when he choked on his food one day, she pretended to choke, the start of a lifelong habit of attention-seeking.

Mitch and Janis are very different people. Janis is quiet, even timid. Mitch is much more outgoing, quick to chat, make a joke and lose his temper. While he was a lively and loving parent, he was not an ideal husband to Janis. He was often away from home, working long hours as a cabbie. When he came in, he had a habit of waking Amy up to play with him, which Janis found disruptive. Yet Mitch doted on Amy, and Amy adored her father. She was Daddy's Girl, later having that phrase tattooed on her shoulder. She copied her father when he sang, and Mitch encouraged her. By the age of five Amy had decided that she wanted to go into show business. She was, as cousin Beryl Winehouse notes, 'definitely an unusual child – very precocious'. At the same time there was a quieter, less confident side to Amy. 'She was always very cheery, but she was also shy,' Janis Winehouse has said. 'She's never been an easy child.'

Amy made friends readily at nursery school, then at Osidge Primary

School, a short walk from home. 'One of our best routines was that one of us would run out of the classroom in tears, and the other would say that they'd have to go out and comfort her. And then we'd just sit in a room somewhere, laughing our heads off,' says one early friend, Juliette Ashby. She also recalled Amy and herself teasing a boy: they told him they wouldn't be his friends unless he pulled his underpants down – which they claim he did to their joy. 'That was when we truly bonded.'*Another friend, Lauren Franklin, remembers Amy as an advanced reader, a spelling-bee champ and a whiz at mathematics (a talent Amy inherited from her mother). Amy took lifelong pleasure in books, puzzles and word games. She also had a precocious interest in boys. 'She was quite a naughty girl,' says Lauren. 'I remember my mum shouting at her in the playground because she had told me stuff that I shouldn't have known at such a young age.' Amy was to become naughtier still, her behaviour linked to a change in family circumstances.

In the short time he'd been married Mitch Winehouse had pursued three careers. He had worked in the gaming industry, as a taxi driver and latterly as a double-glazing salesman. In the last business he worked alongside a marketing manager named Jane, a woman thirteen years his junior (she turned twenty the year she started with Mitch's firm). Jane and Mitch became friends, close enough for Jane to visit the family at Osidge Lane where she met Janis and the children. Mitch says there was no more than a friendship between them 'for ages', but then there was an affair. Janis found out and seemingly tolerated it initially. 'He was a salesman so he was away a lot, but for a long time there was also another woman, Jane,' she has said. 'I think Mitchell [Janis always called him that] would have liked to have both of us, but I wasn't happy to do that.' In 1992 Mitch made the decision to leave home and live with Jane, who turned 28 that year (he was 42 in December). He stayed at home until Alex turned thirteen, and had his bar mitzvah, then he and Janis told the children.

'The children were in shock,' Janis says, of the moment when she and Mitch told Alex and Amy that they were separating. 'They couldn't

* The boy, now grown up, says the story has been exaggerated.

understand it because they didn't see any animosity between us and we never rowed.' Alex withdrew into himself. Amy seemed less disturbed at first, but it became clear that the break-up had a profound effect upon her. As with Kurt Cobain, this could be said to have been the turning point in her young life. Mitch stayed in regular contact with his children after he had left home, keeping a room for them wherever he was living and seeing them frequently, but Amy came to describe her father censoriously, in a 2003 interview with the *Guardian*, as a 'shady' sort of man who 'moved house every two years' after the separation. 'I've no idea what he was trying to run from.'

Part of the problem was that Mitch was in financial trouble. He was declared bankrupt in 1993, around the time he left home, an episode he neglects to mention in his book, *Amy, My Daughter*. He was declared a 'debtor's bankrupt' (meaning he applied to become bankrupt because he could not pay his debts) at the High Court in London on 16 November 1993, discharged three years later. He was described at the time in the *London Gazette* (which publishes London bankruptcies) as a sales consultant and company director of Greenside Close, Whetstone, where the Winehouse family had recently moved. Aside from their previous home in Osidge Lane, two further addresses were given for Mitch in the bankruptcy notice. Over the next few years he continued to move about, living in London, Hertfordshire, Essex and Kent, which explains Amy's comment about his peripatetic lifestyle.

Mitch writes in his book that he felt guilty about leaving his family, and he admits to over-indulging his children to assuage this guilt, buying Alex and Amy expensive gifts, and giving them money. So, Amy suffered the double upset of seeing her parents split up and being spoilt by a father trying to compensate for his misdemeanour. It was a recipe for trouble.

Although the break-up of a marriage is not uncommon, it is very unfortunate for the children, and Mitch Winehouse's decision to start a new life with another woman at a tender stage in Amy's development seems to have shaped her character and behaviour, particularly her attitude to men. For years Amy tried to figure out why Dad had cheated on Mum, expressing her thoughts in a song, 'What is it About Men?', which Mitch concedes is partly about him.

In this song, Amy sings critically about someone who was originally 'a family man', expressing the hope that she will not repeat his mistakes, behaviour that had caused her mother anguish (she referred specifically to her mother in the song). The burden of the deeply personal and revealing lyric was that, while she didn't want to repeat history, she felt almost doomed to do so. And, sadly, Amy proved a faithless and unsuccessful spouse in turn. As Larkin wrote, our parents fuck us up and give us the faults they had.

2

Following her separation from Mitch (they would later divorce), Janis Winehouse enrolled Amy at a Saturday-morning stage school run by a former actress named Susi Earnshaw, who observes that mothers and daughters often bicker after Dad leaves home, the daughter blaming Mum, however unfairly, for driving him away. Typically, Mum feels guilty and tries to do something nice for her daughter, such as, in Amy's case, sending her to stage school. 'It's so common,' says Earnshaw. 'It's a way of making them happy, and it also could be a way that a parent could have a break. It's a Saturday, and it's three hours where your child is happy doing something, and you can have a rest, and they might be in a good mood when they come home.'

Amy was a loud, excitable and energetic addition to the Susi Earnshaw School, a skinny little girl with masses of dark hair, who turned cartwheels in the hall, and ran rings round her mother as Janis tried to have a conversation with other parents at going-home time – she was 'really hyperactive', says Melissa Gillespie, one of Amy's contemporaries. Amy proved an enthusiastic but indifferent dancer, a good, loud singer, and an impressive child actress, outstanding in a school production of *Little Shop of Horrors*. '[Her] comic timing was spot on,' recalls Earnshaw. Amy was a good enough actress to earn a walk-on part in a 1994 English National Opera production of Massenet's *Don Quixote*.

In *Amy, My Daughter*, Mitch writes that he discussed Amy's emerging theatrical ambitions with Susi Earnshaw, but Earnshaw and

Amy's contemporaries at the school have no memory of meeting him during the three years she attended. 'I never saw her dad,' says former pupil Julia Vanellis.

'He never came to the show[s],' agrees Susi Earnshaw, in a round-table discussion with former pupils and staff for this book. 'Her mum was always there ... I never saw her dad, ever.'

Mitch's absence during this period of Amy's life contrasts with the way in which he became ubiquitous after Amy began her professional career. Amy's school friend Lauren Franklin says: 'Let me tell you Mitch wasn't around until his daughter became famous ... But she loved him. That's her dad – absolutely – her dad is her dad. She wanted to make him happy. But, believe me, he was not there ... there wasn't a father figure around.'

If Mitch Winehouse was absent, he was ably represented by his ebullient mother, Cynthia, who encouraged Amy in her show-business ambitions to the extent that she might be described as a pushy stage grandmother, berating one director who failed to cast Amy in *Annie*. The family gathered at Cynthia's flat for dinner on Friday nights, and Cynthia helped Janis bring up the children. Amy saw herself reflected in her forceful grandmother, paying attention to what Cynthia told her, while she tended to ignore or defy other adults. Their closeness mirrored that of Kurt Cobain and his paternal grandmother.

Despite Cynthia's help, the responsibility for bringing up the children rested largely with Janis, who struggled to cope. Ever since she'd had her first child she had suffered with headaches, tiredness and other symptoms that led her doctor to diagnose post-natal depression for which he prescribed anti-depressants. Janis later discovered that multiple sclerosis was sapping her energy. To outsiders she could seem ineffectual. 'I love Janis, but she's a very weak person. She always has been. She's never been able to stand up [to Amy],' says Lauren Franklin. 'I remember [her saying],"Oh, Amy, don't say that." And Amy was going, "Ah, I hate you, you fucking bitch!"... This was, like, when we were very young. She was just very weak, bless her.'

Lauren saw a deterioration in her friend's behaviour after her parents' separation. 'Unfortunately, when Mitch had the affair [Amy] changed … It's a massive part of any kid's life when your parents get divorced. And it wasn't that suddenly she turned to music, or started writing. It was nothing like that. She actually became really naughty.'

The naughtiness became apparent when Amy transferred to Ashmole Secondary School, the same school her brother and father had attended. Lauren, who attended a different, Jewish school, noticed that Amy adopted a new way of speaking after she enrolled at Ashmole. As a child Amy had been 'so well-spoken'. Now she spoke as if she had been brought up on an inner-London estate, even though her school was in the same lower-middle-class suburban area. Amy maintained this *faux*-working-class accent for the rest of her life, broadening it until she sounded like a veritable Cockney. 'None of us speak like that,' says Lauren. It was an attempt to project a worldly image. As a budding writer, Amy also surely found interest in the richly colloquial language of the inner city.

Amy became disruptive in class and started to truant from school, often sloping off home halfway through the day. Like so many indulgent parents, Mitch ascribes his daughter's misbehaviour to being 'bored'. That may be partly true but, as noted in reference to Kurt Cobain, it is also true that disturbed children truant. Happy children attend school. Amy got into the habit of staying up late, which made it difficult to wake her for school in the morning, causing Janis to telephone Mitch in despair. 'Your daughter won't get out of bed.' Amy was more and more in conflict with her parents and teachers and, just as Mitch felt guilty about leaving home, his daughter felt guilty about her misbehaviour, which seems to have stemmed from his having left home. When Mitch celebrated his 45th birthday in December 1995, Amy sent him a card signed 'Your favourite walking car crash of a daughter'. Although the card is jokey, it indicates that she was already developing a negative self-image.

3

Amy's musical tastes were shaped partly by the records her parents and brother listened to. The recordings of Tony Bennett, Ella

Fitzgerald and Frank Sinatra were played constantly when Dad was around, and Mitch would also sing these songs, while Janis liked Carole King. All these artists influenced Amy, as did the mainstream pop acts of the day. Amy and her friend Juliette discovered hip-hop, and formed a singing duo in emulation of the American act Salt-N-Pepa. Meanwhile, Alex Winehouse was learning to play guitar and listening to Ray Charles, Sarah Vaughan and Dinah Washington. Although Alex sometimes seemed impatient with Amy, in the way of older siblings, Amy read the books her brother liked, took up the guitar as he had, and listened to the records he played, which was also Dad's music, songs associated with happy times before her parents had split. Pop, rap and jazz all came together in Amy's mind, helping to form the unique crossover artist she became, and she began to have ambitions as a singer.

Mitch writes that Amy applied to drama school of her own volition, without telling her parents. But Susi Earnshaw remembers a preliminary conversation with Janis, who asked her whether Amy was talented enough to benefit from full-time drama school. 'She [Janis] didn't know herself.' Earnshaw assured Janis that Amy had the talent, and suggested she try for a scholarship to the Sylvia Young Theatre School.

In her application to Sylvia Young, Amy wrote: 'All my life I have been loud, to the point of being told to shut up,' adding that she believed she had inherited her voice from her father, but while Dad was 'content to sing loudly in his office and sell windows' she was determined to develop her talent into a career. The most telling passage of her application is where Amy confesses, 'mostly I have this dream to be very famous ... It's a lifelong ambition.' Fame is a common but dangerous ambition among the young, which is almost bound to end in heartache. There is poignancy in Amy singing 'On the Sunny Side of the Street' at her audition before the eponymous Sylvia Young. There would be few sunny days ahead. She won a half-scholarship to the school, enrolling on 14 April 1997, five months before she turned fourteen.

At the time the Sylvia Young Theatre School was in a former church building behind Marylebone railway station in north London.

Pupils wore regular school uniform for the days they studied academic subjects, Monday through Wednesday. On Thursday and Friday, they changed into less formal attire for dance, drama and singing, which was when the school burst into life as a veritable Fame Academy. Amy loved it. Bumping into her friend Melissa Gillespie at their local swimming pool, Amy exclaimed: 'Melissa! I'm at Sylvia Young's, and I'm going to be famous!' As she spoke, Amy watched herself in the changing-room mirror as if to see whether her transformation had begun.

Amy impressed everybody at Sylvia Young. 'Academically, she was a complete brainiac, almost geekified – she knew everything,' says fellow pupil and friend Ricardo Canadinhas. '[She] was amazing at maths [and a] really great character – she was hilarious.' Staff, too, discerned good qualities. 'I think she had a tremendous brain,' says Sylvia Young. 'Her English teacher, Mr McIntyre, thought she'd be a writer – a novelist.' Amy was a bookworm who read classic and literary modern fiction. *Catch-22* was a favourite. She also enjoyed graphic novels such as Art Spiegelman's *Maus*, a book about the Holocaust. And she wrote, jottings about herself and autobiographical song lyrics.

On the downside, Amy got bored easily, and bucked against discipline. Sylvia Young told her repeatedly to remove her earrings, which were not allowed. 'And she would very nicely take them out, and apologise, and then she'd forget and put them back in again.' Although Young has no memory of this, Amy's friends recall that a bigger issue was the metal stud Amy started to wear in her upper lip. Amy pierced herself, which shocked her friends but which Amy dismissed as no big deal, and over the next few years she acquired several more piercings. It was part of the process of reinventing herself. It was also the start of a worrying habit of hurting herself.

Amy's acting talent won her a small part in the BBC comedy series *The Fast Show* in 1997, but singing was more important. The strength of her voice came home to her theatre school friends at Christmas when the children sang carols in Marylebone station. Amy sang 'Once In Royal David's City' so powerfully that the whole station seemed to stop to listen. 'I remember looking around and everyone

was in tears listening to this [fourteen-]year-old girl,' says Ricardo
Canadinhas. 'Where did that come from?'

As puberty took hold, Amy started to smoke and drink with her
theatre-school chums, especially when they got together for weekend
sleepovers. Her figure had started to develop, and she could pass for
eighteen, as could fellow pupil Amie Schroeter. 'So we'd always go
in and get the booze, take it back to the house [for the party] …
We all drank.' At this stage the teenagers chose sweetened low-alcohol
drinks, and Amy's drinking didn't seem problematic. 'She used to
drink like the rest of us would,' says Amie. 'It wasn't a prominent
feature.'

Weekend sleepovers provided opportunities for sexual encounters.
One of Amy's first tumbles was with Ricardo Canadinhas, who later
became a drag artist on the gay club scene. 'We were quite a naughty
year when it came to things like that. I was possibly the worst,' says
Ricardo, who says he had a fling with Amy when they were about
fourteen. 'She had already been with someone by this stage.' Another
theatre-school boyfriend was Kenneth Gordon, who used the stage
name Tyler James, though it is unclear when exactly they became
lovers. Like Amy, Tyler's family was from the East End where one
of his older relatives had been a member of the Kray gang. Tyler
became a lifelong friend.

Outside school Amy explored her city, gravitating to Camden
Town, only eight stops south of Whetstone on the Northern Line
but a different world from the suburbs. Stepping out of the tube
station Amy stood at the hub of a bustling inner-city area, the radi-
ating roads lined with shops and stalls selling vintage clothes, skull
T-shirts, diamanté belt buckles, leather jackets, distressed jeans,
Converse sneakers, fast food, mobile phones, second-hand records,
comic books and everything else that attracts the young. There were
funky pubs, like the Good Mixer, a hang-out for generations of rock
musicians, as well as cool places to hear live music, like the Jazz Café,
and, tucked away in basements and garrets, there were tattoo parlours,
which typically also do body piercings. Amy got a Saturday job in
one such parlour, and acquired her first tattoo at fifteen, the cartoon
character Betty Boop on her back. Her mother was horrified, but

nothing Janis could do would get the ink out. 'My parents pretty much realised [at that stage] that I would do whatever I wanted.' Over the next few years Amy acquired a dozen or so tattoos, early ones including an Egyptian ankh between her shoulders, a fern on her left forearm and a lightning bolt on her right arm. A middle-class suburban girl was turning herself into somebody who appeared streetwise. 'She was the Rebel Jew. That's what she called herself, when she had the piercings [and the tattoos],' laughs Ricardo Canadinhas.

Camden is also a place to score drugs and Amy started to smoke cannabis around the age of fifteen, which set her apart from some of her suburban girlfriends. 'I just wasn't like that at all ... I was more of a good girl,' says Lauren Franklin. 'There was always something different about her in regards to her intelligence and [behaviour]. When I say naughty, if you told Amy, "No", she'd do it, whether [it be] smoking [or] drinking ... She was *fearless*.' Amy could also be melodramatic, starting arguments for no better reason than that she enjoyed drama. 'She was always very difficult to be friends with ... She was very outspoken, [and she] didn't really care.'

Although Amy enjoyed stage school, she neglected her academic studies to the point at which her head teacher warned Janis Winehouse that Amy might not pass her exams if she stayed at the school. 'The head teacher [was] not happy with her attitude in the academic classes, and nor were most of the teachers happy,' says Sylvia Young. 'He gave the mum the impression that she would be asked to leave. He hadn't passed that by me at all, and I had no idea that had been said, until I got a note from the mum saying that she was going to be leaving, at which time I spoke to the mother and said, "Look, why? It's not a good idea ... Although she may not have been totally happy here, I'm sure she'll be happier here, in this environment, than in any other." She wouldn't be happy in any school.' Nevertheless, Amy transferred to a private secondary school in Barnet, the Mount, where she completed her GCSEs.

Janis was now dating a financial adviser with two teenage children. The families moved into a townhouse at Guildown Avenue, Woodside Park, a short walk from where Janis, Alex and Amy had been living.

The garage was converted into a rehearsal space for Amy, whose behaviour continued to deteriorate. 'I was a shit. I did whatever I wanted. I used to bunk off school, get my boyfriend round. My mum used to come home from work and I'd be lying around the house with my boyfriend in dressing-gowns.' Amy still managed to pass six GCSEs at grades B and C.

Although Amy had now left Sylvia Young's school, Young mentioned her to Bill Ashton, founder of the National Youth Jazz Orchestra, which had been a training ground for numerous professional musicians. He invited Amy to sing for him.

'Hello, my name is Amy Winehouse,' Amy introduced herself in her swaggering *faux*-Cockney accent. 'That's a Jewish name.'

Amy's singing voice was impressive. 'She was absolutely spot-on. She was a very, very good natural singer,' says Bill Ashton, who asked Amy to sing at a pub gig in June 2000. 'She chose to sing a song called "Who's Blue?" [and] she sang it perfectly.' The following month he asked her to fill in at short notice on another gig. She learned the songs on the way to the venue, and gave another fine performance. 'She was a 35-year-old singer in a sixteen-year-old's body,' says Ashton who, in common with others at this stage in Amy's life, doesn't recall seeing or speaking to Mitch Winehouse. 'I don't think I ever met the father.' All his dealings were with Amy's mother. 'I talked to her mum on the phone. I said, "Is there anything you'd like me to do for Amy, Mrs Winehouse?" She said, "Yes. Can you stop her smoking so much?"' That was impossible. Amy was smoking for England. 'She didn't really care about herself. She did not treat her body as a temple,' observes Ashton. 'She was self-destructive.'

Amy's next move was to apply to the BRIT School in Croydon, founded with the backing of the British recording industry along the lines of the New York School of the Performing Arts to educate children who aspired to careers in show business. On her October 1999 application Amy listed Miles Davis, Ella Fitzgerald and Frank Sinatra ('the greatest performer of his age') as her musical influences. In the section in which she had to write about her parents she described her father as 'part-owner of double glazing company.' Hereby hangs a tale.

In recent years Mitch Winehouse had become 'part-owner' of two double-glazing companies, though not successfully. In the late 1990s he became a director and company secretary of Formplace Ltd, which changed its name to Warmglaze Ltd in 1998. The company didn't trade over the following two years and Mitch resigned as director and company secretary in July 2000, the same month that his second wife took over those roles. She resigned four months later and the company was dissolved in 2002. By this time Mitch was involved in another double-glazing company, which got into serious difficulties.

Weatherglaze plc ('where quality costs less') was a large and growing double-glazing company with a turnover of £15 million ($23 million) in 1997.* It nevertheless went bust in February 1998 with liabilities of £3.7 million ($5.8 million). The business was then bought by City Savings & Loans Ltd, which traded under the name Weatherglaze. Mitch became a director of City Savings & Loans in March 1998. He was also sales director. He had two fellow directors, one of whom had also been a director of the ill-fated Weatherglaze. History repeated itself when City Savings & Loans Ltd went bust in 1999 with liabilities of £3.6 million ($5.7 million). The list of creditors ran to twelve pages, including glass manufacturers, hire-purchase, telephone and office-supply companies, newspaper publishers, borough councils and the taxman. The biggest debt was £1.2 million ($1.9 million) owed to the Inland Revenue. 'That figure was for payroll taxes and does not include the liability for VAT [Value Added Tax], which totalled £647,594 [$1 million],' says David Stephenson, a senior manager with the accountants who conducted the liquidation. He explains what went wrong with Mitch's company: 'The report of the directors in office at the date of liquidation cited the causes of failure as mismanagement by [a former director], under-declarations of VAT of as much as £500,000 [$795,000] and loss of turnover following the acquisition of the business from the liquidators of the previous company, Weatherglaze plc.' The former director blamed had resigned prior to liquidation. Mitch was one of two directors still in place

---

* For the benefit of British and North American readers, amounts of money are given in pounds sterling and US dollars at current exchange rates.

and, as it turned out, he and his fellow director were also held responsible for the collapse of the company.

Liquidators spent seven years winding up City Savings & Loans during which time a small proportion of its debts were paid. At the end of the process creditors large and small were left £3.5 million ($5.5 million) out of pocket. One creditor was Glen Day, whose Yorkshire glazing company supplied the glass for the windows Mitch sold. His firm was owed £50,000. Glen Day recalls meeting Mitch in happier times when their companies were doing business: 'Funny. Vibrant. Plenty of chat. If he's a sales director, that's what he needs to be. [But] as a director, of course, he's responsible equally.' Day also recalls angry creditors' meetings at which he and others demanded to know from the directors what had gone wrong. 'I'm sat there owed fifty grand … and the questions are asked, as I asked, I'm sure: *What on Earth were you playing at to rack up a bill like this? You knew you were in financial difficulty. You knew you couldn't pay your way.*' He didn't receive satisfactory answers. Neither did he get his money.

The collapse of City Savings & Loans was sufficiently serious for the secretary of state for trade and industry to take legal action at the High Court against Mitch Winehouse and his fellow directors under the Company Directors Disqualification Act 1986 (Section 7), which deals with people unfit to run a limited company. The case was discontinued in August 2001 when the three directors 'accepted disqualification undertakings' – that is, they promised they would not be a director of a limited company, or take part in the management of a company directly or indirectly, for a period of years. The minimum disqualification period is two years. Mitch was disqualified for three and a half.

That was the unhappy end of Mitch Winehouse's career in double glazing, a subject he skips, along with his bankruptcy, in *Amy, My Daughter*, writing simply that he 'left [his] double-glazing business' to go back to driving a cab. Mitch's business history is relevant, however, in light of his subsequent close involvement in his daughter's business affairs, and the high public profile he maintained after Amy's death by running a charity in her name and asking the public for donations.

4

Amy started at the BRIT School on 29 August 2000, a month before she turned seventeen, arriving complete with piercings, tattoos and the eyeliner that became part of her image, drawn thickly in the style of Elizabeth Taylor as Cleopatra.

Amy's home and the BRIT School were on opposite sides of London. The commute was long and Amy was often grumpy when she arrived at school, if she turned up. 'She wasn't someone who wanted to be institutionalised,' says teacher Adrian Packer. 'We are not talking about someone who is lazy. We are talking about someone who was used to doing things on her own terms.' Still, Amy was an impressive and endearing pupil when she did attend school. 'She was *great* fun to teach, because she was really funny, she was really challenging ... robust and forthright ... an individual who stood out.' At the same time, Packer was concerned: 'Often as a teacher you look at a young person who is presenting themselves in such an upbeat way and think, *Are you really that happy? Are you really feeling that good about things?* And obviously she wasn't.' In fact, Amy was suffering with depression. She asked her pharmacist mother what was wrong with her, and Janis suggested that she might be bipolar (that term again). Amy felt bad enough to take anti-depressants.

By the end of 2000 Amy's commitment to her education was in serious doubt. She agreed with her teachers that she needed to find more self-discipline, but it wasn't forthcoming. She left the BRIT School after nine months in May 2001. It was a momentous year for the Winehouse family: Janis collapsed on holiday in Italy and was diagnosed with multiple sclerosis, which affected her life considerably from then on. She started to struggle with the stairs at Guildown Avenue, and didn't have the energy to fight with her wilful daughter who, having left full-time education, went out to work.

At weekends Amy worked on a clothes stall in Camden market and found part-time employment at World Entertainment News Network (WENN), a small press agency founded by the father of her friend Juliette Ashby. Young freelance journalists were employed on a shift system at the WENN office, behind King's Cross station, to trawl through newspapers and magazines for show-business stories, which were checked, rewritten and sent out 'on the wire' to foreign publications that paid if they used the copy. Working at WENN on the night shift, Amy learned the rudiments of tabloid journalism, of which she would soon become a subject. It was a valuable if limited lesson in how the media works. She also met her first serious boyfriend, a journalist seven years her senior named Chris.

Meanwhile, Amy's stage-school friend Tyler James was attempting to launch his singing career with the help of a public-relations man named Nick Shymansky. When Shymansky suggested that he record a duet, Tyler asked Amy to sing with him. A demo tape duly arrived at Nick Shymansky's office decorated with the type of stickers little girls put on their pencil cases, as well as hearts and Amy's name, as if Amy was seven, not seventeen. When he listened to the tape Shymansky suspected that he was the victim of a practical joke. The voice was so mature and powerful that 'I thought it was a [recording of] an old classic jazz singer.' Assured by Tyler that it was Amy singing, Shymansky called her to arrange a meeting, excited that he might have stumbled upon a star.

Success came relatively quickly and easily after this break. Amy was offered a management deal followed by recording and publishing contracts, giving her financial freedom virtually straight from school. She was not an artist who had to work for years to get started. She did not pay her dues. To some extent she may have been spoilt by easy early breaks. What we don't work for, we don't value, and Amy seemed to put a low value on her subsequent career, behaving in a cavalier fashion seldom found in people who have worked harder and longer for their chance to be heard.

It is sobering to reflect that at this stage, in common with the other principal 27s, Amy was more than halfway through her short but dramatic pocket-battleship life. Her character, interests and psychological quirks had been formed. As she wrote in her notebook, she intended to take full advantage of the opportunities ahead, and 'live like the bombshell I really am'.

Three

THE MAD ONES

... the only people for me are the mad ones, the ones who
are mad to live, mad to talk, mad to be saved, desirous of
everything at the same time, the ones who never yawn or
say a commonplace thing, but burn, burn, burn like
fabulous yellow roman candles ...
Jack Kerouac

1

After childhood, but before they became famous, the 27s met key
people who helped them turn adolescent dreams into careers. For
Brian Jones these were the years 1960–63, from when his parents
kicked him out until the Rolling Stones released their first record.

For the time being Brian worked at a variety of jobs in Cheltenham,
and made an unsuccessful attempt to enrol at art college. No longer
welcome at home, he shared flats with friends. One morning Pat
Andrews came round to Brian's latest digs to discover him in bed
with another girl. She chased him with a knife, though it was usually
Brian who was the jealous one. Still, Pat loved Brian, and she was
now pregnant with his child. A naïve sixteen-year-old, she refused
at first to accept that she was pregnant. 'Strange as it seems, I didn't
know how babies were born.' She persisted in her denial until her
sister took her to the doctor. 'He looked at me and he said, "You're
having a baby." I said, "Don't be stupid. Of course I'm not having

a baby. I'm not married. How can I have a baby?" Then they looked
at each other and must have thought, We've got a right one here.'
The baby, born on 23 October 1961, was given the first names
Julian Mark, Julian in honour of the saxophonist Julian 'Cannonball'
Adderley, one of the Brian's heroes. At nineteen, Brian was now the
father of three children by three women, making no attempt to
provide for any of them. 'I think he was quite proud to be a father,'
says his friend Richard Hattrell, 'although he wasn't a very good
one.'

One night Brian and Richard went to Cheltenham Town Hall to
hear the Chris Barber Jazz Band showcasing Alexis Korner, the first
British musician to sing the blues while accompanying himself on
electric guitar. They went backstage to meet Korner. 'He told us he was
going to start a rhythm and blues band, based on the music of Muddy
Waters, and the first gig would be in March 1962 at the Ealing Club
[in London],' recalls Hattrell. The boys hitchhiked to London for the
show, discovering the Ealing Club to be a basement beneath the ABC
Tea Shop opposite Ealing tube station. Korner's band, Blues Incorporated,
played amplified rhythm and blues in this cavern, with a young drummer
named Charlie Watts. Brian was inspired. He began to hitch up from
Cheltenham every weekend to attend the club, sleeping at Korner's flat,
and soon getting onstage to jam with his new friends under the stage
name Elmo Lewis, after the bluesman Elmore James.

One night two boys came into the club while Brian was performing
a song by one of the first 27s, and one of the fathers of the blues,
Robert Johnson. 'He played "Dust My Broom," and it was electri-
fying. He played it beautifully. We were very impressed,' Keith
Richards recalled in his memoirs, the first and almost the last compli-
ment he paid Brian.

Keith Richards was a spotty, taciturn youth of eighteen from
Dartford in Kent, a satellite town of south London, as was his friend
Mick Jagger, a more personable boy of the same age. Richards was
at art college. Jagger was studying at the London School of Economics.
The boys were as passionate about the blues as Brian and they had
a band, Little Boy Blue and the Blue Boys, in which Mick sang and
Keith played guitar. It was Mick who first spoke to Brian at the

Ealing Club. Brian held significant advantages over the Dartford lads: he was slightly older than Mick and Keith, a more accomplished musician, and evidently highly experienced with the opposite sex. He also had an air of superiority that initially impressed but soon came to irritate.

Brian was now living in London, working sporadically in shops, sacked at least once for stealing, while Pat Andrews worked in a laundry. Unable to cope with baby Julian, the couple put their son into foster care briefly. Brian was more interested in his music than his family. When he advertised for musicians to form a new band his young friends from the Ealing Club, Mick Jagger and Keith Richards, replied and thereby joined a group Brian named the Rollin (*sic*) Stones, after the Muddy Waters song 'Rollin' Stone Blues'. They played their first gig at the Marquee in London in July 1962, shortly after which Mick, Keith and Brian moved into a flat together in Edith Grove, Chelsea, where they shivered through the winter of 1962–63, saved from starvation by the kindness of friends such as Richard Hattrell, who experienced the nasty side of Brian in return for his charity. 'Brian bossed me about quite a bit,' says Hattrell. 'Brian and I were good friends, but he had a vicious streak in him. He had two characters – he could be as nice as pie one minute, and really turn on you the next.' Brian ordered Hattrell to give Keith Richards his overcoat when Keith was cold and made Hattrell pay for everybody at the Wimpy Bar. '[Brian] would make me walk behind the three of them – Brian, Mick and Keith – [and then make] me wait outside [while they ate]. Then he'd come out and expect me to pay for the three of them. If I kicked up a fuss, he just got aggressive ... I can't remember him actually hitting me as such, but verbally he attacked me in no uncertain manner and I'm a pretty sensitive, very emotional person, so that used to upset me a great deal.'

The line-up of the Stones was completed in January 1963 when bass guitarist Bill Wyman and drummer Charlie Watts joined the band. 'The Rolling Stones that I joined was led by Brian Jones,' Wyman wrote in his autobiography, *Stone Alone*, which provides the most detailed account of the band's early years, making it plain that Brian was their leader at this stage. Not only had Brian founded the Stones, he had given the band its name, its musical direction, and he was the front man. But he didn't sing. Mick Jagger held the microphone, which allowed him to command the audience's attention. His position was strengthened by his friendship with Keith, whom Brian condescended to as his understudy on the guitar. Meanwhile, Brian seemed to look down on Bill and Charlie because they were from working-class families. He had an unfortunate knack of upsetting people.

The fact that Mick, Keith and Brian were so young, and living on top of each other at Edith Grove,* made everything more intense. There was a good deal of teasing and jockeying for position. One day Mick made a move on Pat Andrews. Even though she found him 'funny and charming', Pat says she turned him down. But the others made sure that Brian knew what Mick had done, just to annoy him, Brian being pathologically jealous. As an example, he accused Pat of sleeping with a man at work to get money to buy clothes for herself and the baby. And in his jealousy he sometimes became aggressive. As Brian raised his hand to Pat again, she decided to defend herself by hitting him first. She left Brian soon afterwards and brought up Julian alone. Brian didn't seem to care. He had already met someone else.

Despite a weak and neurotic personality, despite his jealousy, faithlessness and violence, Brian had numerous girlfriends, many of whom still hold him in affection. 'You [asked me] why did all these women like him,' his next significant girlfriend, Linda Lawrence, said in an interview for this book. 'Because he was so gentle and very sensual. [He was] the most sweet, gentle guy.' This lovable side of Brian remained obscure to men, many of whom couldn't stand him. 'If Brian wanted to fuck you, maybe it would have been different,' sneers Andrew Loog Oldham, who became the Stones' manager in 1963. Loog Oldham saw Mick Jagger and Keith Richards as the natural leaders of the band and helped them take over. The power games had started and there would be a good deal of cruelty towards Brian before he was edged out. Loog Oldham defends his

* Bill Wyman was married, and lived with his wife. Charlie Watts also lived elsewhere.

part in the manoeuvring by pointing out how young they all were, and when one looks at early photographs and film footage of the Stones their youth is striking, the band members only slightly older than their original fans, most of whom were little more than children. The Stones were essentially still kids themselves in 1963, and they behaved towards each other with the casual cruelty of children. Loog Oldham was nineteen when he started managing the band, the same age as Mick and Keith, while Brian was just 21. As he says, 'When you're children – which is what we were – it's *Lord of the Flies*, dear.'

Loog Oldham altered the band's name subtly, making them the *Rolling* Stones, secured a record deal with Decca and arranged valuable early publicity. The press seized on the Bohemian Stones as an alternative to the slick, packaged Beatles, fast becoming the biggest pop act in the world. Brian was ambitious to match the Beatles' success. When the Stones' début single, a cover of Chuck Berry's 'Come On', charted at a disappointing 21, he muttered about sacking Mick Jagger, as if Mick was holding them back. But events overtook him. The Stones had a rapidly growing following of enthusiastic teenagers, enough to fill every club and theatre they played, and those fans liked Mick Jagger very much. Indeed, it became apparent that it was Brian, not Mick, who was the weak link in the Rolling Stones.

In the history of the 27 Club, a sure sign of trouble comes when artists miss gigs. This happened with Brian Jones at the outset of the Rolling Stones' career. He first failed to attend band rehearsals on 27 August 1963, having 'apparently collapsed from nervous exhaustion', according to Bill Wyman. That night, when Brian didn't show up at the Ricky Tick Club in Windsor, the Stones had to perform without him, as they would many times in the years ahead, deciding ultimately that they would be better off if he left altogether.

2

Jimi Hendrix took longer than most of the 27s to get his break, which gave him time to become the most accomplished musician of the Big Six.

As we have seen, Jimi left home in May 1961 to join the US Army, doing his basic training in California before transferring to Fort Campbell on the border of Tennessee and Kentucky, where he joined the 101st Airborne because parachutists received bonus pay. Jimi had never flown in a plane, let alone jumped out of one, and complained in letters home about the 'dreadful' experience of jump school. 'I can laugh about it now,' he wrote to his father, on 15 December 1961. 'But then, if I laughed, I would be pushing Tennessee around all day – with my hands – push-ups.' Despite a difficult childhood, Jimi's letters to Al Hendrix were affectionate. Jimi was homesick, of course, and some parents are easier to love at a distance.

The best part of being at Fort Campbell was meeting Billy Cox, a soldier from Pennsylvania who played bass guitar and became a close friend. Hendrix and Cox formed a band that performed in and around the base. Jimi's ambition to play music full time reasserted itself and he decided he needed to get out of the army without delay. He told the camp doctor that he was homosexual, as Charles R. Cross revealed in the biography *Room Full of Mirrors*. Jimi persisted in this story, adding other issues, until the army gave up and released him in the summer of 1962. When Billy Cox was later discharged, they formed a band, the King Kasuals, performing on the local club scene. After a while Jimi drifted off to play with other, bigger acts, but he and Billy Cox stayed in touch and they would work together again.

For the next four years Jimi performed on the so-called Chitlin Circuit of African-American clubs in the South, perfecting his skills and learning from musicians he met, including such greats as B. B. King, Little Richard and Muddy Waters. Jimi played in Richard's band for a while. Musicians who knew him during those years of obscurity recall a young man obsessed with the guitar. He'd play 'all night long, all day long, every day, that's all he ever did,' Bobby Womack told the writer Charles Shaar Murray. It wasn't quite all Jimi did. He also started to experiment with drugs, and developed a reputation as a ladies' man.

Jimi relocated to New York in 1964, performing under the stage name Maurice James. That spring he toured with the Isley Brothers, later with Curtis Knight and the Squires. Foolishly, he signed a three-year recording contract with Knight's manager, Ed Chalpin, for a nominal advance of a dollar, a deal that caused problems in the future while doing little to help him in the short term. Indeed, by 1965 he was virtually down-and-out.

'When we met him he was very poor. He had a guitar with no [strap], no amplifier,' says David Brigati, a member of Joey Dee & the Starliters, with whom Jimi toured after the Squires, opening each night with their number one hit, 'Peppermint Twist'. Brigati recalls that Jimi travelled light, with a single overnight bag in which he had a change of clothes and a set of hair curlers. 'He was very shy and quiet ... kind of soft-spoken.' When he did speak, Hendrix had a habit of putting a hand to his face and talking between his fingers. His shyness didn't impede his sex life. Brigati gives examples of Jimi's prowess with women, including the night he met three Indian ladies in an elevator in Buffalo. 'The next day he reported that he slept with all three.' Another night Jimi took part in a threesome with a girl and another man in Brigati's room, while Brigati ate dinner downstairs. 'Afterwards she said it was the best night of her life.' Although Jimi's drug problems are usually thought to have started later, Brigati claims to have received a call one morning from one of Jimi's girlfriends saying he'd overdosed on heroin in her room. 'I said, "Do you love him?" She said, "Yes." I said, "Then call the fucking police." Those were my words. And she did, and he was [revived].'

Jimi Hendrix left the Starliters in 1965, for more money with King Kurtis, but he was weary of this journeyman life. He was in New York when he met the English model Linda Keith, then Keith Richards's girlfriend. The Stones were big now, and Linda had come to New York ahead of the band's summer tour of the United States. She befriended Jimi, introducing him to LSD, which would influence his work significantly, and encouraged him to strike out on his own, assuring him that he could be a star.

He began performing in the clubs of Greenwich Village with two sidemen as Jimmy James and the Blue Flames. Bob Dylan had got his break in the Village, and Jimi was a Dylan fan. The fact that Dylan had become a star with such a quirky voice encouraged Jimi to sing for the first time. Like Dylan, he had a distinctive way of phrasing, part-speaking lyrics, often with a chuckling laugh. Jimi included Dylan's 'Like a Rolling Stone' in his set along with 'Wild Thing'. He began to wear increasingly colourful outfits, letting his hair grow long and performing his stage tricks, including playing his guitar with his teeth, and behind his back. A buzz developed around this extraordinary guitarist.

When the Stones arrived in New York, members of the band came to the Village to see Jimi play. Linda Keith gave him one of Keith Richards's guitars and asked Andrew Loog Oldham if he would manage him. Loog Oldham passed: it wasn't his type of music. Linda Keith continued to sing Jimi's praises to others, including Chas Chandler, bass player with the Animals, who wanted to get into management. Chandler asked Jimi if he would come to England. Jimi wasn't sure. For the time being he continued to scratch a living in New York. The blues musician John Hammond Jr recalls Jimi as being semi-destitute, playing with borrowed equipment and desperate for money. 'He said, "Could you get me a gig?"' So Hammond arranged for Jimi to back him at the Cafe au Go Go on Bleecker Street where he had a residency, showcasing Jimi as part of his set. 'It just turned out that everybody, a who's who in New York at that time, came to the show. It was packed out every night ... Anybody who heard this guy knew he was phenomenal and he was going to go places.'

At the end of the summer, Chas Chandler asked Jimi again to come to England, where he and his partner, Michael Jeffrey, would manage him. Jimi was dubious. He had never been outside North America. But having spent four years working his way up from nothing to penniless obscurity in his homeland, he had little to lose by going abroad. Two months before his 24th birthday he flew to London where his life was transformed.

3

Janis Joplin hitchhiked to San Francisco in January 1963 in search of the adventures Jack Kerouac's characters found in the Bay Area.

She arrived at a time when the subculture was in transition. The heyday of the beats was over, but hippie culture had not yet flowered. In-between was the tail end of the folk revival. Janis slipped into this milieu, singing country blues in coffee houses, relying on the hospitality of friends and lovers of both sexes. This was, as she later wrote, 'my gay period', though she had lesbian partners throughout her life. It was also a drug period. 'Janis called herself a candle burning at both ends,' says her flatmate Linda Gottfried.

Janis became a 'meth freak' in San Francisco, injecting Methedrine to get high. In common with many meth users she believed that speed energy helped creativity, allowing her to work all night on song lyrics and drawings. In the light of day, the quality of the work was often poor, and the user was left with jangled nerves. Many turned to heroin to come down, which may have been Janis's intro-duction to the drug that killed her. Drugs in general came to domi-nate her life. 'I wanted to smoke dope, take dope, lick dope, suck dope, fuck dope, anything I could lay my hands on I wanted to do it, man,' she later admitted, with characteristic candour.

Janis dated a fellow user, Peter de Blanc, who took so much speed he was admitted to an asylum. Janis wanted to marry de Blanc, but she felt that she needed to get clean first, so she returned to Port Arthur in the summer of 1965 to recuperate. She came home in a shockingly wretched state: her body was emaciated, her clothes were dishevelled and her arms were punctured with needle marks. She spent the next few months in Texas trying to live a healthier, more conventional life, enrolling in college, even taking up country-club golf, as she planned for marriage to Peter de Blanc. The romantic fantasy dissolved when she realised her intended was seeing other women in San Francisco. Janis went into a depression and consulted a psychiatrist, telling him that she 'wanted to be like normal people'. The psychiatrist advised her to accept herself as she was, while a doctor prescribed Librium, the same drug Amy Winehouse would take to smooth out her anxieties. Both women were a mass of neuroses. In a letter to Peter de Blanc, Janis wrote: 'I want to be happy so fucking bad.' One can imagine Amy saying the same.

In time Janis forgot de Blanc and started singing again. In March 1966 she accepted an invitation from a friend named Chet Helms to return to the Bay Area where the hippie renaissance was in full swing, the use of LSD having a dramatic effect on fashion, music and design in the city. Helms, who knew Janis as a singer, and was an important figure in the Bay Area music scene, wanted to put her together with Big Brother and the Holding Company, one of a number of happening rock 'n' roll bands he was working with in and around San Francisco. Like the Grateful Dead, Big Brother was a family band whose members lived and worked in a communal house in an atmosphere that was intellectual and drug-oriented. Janis entered this stimulating world with a sense of excitement and foreboding.

Big Brother had two guitarists, Sam Andrew and James Gurley. Janis had a fling with both men, but she developed a particularly close and lasting friendship with Sam, who recalls her mixed feelings about returning to San Francisco after her earlier bad experience: 'She'd failed in San Francisco and she'd gone home, tried to live a normal person's life [and] tried to do everything her mother wanted her to do … She was probably frightened by her early San Francisco experiences. And then Chet wanted her to come back out to San Francisco a second time. She had a lot of trepidation about that … She was afraid that if she came back to the West Coast she would fall back into her same ways and die, and in essence that's exactly what happened.'

Sam describes Janis as 'very *quick*, really quick in her bodily movements, and in her thoughts and in her reactions to everything. She was very *fast*. She was highly intelligent and very focused on her career, more so than we were. We were kind of just a hippie band, and we were kind of stumbling, bumbling around trying to find our way, and she kind of had her eye on the long trajectory, ironically enough. [And she was] a very funny person.' Although Janis's image is of a melancholic, Sam corrects this, saying that everything about Janis was magnified, the highs as well as the lows. In fact she displayed classic bipolar disorder. 'She had more fun than anyone – that I know for sure. She really had a great time.

And then she probably had a really miserable time, more miserable than anyone also.'

Big Brother had a small but loyal following in San Francisco, and some of their fans doubted that Janis was good enough to sing with the boys. There was perhaps some sexism. 'I thought she was a rag … a cheap piece of shit clothing hung on a twig in a middle of a stiff breeze,' says photographer Bob Seidemann, a close friend of the band, who later took an iconic nude photograph of Janis. He remembers that Janis dressed for the stage initially as if she was still at college, not yet wearing the satins, boas and extravagant hats she became known for. 'She looked ratty. Her hair was unkempt. She was wearing a really crummy piece of clothing … She was a mess. She wasn't good-looking, [and] I didn't think her singing was all that good. In fact, the first time I heard her singing with the band I called the drummer over to say, "Get rid of the chick."'

Janis was so nervous that she almost ran home to Texas. She didn't have the experience to sing before large crowds at venues like the Avalon Ballroom in San Francisco. She hardly had any songs prepared. Yet she grew in confidence onstage. 'The music was boom, boom, boom! And the people were all dancing, and the lights [were going] and I was standing up there singing into this microphone and getting it on. And, whew, I dug it.' Janis decided to stay in San Francisco, and Bob Seidemann was one of many who completely changed their mind about her. 'I was lucky enough to be able to ask forgiveness of her, for my original opinion, because I went from a low regard to a high regard.'

4

While Janis Joplin was getting together with Big Brother in San Francisco, the Doors began their career in Los Angeles. There would be rivalry between the Doors and the Bay Area bands in the years ahead – as there always has been between the two great cities of California. The use of LSD, though, was common to all and a vital ingredient in the music being made.

Jim Morrison and Ray Manzarek were both into LSD when they decided to form a band, using the drug to achieve 'nirvana', a word popular with the hippies as it caught the attention of Kurt Cobain decades later. Manzarek believes that he was 'reborn' during his first major trip: 'I was a new Ray Manzarek.' The drug had an equally profound effect on Jim, whom Manzarek invited home to stay with him and his girlfriend as they started to make music together, rehearsing initially with Ray's brother's band. They then recruited drummer John Densmore, whom Manzarek had met at a Transcendental Meditation meeting. Densmore had also dropped acid. Musically, his taste was jazz, which helped form the band's unusual sound. Although not yet complete, Manzarek and Morrison had a name for the group. Manzarek recalls that Jim coined it that first day on the beach: the Doors.

'You mean, like the Doors in your mind … Like Aldous Huxley?' asked Manzarek, referring to Huxley's book about drug experiments, *The Doors of Perception*, itself a quote from William Blake.

'Exactly.'

The naming of the Doors has become a foundation stone of its legend, the literary associations lending gravitas to a band that took itself very seriously. There may have been a more prosaic inspiration. 'I remember their mentioning, "What shall we call the band?"' says actor Britt Leach, who lodged at Manzarek's apartment at the same time as Jim Morrison. 'And we were in a nest of doors [at the apartment]. We were standing in a door. The front door was right there. [Ray] said, "the Doors!" And then, of course, later it became the Doors of Perception … I swear to God that's bullshit.'

The boys needed to cut a demo. Jim approached a friend of his father's for money to make the recording. Admiral Morrison, then stationed in London, had not seen his elder son since his senior year at UCLA and was not pleased to hear about his new career. He wrote Jim a stinking letter, 'severely criticising his behaviour and strongly advising him to give up any idea of singing or any connection with a musical group,' as he later said, 'because of what I considered to be a complete lack of talent in this direction'. It was an unduly harsh response, an indication perhaps of what Jim had had to put up with from his father, and it had a dramatic result: Jim cut all contact with his parents.

Morrison, Manzarek and Densmore somehow found the money to make their demo, which they took around the record companies. The only interest came from Columbia, which signed the Doors to a six-month development deal, during which time the company did nothing to promote them. Meanwhile, the band finalised its line-up, recruiting guitarist Robby Krieger, another acid head who describes taking psychedelics as one of the defining events of his life. Krieger's musical interests were jazz and blues, which complemented Manzarek's and Densmore's. For want of a bass guitarist, Manzarek played the bass parts on his keyboard, which was another important element in the Doors sounding different from other rock bands.

The threat of being drafted still hung over Jim, as it did over thousands of young Americans at the height of the Vietnam War. In May 1966 Jim appeared before the draft board again. Although he had originally been passed fit to serve in the military, government records show that this time he was classified 4-F, meaning he was disqualified.* Like many young men Jim must have pulled a trick to get out of service, possibly pretending to be homosexual, as John Densmore and many others did.

With the fear of being sent to war lifted, the Doors began gigging on Sunset Boulevard in Los Angeles, where further evidence as to the origins of the band's name may lie: the group was billed at the London Fog as the Swinging Doors. 'I don't know if it was them or the club, but the sign advertised them as the Swinging Doors,' recalls Dickie Davis, who came to see the band with a view to managing them. 'It was clearly art rock. It was jazz, a very loose jazz format with Jim holding himself up with the microphone stand, reading poetry into the microphone ... Jim closed his eyes, just went inward. He hung on that microphone stand. It was a strong erotic image. He really sold it.' Davis told the band he didn't think

---

* John Densmore writes in his memoir that Morrison told him he was classified Z, but there was no such classification. Selective Service records reveal the true classification.

he was the right person to manage them, but he became friends with Jim.

A former actress named Ronnie Haran was sufficiently impressed to hire the Doors as the house band at the Whisky a Go Go, further along Sunset Strip. She also invited Jim to stay with her at her bungalow on Westbourne Drive, thereby coming to see herself as one of the 'little girls in their Hollywood bungalows' Jim sings about in 'LA Woman'. Jim was heavily into drugs by this time. 'He was a doper,' says Haran. 'If we were walking down the street and somebody came up and said, "Hey, Jim! Hey, man, take this," he'd take it [even though] he didn't know what it was. [He was] totally reckless.' The couple took acid together and Jim smoked marijuana constantly, littering the bungalow with roaches.

Ronnie Haran says her relationship with Jim was not sexual, surprisingly, possibly because Jim was 'too stoned'. She also suggests that his interest may have lain elsewhere. 'I know he was testing the limits of bisexuality. He used to talk to me about wanting to have an affair with a guy to see what it was like.' Be that as it may, and there is a hint of bisexuality with many of the main 27s, he had numerous girlfriends, often unknown to one another. Around the time Ronnie knew Jim he was also dating a model named Billie Winters, who lived at the Tropicana Motel in Hollywood. When he and Billie parted, Jim took up with her roommate, a model named Enid Graddis, who doesn't recall a problem with impotence: 'I was one of the many girls who thought Jim was the most amazing guy. He was so charismatic … [We] had an amazing relationship.' Then there was Pamela Courson, a delicate hippie chick from Weed in northern California, who wafted into Jim's life around this time and stayed with him until he died. Like Brian Jones, Jim was a man who got on better with women than men.

As the Doors continued to play the Whisky, creating long hypnotic jams for the patrons to dance and trip to, they worked out the definitive versions of many of their most famous songs including 'Break on Through', with its bossa nova beat, and 'Light My Fire', largely written by Robby Krieger. The band reached back to the 1920s to cover 'Alabama Song', by Brecht and Weill, revealing their sophistication. Then there were Jim's original song stories, laced with poetry and philosophy. High on acid, he howled stream-of-consciousness poetry into the microphone at the Whisky until he blurted out the Oedipal section of 'The End', screaming that he wanted to kill his father and fuck his mother. The outraged club owners fired the Doors on the spot.

Fortunately Ronnie Haran had interested a record company in the band. She says that Jac Holzman didn't like the Doors when he first saw them at the Whisky, but he signed them to Elektra Records and teamed them up with producer Paul Rothchild, who did so much to make the Doors a success. Meanwhile, the boys signed a management deal with Asher Dann and Sal Bonafede. Dann was a charming former B-movie actor, once billed as 'Hollywood's handsomest man'. With his acting career behind him, he switched to management and clicked with Jim immediately. 'He was a lot younger than me, but I used to love to go out and I used to love to party, and he saw that in me.'

Jim was essentially a loner. He got along with Asher Dann and Ray Manzarek, whom he had known since college, but he was distant from the other two band members. John Densmore was particularly wary of Jim, whom he considered borderline crazy, and there was evidence to corroborate this view. Whether one believes that Jim set out to live the Dionysian life as a way of making art, or whether he was a pretentious drunken boor, the result was the same. Jim was one of what Kerouac called 'the mad ones'. Many of the 27s were.

An early example of Jim's craziness came when the Doors visited New York to sign their record deal. While they were in the city, Paul Rothchild invited the band home to New Jersey for dinner with him and his wife. 'Jim responded in character by getting stone drunk and coming on to Paul's wife,' John Densmore recalls, in his memoir. As Rothchild drove the musicians back to their hotel after dinner, Jim pulled the producer's hair. He was so out of it that his band mates had to help him up to his room where he climbed out onto the tenth-floor window ledge, 'shrieking like a banshee'. When his band mates coaxed him back inside, he wrestled with them, then urinated on the floor.

5

Kurt Cobain lodged with the Shillinger family in Aberdeen, Washington, over the winter of 1985–86, during which time he wrote songs, some of which he recorded at the home of his aunt Mari Earl, including a tune titled 'Suicide Samurai', which made Aunt Mari fear for her nephew.

There was further cause for concern when Kurt was arrested along with his friend Eric Shillinger for trespassing on a building in downtown Aberdeen. Eric was let go, but the police detained Kurt because he hadn't paid his $180 fine for writing graffiti on the SeaFirst Bank. Eric's father, Lamont Shillinger, declined to post bail for his lodger, so Kurt spent eight days in jail. Not long after this incident he had a fight with the Shillinger boys and left the family home, reverting to sofa-surfing and sleeping rough.

Although only nineteen, and living in close proximity to several family members, including his mother (whom he would visit for meals), Kurt was on the verge of becoming down-and-out. By his own account, he first tried heroin during this unhappy period in Aberdeen. He said he felt drawn to the drug. 'I always wanted to do it,' he told one biographer. 'I always knew that I would.' Trying heroin proved a fateful decision. Of all the drugs abused in the history of the 27 Club, heroin is the one that undoes musicians time and again, playing a significant part in the decline of five of the six main 27s.

Kurt next moved into a shack on East 2nd Street in Aberdeen with friends, living in squalor comparable to that which the Rolling Stones enjoyed at Edith Grove in the early sixties. Somewhat like the Stones, Kurt and his friends made a decision to reject conventional life and live on their wits as artists. Also like the Stones they had no compunction about sponging off friends who had a job, such as carpet-fitter Ryan Aigner. Ryan says Kurt found the idea of a straight life 'deplorable, and didn't want to be traditional … I don't think he ever really embraced the idea that you have an obligation to work.' Much of the time Kurt and his slacker buddies sat around the shack listening to records, stony broke and stoned, cut off from and ignored by the world. 'We didn't really have a lot of places to go, or people calling us, or interested in what we were doing,' observes Aigner (though he had a job). 'We could sit around for days, listening to records, and the phone would never ring ... or we would never even have a phone.' It was, as he says, only music that mattered to Kurt, 'and then music became a job'.

In pursuit of his ambitions Kurt teamed up with a local youth named Krist Novoselic, a punk-rock enthusiast two years his senior and a veritable giant at six foot seven. The Novoselics lived among the better-off Aberdonians on Think of Me Hill. Krist sympathised with Kurt's misanthropy and admired his individualism, describing Kurt as 'one of the most independent people' he had ever known, 'a completely creative person – a true artist'. He particularly liked the way in which Kurt had transformed his shack home into a den of Dada art, a place where he 'sketched very obscene Scooby-Doo cartoons [over the walls], made wild sound montages from obscure records [and] sculpted clay into scary spirit people writhing in agony'.

Krist took up bass guitar. With Kurt on vocals and lead guitar, and a series of friends playing drums, they had a band, though it went by several eccentric names before Kurt hit upon Nirvana. He chose this name after watching a television documentary about Buddhism, which teaches that the life we are living is one of a cycle of reincarnated lives during which humans inevitably suffer. Only by renouncing the attachments of earthly life can a person escape the wheel of reincarnation and aspire to the blissful state of nothingness known as nirvana. Kurt liked the word because it sounded beautiful and was different from other punk band names. He also adopted Buddhism as his faith, attracted by the concept of blissful nothingness, a state of being that the drug-user achieves artificially, and the depressive may look for in suicide.

Kurt's obsession with death remained fundamental to his personality. His notebooks were full of morbid drawings and jottings. He wrote about death and he talked about it. One day Ryan Aigner asked him: 'What do you think you're gonna do when you're thirty?'

'I'll never see thirty.'

'What do you mean, you'll never see thirty?' Ryan was a year older than Kurt and he fully expected to live to thirty.

Kurt was adamant. 'I won't.' And, of course, he was right.

It wasn't so much that Kurt was living for the moment, like the other 27s, experiencing as much as he could as fast as he could. He was barely living at all, and he didn't seem to look to the future with optimism. Perhaps he would have been more cheerful had he got laid.

Kurt had never had much of a sex life. A misanthropic introvert with morbid obsessions, and somewhat unkempt, Kurt was not every girl's dream. 'I never noticed him to be smelly, but he was always dirty-looking, because he was homeless [some of the time], and people knew that. So he couldn't find a girlfriend,' says Aberdeen buddy Mitch Holmquist. 'Before he was big, nobody wanted anything to do with him.' Still, there were girls who looked closer and saw a gentle, intelligent, even quite nice-looking young man. Tracy Marander, a fellow punk-music enthusiast, batted her eyelids at Kurt until he got the message and kissed her. Soon afterwards Kurt moved into Tracy's apartment in Olympia, the state capital of Washington, a university town with a busy music scene, situated roughly halfway between Aberdeen and Seattle. It was in Olympia that Nirvana developed into a tight band with a local following.

Although introverted in everyday life, Kurt was transformed onstage. 'He shocked me when he'd go out and perform, because he was so shy and withdrawn,' says Mitch Holmquist, who attended many early shows. 'He'd be the wild, crazy man out there.' These early performances were not particularly interesting for the words Kurt wrote and sang. He was never a poet of song, like Jim Morrison. Like many punk rockers, Kurt was more concerned with the energy of the music than the lyrics that went with it. Yet his lyrics had interest and, like Janis Joplin and Amy Winehouse, he seemed to mean every word he sang.

As far as Nirvana's appearance and image was concerned, Kurt and his fellow band members wore the clothing of the average blue-collar Aberdeen male: sneakers, old jeans and plaid shirts, clothing layered for warmth in the frigid Pacific north-west. Kurt's high-school contemporary Penny Lloyd recalls how surprised she was when this scruffy attire – which she associated with the men who worked in the mills – became fashionable in the mid-1990s, when Nirvana and grunge rock became all the rage. She and her friends at Aberdeen High had been trying so hard to look like Ralph Lauren models. 'So we thought that was pretty funny.'

As Kurt's band became more proficient they were inevitably drawn to the big city, Seattle. Nirvana recorded a demo in Seattle in 1988 with producer Jack Endino, who passed the tape to a local label, Sub Pop, who put out Nirvana's first single, 'Love Buzz', a *succès d'estime*. As Nirvana's local following grew, the band took to smashing their equipment onstage – an act Jimi Hendrix and others had pioneered in the 1960s but came fresh to their young fans – and in the fall of 1988 Nirvana set out on tour in a van. After years of misery and obscurity Kurt actually started to enjoy himself.

'Dear long lost grandparents: I miss you very much,' he wrote, on a Christmas card to Iris and Leland Cobain at their trailer home in Montesano in December 1988. 'I'm very busy living in Olympia when I'm not on tour with my band. We put out a single just recently and it has sold out already ... I'm happier than I ever have been.'

6

As we have seen, the six main 27s had a difficult start in life. In the years ahead, Jones, Hendrix, Joplin, Morrison and Cobain had little contact with their families. They were adults now, able to make their own decisions, and they didn't need or want interference from their parents. Amy Winehouse was different.

Although her father had left home when she was nine, and was a shadowy figure in Amy's life for the second half of her childhood, as Amy embarked on her professional career Mitch Winehouse became a constant presence. Jewish families often work together; there was some tradition of that in the Winehouse family. Also, Amy was a teenager when she turned professional, so she needed adult guidance. Still, Mitch busied himself in his daughter's career to a remarkable degree from the time she signed her management deal, aged seventeen, with Nick Shymansky and Nick Godwyn, until her death ten years later.

Mitch was clearly very excited that Amy had broken into show-business, a career he had aspired to for himself. In contrast, Amy played it cool. Describing an early meeting with her new managers, Mitch writes, in *Amy, My Daughter*, that Amy 'seemed to take it in her stride, but I could barely sit still'. As Amy's career developed, Mitch often appeared star-struck, while Amy gave the impression that she didn't care what was happening. When people asked her what she was doing, she didn't gush about her management deal, and that she might soon be making a record, but would say casually, 'I'm a jazz singer.' She told her hairdresser that she was 'a wedding singer'.

Amy received a stipend from her management company of £250 a week ($397) while she worked up demos of songs that could be used to get a record deal. The months that followed were a happy time during which she was free to write and record at her own pace with young musicians and producers, such as Stefan Skarbek, with whom she worked at Mayfair Studios in London.

A multi-instrumentalist seven years Amy's senior, Stefan found Amy to be a conundrum. She was in some ways a typical teenager, caught up in dramas with her parents and boyfriend. One of her early unreleased songs, 'Ease Up on Me', was a plea to her mother to cut her more slack, while Stefan also recalls tension between Amy and her father. 'I don't think she was speaking to her dad at that point.' At the same time Amy had an emotional maturity that set her apart from friends of the same age: 'She was very, very wise, emotionally wise, very smart, very, very intelligent [and] funny,' says Stefan, whose father was the noted psychotherapist Andrzej Skarbek while his mother, Marjorie Wallace, had founded the mental health charity SANE, all of which gave him some insight into human behaviour. He identified a fundamental conflict between Amy's craving for normality and her need to express herself. 'I think she was always craving a somewhat normal existence ... that was an internal struggle that was constantly going [on] ... She wanted to make everything homely, making chicken soup, making cups of tea all day long, being a mum. I felt like that was a big attempt by her to be a normal person ... It's a dichotomy ... the two things don't mesh [and] the conflict was what she wrote about.'

Amy wrote in a notebook decorated with pictures of Ella Fitzgerald, Sarah Vaughan and Dinah Washington. Early compositions from the notebook that Amy worked up into songs for her début album, *Frank*, included 'October Song', a lament for her pet canary, Ava, which died one weekend when she was away. Amy's complaints about her boyfriend led to another song, 'Amy, Amy, Amy', the concluding track on *Frank*. 'She came in talking about Chris, and would go into some weird story about something going wrong, and I was, like, "Amy, Amy, Amy, you've got to get serious ..."' says Stefan Skarbek. 'And then we started to write a song of her talking back to herself.' Sexy and funny though the song is, Amy was never satisfied with it. Songs that failed to make *Frank* included 'Ambulance Man', inspired by the drama of Cynthia Winehouse being admitted to hospital. Amy scat-sang in imitation of the ambulance siren. When she and Stefan ran out of ideas they sometimes crossed the road to Regent's Park to visit the zoo (which inspired another unrecorded song, 'Monkey Boy') or went to sit on Primrose Hill with a bottle of wine.

After a while Amy's management sent her to the United States to work with 'Commissioner' Gordon Williams, who'd engineered a successful album for Lauryn Hill. Williams heard Amy singing before he met her and was surprised that such a mature and soulful voice belonged to a white English teenager. 'She sounded like an old black jazz singer ... because all she listened to was jazz.' One of the songs Amy brought to Williams's New Jersey studio was 'What is it About Men?' which addressed her misgivings about her father and men in general. 'I completely did it over, because it was more like a ballad,' says Williams. 'I gave it a little groove and made it a little bit edgy, and she really liked the reggae thing, so it was also kind of finding a way to mix reggae, hip-hop and jazz together in one record.' In this way he helped Amy set her lyrics in a distinctive soundscape that was 'like something from the past but now'.

To record these songs Williams recruited American and Jamaican session players, including reggae musicians who'd worked with Bob Marley, and jazz saxophonist Teo Avery, after whom the track 'Teo Licks' is titled. Avery was struck by how serious Amy was about jazz. She covered two jazz standards on *Frank*, 'Moody's Mood for Love' and '(There Is) No Greater Love', and talked of making a purely jazz album. 'She could have done it, because she had that sensitivity in the way that she sang,' says Avery. 'When you're playing jazz, or singing jazz, there's a high amount of sensitivity you have to have in order to bring the music up to bring it down. It's not like soul, where it's usually a full-on, high-velocity approach to music. She had that sensitivity where she could bring it way down to bring it back up.'

Amy continued work on her album in Miami with Salaam Remi, who played a key role in the making of both *Frank* and *Back to Black*. One of the songs Remi produced for the first album was 'Fuck Me Pumps' in which Amy mocks girls who go clubbing to snare a rich husband. Her humour was equally pointed on 'Stronger than Me', in which she vented her frustration at her boyfriend – Amy made it clear that she had Chris in mind – for not being macho enough. Her wit and enjoyment of wordplay is evident in the very funny line in which she teasingly compares herself, a red-blooded 'lady', to a boyfriend who seems more like a 'ladyboy'.

Gordon Williams never met Chris. 'We were supposed to meet in London, but I don't think he ever did get to the studio. He was probably too embarrassed, to be honest with you!'

During the recording of *Frank*, Amy's managers negotiated two important deals for her: first, a music-publishing deal with EMI; and then, just before Christmas 2002, a record deal with Island/Universal. Although signing a record deal is a red-letter day in the lives of most artists, Amy failed to show up for the meeting. When her manager Nick Godwyn called her to ask where she was, she said she thought she'd already signed the documents. Her attitude was not good, and her working relationship with her managers and record label became strained. 'The truth is she was complicated and difficult,' Nick Godwyn wrote, after her death. 'She could be disruptive and haughty. She liked to challenge you. And she was always kicking against something.'

Mitch Winehouse was very excited about the record deal. Amy asked her father not to tell her grandmother because she wanted to break the news to Cynthia herself. 'I promised I wouldn't,' Mitch wrote in his book, adding that he couldn't help himself. '[I] phoned her the minute Amy left.'

Publishing and record deals earned Amy a combined advance of £500,000 ($795,000), a huge sum for a teenager. A limited company, Cherry Westfield, was formed in 2002 to handle the cash. Amy owned Cherry Westfield outright, her mother being her fellow director. Mitch Winehouse was not allowed to be a company director at this time, as he was still disqualified, but he became company secretary, which he was permitted to do as long as he took no part 'directly or indirectly ... in the promotion, formation or management' of the company. If he did, he could face a fine or jail. Also, Amy was not allowed to take advice from her father in the management of her company. Years later, when his disqualification expired, Mitch was legitimately appointed to the board of directors of Cherry Westfield, and became a director of other companies created to handle Amy's money.

In light of the restrictions on disqualified directors, it is surprising to read in *Amy, My Daughter* how much Mitch involved himself in his daughter's finances while he was disqualified. 'Amy understood very quickly that if her mum and I didn't exert some kind of financial control she'd go through that money like there was no tomorrow,' Mitch writes, and goes on to describe how he and Janis talked to Amy about the benefits of investing some of her money in property. Amy had been sharing a rented flat with her friend Juliette Ashby. When he visited, Mitch found evidence that Amy was smoking marijuana, which was how he belatedly found out about a habit Amy had enjoyed since she was fifteen. Now that her record deal was in place, she bought a maisonette in Jeffrey's Place, Camden Town. Mitch describes this purchase as a collective decision, writing of how *we* put down the deposit, and *we* took out the mortgage. He also became one of the co-signatories on Amy's bank account. Indeed, he gives the impression that he was involved in every major financial and business decision his daughter took from now on, despite his history as a former bankrupt, despite being the disqualified director of a company that had gone bust owing millions.

Amy's new apartment was in a cobbled side-street, the front door accessed through a gated courtyard. She can be seen in the apartment in the photographs inside the *Frank* CD case: rolling what looks like a joint in her kitchen, her clothes, accessories and CDs everywhere. Amy kept a 'floordrobe' rather than a wardrobe, jokes her stylist, Lou Winwood, niece of the musician Steve Winwood. 'She was a mixture between slovenly and fussy-housewifey. So you'd get *Do you want this, babe? Do you want that, babe?* kind of thing. You'd turn up and she'd be cooking chicken soup, which I never did when I was nineteen … She would always say, "I'm Jewish," and fuss about you. But [then there were] things like the cat litter under the letterbox where the letters come through and land in the cat litter, and then the cats would [defecate on them]. I'd be like, "Amy! These are your bills – you've got cat shit on them." So there was always chaos.' Interestingly, the cover photo for *Frank* was shot in Spitalfields where Amy's Russian ancestors had settled.

Amy broke up with her boyfriend before the album came out, and indeed *Frank* is a kiss-off to Chris. At first she was angry and upset about the split, smashing things, tossing nail varnish around her bedroom, then boxing up Chris's belongings for him to collect, as in 'Take the Box'. By the time she came to promote the album in 2003 she seemed to be over the relationship, though she mocked her ex in interviews, ridiculing him in *Blues & Soul* magazine as a 'pussy man'. 'He was seven years older than me and a right woman.' What was most revealing about such comments was that Amy, whose father had left home when she was a child, craved a strong man in her life. Her choices would not always be good ones.

The break-up with Chris aside, the prevailing tone of *Frank* is confident and sassy. In private Amy was not quite the person she presented as. She was prone to bouts of depression, even self-hatred. 'I worry about her a lot,' Juliette Ashby told the *Observer* in 2007, recalling nights when her former flatmate banged her head against her bedroom wall. Amy had also started to drink and smoke cannabis to excess, which didn't help her moods. But she was not yet addled.

She was still a healthy young woman, with a voluptuous figure, clear skin and bright eyes. Many people who worked with Amy at the start of her career recall how well she looked in 2003, and shake their heads at how she changed. As Gordon Williams says, 'You look up and you see a girl you don't even know anymore. How did that happen?'

Four

SUCCESS

… the first wild wind of success and the delicious mist it
brings with it [is] a short and precious time – for when the
mist rises in a few weeks, or a few months, one finds that
the very best is over.
F. Scott Fitzgerald

1

The six principal members of the 27 Club took varying periods of
time to find the formulae for popular success. When they did so, as
they all did in their early twenties, success was sudden and, after a
brief period of elation, proved overwhelming.

The rise of the Rolling Stones was typically meteoric. In March
1963, with one record out, the Stones could still be seen playing
small clubs in England. Within weeks the band were filling theatres,
and within a year they were playing arenas in the United States. Such
rapid success affected all five band members, but it seemed to turn
Brian Jones's head the most. 'Brian was a man of excess,' Keith
Richards has said. 'He got into excess really quickly. The fame affected
all of us – and it still does, no doubt – but it seemed that there was
an extreme personality change, which happened really quickly with
Brian … At the beginning he had considered himself the senior
member of the band. I think he was a very jealous guy, which affected
everything in his life, to the point of self-destruction.'

Initially the public also saw Brian as the leader of the Stones, as did the press and people the band worked with. It was partly the way he deported himself. 'Brian looked like a pop star ... with his extraordinary hair and his white trousers and his rather skinny body,' says Gered Mankowitz, who photographed the Stones for several early album covers. 'He just looked the business, whereas Mick and Keith still looked a little bit studenty. Brian [was also] vain. He fussed about his hair all the time. He was the only one who actually carried a bit of makeup.' Brian's contribution to the sound of the group was also vital at this early stage. Bill Wyman writes that he and Keith Richards agreed that Brian's bottleneck guitar helped make their second single, 'I Wanna Be Your Man', a hit.

Brian took full advantage of his good fortune. He moved to an expensive address in London's Belgravia, bought outlandish clothes and a fancy car, and became a face on the club scene alongside the Beatles and the other pop luminaries of the day. 'He thought he'd made it when he just got to London and had that big audience. He was quite happy,' says his girlfriend Linda Lawrence. Most of the 27s enjoyed a similar golden period before they became weighed down with the burdens of fame. For Brian, as with others, this shining period was brief. 'Money and power and fame took over,' sighs Linda.

That summer Linda gave birth to Brian's fourth illegitimate child, a son. Although Brian took no more care of this boy than he had his previous children, Linda defends Brian within the context of the hippie era, going so far as to liken him to mythological Pan. 'It's only society that judges the way we [behave],' she says. 'But if you put it in mythology, and into a higher level of thinking, [Brian] was a very special being that came in and fertilised many women ... He was Pan.' Brian and Linda named their son Julian. Perhaps Brian had forgotten that he already had a son of that name, by Pat Andrews. In any event he all but ignored Julian II (as we might think of him), as he ignored Julian I (whom Pat chose to call by his middle name, Mark). Pat and Linda would have to go to law to compel Brian to help support them and the two Julians.

Meanwhile Brian went on his merry way, dating other women, including the French actress and model Danièle Ciarlet, better known as Zouzou. Brian met Zouzou in Paris when the Stones were on tour and invited her to stay with him in London. He neglected to mention that he was living with Linda Lawrence. The actress found out about Brian's domestic arrangements when she arrived on his doorstep. 'Linda was there [and] they had a baby. Oh, my God! If he had told me he had a girlfriend, and all of this, I wouldn't have come.' Still, Zouzou became part of Brian's complicated private life. Like his other lovers, she found him to be sensitive and deeply insecure. One of his many hang-ups was that he was short (barely able to peep over the steering wheel of his Humber Super Snipe, according to Keith Richards who says that Brian sat on a cushion to drive). So that Zouzou didn't tower over Brian she wore flat shoes and walked with a slump when they were out together. There were other neuroses: 'He had depression sometimes at night, because he thought he was ugly, and he wanted to have the bags [under his eyes] done. I had to put makeup [on him] every time we went out. I cut his hair – one millimetre by one millimetre.' She laughs affectionately. 'I knew it was crazy.'

During a tour of the United States in 1964 Brian complained of feeling unwell, checked into hospital and missed four concerts. By necessity Mick Jagger and Keith Richards took on more and more responsibility. A key element in their ultimate take-over of the band was that they also started to write songs. Previously the Stones had recorded covers of songs by other artists, including Lennon and McCartney's 'I Wanna Be Your Man'. Seeing how much money Lennon and McCartney earned as songwriters, as well as performers, Andrew Loog Oldham urged the Stones to write original material. While he had good ideas, Brian didn't have the inclination or talent to write songs. But Mick and Keith were willing to try their hand. Their first real success was with 'As Tears Go By', which became a hit for Marianne Faithfull, a *protégé* of Loog Oldham who became Mick's girlfriend. Then they wrote 'The Last Time', which the Stones took to number one in the spring of 1965.

Brian began to feel 'redundant and underappreciated', says Loog Oldham, who urged Mick and Keith to write more hits. Brian mocked their lyrics as 'moon and June' piffle, further estranging himself from his colleagues. Indeed, Brian increasingly seemed like the odd man out in the band. Some of his contemporaries sympathised. 'I found [Brian] to be the most musical of all of them,' says Zoot Money, leader of the Big Roll Band. 'In a way, I thought it was the wrong band for him to be in.' Now that he was perceived as being weak, and uncongenial, Brian was mercilessly teased and mocked by Mick and Keith. They made fun of his stature, his pomposity and pretensions. He irritated Keith in particular for not thanking him when Keith covered for him. 'Mick and I had gotten incredibly nasty to Brian when he became a joke, when he effectively gave up his position in the band,' Keith Richards writes in his autobiography. Isolated and ridiculed, losing status and confidence, Brian became paranoid. At the same time he was drinking, he was using amphetamines, and he became one of the first British rock stars to use LSD heavily, none of which helped his mental health.

As we have seen, Linda Lawrence maintains that Brian had an underlying personality disorder in that he was bipolar. Unhappy at work, and under the influence of drugs, he became increasingly volatile and was often violent, throwing a fit at a press conference in the United States when a journalist asked him a question he didn't like. 'He was threatening to use a glass on the guy and had to be restrained,' says Gered Mankowitz. 'Suddenly one was aware of this extremely violent side to him.' Brian also turned his violence on himself.

Freud wrote that the suicidal person initially wants to kill others. When thwarted, they turn their rage inward. Many of the 27s exhibited such anger (Kurt Cobain developing a murderous rage against one unfortunate journalist) before ultimately destroying themselves. As his personality crumbled, Brian threatened suicide, telling friends that he wanted to cut his wrists, drown himself in the Thames, or throw himself from a hotel window. It has been claimed in one history of the band, by Stephen Davis, that Brian actually cut his wrist in 1964 to punish Mick and Keith for ignoring him. But it was a superficial cut, a suicidal gesture rather than a serious attempt to end it all, and indeed Brian's suicidal talk at this point seems to have been intended to gain attention. If he was serious, he could have done away with himself easily enough.

The stoic philosopher Seneca argued that death can always be achieved, by a variety of means, if one is determined. 'In whatever direction you may turn your eye, there lies the means to end your woes,' he wrote. 'See you that precipice? Down that is the way to liberty. See you that sea, that river, that well? There sits liberty – at the bottom. See you that tree, stunted, blighted and barren? Yet from its branches hangs liberty ... Do you ask what is the highway to liberty? Any vein in your body!' When his problems became insurmountable, Seneca was true to his philosophy and dispatched himself by opening his veins. He found that this was not as easy as he had supposed, but die he did. Somebody like Brian, who is forever threatening suicide – an alarming cry that soon becomes tiresome – may never have the courage to do it. Alternatively, he may be giving utterance to where he may end up and, as noted in the Prologue, suicide can be achieved by negative as well as positive action. By abusing his body with drugs Brian's life had already started to take on the shape of what Al Alvarez described in his insightful book on suicide as the 'gradual, chronic suicide of drug addiction'.

Brian's behaviour continued to deteriorate. He walked out on the Stones for three days during a tour of North America in the spring of 1965, and when the band got to Florida in May, he beat up a girlfriend in his motel room. '[Apparently] Brian was frequently impotent as a result of drugs,' says Gered Mankowitz, who travelled with the Stones at the time. 'When I say frequently impotent what I mean is he was too stoned to get it up. I think that became a big problem, and whether he took that out on women, I don't know.' Marianne Faithfull adds corroboration. In her memoir, *Faithfull*, she describes a fumble with Brian at his London flat when they were high. Brian got as far as groping her after which his interest 'fizzled out'. She writes: 'He was a wonderfully feeble guy, quite incapable of sex.' That Brian had fathered so many children demonstrates that this was not always the case.

Still, Brian retained an attraction. On tour in Germany he met a model named Anita Pallenberg and cried on her shoulder about how mean the Stones were being to him. Pallenberg promptly moved into his London apartment, which put paid to Linda Lawrence. 'I was very upset about it,' says Linda, who had considered Anita a friend. This time Brian was in love. Anita was a cultured, statuesque beauty of aristocratic heritage, whose blonde good looks complemented his own. He was proud of having a partner whom his friends admired and were nervous of, for Anita exuded danger. Even Mick Jagger seemed frightened of her. This was also a love affair marked by violence. As we have seen, Brian had a history of hitting women. Anita apparently hit back. Their rough-house lovemaking became notorious, as Stones employee Ron Schneider recalls: 'When he was with Anita, there would be many a time that the hotel would call me and say, "Mr Schneider, could you help us, please? The room that Mr Jones is in, the door's been locked overnight, and all day, and all we hear is screaming and fighting …"'

By now Brian had effectively lost the leadership of the Stones to Mick Jagger and Keith Richards, who had come into their own as songwriters with compositions including '(I Can't Get No) Satisfaction', number one in May 1965. At the end of the year the band went into the RCA studios in Hollywood to record the *Aftermath* album, every track of which was by Jagger-Richards. Brian's contribution can still be heard – playing sitar on 'Paint it, Black' for example – but he was marginalised. Andrew Loog Oldham says that Brian was absent for days on end during the sessions, and when he did show up he was so stoned that he just about managed to plug in his guitar before collapsing on the floor. The instrument hummed uselessly in his hands until Loog Oldham withdrew the lead.

2

Jimi Hendrix arrived in England on 24 September 1966, stopping off at the West London home of Zoot Money to borrow a guitar on his way into town from the airport. Jimi jammed that night at the Scotch of St James, one of London's trendy new nightclubs, then went back to his hotel with a woman he met at the club, Kathy Etchingham, who became his steady English girlfriend. It was a busy first day.

Over the following weeks Jimi played in front of the élite of British pop at several London clubs, impressing everybody who heard and saw him, and making important new friends, including Brian Jones. With their shared love of the blues, the two guitarists became close over the following months, as Jimi's career burgeoned and Brian's wilted. They were headed in opposite directions, yet both would be dead within four years.

Although he took longer to get his break than the Stones, and indeed the other principal 27s, Hendrix's career took off like a rocket once he came to England. He went from obscurity to being one of the biggest acts in popular music – the first black rock star – in a few months, creating all the amazing music he is known for between his arrival in London in September 1966 and his death in September 1970. Between those dates Hendrix 'zoomed off in a spaceship round the world', as Zoot Money says. The metaphor is apt. Hendrix was a science-fiction fan who incorporated space imagery in his work at the time of the race to the moon.

The Jimi Hendrix Experience was assembled quickly in London with the recruitment of two British sidemen: chirpy former child actor John 'Mitch' Mitchell on drums, and the lugubrious Noel Redding on bass. The trio's first release was an elemental electric blues, 'Hey Joe', just before Christmas 1966. Gered Mankowitz took the publicity photos at his studio next to the Scotch of St James. He recalls how happy Jimi was on the brink of success, despite his intense stare in the photographs. 'He wasn't a hit yet. But he was clearly at a fantastic moment in his life and he was really relishing it, so he was happy and everything was clicking. It was all falling into place. And he was excited, and it seemed like an extremely positive, good energy, and a really great moment to have been with him.' Sadly, the happiness did not last. 'His decline was terribly rapid, when you think about it. I mean, [four] years after my session he was dead!'

Around this time Mankowitz also photographed the Rolling Stones for their *Between the Buttons* album, taking the cover picture on Primrose Hill, where Amy Winehouse would spend carefree summer days in the 21st century. The Stones shoot took place in the winter of 1966 at a time when Brian was increasingly unhappy. Wrapped up in a fur coat like a querulous old woman, he sulked throughout, which was typical of his disobliging behaviour nowadays. 'He had a big brown fur coat and it was very, very cold and he wrapped himself up in this coat and sort of hid in the collar and turned his back to the camera and started reading the newspaper,' recalls Mankowitz. 'I said to Andrew [Loog Oldham] that I was worried that Brian was fucking up the session.'

It was not long after this that the authorities began to create significant problems for the Stones, with the police conducting a dramatic drugs raid on the country home of Keith Richards in February 1967, resulting in charges against Keith, Mick Jagger and their friend Robert Fraser. In the aftermath of this bust, while awaiting trial, Keith decided to go on a road trip to Morocco with Brian and Anita.

They travelled in Keith's Bentley, chauffeured by Stones employee Tom Keylock. On the drive south through France, Brian complained of feeling unwell and checked into hospital near Toulouse. Keith and Anita continued without him to Spain. 'In the back of the Bentley, somewhere between Barcelona and Valencia, Anita and I looked at each other [and] the next thing I know she's giving me a blow job,' Richards writes in his autobiography, *Life*. Keith and Anita slept together that night, then continued to Tangier where the affair intensified. Richards found himself falling in love with Anita, but he worried about the effect this would have on Brian and the band. Anita also seemed concerned. She flew back to France to pick Brian up, taking him to London for medical tests, before they both flew on to Morocco to rendezvous with Keith, Mick Jagger and other friends in Marrakesh.

His mind poisoned with jealousy, Brian attacked Anita at the Es Saadi Hotel in Marrakesh. Keith Richards heard them fighting. Brian tried to get Anita to participate in an orgy with two Moroccan whores. When she refused, he threw room-service food at her and she fled to the sanctuary of Keith's room. Together they planned an escape.

Keith arranged for Brian to take a trip to the Square of the

Dead to record local musicians. While he was thus occupied, Tom Keylock drove Keith and Anita towards Tangier. When Brian discovered he had been cuckolded by Keith, and that Anita had deserted him, he was crushed. Not only had Mick and Keith taken over his band, Keith had stolen his girlfriend, perhaps the one woman he had loved. That he had mistreated Anita didn't lessen the humiliation.

After returning from Morocco, Brian invited a French playboy friend named Prince Stanislas Klossowski de Rola, known as Prince Stash, to stay with him at his London apartment. Brian whined about losing Anita, whom he tried but failed to win back, and consoled himself by taking inordinate amounts of drugs in what had become, at least for the music industry, an era of hedonism and experimentation. As Prince Stash says, 'One lived dangerously and fully and madly, and that's the way it was.' It was also a time when Scotland Yard was targeting celebrity drug-users. Following the bust at Keith Richards's house, Brian was on a police list of stars to be raided. Sure enough, on 10 May 1967, detectives called at his London flat, and searched it, charging Brian and Stash with possession of cocaine and cannabis; Brian was also charged with possession of Methedrine.

'The drug bust that he and I went through was the beginning of the end,' says Prince Stash, who claims that the police planted the evidence. 'Brian went through a catastrophic change during the aftermath of that bust.' While a trial was pending Brian was advised not to contact Mick Jagger and Keith Richards, who were facing separate charges over the raid on Richards's home, and thereby found himself more isolated than ever. 'He would ask me, "What are the Stones doing?" as if it was not his own band,' says Prince Stash. Brian started to use Mandrax to calm his nerves, with deleterious consequences for his physical and mental health. Prince Stash again: 'Brian was bending to the point that he would soon break, and he had a real kind of nervous breakdown.' Stones employee Ron Schneider says Brian was so freaked out that he had to hold his hand to comfort him as he tried to sleep. 'He wasn't the same after [the bust], that's when he started going into the real depressions.'

3

While Brian's life was falling apart, Jimi Hendrix's was in the
ascendant. Just before his first album, *Are You Experienced?*, was
released he and Kathy Etchingham gave a party at their London flat
so that their friends could hear the music on acetate disc before the
general public. The album was truly ground-breaking and extraordinary, full of what have become classic tracks, including 'Foxy Lady'
and 'Manic Depression' (as well as 'Purple Haze' and 'Hey Joe' on
the version sold in the United States). Brian Jones and Prince Stash
were among those lucky few who attended the acetate party. Prince
Stash recalls a shared sense of 'excitement filled with wonder' as they
listened for the first time to amazing new music.

A few days later Brian accompanied Jimi and his band to the
United States. They landed in New York where the musicians spent
a few days clubbing and seeing friends. One of the acts Jimi caught
at Steve Paul's Scene, a fashionable basement club on West 46th
Street, was the Doors. The band was in town promoting their début
album, which gathered together Jim Morrison's and Robby Krieger's
strongest songs, tunes honed in the clubs of LA, and recorded in
only six days by Paul Rothchild. The result is the best album the
Doors ever made, though the opening cut, 'Break on Through',
initially failed to make an impression on the charts. Then Elektra
released an edited version of 'Light My Fire', which became an AM
radio hit, while FM stations began playing the longer, trippier album
version as well. At the time Hendrix dropped into the Scene, 'Light
My Fire' was on its way to number one, and *The Doors* album would
follow it to the top of the charts.

The inner world of 1960s rock was intimate and many of the
central characters knew one another. While they were in New York,
Brian Jones introduced Jimi Hendrix to a friend named Deering
Howe, a hip young millionaire, whose fortune came from the
International Harvester company. Brian had stayed with Howe on a
previous visit to New York. Howe recalls Brian entertaining a girl in
his room when Anita Pallenberg showed up, broke down the bedroom

door and brained Brian with a Coke bottle. Blood streamed down his face. 'It was insanity,' sighs Howe, whose social circle also included Jim Morrison. Now that Anita had gone, Howe found Brian in a terrible shape: 'Sadly, he was pretty much out of it with the drugs and alcohol. On a day-to-day basis, Brian didn't make much sense.'

While they were in New York, Brian and the Experience went out for a pleasure trip in Deering Howe's boat. 'We used to get whooped up and take the boat up and down the Hudson river. When we turned around we'd do a head count to make sure we had as many people as we started out with.' Hendrix and Howe became unlikely friends. '[Our friendship] developed over one thing, which was mutual respect and a love of music,' says Howe, noting that it would be hard to find two more different people. 'Here I was, a young twenty-something white millionaire and he was a young black guy ... whose mother was basically a hooker, and [he] had never had two cents to rub together his whole life. [But] we always had some kind of common ground. I was able to teach Jimi some things when he started to make some money, about how to handle it, and how to act, and how to go to a restaurant and order a bottle of wine – basic stuff that to me was second nature, but Jimi wouldn't have had a clue.'

Saying goodbye to Deering Howe for the time being, Brian and Jimi flew on to California for the Monterey International Pop Festival.

Monterey Pop was a relatively small event, held over the weekend of 16–18 June 1967 at the Monterey County Fairgrounds south of San Francisco, which accommodated 8,500 people. The biggest names in rock did not attend. There were no Beatles, no Stones, no Bob Dylan, though Brian Jones made a guest appearance, while Paul McCartney and Andrew Loog Oldham had a hand in the organisation. Nevertheless, Monterey Pop was a considerable success, a bijou event that inspired the larger, though often less successful, rock festivals that followed.

Although the biggest acts in pop were absent from Monterey, many significant artists performed, their sets preserved for posterity on film by D. A. Pennebaker. His movie is part of the reason the festival is remembered. What is often overlooked is how many of the performers at Monterey died young – including Brian Cole of the Association, Cass Elliot of the Mamas and the Papas, Keith Moon of the Who, and Otis Redding, plus four members of the 27 Club.

Taking the 27s in order of appearance at Monterey, Canned Heat performed at the festival on Saturday afternoon. This band had been formed in California by two friends, Al Wilson and Bob Hite, the latter a larger-than-life character known as the Bear. Al Wilson was the antithesis of the Bear: a slight, introverted young man, whose poor eyesight earned him the nickname Blind Owl. The two very different men were united by their love of the blues. Both sang with Canned Heat, Al Wilson additionally playing harmonica and lead guitar. Wilson did not look like a rock star. Indeed, he appeared out of place onstage at Monterey, with his glasses, short hair, sensible clothes and impassive demeanour. But he was a superb musician and singer, his high tenor voice immortalised in the band's hits 'On the Road Again' and 'Goin' Up the Country'.

Canned Heat enjoyed considerable artistic and commercial success over the next couple of years, crowned by an appearance at Woodstock in 1969. But Al Wilson was a troubled young man. Like many 27s he was estranged from his family; he lacked confidence and he suffered with depression. He twice attempted suicide, according to the band's drummer, Fito de la Parra, who further claims in his memoir, *Living the Blues,* that 'Alan often talked about death.' This is characteristic of the 27s. Wilson knew he had problems. He consulted a psychiatrist and took anti-depressants. He even quit the band briefly, wondering if that was the cause of his problems, returning when he realised that it was the band he really loved. One of his eccentric habits was sleeping outdoors when staying with friends, as he did latterly at Bob Hite's house in Los Angeles. Wilson's body was found in Hite's yard on 3 September 1970, a day after he was due to fly to Germany with Canned Heat. His hands were crossed over his chest and there was a bottle of Seconal by his side. Cause of death was officially given as an accidental overdose of barbiturates, but Fito de la Parra believes Wilson committed suicide, at age 27.

Big Brother followed Canned Heat on stage at Monterey on Saturday, 17 June 1967, playing again on Sunday for the film cameras. Janis Joplin gave her all to these two performances, seemingly reaching the brink of nervous breakdown on 'Ball and Chain' during which she whispered, pleaded and wailed her love for a man, her face a picture of suffering. Mama Cass watched open-mouthed. 'Wow!' she exclaimed as the audience rose to give Janis an ovation. Janis grinned with joy and skipped offstage a star.

Among those watching was John Byrne Cooke (son of the journalist Alistair Cooke), who was D. A. Pennebaker's sound man at Monterey. Having heard both performances of 'Ball and Chain', on Saturday and again on Sunday, Byrne Cooke couldn't decide which was best. 'You listen to one and you say, "My God, that's the crowning performance of 'Ball and Chain'." And then you listen to the other one and you say, "Well, that one's it." They are the only group that got to perform twice, and it was in order that they would be in the movie, and she knew, and the band knew, it was just as important to knock everybody out on the Sunday-evening performance.' Byrne Cooke was so impressed by what he heard that he became the road manager for Big Brother, working closely with Janis until she died. 'People really noticed Janis [after that]. Janis was known in San Francisco … but after that it was the world.'

Several other Bay Area bands performed at Monterey that weekend, including the Grateful Dead on Sunday night. Their keyboard player, Ron 'Pigpen' McKernan, was like Janis Joplin (with whom he was friendly) in that he was a sensitive, somewhat unsightly character with a drink problem. He was also scruffy and odorous, hence the nickname. Beneath the beard and biker jacket, though, Pigpen was a gentle soul with a melancholy typical of alcoholics.

Pigpen was a founding member of the Grateful Dead. He got together with Jerry Garcia and Bob Weir in 1964 to form a jug band that developed into a rock 'n' roll group associated with Ken Kesey's acid tests. Under the influence of LSD, the Dead took to playing long improvisational sets that became the epitome of psychedelic rock. Pigpen wasn't into drugs as much as the others. He was a boozer. He started drinking when he was twelve and by his mid-twenties he had cirrhosis of the liver, ulcers and other health problems.

Alcoholism is found almost as commonly as drug addiction in the history of the 27 Club, and many would say that one is as bad as the other. These days, alcoholism is blamed on all sorts of things, sometimes ascribed to genetics, most fashionably called a 'disease', as if anybody might develop the condition through no fault of their own. But life shows us that alcoholism is the result of a bad habit taken to excess, and that people who drink to excess, and abuse narcotics, typically do so because they are unhappy. People get drunk to forget themselves, 'to send myself away', as Samuel Johnson said. And they keep drinking despite the warnings because they can't stand themselves sober.

After a lifetime of boozing to send himself away, Pigpen was admitted to hospital with a perforated ulcer in 1971. Afterwards he performed intermittently with the Grateful Dead. Towards the end of his short life he eased back on the drinking but, as with many 27s, there was a sense that he had tired of life. In his last months he wrote a song about 'no tomorrow' and broke up with his girlfriend, explaining, 'I don't want you around when I die.' Pigpen was on his own at his apartment in Corte Madera, overlooking San Francisco Bay, when the end came on 8 March 1973. He died of a gastro-intestinal haemorrhage with cirrhosis an underlying factor. He had been dead for up to two days when his landlady found him.

If none of those artists had performed at Monterey, the festival would still be remembered for the incendiary performance by the Jimi Hendrix Experience on Sunday night. Beforehand, Jimi argued with Pete Townshend of the Who over which band should play first, neither wanting to follow the other. The Who won a coin toss, Jimi warning them that he would pull out all the stops. Townshend says Hendrix was 'out of his head on acid'.

Brian Jones introduced Jimi to the festival audience. Always an extravagant dresser, Brian appeared onstage at Monterey in a gold cape trimmed with pink fur, looking like a dissipated drag queen. He described his friend warmly as 'the most exciting guitar player I've ever heard'.

Wild as Brian looked, he was outdone by Jimi Hendrix himself. Nobody at Monterey looked as *different* as he did that weekend in June 1967. That Jimi was a black rock star made him immediately distinctive in an event dominated by white artists, but his stage clothes were also truly extraordinary. He wore an orange shirt, skin-tight scarlet pants, a jacket decorated with eyes (a garment he removed to reveal an equally elaborate waistcoat), a patterned bandanna and a pink boa. Although Pete Townshend says Jimi was high, he appeared relaxed and in control onstage, the seasoned pro, chewing gum and chatting to the audience as he warmed up. But his set was not at all laid back. It surged with power, his dextrous fingers creating a massive guitar sound, as huge as a Gothic cathedral and as delicately detailed, as Mitch Mitchell and Noel Redding kept time.

Jimi performed all his tricks at Monterey, playing his guitar with his teeth during 'Hey Joe'. He prefixed 'Wild Thing' by promising he was going to 'sacrifice something I love' at the end, then played an intro during which he made his Fender screech like a bird and bellow like an elephant. Midway, he picked out the tune of 'Strangers in the Night' one-handed. Then he went into his closing act: grinding his guitar against his amplifier; straddling the instrument; dousing it with lighter fuel and setting it on fire; finally smashing it and throwing the pieces to the audience, who looked on with shock as if he had gone mad. In fact he had planned and rehearsed the act, having set fire to a guitar onstage previously in London. Still, this performance was in front of film cameras. Along with Janis Joplin, Jimi Hendrix was the break-out star of Monterey.

4

The Doors were disappointed not to be invited to Monterey, snubbed because of a falling-out with the organisers. With 'Light My Fire' and their début album at number one, the band was, however, on top of the world.

Along with the quality of their music, Jim Morrison's emergence as a pop idol played a part in the Doors' breakthrough. The publicity department of Elektra Records made the most of the fact that Jim was a handsome young man, making a doe-eyed photograph of the singer the focus of the album cover and putting him on a billboard above Sunset Boulevard – the first time a rock band had been promoted in this way. A series of cheesecake publicity photos of Jim, by Joel Brodsky and others, were distributed to the press and teen magazines. In the most famous Brodsky shot Jim posed without his shirt, his arms spread like Christ's on the cross. This picture has been reproduced endlessly over the years, on posters, T-shirts, book jackets, magazine and album covers, becoming truly iconic. With his long curly hair and lithe body, Jim was at his most photogenic, and the picture helped make him a star – at a price.

'He hated that picture,' says Danny Fields, the Doors' publicist. Fields says Jim never looked quite as good in life as he did in the Brodsky photograph. He was heavier-set normally, later distinctly overweight, but fans expected him to look as he did in the Brodsky picture. Fields believes Jim came to resent this, taking the view that '"I don't look like that, I never did, I never will …" Angry about it …You can't say that to a fan who says, "Sign this picture of yourself." He felt that way, but can't say it.' In a 1969 interview with *Rolling Stone*, by which time he was heavy and bearded, Jim remarked, 'A photograph can make any person look like a saint, an angel, a fool … And a lot of it is idolatry.' He may have imagined initially that the shirtless photos presented him as a modern-day Dionysus. Some fans saw the pictures that way. Looked at from another angle, he had allowed himself to become a teen idol, which was demeaning for an intellectual and a poet.

Jim's family found out about his new celebrity when Andy Morrison brought *The Doors* album home. Having told his son that his musical ambitions were ridiculous, Admiral Morrison had a change of heart and telephoned Jim to congratulate him. Jim responded coolly. The admiral said it was a conversation during which 'nothing of consequence was discussed'. In fact, father and son never communicated again. Clara Morrison was not so easily deterred. She called Elektra Records asking to speak to Jim. Her call caused surprise in the office because Jim had told everybody that his parents were dead.

'[So] I get a call from his mother at the Elektra office,' recalls former label executive Steve Harris. 'They were playing in New York, and she said, "I need to talk to Jim, it's important to me." I said, "Who's calling?" "His mother." I didn't want to say, "You're supposed to be dead."' Persuaded that the caller was genuine, Harris gave Mrs Morrison the number of the hotel where Jim was staying. The next day members of the band told Harris that Jim was so upset by hearing from his mother that he'd got rotten drunk after her call. An edict went out that any further calls were not to be put through.

Clara Morrison remained determined to make contact with her boy. When the Doors performed at the Hilton in Washington DC on 25 November 1967, she went to the show with her second son, Andy, and his date, and introduced herself backstage to the band's manager, Asher Dann, who asked her to wait while he told Jim she was there. He assured Jim that there was time to meet his mother after the show, if he wanted. Jim had no intention of meeting her. He asked to be driven to the airport as soon as he came offstage. Dann went with him, without telling Clara Morrison that Jim wouldn't be meeting her. 'I guess she got the message [when] I didn't come back,' he says. 'It's a sad story, but I guess that was part of his make-up, one of those demons inside his head …' Looking back, Dann concludes that Jim hated his parents. 'Probably hated them. You know, "The End" related to his parents.'

Clara Morrison was crying as she walked back to the car where Andy was waiting with his date. Andy agrees that his mother was hurt to be snubbed by Jim, but hastens to add that she was tough. 'She got over it.' Here is an insight into the psychology of the Morrison family, a family whose emotions were subjugated by military discipline to the point at which a child could turn his back on his parents, and a mother was expected to face rejection by her son with equanimity.

During the next four years Steve and Clara Morrison followed Jim's career closely in the press. '[Mom] kept all the newspaper articles and all the magazines,' says Andy. 'They were proud of him.' But they didn't see or speak to Jim again. Unhappy family stories are found in the background of all the main 27s, but few stars had such a sad and peculiar relationship with their parents as Jim Morrison did with his mother and father. It is tempting to think that there may have been something in the relationship that made him self-destructive.

Five

KURT AND COURTNEY,
AMY AND BLAKE

Set me as a seal upon thy heart,
as a seal upon thy arm:
for love is strong as death,
jealousy is cruel as the grave.
Song of Solomon

1

Although their careers belonged to different eras, Kurt Cobain and
Amy Winehouse achieved success at around the same age as each
other, and their 1960s forebears. As with the earlier stars, once Kurt
and Amy had found their voices, their rise to the top was rapid, and
in becoming celebrities they took up with partners who shared their
weaknesses, which exacerbated their problems.

The first Nirvana album, *Bleach*, was recorded quickly and cheaply
in Seattle in December 1988, with a $600 loan from a friend of
the band, Jason Everman, who'd saved the money working as a
commercial fisherman. *Bleach* has a freshness and energy that
remains endearing. The guitars are loud and the tunes melodic,
which would be a recipe for mainstream success. Kurt's rasping
vocals suited this music well, while his lyrics – though sketchy and
repetitive – were not without interest. A sense of humour is a boon
to any writer, and Kurt's sly wit was evident on such numbers as

'Floyd the Barber', which describes a visit to a barber's shop as nightmarish as Sweeney Todd's.

Jason Everman was rewarded for his financial help by having his name and picture on *Bleach*, though he didn't play a note on the album. He did join the band on tour, though, as a second guitarist, 'playing small bars in front of five people and not being paid enough money to both eat and buy gasoline to the next town, things like that; sleeping on floors, sleeping in the van, sleeping outside at rest areas', as he describes Nirvana's first extensive trek across America in the summer of 1989. 'I remember getting shaken down by police in Texas somewhere – it might have been Houston or Dallas – basically for taking the wrong turn and being in a nicer neighbourhood, these four probably dodgy-looking guys in a beat-up old van. We got pulled over and searched, hands on the hood, that whole deal.'

Everman didn't stay with Nirvana, and there were changes of drummer before the final line-up was achieved. Chad Channing was drumming with the band when they went to Europe for the first time later that year. The maxim that a prophet goes unrecognised in his own land proved true for Seattle's Jimi Hendrix, who had had to go to London to become a star. Nirvana's Seattle-based record company, Sub Pop, tried to achieve the same result by sending Nirvana on package tours to Europe when the group had a tiny following at home. Sub Pop also courted the British music press with the result that journalists, including Everett True of *Melody Maker*, became important early champions of grunge rock in general and Nirvana in particular. True claimed to be the first to apply the word 'grunge' to the new bands coming from Seattle, of which Nirvana was only one.

As Nirvana started to gain greater recognition Kurt's eccentricity was magnified. His *outré* interests in pornography, disease, disability and suicide increased. He exhibited the mood swings of bipolar disorder, being semi-catatonic offstage and crazed in front of an audience. When Nirvana played Rome in November 1989, Kurt freaked out during the show, smashed his guitar, climbed up onto the speaker stack and threatened to throw himself off. Some watchers feared he was having a nervous breakdown.

The following year there were major developments in Kurt's life.

He broke up with his girlfriend, Tracy Marander, and Nirvana recruited David Grohl as their drummer, thus completing the line-up that became famous. A second European tour followed. Although it was a success, Kurt was increasingly unhappy. His love life was a mess – he doubted he would ever find the right companion – and, like many 27s, he was tortured with self-doubt. Reviewing his life at 23 he wrote in his journal: 'I am obsessed with the fact that I am skinny and stupid.' His problem with body image, thinking himself unattractively puny, was comparable to the agonies suffered by Brian Jones, Janis Joplin and Amy Winehouse. All disliked and worried about their appearance to a degree that was excessive, even irrational.

Kurt also continued to grouse about stomach pain. He consulted a specialist in 1989 who found nothing wrong with his stomach, and went on to see several gastroenterologists, writing in his journal that they located 'an enflamed [sic] irritation' in his gut, but failed to alleviate the pain. Kurt's stomach problem was never diagnosed. There may have been nothing much wrong, other than that he lived on his nerves and ate too much junk food. In any event, he used his real or imaginary stomach pain as an excuse to turn to heroin in the fall of 1990, not as a one-off high, but self-medicating on smack on a regular basis from now on. 'When I got back from our second European tour with Sonic Youth I decided to use heroine [sic] on a daily basis because of an ongoing stomach ailment that I had been suffering from for the past five years that had literally taken me to the point of wanting to kill myself. For five years every single day of my life,' Kurt wrote in his journal. Here was the old obsession with suicide, while his extraordinary conscious decision to become a junkie was in itself a significant act of self-harming.

Kurt's willing descent into drug addiction began at the point when Nirvana started to see glimmerings of success. This is the pattern with many 27s. Like other club members, Kurt craved success. He was every bit as ambitious for Nirvana as Brian Jones had been for the Rolling Stones. Yet both musicians lacked the mental toughness to cope with success when it came. As Mick Jagger has observed, some people simply aren't psychologically suited to be rock stars. He was. Kurt and Brian weren't. Neither was Amy Winehouse.

Nirvana now signed with a new management company, Gold Mountain, run by Danny Goldberg and John Silva, who would guide them to worldwide fame. Looking back, Goldberg sees three distinct elements in Kurt's character. First, he emphasises how motivated and ambitious Kurt was, involving himself in every aspect of Nirvana's career from songwriting to the design of their CDs. 'Although he didn't like some aspects of being successful, he was driven to be successful.

'The second aspect of his personality was that, when he was not on drugs, he was a very, very nice person: very thoughtful ...' The corollary of this was that drugs distorted his personality. 'Then the third aspect was that he was prone to deep depression.'

One day when Kurt was looking miserable, John Silva asked him why he was in a bad mood. 'I'm awake, aren't I?' Kurt snapped, in a way that made his managers realise he wasn't just down in the dumps but seriously depressed. 'And that was sort of a-ha!' says Goldberg. 'This is somebody who, when he gets bummed out, gets very bummed out.'

Under new management, Nirvana left their independent record label and signed with Geffen Records, which released their break-through album in 1991. Geffen had modest ambitions for *Nevermind*, being far more concerned with *Use Your Illusion*, the two-volume Guns N' Roses album also due for release that September. Geffen had invested a lot of money in Guns N' Roses. It so happened that there was a marketing meeting at the company's headquarters in Los Angeles to talk about *Use Your Illusion* on a day when Nirvana would be performing at the Roxy, on the other side of Sunset Boulevard, in the evening. After the meeting Geffen executives crossed the road to take another look at Nirvana and were impressed by what they saw. 'That's when everybody said, *Holy shit!* ... We were way more interested in Nirvana at that point than Guns N' Roses,' recalls former Geffen executive Michael Maska. 'I was literally pinned up against the back wall of the Roxy watching kids jumping onstage. Kurt was hitting people with his guitar ... he was slightly out of control, and very edgy and very loud and really good.'

There was an anger about Kurt's performance that commanded

attention. 'His style of singing was rage, you know?' says his friend
Eric Erlandson. That rage is heard clearly on 'Smells Like Teen Spirit',
the first single from *Nevermind*, released in the summer of 1991.
The song caught on with radio listeners, sales propelled by a video
played frequently on MTV. The single sold the album. Geffen's
modest expectations for *Nevermind* meant that the company had
shipped only 50,000 copies. Demand outstripped supply as *Nevermind*
became the hottest album of the year, a number-one bestseller that
ultimately sold in millions at home and abroad. Kurt's dreams of
success were fulfilled far beyond his expectations, and beyond what
he was able to deal with.

It was at this crucial point in his career that Kurt teamed up with
the woman who became his wife, the mother of his child, and his
partner on the helter-skelter ride of fame. It is not possible to write
further about Kurt without also writing about Courtney Love.

2

Courtney Love is the stage name of Courtney Harrison. She was born
in San Francisco in 1964. Her father, Hank Harrison, fleetingly
managed the band that became the Grateful Dead, and counted Pigpen
McKernan as a friend, one of several 27 connections in Courtney's
curious life. Her mother, Linda Carroll, later became a well-known
therapist. After her parents broke up, when she was five, Courtney
lived an itinerant childhood in various states, and different countries,
suffering by her own account from a lack of parental discipline.

At the age of twelve Courtney was sent to a juvenile detention
centre for shoplifting. In her late teens she claims to have worked as
a stripper in places as far apart as New Zealand, Los Angeles and
Alaska. She also dabbled in drugs. By the 1980s, she was in Liverpool,
where she became part of the alternative music scene, hanging out
with bands such as Echo and the Bunnymen, whose drummer, Pete
de Freitas, died at 27 following a motorcycle accident, forming
another Club connection. Courtney tried her hand at acting,
appearing in the 1986 British movie *Straight to Hell*. Three years

later she was back in America where she formed and sang with the punk band Hole, which played the same circuit as Nirvana.

Kurt and Courtney bumped into each other as their bands did the rounds, getting together as a couple in 1991. Some observers believe that Courtney latched onto Kurt for career reasons, his band being bigger than hers. Kurt's uncle, Chuck Fradenburg – whom Kurt took Courtney to meet – calls her 'a gold digger'. To Kurt's grandfather, Leland Cobain, Courtney is 'a bitch'. She is a woman who induces strong and often negative reactions. Hole guitarist Eric Erlandson, Courtney's lover at one time, describes a more nuanced character, 'a loud woman [who can] charm your socks off'. He believes that Kurt and Courtney complemented each other, understanding their common 'darkness'. He also notes that Kurt chose Courtney as much as she chose him, arguing that Kurt used his girlfriend to deflect attention from himself. 'Having a loud woman, or even a strong woman to defer to, takes a lot of your load off,' says Erlandson, citing what he calls the Yoko Ono Syndrome. 'I'm not putting down Yoko Ono, I'm just saying that Yoko is that archetype: the person you want to blame for breaking up the band, or fucking up someone's life. And Courtney knew she had that thrust upon her...'

As *Nevermind* went platinum, and Kurt's sad little face became world famous, a strong, controversial partner strode beside him, a woman whom many people disliked on sight, and blamed for his subsequent self-destruction, even though that process had started before they met. It is a story mirrored a decade later in the life of Amy Winehouse.

3

Named *Frank* as a nod to Frank Sinatra, and for the directness of its lyrics, Amy's début album was released in Britain in October 2003. Although it featured good songs, received positive reviews and garnered an Ivor Novello award for 'Stronger than Me' (Best Contemporary Song), Amy was never happy with *Frank*. Too many musicians and producers had been involved in making the record, over a long period, creating a 'shit show with her in the middle,' says contributor Stefan Skarbek. The resulting album lacks cohesion. Amy was unhappy with the track selection; she didn't like some of the songs because they reminded her of her ex-boyfriend, Chris; and she was disappointed that Island didn't release *Frank* in the United States, not thinking her ready for the US market.

Nevertheless, Amy set out to promote *Frank* with interviews and concerts, including a showcase event at the Bush Theatre in London in December 1993, to which family and friends were invited. One of the relations who came was Amy's surgeon cousin, Jonathan Winehouse. This was the first time Jonathan had met his younger cousin in adult life and, drawing on his medical knowledge, he was immediately concerned about her. 'She was very distant, and she was really sort of out of it, even at that stage,' he says. 'It was very difficult to communicate with her. I said a few words to her, and she asked whether we enjoyed the show, and things. I had a brief conversation. Then when I went to say goodbye she was just really, really distant, sort of in another world.' Jonathan was so worried that he called Amy's manager. 'I wanted to get her some advice. I said her stage presence needed work, and she needed psychological support, and I just felt she was very insecure, and I didn't see any reason why she should be because she was bloody brilliant. That's what the conversation was about — it was about me trying to get him to get her some sort of psychological support really, and stage training.' Jonathan says Amy's manager agreed with him, but said Amy would go her own way. Over the next few years, as he became more concerned about Amy, Jonathan tried repeatedly to talk to Mitch Winehouse, but says Mitch was never receptive to his advice.

Amy proved an outspoken interviewee when it came to publicising *Frank*. Apart from mocking her ex-boyfriend, and making it clear that 'What is it About Men?' was partly about her father's shortcomings, Amy was outrageously rude about contemporary artists she considered dull, fake, or past-it, saying that Dido made her sick, Katie Melua was shit and Britney Spears a joke. She was equally forthright about her record company and management. In an interview with the *Sunday Times*, Amy ridiculed Simon Fuller, the owner of her management company, comparing his pristine appearance to a plastic Ken doll. As for her record company, Island was staffed by 'fucking morons'. Warming to her theme Amy complained to the *Observer* that the marketing of *Frank* had been a shambles. 'It's so frustrating, because you work with so many idiots.' They were 'nice idiots', but idiots nonetheless, and 'they know they're idiots'. Amy wasn't the first pop star to insult her record company in public – the Sex Pistols did so famously – and, like the Pistols, she may have spoken out to get publicity. At least one musician who played with Amy believes that she drew on her brief journalistic experience to manipulate the press. Still, her candid comments did her as much harm as good. Her manager Nick Godwyn says Amy's remarks 'alienated' people at Island, while his own relationship with her deteriorated. Producer Gordon Williams agrees that Amy's attitude 'hampered the success' of *Frank*.

As she emerged into the public eye Amy started to drink more. There were several reasons for this. As is generally true of the 27s, Amy had been experimenting with drink and drugs since her teens. Once her professional career started, it was natural to want to celebrate success and to have a drink to cope with the pressures. It is also true that pop musicians work in an environment where drink and drugs are readily available and part of the culture. More specifically, Amy was a nervous performer, prone to stage fright, who drank to calm down before a show. Her stage fright became worse over the years until she got into the bad habit of drinking both before and during the show. Then, when she wasn't performing, she had a lot of free time. With nothing much to do during the day, and money in her pocket, she went to the pub.

Amy's favourite pub at this stage was the Good Mixer in Inverness Street, Camden Town, not far from her flat. If she was at home she would typically wander over to the pub shortly after it opened at noon, stopping *en route* to chat to her friend Catriona who worked in a vintage clothes shop on the corner of Inverness Street, and calling, ''Allo, gorgeous!' to the men who sold fruit and veg on the market stalls. The Good Mixer became a second home for Amy who sometimes did her makeup sitting at the bar. She brought her guitar in and played songs she was working on, asking the staff what they thought of them. She became friendly with the landlady, Sarah Hurley, Sarah's fiancé, John, and the bar staff. When it was quiet in the pub Amy and the barmen discussed books they were reading, forming an informal reading group, which Amy mentions in the liner notes to *Back to Black*, reminding us of her lifelong interest in books. 'Thank you to the founder of PWRB (People Who Read in Bed), Gilly Mixer.' Gilly was one of the Australian bar staff at the pub. With one thing and another, Amy could spend most of her day in the Good Mixer, and often half the night.

She was a big drinker from the start, drinking shots rather than wine or beer, and usually ordering doubles. Jack Daniel's was her favourite tipple when she started frequenting the Mixer. Then she developed a taste for sambuca, vodka, tequila and Jägerbombs – a shot of the green liqueur Jägermeister in Red Bull. After a while she was drinking everything mixed together in a pint glass. Although physically small, Amy could consume huge quantities of booze, drinking 'flat out', as former Mixer bar-keep Bradley Leckie recalls: 'Everyone got pissed. Everyone would fall over,' he says, of the nights he spent with Amy in the Mixer and afterwards at her flat, where the party would continue until dawn. 'You're young. You have fun, don't ya?'

That summer – the summer of 2004 – Amy got falling-over drunk many times. One night she banged her head so badly that a friend took her to hospital, and then to her father's house in Kent to recuperate. According to Mitch Winehouse, there was a meeting as a result of this accident with Amy's managers, Nick Godwyn and Nick Shymansky, who spoke to him about Amy's 'drinking problem'. Mitch writes that Godwyn suggested Amy should go to a rehabilitation centre, which was apparently the first time the idea had been raised.* Amy said she didn't need help, and at first Mitch agreed. Still, she was persuaded to visit a rehab centre in Surrey. Amy made this brief visit the subject of her song, 'Rehab',

---

* Godwyn gave a different account of this in a 2011 article for *The Times*, stating that the first attempt to get Amy into rehab came after her initial break-up with Blake Fielder-Civil. This seems incorrect. She didn't meet Blake until 2005.

in which she describes her interview with a counsellor who asked her why she was drinking, and suggested that she might be depressed. She agreed sarcastically, 'and the rest!' In life, as in the song, Amy was told that the treatment programme lasted seventy days, which she considered out of the question. 'No! No! No!' she told the therapist. Then she left the clinic. Amy believed that only she could deal with her problems.

Amy turned 21 in September 2004. Although she'd had a busy year, *Frank* had not been a hit and her recording career seemed in danger of petering out. Mitch appeared concerned. It seemed to matter less to Amy, who carried on in her own sweet way, singing for fun as much as for money, hanging out in the Good Mixer, drinking, playing pool and flirting with men who took her fancy, which was how she met Blake Fielder-Civil.

4

The love of Amy's life was born Blake Fielder in Northamptonshire, on 16 April 1982, making him seventeen months older than her. His father was a restaurateur named Lance Fielder. His mother, Georgette, was a hairdresser. The Fielders were living in Spain when Georgette became pregnant. She came home to Britain to have the baby and, after an acrimonious break-up with Lance, took the child to live with her parents. Blake had little contact with his natural father while he was growing up. He came to see Georgette's new husband, teacher Giles Civil, as his dad, and took his surname.

Georgette considered Blake to be an unusually clever child and had high expectations for him. He was privately tutored at primary level, and when Giles Civil got a job at a prep school in Surrey, Blake was enrolled as a pupil. It was at this stage that Blake started to go astray. He disliked the prep school and was apparently upset when his mother and stepfather had another son, when he was ten, a third when Blake was eleven. The arrival of these half-siblings made Blake feel left out, in addition to which he became conscious of the fact that Giles wasn't his genetic father, which also unsettled him.

In later life, Georgette questioned whether she had let Blake down as a mother. As an adult, Blake formed a closer bond with his natural father and went by the hyphenated surname Fielder-Civil, later reverting to his real father's surname.

The Civils moved to Lincolnshire where Blake attended grammar school. He had lost interest in his studies by this time and left school at seventeen to go to London – to get away from home, he says. This is seemingly when Blake first used drugs. He worked in a hairdressing salon in the capital, sharing a flat with a girlfriend, but the job didn't last, and his mother lost track of where he was staying because he moved so often.

Blake had long been told that he was talented, and he harboured ambitions to be a novelist. Like Amy, he read literary fiction. *Lolita* was his favourite book – later Amy gave him a valuable first edition. Blake aspired to be a writer in the style of Nabokov or, more so, William S. Burroughs, who documented his experiences as a drug-user in *Junky* and other books. It was some time before Blake grasped that he didn't share Burroughs's talent, only his weakness. 'I had to accept that the only similarities between me and Burroughs was the ingestion of drugs,' he wrote to this author, describing this as a 'devastating' realisation. As a young man in London, Blake still harboured literary ambitions. While he waited for them to come true, he worked for a video production company and hung around the bars of Camden Town. He dressed to match the hipsters on the scene, getting tattooed, using drugs and altering his speaking voice, that of a grammar-school boy from Lincolnshire, so that he sounded like a Londoner. Young men he met in the capital tended to distrust Blake. 'I could see why people wanted to kick his arse,' says Good Mixer barman Bradley Leckie. 'He seemed to get along better with the chicks ...'

Women found Blake attractive. 'He was definitely a figure in Camden ... definitely seen as a Jack the lad,' says Sarah Hurley, landlady of the Good Mixer. Amy and Blake first set eyes on each other one day in the Good Mixer when Amy was playing pool. She loved to play pool, and was good at the game. She saw a pale young man, tall with short dark hair and a skinny but muscular physique, his arms smothered in tattoos. Amy loved tattoos. She'd recently added a tattoo of her grandmother, Cynthia, in the form of a 1950s pin-up, to her right shoulder, balanced by a horseshoe and the words *Daddy's Girl* on her left.

They exchanged looks. Blake asked a friend about Amy. His friend told him he was 'ten years too young and the wrong colour' for Amy, who had been dating an older black man, but he was wrong. 'God almighty, she found him sexy! There was a hell of a lot of lust there,' says Sarah Hurley, who watched the romance unfold. 'Blake was very popular [with women]. And [he] found it very hard to stay faithful, but for Amy it was a challenge. And she got him ... she really wanted him, and she got him. She liked to vaguely mother him, definitely, but she loved being his woman. He was the man and she was the woman. She liked that role. I think that was very important to her. Even though she went out onstage and did what she had to do on her own as a woman, at the end of the day she wanted to be *his* woman.'

Not long after they met, Blake moved into Amy's flat in Jeffrey's Place where drugs became an issue. Mitch Winehouse believes that Blake was smoking heroin in the flat at this early stage in the relationship, and that he offered Amy cocaine. It is unclear whether she tried it at this point. Alcohol and marijuana were her drugs of choice. When she sang about 'blow' (cocaine) and 'puff' (marijuana) in 'Back to Black' she was describing Blake's and her own respective drug preferences. But it would have been in character for her to try cocaine.

The first crisis in the relationship came when Amy discovered Blake was seeing an ex-girlfriend. Amy was in despair, weeping and drinking herself insensible. Mitch invited Amy on holiday to Spain with himself and his second wife in the hope that his daughter would benefit from the break. No sooner had they arrived than Amy was on the phone to Blake discussing a reunion.

When she wasn't on the phone to her lover, she was writing songs about their relationship. She composed three important *Back to Black* songs in Spain, 'Love is a Losing Game', 'Wake Up Alone' and 'You Know I'm No Good'. These are dark love songs, written in original and poetic language that showed a new maturity. Gone was the sassy young girl of *Frank*. Amy was now a woman, as passionate about love as Janis Joplin, and likewise as prone to depression.

In 'Wake Up Alone' Amy evoked the misery she suffered after Blake went back to his ex. She wrote that she tried to keep busy during the day, to save herself from thinking about him and from drinking. But after sunset depression descended like night. The writing is sophisticated. In a few words Amy managed to evoke all the agony of an unhappy love affair, laced with lust and self-doubt. We see Blake as a vision swimming before her eyes, mesmerising her in a sexual fantasy. She wants to 'pour myself over him' – an appropriately liquid image for a sex dream, and for a boozer. None of this is tacky. One of Amy's achievements as a songwriter was to address sex in a way that was explicit and erotic, but not seedy. Her honesty saved her from sounding cheap. Indeed, the song is romantic. When Amy sings of the moonlight coming into her room, she evokes a scene reminiscent of *Romeo and Juliet*, in contrast to the depression of waking up alone at the start of a new day. With this and other songs written at this time, Amy showed herself the equal of the best female songwriters of the twentieth century, as good as Carole King or Joni Mitchell.

The third love song written in Spain evokes what was, no doubt, in Amy's mind, the alluring image of Blake in his 'skull T-shirt', sleeves rolled up to reveal his tattoos. With this song Amy displays her talent for unusual images and rhymes, finding unexpected rhymes for Tanqueray gin and Stella Artois lager, and creating a convincing picture of pub life in the process. One can almost smell the booze, and taste the junk food consumed on the way home to soak it up. There is also a reference to the casual violence so common in London when young people drink. Amy refers to her lover tearing men apart, as if it turned her on to watch Blake putting the boot in. Like Ray Davies of the Kinks, Amy did not attempt to sound transatlantic in this and other songs. She wrote and sang about her London life in vernacular English, which added to the sense that she was telling the truth. And part of that truth was that she didn't like herself. The title of this song said it all: 'You Know I'm No Good'.

Amy got back with Blake when she returned to London. The

couple were a familiar sight in Camden, lurching down the street hand in hand, or with their hands buried in each other's back pockets, lanky Blake with his gargoyle face towering over tiny Amy, who had recently taken to wearing her hair in a beehive. She looked happy when she was with him.

Apart from frequenting the local pubs the couple would often pop into Pat's News near Amy's flat where Amy would buy tabloid newspapers, rolling tobacco and Rizla papers for joints, as well as the kind of cheap chews school children enjoy. Amy's favourite sweet was strawberry laces. There was always a childish side to her (though it is also true that drug-users develop a sweet tooth). Blake got into trouble with the Patels who own Pat's News when he appeared to take sweets from their shelves without paying. When Vidia Patel protested, she says Amy scolded Blake and paid for him. '[Amy] would tell him, "Don't do that in this shop."'

During the early stage of the romance, in the late spring of 2005, Amy and Blake went to an exhibition of landscape paintings by John Virtue at the National Gallery. The exhibition made a big impression on the lovers. Then they broke up. A short time later, when they were apart, Blake returned to the gallery to have another look at the exhibition and was surprised to find Amy there. It felt as if they were meant to be together, and so they were reunited.

Although some people take the view that Blake latched on to Amy because of her success, as some believe Courtney Love set her cap at Kurt Cobain for the same reason, friends see these relationships as true romances. They may not have been healthy love affairs, but they weren't without substance. 'I think he did love her. From what I could see, they seemed very happy. He was affectionate,' Sarah Hurley says of Blake and Amy. 'If she got up, his eyes would follow her.' Like many lovers, the couple used pet names for each other. Amy was Lioness, because she was wild like a lioness. He was Christopher Crocodile. To demonstrate the sincerity of her love Amy had another tattoo applied to her much decorated torso. She asked Mirek vel Stotker, at Eclipse in Camden, to draw a pocket over her heart, and above the pocket she had him ink *Blake's*. Blake felt flattered.

Then they argued, and broke up again. It became a wearisome pattern. This time it was Amy who told Blake to go, taking up instead with a mild-mannered chef named Alex Clare, whom her girlfriends liked and thought good for her, but whom Amy seemed to find a little dull. It was Blake she craved. Blake was her obsession, and he was the inspiration for the album that made her a star.

Six

EXCESS

'I wonder, Madam,' replied the Doctor, 'that you
have not penetration enough to see the strong inducement
to this excess; he who makes a *beast* of himself gets rid of
the pain of being a man.'
Samuel Johnson on drunkenness

1

The week after the Monterey Pop Festival, the Jimi Hendrix
Experience performed at Bill Graham's Fillmore West in San Francisco.
Big Brother was in town at the same time. It is said that Jimi Hendrix
and Janis Joplin got it together backstage at the Fillmore, presenting
the intriguing vision of two principal 27s in an intimate encounter.
Even at a time of free love, Jimi and Janis were notably promiscuous.
Janis propositioned men on a daily basis – often men who were
obviously unsuitable – as if to prove to herself that she was attractive.
She boasted of her exploits, announcing onstage that she had slept
with two thousand men, more or less, 'and a few hundred chicks'.
There were countless one-night stands for Jimi, too, though there
was more to his relationship with Janis than sex.

'They had a closer connection. They were trying to have a romance,'
says Jimi's friend Anthony Atherton. 'I was in San Francisco with
him and we went to Janis's place. But they had another thing going
on: a working relationship that was really close. Janis just fell in love

with his style of music.' Atherton believes that racial prejudices prevented Janis and Jimi being a more public, stable couple, though their work schedules were probably a bigger issue.

Jimi worked incredibly hard. Many of his associates blame Michael Jeffrey – who managed the Experience with Chas Chandler initially, then bought Chandler out – for greedily overworking the guitarist. The tour schedule Jeffrey set the Experience on was relentless, even by the standards of the 1960s when bands generally worked harder than they do today. Musicians used drink and drugs to cope with the strain of constant travelling and performing, which was one of the reasons drugs began to play a major part in Jimi's life. There were additional reasons.

In his memoir, *Are You Experienced?*, Jimi's bass guitarist Noel Redding wrote that he, Jimi and the drummer Mitch Mitchell were all of the opinion that they had to be 'properly stoned to play properly. Good dope equalled good music …' Many contemporaries shared this view, which is a variation on the belief common among artists of all kinds that they need to maintain habits they have developed to function creatively, whether it be the novelist who claims not to be able to write without a cigarette, or Amy Winehouse who feared she would lose the ability to compose songs if she submitted to therapy in order to stop drinking. The belief that drugs were essential to creating good music was particularly prevalent in the rock community of the 1960s, and partly explains the fatality rate. There was even a competitive culture in which rock musicians vied with one another to see who could take the most dope, as young men will indulge in drinking contests (by and large such behaviour is the folly of men). So, Jimi and his band took an astonishing amount of drugs. Noel Redding reports that they returned to Britain from their first US tour, in August 1967, 'very pissed. Very stoned. Very shattered.'

In contrast to the Experience, the Rolling Stones were taking an extended break from touring, which was fortunate for Brian Jones, who was in no state to perform. His drug abuse had escalated alarmingly since he had lost Anita Pallenberg to Keith Richards and, ironically, since being busted for drugs. Brian's nerves were shot and, although he was still young, his face was haggard under his mop of blond hair, while the bags under his eyes had become darker and heavier. Yet he still had admirers.

Brian was dating two models, Suki Poitier, who had been with the Guinness heir Tara Browne the night Browne died in a car crash, an accident that had partly inspired the Beatles' song 'A Day in the Life', and Amanda Lear, who recalls Brian as being extremely neurotic. 'I've never seen anybody so complex.' This is quite something, coming from a woman widely believed to have started life as a boy.* 'Everything was taken wrong, in the wrong sense. He wouldn't go out if the wind was blowing his hair. He had to have that hair style, with that heavy fringe covering his [brow]. On top of it he was putting a hat. So he was all day long with my blow dryer getting his hair together, and he was afraid to go out, and to be seen in the daylight. I don't know, he was so full of complexes! And at night he was having nightmares when he was asleep. He was waking up screaming, "Where am I? Who are you? What are you doing here?"'

Within a month of the Monterey Festival, worried about his forthcoming drug trial, Brian checked into a clinic. From now on Brian used private clinics like hotels. Amy Winehouse was the same, often frequenting the same establishments decades later, demonstrating that while patients come and go the lucrative business of looking after unhappy people rolls along indefinitely. Brian was in such a bad way that he was referred to the Priory Clinic in Roehampton, south-west London, for more specialist treatment. Amy, too, would find her way to the Priory.

Brian's criminal case came before the Inner London Sessions on 30 October 1967. The Crown didn't proceed against his friend and co-defendant, Prince Stanislas Klossowski de Rola, and Brian's not-guilty plea to possession of Methedrine and cocaine was accepted. However, he had little choice but to plead guilty to possession of cannabis, and to allowing his home to be used for smoking the drug, only hoping that he would be spared a custodial sentence. In his defence, Brian's barrister told the court that his client had suffered a

---

* Though her gender at birth has been the subject of much debate, Amanda Lear has always denied being a transsexual. See Source Notes, page 322.

nervous breakdown since his arrest, and had been under the care of psychiatrists at the Priory. Dr Leonard Henry gave evidence that Brian was depressed and agitated to the point of incoherence, and had had to be tranquillised. The doctor believed that if he was sent to jail he might go into 'a psychotic depression … and he might well attempt to injure himself'. A second psychiatrist, Dr Anthony Flood, concurred. Nevertheless, the chairman of the court made an example of Brian, sentencing him to nine months in prison. Brian was taken directly to Wormwood Scrubs, but freed on bail the following day after his psychiatrists came before an appeal-court judge.

Further evidence of the dire state of Brian's mental health came at the full appeal hearing later in the year. This time his barrister spoke of the strain fame had put on Brian's 'already fragile mental make-up'. Dr Flood said he had found Brian 'anxious, considerably depressed and potentially suicidal' when he had first treated him. He added revealingly: 'He was easily depressed and easily thwarted. What to him seemed overwhelming problems made him anxious and depressed. He was not able to sort his problems out satisfactorily because he became anxious and depressed. He has a history of depressive mental illness.' The appeal was successful. Brian was released with a fine on the condition that he continued to receive psychiatric treatment.

Even allowing for the fact that Brian's barrister was calling witnesses to keep him out of jail, the evidence of the psychiatrists at the appeal hearing is striking. Here was one of the leading pop stars of the 1960s, one of the core group of musicians who went on to die at 27, described at the age of 25 as a man with 'a history of depressive mental illness' who was 'potentially suicidal'. The words are worth bearing in mind as we follow Brian's life to its conclusion.

2

All performers face the challenge of getting psyched up for a show, then having to come down from that high before repeating their performance the next night, or as required. It is an emotionally exhausting regime. There are healthy ways of managing the up-and-down cycle, involving diet and exercise, and less healthy ways, using drink and drugs. Amy Winehouse tried both methods. Ultimately, like other 27s, she fell back on substance abuse with fatal consequences.

In many ways the stars of the 1960s had a harder time because, as touched upon, they worked harder. Amy released only two albums and gave precious few concerts. One of her former managers has remarked ruefully that 'you were lucky if Amy did thirty days a year'. By comparison the Rolling Stones gave hundreds of shows in the sixties and still found time to record nine studio albums while Brian Jones was in the band, though he contributed less and less. The Doors didn't tour intensively by the standards of the day, but they cut six studio albums in four years. Janis Joplin released three albums. So did Jimi Hendrix, plus the live *Band of Gypsys* (*sic*) album. In brief gaps in a virtually continuous concert schedule, the Jimi Hendrix Experience found the time to record a second sensational album in 1967, *Axis: Bold as Love*, released in Britain only seven months after their début LP. By comparison there were three years between Amy Winehouse's two albums. Hendrix also toured more than any other 27. From October 1966 until February 1969 he was onstage almost every night, sometimes playing a matinée as well. Only in the last months of his life did he get significant time off the road, and he spent most of it in the studio.

Inevitably, Jimi's workload affected his behaviour. He cracked up after a show in Gothenburg, Sweden, in January 1968, according to Noel Redding, who wrote in his memoirs that Jimi got stinking drunk and suggested that Redding and Mitch Mitchell join him and a Swedish journalist in an orgy. Redding says that when he and Mitchell turned him down the guitarist went berserk and smashed up his hotel room. 'You could hear the noise all over the hotel,' Redding wrote, adding that the police were called when his band mates failed to calm Jimi down. Mitchell doesn't mention the orgy suggestion in his book, but he agreed that Jimi wrecked his room.

Redding also gives an alarming account of the substances the trio consumed on the road. 'Just how do you get down after the show

so you can sleep?' Redding writes in his book. '[A] few stiff drinks
and a sleeper sped you on your way. But plane time would come
long before the sleeper wore off, hence the leapers. But the flights
are terribly boring when you're up, so a creeper rounds off the edges
and a lot of drink takes a bit of the cotton wool out of your mouth.
But booze (well over a bottle of vodka a day now) makes life a bit
grim, so "just a bit" of acid makes you feel all tingly and good. But
it's hard to concentrate on acid, so a quick sniff of coke (just becoming
trendy …) brings the brain briefly to attention while you smoke
some grass or hash to take the nerviness out of the coke. Then, as
you're beginning to feel a bit tacky by the time the flight's over, the
hotel is found, and it's gig time: a bath, a snort of Methedrine and
a big tobacco joint puts you onstage. Repeat as necessary.' Redding
may have been exaggerating for effect. But if half of what he wrote
was true it would help to explain why all three members of the
Experience died before their time. Redding developed cirrhosis of
the liver and died at 57; Mitchell died on the road at 61 after years
of heavy drinking; while Hendrix, of course, bowed out at 27.

The most gruelling Experience tour – 'the one that did us in,'
wrote Redding – began in January 1968. This was a two-month trek
across the United States during which the band played virtually every
night. In mid-February the tour brought Jimi home to Seattle and
a reunion with his father, whom he hadn't seen since he'd joined the
army. Al Hendrix had remarried. His new wife was Japanese, Ayako
'June' Jinka, who had five children of her own: Willie, Marsha, Linda,
Donna and Janie. The whole family turned out to greet Jimi and his
band as they arrived at Sea-Tac airport.

As we have seen, several of the 27s had strained relationships
with their parents. In the normal course of events they may have
had little or nothing to do with their families in adult life, as
indeed Jim Morrison didn't. But success introduced a new dynamic.
Jim Morrison's face on an album cover was enough to make Admiral
Morrison telephone his son to try to patch up their relationship.
Mitch Winehouse became ever present in Amy's life when her
recording career began. And there was a marked change in Al
Hendrix's relationship with Jimi now that he was a star. 'Mr

Hendrix finally accepted him, but he accepted him only after he had made it,' says Anthony Atherton. 'That wasn't a good basis for a good relationship. I don't think that [Jimi] really held that against his father, but I think they could have been closer.'

The first Al knew of Jimi's new life was when Jimi telephoned from Britain in 1966. Al didn't welcome the call, according to Jimi's girlfriend Kathy Etchingham, who says he admonished Jimi for calling collect, suggested that he write instead and hung up. One of his stepsisters, though, gained a different impression. 'I was in the living room when Jimi called,' says Janie Hendrix, crossly. 'I heard the conversation and I got to talk to Jimi, and he was *so* excited, and there was no wet cloth thrown on his exuberant news of he's made it.' Her memory of events may not be perfect as she was only five or six at the time. 'My dad was very, very supportive [of Jimi].' Janie is defensive of the memory of Al Hendrix, whom she refers to as 'Dad' although there was no blood relationship between her and Al, any more than there was between her and Jimi, whom she refers to as her brother. Nevertheless, she would inherit and control Jimi's musical legacy, making her a significant figure in his story.

By the time Jimi returned to Seattle, the extent of his success was clear to everybody, Al included, yet the family were taken aback by his prosperity. The guitarist arrived home wearing a vintage military jacket and an elaborate silver and turquoise belt. Janie Hendrix recalls Jimi showing off his belt to the family, saying that it had cost several hundred dollars, to their amazement, and telling his father, 'When I'm not here, it's yours.' Janie interpreted this to mean that Jimi knew he wouldn't live long. 'It always seemed as though Jimi just felt like he wasn't going to be here, and perhaps there was a time limit, and it seemed like he knew what that was.'

Mitch Mitchell recalls Jimi's surprise upon meeting the new family members, but gained the impression that Al was 'genuinely pleased to see his son had made good'. The kids had drawn a 'Welcome Home' banner on butcher's paper, which Jimi displayed onstage that night when he played Seattle's Center Arena. The family sat in the front row. Afterwards there was a party at Jimi's hotel, and the next day he was guest of honour at his old high school, before leaving town to continue the tour. Jimi would return to Seattle three more times. He was generous with his family, giving Al money to buy a truck and a car. But the visits were not entirely happy. Jimi was concerned to see his younger brother Leon in trouble with the police, and there was friction between father and son, while friends couldn't help but notice how differently Al Hendrix behaved towards Jimi now. 'When he came back everybody was in awe of him, you know, that's just human nature,' says Jimi's friend Sammy Drain. But Al's reaction was pronounced. Sammy imitates the old man: 'My boy! My boy! ... That's my boy!'

3

Like some other members of the 27 Club Jim Morrison seemed obsessed with his mortality, though it wasn't always clear whether he was truly morbid or if he was talking about death to make an impression.

After a Doors show at the Fillmore West in 1967, just before the band hit the big-time, Jim took Elektra Records executive Steve Harris aside and said, 'Let's pull a death hoax,' meaning they should tell the press he'd died, then announce that he was alive, after all, for publicity.

'It's a great idea, Jim. What a wonderful idea. Except for one thing.'

'What?'

'Nobody really knows who you are yet.'

Though this was a jokey exchange, Jim's obsession with death and indeed suicide rivalled that of Kurt Cobain. Jim's band mate Robby Krieger recalls a night in Los Angeles with Morrison and the Doors drummer John Densmore when Jim 'was very depressed and he was talking about killing himself, which wasn't that unusual, but we believed him. He just didn't think it was worth it anymore, and life was horrible ... And so we spent all night talking him out of killing himself ...' In the morning the musicians went outside to watch the sun rise, at which point Jim cheered up considerably. Indeed, he was inspired to write a song, 'People are Strange', which the Doors recorded the following day.

There is no doubt that Jim Morrison enjoyed playing mind games with his band mates, especially Krieger and Densmore. But there is evidence that he did suffer with depression, exacerbated by his drinking and use of drugs, which increased after he became famous. 'He became downright crazy. He got way too drunk,' says Dickie Davis, who knew Jim before he was a star, and shudders at the memory of how his friend abused drink and drugs during the years of his celebrity. Jim had always been a hedonist, but he was much worse now. 'It was a tragedy. Tragedy is so romantic when people write about it, but it is horrible to see. There's nothing pretty about a person destroying themselves. And it gets romanticised. Everybody thinks, Oh, it must have been wonderful to know [Jim]. It was, up until it became a tragedy, and then it was impossible to know him.'

One symptom of dissolution was getting into trouble with the police. All the principal 27s had brushes with the law, mostly when under the influence, and Jim was no exception, though his first arrest as a star was not his fault. He was making out drunkenly with a girl backstage before a show in New Haven, Connecticut, in December 1967, when a police officer ordered them to leave the area, not realising who Jim was. Jim's mistake was to tell the cop to 'eat it'. The cop sprayed him with Mace.

When he came onstage Jim told the audience what had just happened, incorporating the story into a performance of 'Back Door Man', effectively taunting the police and turning the crowd against the officers at the venue. Fearing a riot, the police turned on the house lights and arrested Jim, on charges that were later dropped. They punished him in a more direct way backstage. 'I saw them pounding Jim. There was this guy holding him, and one pounding his back and another punching his face,' says Vince Treanor, later the band's road manager. Luckily Jim was so drunk he hardly felt it.

Jim wore leather onstage in New Haven. It had become his look, complementing his image as the Lizard King. The moniker derives from his poem 'The Celebration of the Lizard', also sung in concert, in which Jim proclaimed: 'I am the Lizard King/ I can do anything'.

Jim bought his leathers off the peg initially, but as the Doors became more successful he had his outfits tailor-made, with bespoke features such as stash pockets for his dope. Many of these outfits were made by Mirandi Babitz, a friend of Jim's girlfriend Pamela Courson, who ran a boutique in LA. Mirandi came to know Jim well, getting a unique insight into the domestic life of the Lizard King when she and her musician husband, Clem Floyd, stayed briefly with Jim and Pamela.

Jim and Pamela were renting a funky little wooden house in a side-street in Laurel Canyon, above Hollywood, an address Jim sang about in 'Love Street', though the actual address was Rothdell Trail. Considering Jim's wild-man image, his home was surprisingly neat and tidy, a pretty little 'hippie castle', says Mirandi, with pine furniture draped in gingham and Madras-cotton throws. Pamela had made a cosy nest for herself and the man she wanted to marry. Marriage wasn't considered particularly cool for people in and around the music business at the time. Mirandi had married her British husband for visa reasons, but she says Pamela very much wanted to marry Jim, and she was frustrated that he wouldn't make her his wife. It was one of the causes of tension in a tempestuous relationship.

Drink and drugs were problems too. Jim was a drunk with a fondness for marijuana and LSD while Pamela used heroin. Drinking and drug abuse made the relationship explosive. When they were high Jim and Pamela were prone to extravagant arguments that saw them tear their house apart. 'The drug use was, like, so heavy, and the drinking was so heavy, and the wild running off into the night, fighting with each other, throwing things around … It was really tempestuous, just dramatic,' says Mirandi. Sexual jealousy was also an issue. '[Pamela] would do things like cut up his clothes. He was unfaithful, and so was she, but they were both supposed to be faithful … He also had his back-door man thing going on,' she adds, referring to Jim's apparent predilection for anal sex, which Pamela didn't think cool. '[So] she wrote "fag" across his clothes and cut them up.'

Mirandi, too, was a drug-user. Later she cleaned up and became a therapist, counselling addicts. Looking back, she believes that Jim had a range of problems, including 'bipolar disorder, depression [and] total addiction'. His conversation was also morbid, as was true of Pamela. 'Him and Pamela, the two of them together were just always talking about death, [and] they talked about dying together.' The couple acted out suicide fantasies on the twisting roads of Laurel Canyon. 'They did things like take the cars up on Mulholland Drive and play chicken, you know, *We'll drive towards the cliff, and we're totally stoned on acid, and we'll see if we can stop in time, and maybe we'll die together.*'

These stories add to the picture of Jim Morrison as a man bent on self-destruction, his death at 27 the inevitable result of reckless living. Clem Floyd agrees with his ex-wife that Jim was a depressive and reckless, but he is not convinced about Jim's obsession with death. 'He wasn't really obsessed with death – until he got killed,' he quips. 'Now he's obsessed.' Rather, Floyd saw a young artist who hadn't learned to leave his act on stage. 'Morrison was kind of depressed under the weight of his stage image. He was trying to carry that personality around with him. You can't do that. You have to drop it when you get off stage,' says Floyd, who didn't warm to Jim personally during the time he and Mirandi stayed with the rock star. 'I didn't like being around him, because you never knew what goddamn stupid thing he was going to do next.'

While the Doors were now very successful, there was a growing sense that Jim was already tiring of his role as the band's front man, and finding it difficult to come up with new songs. He had used his best ideas on the first two albums. Now he felt he was on a treadmill to churn out product. As he complained to an interviewer in 1969, 'there's not the time to let things happen as they should.' The Doors were contracted to deliver several more albums to Elektra on a tight schedule. Recording sessions became long and difficult.

The third Doors album, *Waiting for the Sun*, was a particular struggle. Jim got into the habit of bringing friends into the studio to relieve the boredom and tension, turning recording sessions into parties. One of the people he invited over was the young millionaire and friend to the stars Deering Howe, who spent a wild night in LA with Jim after they had left the studio. 'The last thing I remember that night is waking up about four in the morning in somebody's house underneath the table, and sitting at the table above me was Jim Morrison, and some guy I had never met, and they were playing Russian roulette with a loaded fucking gun. OK, time for me to leave …' In an attempt to get Jim to finish *Waiting for the Sun*, the Doors engaged the musician Bob Neuwirth to keep an eye on him. But Neuwirth was almost as dissolute as Jim. 'Bobby Neuwirth needed a keeper himself,' says Deering Howe. 'This was like the blind leading the blind. My God!'

John Densmore became so frustrated that he quit the Doors briefly during the making of *Waiting for the Sun*. When the album was finally finished it was weaker than *Strange Days*, which in turn had not been as impressive as the Doors' début LP, showing a band in artistic decline, though not yet in commercial trouble. The album and its single, 'Hello, I Love You', both went to the top of the charts.

When the Doors went to New York to promote their records, Jim visited Steve Paul's Scene, on West 46th Street, where he drank to excess and acted the fool in the company of fellow stars. One night he got onstage with Tiny Tim, grabbed the microphone and swung it around his head like a lasso, a dangerous trick he often performed when drunk, occasionally hitting people. He accidentally hit the promoter Bill Graham at a show in San Francisco. After interrupting Tiny Tim's set, Jim got into a fight with his manager, Sal Bonafede. The men starting brawling, 'like an old Western thing,' says Bonafede's partner Asher Dann, who separated them and escorted Jim back to the Warwick Hotel where Jim punched him. 'All of a sudden he spins me around and throws a punch at me. I go – *boom* – down he goes … He was a handful.'

This was only one example of Jim's misbehaviour at Steve Paul's Scene. Musician Harvey Brooks, who played bass with the Doors in the studio and on stage, recalls Jim grovelling at his feet one night when he was jamming at the club. 'At one point he licked my toes. Don't ask me why.'

The most famous incident at Steve Paul's Scene involved Jim in a drunken encounter with Jimi Hendrix and Janis Joplin, presenting the fascinating image of three principal 27s together during a night out. Hendrix was in New York working on his third and final studio album, *Electric Ladyland*. Despite his intensive schedule, he would drop into clubs like the Scene late at night to jam for pleasure. One night in the spring of 1968 a drunken Jim Morrison got on stage with Hendrix. Steve Harris of Elektra Records says Morrison grabbed Hendrix's hat before repeating his trick of taking the microphone and swinging it around his head. 'The audience had to duck.' Another witness, Doors publicist Danny Fields, says Morrison made a drunken pass at Hendrix. 'Morrison crawled on his stomach to the microphone, got onstage … put his arms around Jimi's hips and said, "I want to suck your cock." And Jimi was, like, so shy, he was, like, embarrassed, but a professional, and he tried to keep playing.' Morrison then tumbled into the table where Janis Joplin was sitting, knocking her drink over. Some say Joplin was so incensed that she broke a bottle over Morrison's head.

The story has become confused in the telling, and may well have been exaggerated, but evidently something happened between Morrison, Hendrix and Joplin at the Scene, and it certainly wasn't the only time Jim Morrison and Janis Joplin had an altercation. Janis told her publicist that she hit Jim with a bottle one time after he'd yanked her hair, while Big Brother guitarist Sam Andrew remembers two such incidents: 'Jim Morrison was a brat. He was really ill-behaved … You know, at a party he came over to Janis and pulled her hair down to the floor. I don't know what he was thinking. That's just like really boorish behaviour. I think he was trying to shock people … But he was going too far. His father was an admiral, so he knew what correct behaviour was.'

At the time Janis was working on the *Cheap Thrills* album for CBS, Big Brother having signed to the label after Monterey. They had also signed with the premier manager of the day, Albert Grossman, whose clients included Bob Dylan. Grossman warned the members of Big Brother at the outset of their relationship that he wouldn't tolerate his clients using heroin. They nodded agreement. 'When he said that to us, you know, we all said yes, but at least three of us out of the five in that room were already doing it,' says Sam Andrew, who was one of those using heroin, as was Janis.

Despite several overdoses Sam Andrew was fortunate to live to old age. Heroin killed Janis and many of their friends in their prime. One wonders why so many musicians abused heroin, knowing how dangerous it was. 'It's an opiate and Janis was really fast, in all of her reflexes, and thinking and everything. So to a person like that who is fast and kind of anxious and quick, any kind of opiate is gonna be very attractive, because it gives them a chance to relax,' explains Sam, who offers an image of how good heroin made them feel: 'It's like a really warm summer day and everything is beautiful and kind of warm and dreamy.'

Fans of Big Brother empathised with the band's dreamy, druggy music. Others saw Big Brother as amateurs, complaining that they played out of time when they were stoned. This became an issue for Janis as her popularity and ambitions outgrew the band in the build-up to the release of *Cheap Thrills*, her first significant recording.* The original idea had been to make a live recording of Janis and Big Brother, but the band was so loose in concert that most of the album had to be recorded in the studio with the audience sound overdubbed. Producer John Simon lamented Big Brother's lack of musicianship. 'I always thought they were a great performance band, but I didn't think they made it as a recording band.'

Janis initially wanted the album titled *Sex, Dope and Cheap Thrills*, playing up to her libertine image. This was abbreviated to *Cheap Thrills*, the cover illustrated by her friend the artist Robert Crumb who was saddened by Janis's subsequent decline. 'She was a tough, hard-drinking girl, but soft inside. She liked getting fucked up too much, obviously. She ended up surrounded by blood-sucking sycophants and scary parasite types, both male and female. Poor thing, she didn't stand a chance.' The musicianship on *Cheap Thrills* may have been crude, but the album succeeded in capturing the energy of Janis's performances, her impassioned vocals sounding especially impressive on 'Summertime', 'Piece of My Heart' and 'Ball and Chain'. And

---

* An earlier album, *Big Brother and the Holding Company*, was released on the minor Mainstream label in 1967.

the album was a commercial success, number one in the US charts for eight weeks in the summer of 1968.

The Doors' third album, *Waiting for the Sun*, and Jimi Hendrix's *Electric Ladyland* were released within a couple of months of *Cheap Thrills*. All three made number one in America, uniting Joplin, Hendrix and Morrison at the apex of their careers, at roughly the same age. They were all between 24 and 25. In many ways it was downhill from now on.

That autumn Jim Morrison confessed to Ray Manzarek that he wanted to leave the Doors, as Manzarek recounts in his autobiography, *Light My Fire*. Manzarek couldn't understand why Jim wanted to quit when they had an album and a single at number one.

'I just can't take it anymore,' said Jim.

Manzarek reminded his friend that they had it good. They didn't tour much. And recording wasn't that onerous. When Manzarek pressed for an explanation, Jim made a significant admission.

'I think I'm having a nervous breakdown,' he said.

Manzarek refused to believe it. 'Oh, man. No, you're not. You're just drinking too much. It's starting to get to you.'

'No, Ray. I'm telling you ... I'm having a nervous breakdown. I want to quit.'

Manzarek persuaded Jim not to do anything hasty. The conversation ended with him agreeing to stay with the Doors for six months. As it turned out, he stayed longer. But the die was cast. Jim wanted out.

The Doors flew to Europe in September 1968 to play some gigs with the Jefferson Airplane. The bands gave two shows at the Roundhouse in London, a former train shed on Chalk Farm Road in Camden that would feature in the lives of three 27s. Brian Jones was one of those who came backstage to meet Jim Morrison, along with his French girlfriend Zouzou, who recalls Jim looking fit and handsome. 'He was so sexy on stage.' Later she would encounter a different Jim in Paris. By comparison Brian looked awful. He was baggy-eyed, nervous and paranoid, having recently been busted for cannabis for a second time. ('Why do you have to pick on me?' he whined to the police officers who raided his home. The result was another conviction and fine.)

After their London shows, the Doors and the Airplane travelled to continental Europe. They played Frankfurt, then Amsterdam on 15 September 1968. Before the Amsterdam gig, Jim swallowed a block of hashish, possibly given to him by a member of Canned Heat, who had been on the bill in Germany the previous night. (The members of Canned Heat were notorious for their drug use, save Al Wilson, ironically, who would die of an overdose.) The hash reacted with the booze Jim had been drinking sending him high as a kite. He appeared on stage unexpectedly during the Jefferson Airplane's set, performed what Ray Manzarek describes as a 'whirling dervish dance', then collapsed.

As an ambulance transported Jim to hospital, the remaining Doors were obliged to take the stage without him. Manzarek and Krieger sang Jim's parts as well as playing their instruments. After they'd got over the shock of working without him, they enjoyed the experience. For the first time Densmore, Krieger and Manzarek basked in the attention and applause usually focused on Jim, and they received good reviews.

The fact that the Doors had done well without Jim seemed to depress the singer when he came round the next day. He was also coping with a monumental hangover. 'When I walked in he had his head on a piano, and he was plunking one key [repeatedly] and he was in bad shape, really bad. I think had they not got him to the hospital he might have gone that night,' says Vince Treanor. He further believes that the fact the Doors proved they could perform without Jim fundamentally undermined his confidence. Indeed, a feeling began to grow that the group might have a future without him.

4

At this point in the history of popular music, virtually all the big rock bands were intact, including the Beatles and the Rolling Stones. There was a prevailing belief that, despite personality clashes, the major bands would continue together for the common good. This fantasy would be broken by the Stones, who had all but given up on Brian Jones by the end of 1968 when they released *Beggars Banquet*.

'Brian wasn't really involved on *Beggars Banquet*, apart from some slide [guitar] on "No Expectations"; that was the only thing he played on the whole record,' says Mick Jagger. 'He wasn't turning up to the sessions and he wasn't very well. In fact we didn't want him to turn up, I don't think.' *Beggars Banquet* was the group's strongest album yet, with Mick and Keith showing a significant musical and lyrical development on songs such as 'Sympathy for the Devil' and 'Street Fighting Man'. This was the beginning of the band's glory days, when they became a swaggering creative unit with a unique sound. Brian, who was not part of this development, was merely called upon for promotional duties, including attending the launch party for the album in December 1968, which culminated in a food fight for the press photographers. Symbolically, Mick Jagger plunged the first cream pie into Brian's face.

Two weeks before Christmas the Stones recorded a concert film in a London TV studio dressed to resemble a circus tent. *The Rolling Stones Rock and Roll Circus* brought together artists including Eric Clapton, John Lennon and the Who in a circus-themed show before a live audience that culminated in a set by the Rolling Stones. The night before the recording, Brian telephoned the director Michael Lindsay-Hogg in tears, complaining that the Stones were being horrid to him and saying he didn't want to appear in the film. Lindsay-Hogg, who had known the band since they first appeared on *Ready Steady Go!*, a TV show he had directed, talked Brian round, but the guitarist was in a sorry state during filming – a weary, depressed little man, chubby now, with a drawn face.

'He changed,' says Lindsay-Hogg. 'I met him first on *Ready Steady Go!* in April '65 when he was still himself. But he had become a very, very different person in only three years. His looks were shot. His connection to other people was shot. And he just seemed to be fading as a person, unlike Mick and Keith, who were coming into their own at that time. They'd all become famous [at the same time], and they still were very young, but they had had life experiences at that point which often people in their fifties and sixties had never had. Mick and Keith were talented and tough, with great will power, and Brian had none of those things to the degree the other two had.'

The Rolling Stones Rock and Roll Circus would be Brian's last public appearance with the band.

5

Although she had thrown her son out of the family home when he was an obstreperous teenager, Wendy O'Connor, in common with other 27 parents, revelled in Kurt Cobain's success. 'I just received a phone call from my son, Kurt Cobain, who sings and plays guitar with the band Nirvana. They are presently touring Europe. Their first album with Geffen Record Co. just went "Platinum" (over 1 million sales),' Wendy O'Connor wrote to her local newspaper, the *Daily World*, in November 1991. 'Kurt, if you happen to read this, we are so proud of you and you are truly one of the nicest sons a mother could have. Please don't forget to eat your vegetables or brush your teeth and now you can have your maid make your bed.'

At the time, Kurt was in Europe with Nirvana, and he and Courtney were using heroin. Kurt said they'd started using together in Amsterdam around Thanksgiving 1991. 'It was *my* idea,' he told his biographer Michael Azerrad, always keen to shield Courtney from blame, though he said she scored. 'I didn't really know how to get it, so Courtney was the one who would be able to somehow get it.' Here, then, was a love affair steeped in drug abuse from the outset. Back in the USA in December, Kurt overdosed, as he would time and again during the remaining two and a half years of his life, as Janis Joplin had before him. In both cases doctors warned the artists that one day they might never wake up. Still, they carried on taking heroin.

The seriousness of Kurt's problem became apparent to his close associates when his management, record-company executives and family gathered in New York in January 1992 for Nirvana's appearance on *Saturday Night Live*. 'The first time I knew he was doing hard drugs was around the first time the band did *Saturday Night Live*,' says Nirvana's manager Danny Goldberg. 'It was clear to me he was stoned.' Drummer David Grohl says he hadn't realised how bad things had become until he visited Kurt and Courtney in their hotel room prior to the recording and found them 'nodding out in bed, just wasted'. Others realised what was going on when Kurt reached the NBC studio. He was throwing up, and spending an inordinate amount of time in the toilet. 'Frankly, he looked strung out. He looked unhappy,' says Geffen executive Michael Maska.

Kurt, who had dyed his hair red for the TV show, didn't appear entirely present as he performed 'Smells Like Teen Spirit' for the cameras. For their second number Nirvana played 'Territorial Pissings', at the end of which they went through the motions of breaking their equipment. That night Kurt overdosed again.

Kurt and Courtney moved to Los Angeles where they detoxed after *Saturday Night Live*. In Courtney's case there was a special reason to get clean. She was pregnant. There wasn't time to address Kurt's problems properly, however, without putting Nirvana on hiatus. The band was about to tour Australia and Japan. Courtney joined Kurt on tour, travelling with him to Hawaii where the band also had concerts. On 24 February 1992, Kurt and Courtney married on Waikiki Beach. Kurt took heroin before the ceremony, literally and symbolically making heroin part of their union.

Noticeably absent from the Hawaii beach wedding was Kurt's band mate and, for several years, his best friend, Krist Novoselic. Krist and his wife Shelli had fallen out with Kurt and Courtney after Shelli had criticised the couple's drug use. She was particularly concerned because Courtney was pregnant, though whether she used heroin when she knew she was pregnant would become a contentious issue. Kurt and Krist were further estranged by an argument over money. As the main songwriter in Nirvana, Kurt now asked for a larger percentage of publishing income than his band mates received. The argument almost broke the group. Kurt's drug problem compounded these issues and made for an increasingly difficult relationship between the musicians.

It was at this stage that Kurt's managers staged their first intervention to try to get him off drugs. In what was then a fashionable method of dealing with drug-users, Kurt was confronted with his problem, and warned of the consequences if he did not stop. He was persuaded to check into Cedars-Sinai Hospital in Los Angeles for methadone treatment, but he rejected the Twelve Steps programme, by which alcoholics and other addicts admit that they have a problem they can't control and give themselves up to a higher power/ God. The quasi-religious aspect of the programme is a barrier to many addicts, as is the group therapy. Kurt was uncomfortable with the programme. He quit treatment early and returned to his heroin habit, which became more ferocious than ever.

On tour in Europe that summer Kurt collapsed and had to be hospitalised again. A number of shows were cancelled. Returning to Los Angeles, he went into a suicidal depression, bought himself a gun and contemplated blowing his brains out. He was obsessed with this dramatic and violent form of suicide, which is more common in the United States than in most countries due to the availability of guns. If one is serious about suicide, a bullet in the head is also a highly effective method – not a suicidal gesture, like slitting your wrists or swallowing a random number of pills, which may well fail – though not necessarily fool-proof. (Approximately three-quarters of suicide attempts with firearms prove fatal. A significant minority survive, often with severe injuries.) Two of Kurt's uncles successfully shot themselves dead and Kurt had recently been obsessively watching a video of a gunshot suicide, no doubt ideating his own exit. But he didn't pull the trigger. Not yet. He went back to Cedars-Sinai to detox. Almost simultaneously Courtney checked into the maternity ward of the hospital to have their baby. She ordered Kurt to attend the birth, which took place in chaotic circumstances on 18 August 1992. Drug sick, Kurt passed out during the delivery.

The fact that the child, Frances Bean Cobain, was born healthy was a relief to everybody, but there was an immediate related drama. While pregnant Courtney had given an interview to *Vanity Fair* in which she seemingly admitted to using heroin during her pregnancy. Reading an advance copy of the feature, she was dismayed to see herself characterised as an avaricious and boastful 'train-wreck personality'. The article reported that many people considered her 'a charismatic opportunist', who had pursued Kurt, and possibly introduced him to heroin (which he denied). The real bombshell came in Courtney's account of using heroin with Kurt. She was quoted as saying that they were using in New York in January when Kurt had recorded *Saturday Night Live*, as Kurt corroborated. 'After that, I did heroin for a couple of months.' If true, this meant that Courtney was still using heroin when she was pregnant, which exposed their baby to health risks.

Kurt and Courtney were furious and scared: furious at *Vanity Fair* journalist Lynn Hirschberg for having the temerity to take a critical look at Courtney, who had expected the magazine to publish a puff piece about her, and scared that the authorities would see them as unfit parents. They had discussed what they would do if their baby was taken away, deciding upon a catastrophic response.

Kurt appeared at Courtney's side in Cedars-Sinai with a gun, reminding her that they had made a suicide pact. They argued over who should go first.

'I'll go first, I can't have you do it first,' Courtney told Kurt.

Kurt gave her the gun. Courtney held the weapon and reflected on what it would mean to leave Frances without parents. She had second thoughts and tried to talk Kurt out of the pact.

Kurt became angry. 'Fuck you,' he said, 'you can't chicken out. I'm gonna do it.'

But neither did. Courtney gave the gun to their friend Eric Erlandson for safe keeping. Kurt wandered off to get more heroin. Amazingly, this mad scene was taking place in hospital.

Kurt and Courtney's fears came true when social services intervened in the care of Frances Bean after the publication of *Vanity Fair*, which sent them into another suicidal depression. The authorities wouldn't let them take the baby home without supervision, only allowing Frances to leave hospital when nannies were in place to care for her. Kurt and Courtney would have to go to court to get exclusive custody of their daughter. Meanwhile, Courtney protested that the *Vanity Fair* article was mostly 'unsaid and untrue', which was not a denial of the central allegation, and the publishers stood firm. In retrospect the article reads as fair and balanced, showing Courtney to be a complex character who, for all her faults, came across as more rational than her husband, who raged hysterically in the aftermath of the affair that he wanted to track down journalist Lynn Hirschberg and murder her dog, 'then shit all over her and stab her to death'.

In the wake of this mess Nirvana went back on tour in Europe and the United States, the US tour bringing Kurt home to Washington state and a family reunion reminiscent of Jimi Hendrix's Seattle homecoming. Nirvana was playing the Seattle Center Coliseum in September 1992 when Don Cobain showed up backstage. Don hadn't seen Kurt for seven years. He had made repeated efforts to contact his son, but had been rebuffed. Now that they stood face to face Kurt seemed to have nothing to say to his dad, nothing pleasant. He apparently told Don to 'shut the fuck up' when he spoke to Courtney in a way Kurt didn't like. As with other 27s, one of the fundamental relationships in life, between child and parent, was broken.

It was time for Nirvana to record their third album. Kurt had some powerful new songs including 'Serve the Servants', which addressed his relationship with Don. Kurt rasped that he had wanted a father in his life, but unfortunately 'I had a dad'. This was a sharp rebuke to Don, delivered with a typical economy of language. Kurt went on to sing that he didn't hate his old man anymore, suggesting that the subject of divorce had become boring. Yet it was the event upon which he brooded, the quagmire from which grew the weird tree of his adult life, his drug abuse, his rage, and his obsessions with guns and suicide, among the strange fruit it bore.

Kurt wanted to call the new album *I Hate Myself and I Want to Die.*

Seven

DISTRESS

What is a poet? An unhappy person who conceals
profound anguish in his heart but whose lips are so formed
that as sighs and cries pass over them they sound like
beautiful music.
Søren Kierkegaard

1

Drinking was a problem for Amy Winehouse long before she became
a notorious alcoholic. In the period between the release of her first
album, *Frank*, and her second, *Back to Black*, the record that made
her a star, Amy steeped herself in booze, and then she started using
hard drugs.

One of Amy's haunts was the Ten Room at the Café Royal on Air
Street in London, a private club run by two veterans of the music
scene, Patrick Alan and John Altman, for the entertainment of their
fellow musicians and celebrity friends. Alan and Altman recognised
that Amy had great talent. 'Amy sings with a low register,' explains
Patrick Alan, whose career credits include working with the Drifters
and Michael Jackson. 'Because she has that nice meaty bottom end
when she goes to her highs it's really impressive ... It just moves you.'
But drink sometimes got the better of her. 'With Amy, I could see
early on that she drank,' says John Altman, who jammed onstage with
Jimi Hendrix in the sixties as he now jammed at the Ten Room with

Amy. 'Sometimes she would get up and she'd be unable to perform, [or] I'd have to play through a lot of what she was singing to keep her on track, because she'd lose her place, because she was drunk.'

At this stage in her career Amy would sing at private functions and small venues in Britain and abroad to boost her income. In the summer of 2005 Patrick Alan got Amy a gig with fellow singer Natalie Williams in Greece. Unfortunately, Amy started drinking as soon as she arrived in Skiathos and passed out drunk backstage during the interval on the first night. '[They] couldn't wake her up,' says Alan, who had to deal with the irate promoter. 'They were supposed to do three nights. He was so upset, he sent her home the next day [without pay].' This was a foretaste of trouble to come.

Amy had always suffered mood swings, and drink made her more volatile. When she sang in aid of charity at the Cobden Club in London in November 2005 she was in a particularly grumpy mood, telling her audience to be quiet and leaving the stage after three songs. Her surgeon cousin Jonathan Winehouse was in the audience, and once again he felt concerned. 'I saw in her all of those things I'd learned in medical school,' he says, noting a decline in Amy's health and behaviour that worsened over the next few years into what he calls a 'stepwise deterioration'. '[People] talk about her death being totally unexpected, but if you actually look at the history of what she did, and study the chronology of what she did, you'll see that stepwise deterioration. Sometimes she was able to hold it together, and other times she wasn't, and she ended up at the point she ended up, and died. There's a lot of denial, unfortunately, both with her and the people around her as well, and that's half the problem with alcoholic people.' Again, Jonathan tried to talk to Mitch Winehouse about his concerns. 'He just wasn't receptive to hearing it.'

In truth, it wasn't easy to tell Amy what to do. She hadn't forgiven her manager Nick Godwyn for trying to get her into rehab after *Frank* was released. 'After that my relationship with her definitely changed. She hadn't wanted to go, didn't think she needed it and she lost her faith in me,' Godwyn wrote, after her death. Amy dropped him and signed with a new management firm, Metropolis Music, run by Raymond 'Raye' Cosbert, who ingratiated himself by sending Amy champagne and getting friendly with Mitch at football matches. Amy grew fond of her 'Raye-Raye', as she called him, but Cosbert struggled to impose discipline on his artist. Perhaps nobody could. 'I'll tell you one thing, God couldn't manage Amy Winehouse,' says musician and filmmaker Don Letts, a mutual friend of Amy and her manager. 'Raye did the best he could ... It was more about damage limitation, trying to guide her.' And, when all was said and done, Raye Cosbert guided Amy to worldwide success with her second album.

Amy had been writing songs for the album throughout her relationship with Blake Fielder-Civil, and after they broke up. When it came time to record she collaborated with a DJ and producer eight years her senior. Like Amy, Mark Ronson had been born in London to a Jewish family. His was wealthy and well connected. Relatives included two former British government ministers, Lord (Leon) Brittan and Sir Malcolm Rifkind. After his parents divorced, Ronson's mother married Mick Jones of Foreigner and settled with her children in New York, where Ronson established a recording studio. Amy paid him a visit in March 2006.

Amy showed Ronson the lyrics to 'Back to Black' and he came up with chords that fitted, thus completing the song. Amy was delighted and extended her stay in New York so they could work together further. They were out shopping one day in Manhattan when she told Ronson the story of how her management had tried to get her into rehab, explaining how she had replied emphatically and repeatedly in the negative. *No. No. No.* 'It was so funny, the way she said it,' Ronson said. 'I was, like, that could really be a song, you know.' To set Amy's words to music, he drew on their mutual love of classic American soul, taking Amy to Brooklyn to record with the Dap-Kings, a band who lived for this music. They recorded six of the eleven songs on *Back to Black* at the Dap-Kings' studio, including 'Rehab', 'You Know I'm No Good', 'Love is a Losing Game' and 'Back to Black' itself. Amy recorded the rest of the album with Salaam Remi in Miami, with overdubs in London.

All the tunes on *Back to Black* are catchy, the Ronson songs in particular having a retro feel without degenerating into pastiche. Although the songs were recorded by two producers the album is cohesive, while the way it was made with musicians playing live in the studio, as opposed to using sampling and digital tuning, was a return to a traditional way of recording. 'We do a lot of these recordings but this one stood out because it sounded so real. It was all live drums and live rhythm section, [and] because so much of it these days is programmed, it was almost old-fashioned,' says Jamie Talbot, who played tenor sax on 'Rehab'. 'You go in and it's the same old, same old, boy bands and this sort of thing, kids that are making records and they are just being processed, and they sound like it. But this sounded real. It was an honest, old-fashioned pop song. It was great.'

The lyrics matched the quality of the music. Amy became a poet of song on *Back to Black*, relating the story of her romance with Blake in original and evocative language that brought each stage of the affair to life, from the initial sexual excitement and joy to the pain of separation and resulting depression. The darker aspects of the relationship give *Back to Black* its tone. At times Amy sounds distraught, almost mad with grief. There was another event in her life during the making of the record that contributed to this downbeat mood. Her grandmother, Cynthia Winehouse, died of cancer in May 2006.

Amy's writing talent shines through all the tracks on *Back to Black*, but her vocabulary is particularly interesting on 'Me and Mr Jones'. In this song Amy invents a word, 'fuckery', to describe the unreliability of her lover, asking: 'what ... fuckery is this?' This twist on a well-worn vulgarity – simple, yet very expressive – may earn Amy a place in the *Oxford English Dictionary* in time. She sang the line beautifully, with a raised eyebrow of contempt for a man fallen below expectations, as so many men had and would. Yet Amy wasn't perfect. She was indulging in fuckery by the summer of 2006, by sneaking around behind her boyfriend's back with her ex.

2

Blake was using cocaine, crack and heroin by the time he and Amy starting seeing each other again that summer, behind Alex Clare's back, and they were soon using hard drugs together. Pandora's box was opened one day when they were in a pub in the West End of London listening to tracks from the forthcoming album, songs about Blake, of course. 'I think I had a little bit of coke, one of my pals had a bit of coke, and she wanted some,' Blake said, in a 2009 television interview, in which he gave an unusually detailed and direct account of their drug history. 'As far as I know, she only took it on certain occasions. She didn't always take it when I was with her. It took months – six, seven, eight months – before she got bad.'

During this period, photographer Mischa Richter and stylist Lou Winwood visited Amy at her Camden flat to discuss the photo shoot for her new album cover. Amy was in the bath when the photographer arrived at Jeffrey's Place. He waited downstairs in the living room, chatting to Alex Clare. 'And all of a sudden I heard water dripping,' he says. 'I look up and there's a big hole in the ceiling and water is rushing out of this hole.' Clare and Richter ran to get pans to catch the water. As they did so Amy sauntered downstairs with her hair in a towel, 'and paid no mind at all to the fact that water was pouring down,' laughs Richter. 'I loved that.'

Amy looked very different from the girl who had made *Frank*. Most obviously she had lost weight. Lou Winwood says that when she first dressed Amy in 2003 she had worn size ten or twelve (UK), fairly small but not unhealthily so. Now Lou was obliged to go to children's shops to find items for Amy to wear because she was so thin. Amy had also perfected her image. She had a preference for 1950s-style clothing. She had many more tattoos than previously, up and down both arms, which she liked to show off in short-sleeve tops; she had refined her Cleopatra eyeliner, and had taken to adding extensions to her hair, which she piled up in a tower. These elements came together to create a unique look that became familiar to millions of people.

Lou brought a selection of tiny garments to Mischa Richter's north London house a few days later for the *Back to Black* photo shoot, but there was no sign of Amy. Instead of getting an early night so she would look her best for the most important photographic session of her life, not to mention wanting to be on time (she rarely was),

she had partied until dawn after a wedding in Essex and crashed out
in a country hotel where she was finally located. A driver was sent
to collect her. She tipped up belatedly at Richter's house in Kensal
Green very much the worse for wear. 'When she arrived I was having
to pick coke out of her nose, and stuff like that,' says Lou, 'brush
her up a bit.'

The cover photo for *Back to Black* was taken in the front bedroom
of Richter's house, which happened to have a black carpet and a
cupboard he'd painted black for his children to chalk on. The use of
the black room with its blackboard was a happy accident: Richter
didn't know what the album would be called. The chalk marks on
the board had been made by his five-year-old daughter, Elsie, and
her friend, Honer, whose name can be deciphered on the CD sleeve.
The inside pictures of Amy in a purple top were taken in the back
garden, while the shots of Amy in a red and white dress were taken
by the front door. Having started the day hung-over, and in a difficult mood, Amy had loosened up by the time these pictures were
taken, becoming coquettish and chatty with the photographer as she
perched on his garden wall, one hand behind her head, showing a
bit of leg, looking like a Reader's Wife. 'She's talking about Blake
this whole day, and how it was a bit naughty of her ... She was full
of Blake,' says Richter, who felt sorry for Alex Clare, 'because I
thought he was cool and I liked him ... She was saying to me, "I'm
doing something [bad]. I don't care. I've got to see him."'

Amy's sneaky affair with Blake continued while she assembled a
band to promote *Back to Black*. As her musical director, Amy hired
bass guitarist Dale Davis, whom she knew from the Ten Room, and
he helped her select seven more musicians, mostly men with a jazz
background, including two horn players and two backing vocalists,
Ade Omotayo and Zalon Thompson. A third horn player was added
later, and sometimes Amy worked with three singers. In keeping with
the retro sound of her songs, the musicians wore suits and ties for
the stage, which was dressed to look like an old-time jazz club.
Musicians came and went from Amy's band over the next five years,
but Davis, Omotayo and Thompson remained constant, while several
others served long stints. Amy endeared herself to her band. She

didn't set herself apart from the musicians, although she was clearly the boss. She chose them and paid their wages, cheques coming from her company, often signed by her mother. Amy's knowledge of music, her love of singing and her sheer talent impressed everybody. 'Many times she made the hairs on the back of my neck stand up on end, just down to the timing of her phrasing,' says Aaron Liddard, who played tenor and baritone saxophone and flute with the band.

Drummer Nathan Allen, a veteran of the *Frank* band, was one of those who were taken aback by how much weight Amy had lost. 'I was like *wow*. I didn't say anything. But, yeah, there was a drastic change.' Amy explained her altered appearance by saying she was using the gym more often, confiding in Aaron Liddard that she was exercising to cope with mood swings. 'She knew she was bipolar, and she knew how to deal with it healthily,' says Aaron, who was himself slightly bipolar. 'I think I was asking her why she was going to the gym all the time, she don't need to lose any weight. She's like, "I don't do it for that. I do it because it helps me to feel stable. I'm self-medicating. That's why I go and do it. It makes me feel good."' This was not the whole story. In truth, Amy suffered with eating disorders. She binge-ate and then made herself vomit.

Amy also spoke about drugs. 'She knew that if she ever started doing Class A, it would kill her,' says Aaron. 'She said, "I don't do weed anymore. I just do alcohol. I won't do any A-Class. I'm too addictive a character. If I did A-Class, I would like it too much and it would kill me."' Again, it seems that Amy wasn't being entirely candid. Or perhaps she was expressing a *desire* to keep off drugs. She had already started to use cocaine with Blake, and never really stopped using marijuana. But alcohol was still her preferred drug. A drink with the band and crew after the show was a social pleasure that helped draw everyone together. 'We'd all go out and get plastered,' says production manager Dave Swallow, pointing out that this is what young people typically do in Britain. 'She was out there having fun. She was getting paid to sing in front of people. What do you expect?' These were indeed fun times, before the stress of her career overwhelmed Amy. She travelled with the boys, typically sitting up late on the tour bus as they drove through the night to the next gig, singing to the accompaniment of Dale Davis. The songs were like lullabies sending the rest of the band to sleep.

Yet Amy was a nervous performer who found talking to her audiences surprisingly difficult, considering how witty she was. Like Janis Joplin, she got into the habit of having a drink before the show to settle her nerves. Then she started to drink on stage. As the shows wore on, and her glass was refilled, she became erratic. The musicians noticed that Amy could drink a bottle of vodka in no time, with a thirst that went beyond having fun, and decided it was better not to drink in front of her lest it encouraged her. But nobody seemed able to tell Amy when she'd had enough, including her father.

'I didn't see him saying no. I saw him a couple of times, and it's not like when we were in rehearsal and she was drinking her bottle of vodka he was going, "Hey, daughter, what the hell are you doing? Give me that." No, he was just letting it happen,' says Jay Phelps, who played trumpet with Amy's band for a time. 'Maybe she would have switched on Mitch if he had done something like that. But you know you do that as a parent. You have to be hard on [your children]. It's not like she was a big ol' thirty-odd-year-old woman who was completely experienced in life. She was still a young girl. [And] it didn't seem like Raye [Cosbert] was doing too much. I can only say what I saw at the times when I was there, but I would've liked to have seen someone *not* give her a drink. Or say, "You can have just that, and that's your lot until maybe after the gig." Maybe after the gig, then let's have some fun ... But like before the gig, during the gig, after the gig, until you just conk out? You know, it's a bit much.'

The material was part of the problem. Amy had made a rod for her back with *Back to Black*, an album comprised of sad songs about her break-up with Blake. She was obliged to sing them every night, and she found 'Back to Black', 'Wake Up Alone' and 'Some Unholy War' particularly upsetting. So she incorporated lighter material in her set, including upbeat ska songs made famous by the Specials, usually ending with a romp through 'Monkey Man', which lifted the mood. 'What she said quite regularly to audiences was, you know, "The trouble is I've written all these depressing songs, and I've got to go and sing them,"' recalls Aaron Liddard. 'The first two tunes were quite tough, and then you'd have about forty minutes of depression, and then finally you'd get to play "Monkey Man", and "Monkey Man" was for all of us a release.'

Interest in Amy and her darkly unusual album grew in Britain during the autumn and winter of 2006, the press seizing on her as a talented and entertaining new celebrity, who was photogenic, articulate and uninhibited. Her antics offstage started to make headlines. An early example came when Amy heckled Bono at the *Q* magazine awards in London in September, telling the U2 singer to shut up while he gave a speech. 'I don't give a fuck!' she yelled. What wasn't mentioned in the press coverage was that Amy was also rolling joints at her table at the Grosvenor House Hotel during the ceremony. 'I mentioned I wouldn't mind a spliff, and Amy pulled a big bag of weed [out of her handbag] and starts grinding up and making a spliff at the table,' laughs Don Letts, who sat with her.

In October Amy was invited onto Charlotte Church's television show, filmed before a studio audience at the LWT building on London's South Bank. A memorable day started with an interview for morning television – and a drink. 'If I remember right she had a Jack Daniel's with Coke at breakfast time, at nine o'clock in the morning. I don't know why nobody said, "Don't,"' says Lou Winwood. 'And then the record company took her out for a lunch … I think that turned quite boozy. Then we went to a pub and played pool. *Then* we went to Charlotte Church. Hence you can see at that point [she was drunk]. She had been drinking all day. But nobody stopped that. You want to keep her onside … people found it hard to stand up to her when she said, "I want another Jack Daniel's and Coke."'

Amy was supposed to sing 'Beat It' with Charlotte Church, a big production number with horns and backing singers and a blitzkrieg of stage lights that would close the show. But she hadn't learned the song and was so sloshed by the time it came to record that she couldn't read the autocue.

'Is she *drunk?*' a stage manager asked her entourage.

'Er, yeah,' replied Lou Winwood. Anybody could see *that*. The stage manager was horrified, but a girl on the lighting desk was crying with laughter.

Amy seemed unaware of the havoc she was causing as she made repeated, cheerfully hopeless attempts to sing 'Beat It' with her host Charlotte Church, who watched her like a hawk. Finally, Amy marshalled her thoughts and belted out one semi-useable take of the song, which was televised, even though Amy looked and sounded like a drunk in the pub on karaoke night. Naturally, this made headlines, increasing Amy's celebrity.

When 'Rehab' went to number seven in the charts a decision was made to make 'You Know I'm No Good' the second single from the album, with Amy obliged to shoot a quick promotional video. Beforehand, Lou Winwood took a couple of rails of tiny clothes to Amy's flat for her to select what she wanted to wear. She walked into a blazing argument between Amy and Alex Clare.

When the girls were alone, Amy confessed to her stylist that she had been with Blake, they'd done crack cocaine, and Alex had found out. 'And so there was this enormous fight going on.' At the same time Amy was trying to cook dinner for Alex, and they had a guest coming, so the flat was in chaos. As Amy undressed to try on outfits for her video, Lou noticed carpet burns on the singer's body. 'She had marks down her back from where she'd been with Blake on the floor, she told me. She was trying to hide them from Alex.'

Blake started to show up backstage at Amy's gigs, making furtive appearances in the wings after Alex had left for his evening job as a cook. Although some friends believe that Blake truly loved Amy, his attitude seemed cold and distant in contrast to Alex's: the latter obviously adored Amy. '[Blake] was definitely not all over her, not in your wildest dreams,' says Lou Winwood. 'When he did turn up, she was, like, all over him. But we liked Alex. Alex was lovely. It was a little bit odd to see Amy chatting to Alex one minute – he'd go off to work – and Blake would turn up, and she'd be all over him.'

Drink and drugs complicated Amy's relationship with Blake. 'I mean, she was drinking a lot and she was snorting a lot of cocaine,' says Blake. 'She was worse than any of us for the drink. And so, like, when she started getting on the coke, it was double bad.' What most people find hard to forgive is that Blake introduced Amy to heroin, though it was her decision to take it. By Blake's account their mutual heroin use started one night when they were in a London hotel, 'just having one of our mad little nights', no doubt behind Alex Clare's back. 'We had a bottle of rosé champagne, had a bath. I had a couple of stones of crack and a few bags of brown [heroin] for myself, and I was smoking it, and she said, "Can I try some?" I was out of my fuckin' nut. I said, "Yeah, of course."'

Excessive drinking, career pressure, love-life problems, and now crack cocaine and heroin altered Amy's appearance and behaviour dramatically. She walked offstage in London in the new year, after singing one song, to be sick, and she was in a fearful state when she returned to the BRIT School in Croydon, where she had once studied, to perform for the students. 'I remember seeing her arrive, seeing her in the car, she was just utterly miserable,' says her former teacher Adrian Packer, who was distressed by what he saw. 'I found it all very difficult.'

Backstage Amy created a scene. 'She turns up and she literally looked like a plucked chicken. All her extensions had come out of her hair. It was all sticking up on her head. And she'd been crying, and there was, like, black makeup all down her face, and she was just in a terrible state … She was shouting at her tour manager, "I'm not doing this. I'm getting the train now." Because she'd had a row with Alex,' explains Lou Winwood. 'So she walked out.'

Amy stomped out of the dressing room, slamming the door behind her. Unfortunately, she walked into a cupboard. She re-emerged, glaring at her entourage as if to dare them to say anything. Finally the boldest did.

'Wrong door,' said her stylist.

'Oh, Lou!' exclaimed Amy, and flounced out by the right door.

The scene was funny and exhausting. Lou Winwood sat down and cried when Amy had gone. 'Because it had been intense, it had been uncomfortable, and it had been like being at the top of a roller-coaster. There were moments of magic, and she was a great person, but there was just difficulty and chaos … the whole thing was stressing me out a lot more than I realised … That was that for me. I sent her a text message, [but] I never spoke to her again.'

3

Sometimes Amy's misbehaviour was funny; then it became disturbing. One worrying incident occurred when Amy and her band were having a drink in a nightclub after a show on tour. Amy's mood darkened. 'She got a bottle. *Smash!* The whole place went [silent],' remembers saxophonist Aaron Liddard. 'And then she makes out that perhaps she's going to cut herself.' The band hustled Amy outside before anything worse happened, but this was not an isolated incident and the musicians were not always able to save Amy from herself. 'She did self-harm,' says Aaron. 'There were cut marks.'

'Self-harming' is a broad term covering behaviour up to and including a suicide attempt. Self-cutting, typically scoring one's forearms with razors, knives or glass, is usually less serious. It is behaviour typically associated with overwrought young women, though young men do it, too. Blake Fielder-Civil says he has been cutting himself since he was nine years old, describing the experience as a 'release'. His arms are criss-crossed with scars. When freshly done, cuts bleed profusely. This creates drama, and gets the victim attention, while not being life-threatening. Such behaviour is, however, a warning. People who self-harm are estimated to be one hundred times more likely than the general population to take their life.

The most notable example of self-harming in the history of the 27 Club is Richey Edwards of the Welsh band the Manic Street Preachers, a young man who became notorious for mutilating himself, often in public. Edwards suffered serious mental illness and went missing in 1995 after a period of instability. Although his body was never found, he is presumed to have committed suicide. We shall return to his sad story later.

Amy's self-harming was therefore concerning. But, like so much of her odd and wayward behaviour, it was observed but mostly ignored. Crew member Dave Swallow says that he noticed the scars on Amy's arms, as Aaron Liddard did, but he doesn't recall anybody discussing the issue with Amy.

Meanwhile, Amy's career went from strength to strength. *Back to*

Black made number one in the UK in January 2007. 'Rehab' was being played constantly on the radio, and Amy was in the papers almost daily. She won Best British Female Solo Artist at the BRIT Awards in February, which she attended with Alex Clare, her manager, parents and band members. Mitch and Janis congratulated Amy warmly, and she thanked them from the stage, but at least one band member sensed that Amy's relationship with her father was not without issues.

'I think that as children we all know that we have elements of our parents in our own character, whether we like them or not, and girls would like to respect their fathers, and I'm not sure how much respect there was. There was a lot of love, a lot of buddiness, a lot of friendship, but I'm not sure how much respect there was [for her father],' says Aaron Liddard, who observed Mitch at the BRITs, accompanied by the woman for whom he had left Janis, an episode that had caused pain for the family. Now Amy was repeating history by cheating on her boyfriend with Blake, something she vowed in 'What is it About Men?' that she would never do. 'I got the impression she might have recognised herself as being a little bit more like her dad, and a little bit less like her mum,' says Aaron, 'not in a way that she particularly liked.'

4

While Amy was a rising star in Britain she was so far virtually unknown in the United States. Her first promotional performance in the USA took place at Joe's Pub in New York in January 2007, backed by the Dap-Kings. 'Really nobody knew who she was other than some people who were from Britain,' says Maurice Bernstein, whose marketing company was hired to build interest in Amy in advance of the US release of *Back to Black*. 'Some people were a little resistant. "Oh, she sounds like she's trying to be African-American. Is that really her voice?"'

Bernstein had to work hard to fill Joe's Pub for that first show, and he found Amy a nervous performer. But she did well enough to be invited onto *Late Night with David Letterman*, one of a series of promotional appearances she made in America in the spring of 2007. In March she played the Roxy in Los Angeles, where Nirvana had once impressed the executives from Geffen Records. Kurt Cobain's widow, Courtney Love, was in the audience to see Amy. There was another crossing of paths with the 27s when Amy checked into the Chateau Marmont on Sunset Boulevard, a hotel Jim Morrison had frequented. In May, Amy was back in New York to play the Highline Ballroom. There were already signs in her stage manner that all was not well. 'It was the first time I had seen her where I felt, *hmm*, she was a bit off,' says Maurice Bernstein. Still, *Back to Black* had entered the *Billboard* chart at number seven, the highest entry position ever for a British female artist. It was a promising beginning.

Around this time Amy broke up with Alex Clare and became engaged to Blake. When she went back to the USA to do further promotion for her album, Blake was by her side during interviews and photo sessions for *Rolling Stone* and *Spin*, both of which put Amy on the cover, reflecting growing American interest. But again there were worrying signs. When the journalist from *Rolling Stone* asked Amy about the scars on her arms she said they were old marks from cuts made in 'desperate times', seeming embarrassed by the question. But she flaunted her self-cutting during her photo session with *Spin*, posing with shards of broken mirror, which she scratched across her belly to write, 'I love Blake'. A few days after this odd and unpleasant display of affection, on 18 May, Amy and Blake married in Miami. She did not ask her parents to be there.

Returning to England, Amy was invited to appear on stage with the Rolling Stones at the Isle of Wight Festival during the band's summer tour of Europe. This was the Stones 37 years on from the death of Brian Jones, with Ron Wood filling Brian's shoes, and Bill Wyman retired from the band. The spotty lads Brian had recruited in 1962 were now grizzled old men, rich beyond the dreams of avarice, living on their legend. On the evening of Sunday, 10 June, the Stones performed a cover of 'Ain't Too Proud to Beg'. After the first verse, Amy sashayed onstage to join Mick Jagger in a duet. The crowd roared approval when they saw Amy, showing how popular she had become in a short space of time. She delivered her opening lines with panache, then lost her way in a song she didn't seem to know any better than 'Beat It'.

A few nights later there was another echo of the past when Amy met Ray Manzarek of the Doors at the *Mojo* magazine awards in London. She sat on the lap of the 68-year-old keyboardist, who, like the Stones, was living on music made decades ago, and discussed the possibility of a posthumous duet with Jim Morrison on a remixed 'People are Strange'. It never happened.

Two days later a violent incident threw Amy's life into crisis. Blake attacked a man in a London pub, a serious assault that led to a charge of Grievous Bodily Harm with intent (GBH). If convicted, he faced a possible prison sentence. In the aftermath of this nasty business, Amy's career fell apart. She started to cancel shows, sometimes at the last minute. 'She was ill. There's no two ways about it,' says tour production manager Dave Swallow in her defence. 'At some point it felt like she didn't want to be there.' The truth was that her drug use was getting out of hand, and Blake's nefarious activities helped destabilise Amy's fragile sense of well-being. Amy and Blake were together at her flat on the evening of 6 August 2007 when she suffered the first of what became a series of drug-induced seizures. Blake called Amy's friend, Juliette Ashby, who took Amy to hospital where her stomach was pumped.

The next day Mitch Winehouse took Amy to the Four Seasons Hotel in Hampshire to recuperate. Blake joined Amy, and they got high. A doctor summoned to examine Amy informed Mitch that his daughter had probably been using crack cocaine, which was how he discovered Amy was using Class-A drugs. Others say they had known for a while. 'We did tell Mitch, through my family, but Mitch basically said he only thought she was smoking marijuana, and thought it was a load of nonsense, that people were just gossiping,' says Jonathan Winehouse.

Amy's mother and brother came to join the grim party at the Four Seasons, as did Blake's mother and stepfather, Giles Civil. The two families clashed over which child was to blame for the pair using drugs. It looked like Mitch and Giles were going to have a fight.

'I was so angry with Giles I was shaking,' Mitch admits in his book. In contrast Janis Winehouse seemed resigned to seeing her daughter destroy herself. 'A part of me has prepared myself for this over the years,' she told the *Mail on Sunday* that month. 'She has said to me, "I don't think I am going to survive that long." It's almost as though she's created her own ending. She's on a path of self-destruction, quite literally.' This proved absolutely correct. While Mitch tended to talk most about his daughter, Janis seemed to know Amy better.

Blake and Amy were persuaded to go to a rehabilitation centre in Essex, but they didn't stay. Instead they fled to London where they checked into the fashionable Sanderson Hotel, north of Oxford Street. Alex Winehouse came to see his sister there in mid-August and they rowed about Amy's drug use. In the early hours of the following morning, Blake and Amy had an argument while high. Blake got into a rage. 'I smashed a bottle and took a chunk out of myself.' Then Amy cut herself. 'I think she just looked at me and out of love, or fear, or whatever it was, or some fuckin' weird sense of loyalty, just did it to herself.' The couple stumbled out of the hotel in the middle of the night and were photographed by a waiting *paparazzo*. Photographers had begun to follow Amy everywhere, a reflection of how colourful her life had become, and how much media and there-fore public interest there was in her. Amy and Blake were a shocking sight. Blake's wild eyes showed him to be high, while his face and neck bore what looked like fingernail scratches – not deep, but bloody. Amy's mascara was smeared as if she'd been crying. Her left wrist and forearm were bandaged. Her trousers were scuffed, with blood showing at the knee. Blood was also soaking through her ballet pumps. It was suggested in the press that she had been injecting drugs between her toes, which Blake denies. He says blood simply dripped onto her shoes. But why was she bleeding? Amy texted a disturbing explanation to the blogger Perez Hilton: 'I was cutting myself after [Blake] found me in our room about to do drugs with a call girl and rightly said I wasn't good enough for him. I lost it and he saved my life.'

Following this bizarre and grisly incident, Blake and Amy flew to the Caribbean island of St Lucia where they lay low while a series of concerts, including an entire US tour, was cancelled.

The Rolling Stones are seen here at the start of their career, in 1963, gathered around their founder, Brian Jones.

A young Jimi Hendrix is seen in London in 1966, the year the Jimi Hendrix Experience was formed.

Janis Joplin was a beatnik college student in Austin, Texas, when this photograph was taken in 1962.

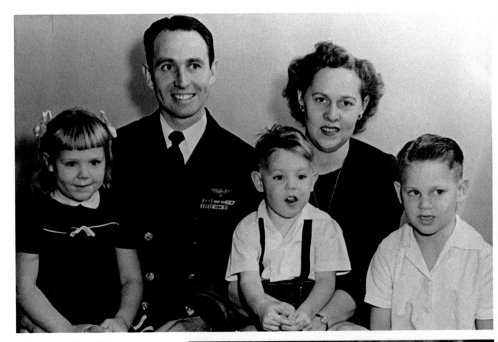

The young Jim Morrison is pictured (far right) with his naval officer father, Steve, mother Clara, sister Anne, and brother Andy. Jim would sever contact with his parents in adult life.

Kurt Cobain was seven in this family group, with his father Don, mother Wendy, and sister Kimberley. Kurt had a complicated relationship with his parents.

As a boy growing up in Aberdeen, Washington, Kurt had the cheerful, innocent appearance of a member of the Brady Bunch. But he was traumatised by his parents' divorce.

Aged about ten in this photograph, Amy Winehouse was a vivacious and precocious child.

Jimi Hendrix is seen here on the cusp of fame in 1967. 'He wasn't a hit yet. But he was clearly at a fantastic moment in his life and he was really relishing it,' recalls the photographer Gered Mankowitz.

The careers of Janis Joplin and Jimi Hendrix were boosted by their appearance at the Monterey Pop Festival in 1967. Janis is seen on stage with Big Brother and the Holding Company.

Jim Morrison poses with his fellow Doors, in a typical beefcake publicity photograph, at the time of their first album. Behind him are (clockwise from bottom): Robby Krieger, Ray Manzarek and John Densmore.

Kurt Cobain was happy on tour with Nirvana in 1989, just as they were getting started. Krist Novoselic sits at the back.

Amy Winehouse was a healthy young woman when she attended the Mercury music awards in 2004, following the release of her début album. She would soon be an emaciated drug addict.

Amy Winehouse's stylist took this candid picture of Amy at her Camden flat as she tried on outfits for the 'You Know I'm No Good' video. Amy was in the middle of a row with her boyfriend.

Self-harming scars are visible on Amy Winehouse's forearm as she embraces Blake Fielder-Civil, on tour in the USA, April 2007.

Amy and Blake emerged cut and bleeding from the Sanderson Hotel in London after self-harming in the middle of the night, August 2007.

Amy celebrated her multiple Grammy Awards win with her family in February 2008. Left to right are her brother Alex, mother Janis (front), stepmother Jane (behind), father Mitch, and aunt Melody.

Looking like a trapped animal, Amy was photographed in the window of her Camden flat in June 2008.

Amy Winehouse presented a horrifying spectacle at the Berkeley Square Summer Ball in September 2008. Death seemed close.

5

During this turbulent period in her life Amy enjoyed her biggest UK hit with 'Valerie', a wistful love song by the Zutons, which she recorded with Mark Ronson. It went to number two in the singles charts in the autumn of 2007 as she made a shaky return to live performance. There was trouble almost immediately.

Three nights into a European tour Amy and Blake were arrested in Norway for possession of marijuana, which they'd been smoking in their hotel room. The couple spent a night in the cells before paying a fine. Although this might appear a minor matter – par for the course for rock stars – Amy was denied a US visa as a consequence, which meant she couldn't tour America. In fact, she never visited the United States again. *Back to Black* continued to sell in America on merit, and Universal belatedly released *Frank* there, but Amy was unable to promote herself, which hobbled her career. 'To become a huge star in the States you've got to work it. And she wasn't available to work,' says her US publicist Maurice Bernstein, who believes that the record industry was partly to blame for what subsequently happened to Amy, and the 27s who came before her.

'I think the music industry has a lot to answer for. It's quite obvious that all [these artists] had abuse problems, and I don't think that the music industry always, with their hands on their hearts, can say they acted in the best interests of getting these artists healthy. I know ultimately it is up to the artists. Addiction is a very touchy thing, and you've got to want [to get clean]. But I can't say that the industry has always acted responsibly either.'

Drugs take over the life of the user, the business of scoring and consuming becoming a daily chore. Blake scored for Amy and himself. He took perverse pride in it, as he explains: 'As mad as it sounds, it's the only thing I was bringing to the table for a while, cos I mean I couldn't match her financially.' As Amy became dependent on drugs, and on Blake as her supplier, she lost interest in her career. It was touch and go whether she would turn up onstage each night, and often the only person who could influence her was Blake. He seemed to enjoy this power, and would bring his wife offstage if he had a mind to, as he did at a show in Zürich in October 2007. The couple's hairdresser friend Alex Foden has said that a further compli-cating factor was that Amy had been trying for a baby, and had just found out that she wasn't pregnant, which upset her. She certainly looked unhappy.

The band found Blake and Amy's hanger-on friends a nuisance. 'I think there was a certain amount of sort of emotional blackmail going on, and it would upset the show sometimes,' says Troy Miller, who took over as Amy's drummer at this time and worked with her until she died. 'Obviously, she was in love with someone who wasn't very supportive, let's say, of her music and her career as a whole. So that made things difficult. That was part of the reason some of the shows got pulled.'

Then Blake got arrested *again*. The police came looking for him at Jeffrey's Place first, breaking down the door of Amy's apartment, but Amy and Blake were not at home. Officers caught up with them at a flat in east London, arresting Blake on suspicion of perverting the course of justice. The allegation was that he had conspired with others to bribe the man he'd allegedly assaulted in a pub earlier in the year not to give evidence against him in court. This was even more serious than the original GBH charge, carrying a potential sentence of life imprisonment. Disaster was heaped upon disaster, and Amy was beside herself.

Her mental disintegration was apparent at a concert in Birmingham. Amy came on stage late and complained to her audience about Blake being held on remand, as if the charges against him were petty. She was blind to the facts, and the audience showed little sympathy, heckling and booing. Amy became indignant.

'First of all, if you're booing, you are a mug cunt for buying a ticket,' she told them. 'Second of all, to all them people booing, wait till my husband gets out of incarceration. I mean that.'

The audience howled with laughter.

In subsequent shows Amy incorporated Blake's prison number into the lyrics of songs. Audiences came to expect eccentricity, many coming to her shows to see what crazy thing she would do next, as they had once come to gawp at Jim Morrison. Amy wearied of this and cancelled the tour. She got a reputation for cancelling. 'She would always pay us for the whole tour, even if it got cancelled. She was very good like that,' says Troy Miller, who insists that Amy felt bad about cancelling concerts. 'She realised that it was disruptive. But I don't think she had much control over it, that's the problem.'

With Blake in prison Amy let herself go, getting stoned day and night. *Paparazzi* set up camp outside her flat, taking pictures of her lurching about in a state of inebriation. Her appearance had deteriorated significantly in a short space of time. Her skin was bad and her eyes were wild. She had also lost a tooth. At her worst she looked like a homeless junkie. So wretched had she become that a website was set up in the USA inviting the public to predict the date of Amy's demise, which seemed imminent. Amy surrounded herself with fellow users at Jeffrey's Place, including the singer Pete Doherty, whose drug problems were notorious. Although Amy told one friend that she thought Doherty an arsehole, they spent a lot of time together while Blake was in prison, and by Doherty's account they became lovers.* Certainly Amy seemed less committed to Blake than she had been.

In the months ahead Amy angered her husband by arranging to see him, then failing to show up, even though she lived fifteen minutes from Pentonville Prison. She may have been advised to keep her distance. Detectives were investigating her possible involvement in the conspiracy Blake was charged in connection with. He had apparently offered the man he assaulted £200,000 ($318,000) not to give evidence against him. Detectives wondered where unemployed Blake expected to get this money. Amy was questioned under caution in December, but not charged.

She flew to the Caribbean for Christmas, having swallowed packages of heroin before boarding her flight, according to an interview her friend Alex Foden gave the *Daily Mirror* after Amy died. She was interviewed by detectives again when she came home.

* During the writing of this book, Doherty offered to sell an account of his 'liaisons with Amy during [Blake's] little HMP chez da Ville [*sic*]' in exchange for money to get his car fixed.

Finally, her record company had had enough. Lucian Grainge, the chairman of Universal Music, decreed that Amy should not perform again until she'd been to rehab. Otherwise he would stop her working. As a result, on 24 January 2008, Mitch drove his daughter to the Capio Nightingale private psychiatric hospital in north London. She did not want to go, and threatened to kill herself *en route*. When she repeated her threat in the hospital, the staff discussed having Amy sectioned under the Mental Health Act. Things had got that bad. In the end she was sedated. Over the next few days Amy was treated both at Capio Nightingale and the London Clinic on Harley Street, which became her preferred bolt-hole in a crisis.

All this was happening in the build-up to the biggest music ceremony of the year, the Grammy Awards, which were held at the Staples Center in Los Angeles on 10 February 2008. Amy was nominated in several categories and her management had been trying to get her a US visa so she could appear live on the show. When the visa was denied, because of her drug history, arrangements were made for her to perform via satellite from London. She won five Grammys on the night, including Best Pop Vocal Album for *Back to Black* and Record of the Year for 'Rehab'. Her parents and brother celebrated this remarkable success with her. 'For the first time in God knows how long, my parents were truly happy, and Amy was, too,' Alex Winehouse said, in one of his few public comments about his difficult sister, revealing something of what Amy had put the family through. 'We hugged and kissed and suddenly the world melted away. We were alone, a loving family that has suffered so much.'

The Grammys win was incongruous. It was the ultimate celebration of success at a time when Amy's career was actually declining. She had achieved more in America than any British female artist in recent years, becoming an international superstar at 24. American sales of *Back to Black* rose dramatically on the back of the Grammys. Yet Amy was unable to tour America, and virtually unable to work at all because of her drug problem. The woman celebrating her multiple Grammy win had threatened to kill herself days previously, becoming so crazed that she had almost been sectioned.

6

Although she disliked being told what to do, in her more lucid moments Amy recognised that she had a problem and began to make tentative efforts to quit drugs. In March 2008 she moved out of her flat in Jeffrey's Place in Camden – which she continued to own – into a townhouse around the corner on Prowse Place. She decided to take a cure there. Doctors were consulted, including Dr Cristina Romete, a private general practitioner who would treat Amy from now on; a drug-replacement programme was prescribed and private nurses were engaged to care for Amy while she got clean. But she had to stop using heroin, and stay off it for twelve hours, before the cure could begin.

It was a tall order to get clean of heroin and pursue a career at the same time, yet this is what Amy tried to do. While she was attempting to kick heroin she was supposed to be writing and recording a theme song with Mark Ronson for the James Bond film *Quantum of Solace*, a prestigious commission everybody thought she should do, though Amy didn't seem keen to write a song to order. Frankly, she was in no state to try.

Mark Ronson was at the Dog House recording studio in Henley-on-Thames waiting for her to start work. Amy turned up with two nurses. Although she had said she wanted to detox, she continued to use crack and heroin during her stay at the studio with the result that she was often incapable of work. When Mitch Winehouse visited on 11 April 2008 he found Amy in a terrible state: strung out, emaciated and physically filthy. She was also clashing with Ronson. After one row, she invited Salaam Remi to the Dog House to work on a different song, 'Between the Cheats', in which she sang about her undying love for Blake. The song was arranged with doo-wop backing vocals to sound like classic 1950s R&B. It is the best indication of what a third Amy Winehouse album might have sounded like.

While she was at the Dog House Amy had a fling with a young man named Alex Haines who was working for her manager. The *News of the World* published a lurid account of the affair in which

Haines was quoted as saying that Amy reached for her crack pipe as soon as she woke up; she lived on junk food, which as a bulimic she then forced herself to vomit; she cut herself, and attacked people when drunk. Haines was further quoted as saying: 'She reckoned she would join the 27 Club of rock stars who died at that age.' This stilted quote reads as if he was prompted by a journalist. But, for what it's worth, Amy's friend Alex Foden said the same.

Returning to Camden, Amy went on a bender with friends, during which she hit a man who wouldn't give way to her on a pool table and slapped another in the street, as a result of which she was arrested. A police doctor decided she was unfit to be questioned so she was locked in the cells overnight. Amy eventually accepted a caution for common assault. This was not the end of her problems with the police. The following month she was charged with possession of crack cocaine, though the case did not proceed to court.

Between visits to the police, Amy returned to the Dog House in a desperate attempt to record the James Bond theme. While she was at the studio she spoke to Blake by telephone, confessing her adulterous fling with Alex Haines. The conversation upset her badly, triggering a breakdown. 'I had never seen Amy so bad,' her father writes of the ghastly scene he encountered at the studio. 'She had cuts on her arms and face; she had stubbed out a cigarette on her cheek, and had a bad cut to her hand where she had punched a mirror.' Mitch restrained Amy while nurses bandaged and tried to calm her. He later told a journalist that he was so disturbed by what Amy had done to herself that he tried to have his daughter sectioned, but by the time the requisite doctors had been summoned Amy had calmed down.

The Bond theme was abandoned. Amy returned home where she suffered another seizure and had to go back to the London Clinic. She now had emphysema among other problems. She was allowed out on 27 June for a concert in honour of Nelson Mandela's ninetieth birthday, singing before Mandela and an audience of 42,000 people in Hyde Park. Amy showed that she had not lost her sense of humour when she altered the lyric of 'Free Nelson Mandela' to 'Free Blakey, my fella'.

The following day she performed at the Glastonbury Festival, the penultimate act on the Pyramid stage on Saturday night. Amy was escorted to the gig by her nurses and a team of minders, who now accompanied her everywhere. She was *compos mentis*, but agitated. 'She had this kind of fragmented manner about her, like a nervous energy. It almost put me on edge,' says Don Letts, who hung out with her backstage. 'That wasn't how she was when I first met her.' When the headliner Jay-Z came into the dressing room to say hi, Amy told him that he reminded her of her late grandmother. Sometimes it was hard to know what was in her mind.

Amy sang a full set at Glastonbury, telling the crowd with girlish pride that Blake was getting out of jail in two weeks, which was an optimistic view of his forthcoming trial. She was drinking. 'It wasn't among the best shows, but I thought it went well,' says drummer Troy Miller. 'Sometimes she'd have a drink during the show, so she became progressively less in control towards the end, but it was usually never completely out of control.' The booze showed by the time Amy got down from the stage to sing 'Rehab' while greeting members of the audience. When a fan made a grab for her, she elbowed him back angrily, then threw a punch at the man before she was pulled away.

Like many addicts Amy had a tendency to construct a fantasy world. Her belief that Blake was about to walk free from prison, an innocent man, was a prime example of her self-delusion, common to stars who are pampered and spoiled by a sycophantic entourage. In fact Blake pleaded guilty in court in July to GBH and perverting the course of justice and was sentenced to 27 months. Although he would be out sooner, Amy's fantasy was shattered, and she descended into further debauchery.

Record-label boss Lucian Grainge – a voice of reason – had already told Mitch Winehouse and Raye Cosbert that he didn't want Amy performing live until she was well. Mitch, who had effectively become part of his daughter's management team, makes it clear in his book that he clashed with Grainge about this issue in a 'heated' conversation. It was the summer festival season, and Cosbert had bookings lined up. Although Mitch writes that Cosbert was himself worried about

Amy performing, she played several festival shows that summer, though she sometimes looked shaky and seemed reluctant to perform. Mitch writes that Cosbert had to 'persuade' her to sing at the V Festival in August. Typically, Amy arrived late. Her band was already onstage when her Range Rover pulled up. Amy had got into the habit of changing into her stage clothes in the car while the band played her intro. She would join them at the last minute. There was a crisis at one festival when Amy got out of the car and wandered off in the wrong direction. 'So we'd already been given the signal to start, and we were literally on stage playing this intro for [what] felt like an hour,' says Troy Miller. The crowd booed and threw things. 'I had a bottle of piss thrown at the drums ... [But] we loved her. And the thing that we had was the hope that she'd get better, really, and we always clung to that.'

Amy had always been a nervous performer. Now she seemed to have lost her nerve completely. Just as she had once avoided going to school, she now employed a variety of childish stratagems to get out of touring, including hiding from her manager.

'Quite often when Raye would be trying to track her down, and she was supposed to be picked up, she'd be hiding in our flat. She'd be hiding in my bed, or hiding in the toilet, not wanting to go on tour,' says Doug Charles-Ridler, landlord of the Hawley Arms in Camden Town, which had become Amy's favourite pub. 'Raye would come down and I'd just go, "Yeah, she's here. Give me five minutes. I'll sort her out."... Amy would say, "Oh, I gotta change ..." like, delaying tactics all the time, and then she'd lock herself in our toilet. We'd be, like, "Amy [coaxing voice]? You've gotta go." And she'd be, like, "I'm just changing, I'm just changing." And then she would do, like, her eye makeup – she used to take hours – and I'd be, like, "Raye, she's coming ..." It was really difficult. She was like a friend, whereas I was friends with Raye as well. So it was a real difficult situation, because I wanted to always make sure Amy was OK. And also Raye is quite an imposing guy.'

In recent months Amy had befriended a child singer from south London named Dionne Bromfield. Amy referred to Dionne as her goddaughter though she wasn't in the religious sense. Rather, Amy had decided to mentor the girl, who was signed to Amy's record label. Amy relaxed with Dionne, giggling with her as if she was a child, too. The relationship was part sisterly, part maternal, Amy deriving pleasure from Dionne's youth and innocence, which contrasted with her debased and wretched self.

In September 2008 twelve-year-old Dionne was hired to sing at the Berkeley Square Summer Ball where Amy's friends from the Ten Room, Patrick Alan and John Altman, were also due to perform. Amy agreed to make a guest appearance with them all. The Berkeley Square Ball is a grand annual event in Mayfair, held beneath the square's plane trees, with many wealthy and well-known people attending in evening dress, including Kate and Pippa Middleton in 2008. The dinner menu was by Marco Pierre White, and after dinner there was music and dancing.

Amy stumbled into this classy event wearing ragged shorts and a black vest that revealed her skeletal torso. 'She looked like a concentration-camp inmate,' says John Altman. 'I mean, she looked *dreadful*, absolutely terrible.' Amy had a posse of hangers-on with her, including the comic Russell Brand, band members and minders. She saw Patrick Alan and gave him a hug. 'She literally was hunched over like a homeless woman ... I was just in shock to see her that way.' Patrick asked Amy if he could get her a drink, out of politeness, realising at once that he'd put his foot in it. 'I swear to God every one of her people looked at me – it was like a Monty Python movie – they looked at me. *Shush!* But without making any noise. *No!* Cutting their throats. *What are you doing?* I was, like, *Oh, my gosh!* And she reeled off, like, eight things she wanted: a vodka tonic, a bottle of this, a bottle of that ...'

Patrick Alan and John Altman went on stage with members of Amy's band and Dionne Bromfield, who was going to sing Motown songs. The audience applauded politely. Then there were gasps as Amy appeared along with her friends, looking like the walking dead, followed by the sound of chairs being scraped back as people got up from their tables and ran to the front to stare at this spectre. Amy was clearly high. Her eyes were wild. Her movements were jerky as she danced and sang.

Backstage Amy got into a fracas with a woman who complained to police that Amy had punched her. Amy was acquitted at trial. During an eventful evening she also spoke with John Altman, telling him something sad and revealing. 'She said, "I didn't want all this. I just wanted to make music with my friends."' Success had not made Amy happy, any more than it had brought happiness to Brian Jones, Jimi Hendrix, Janis Joplin, Jim Morrison and Kurt Cobain. Looking at Amy at the Berkeley Square Ball, John Altman doubted that she would live to see Christmas.

Part Two

Death

Oh, lonely death on lonely life!

Captain Ahab, *Moby-Dick*

Eight

IN WHICH BRIAN IS ENTIRELY SURROUNDED BY WATER

There was a loud splash, and Eeyore disappeared.
A. A. Milne

1

So far we have followed the principal 27s from their difficult childhoods, through early success, to the point in their mid-twenties when they were dosing themselves with alcohol and drugs to stabilise their moods, and cope with the pressures that came with fame. Now we turn to the end of these lives. All six artists met different deaths. Yet each was a shade of the same colour.

When British pop stars of the 1960s started to make money they tended to buy country houses tucked away down leafy lanes where their fans and the press would struggle to find them, but still within driving distance of London. Members of the Beatles and the Rolling Stones all bought such homes, and Brian Jones was no exception. In late 1968 Brian purchased Cotchford Farm just outside Hartfield in East Sussex, fifty miles south of the capital. The house is at the side of a valley, overlooking a stream, on the edge of Ashdown Forest. The oldest part dates to the sixteenth century, including a beamed living room with an inglenook fireplace. Over the years owners have expanded the property to create a rambling six-bedroom house that seems to grow naturally out of the countryside.

Brian loved Cotchford Farm and he took pride in the fact that A. A. Milne had lived there in the 1920s, writing his Winnie-the-Pooh stories, inspired by his son Christopher Robin and his toy animals. The landscape around the house – which Brian bought with eleven acres – was the landscape of Pooh. The '100 Aker Wood' was Ashdown Forest; Eeyore's Gloomy Place was the soggy ground at the bottom of the garden by the stream, forded by the bridge upon which Christopher Robin, Piglet and Pooh played Poohsticks. This was where Eeyore the neurotic donkey, a character Brian resembled in certain respects, fell into the water in *The House at Pooh Corner*. All these places were immortalised in Milne's stories and in the original illustrations by E. H. Shepard, who visited Cotchford Farm for inspiration. It is a striking irony that Brian Jones's debauched life as a rock star ended in a place associated with childhood innocence.

After *The Rolling Stones Rock and Roll Circus* was filmed in December 1968 (though not shown for many years), Brian played little part in the band he had founded. He turned 27 in February, and was back at the Priory in March 'suffering with depression', according to Bill Wyman, when the Stones began recording *Let it Bleed* at Olympic Studios. Brian attended on occasion, playing autoharp on 'You Got the Silver' among other bits and pieces, but he was now a peripheral figure.

As far as his personal life was concerned, Brian's relationship with Suki Poitier ended, but he did not lack female company. On a trip to Paris in the spring of 1969 he caught up with Zouzou, who found Brian depressed, drinking heavily and using drugs to excess. 'He was really, really fucked up ... He said, "I asked Mick to put me in a mental hospital," to do a cure or whatever, and Mick told him to fuck off.' Zouzou says Brian knew the Stones wanted to be rid of him. 'He wanted to see how they were going to tell him.' Back in England, Brian was seeing a 22-year-old Swede named Anna Wohlin. She came to stay at Cotchford Farm in May, and was Brian's companion during his final days.

In London, the Stones were recording 'Honky Tonk Women' with Mick Taylor, whom Jagger and Richards chose as Brian's replacement in the band. It was time to tell Brian.

After work at the studio on 8 June 1969, Mick Jagger, Keith Richards and Charlie Watts drove to Cotchford Farm where they spent half an hour talking with Brian in the living room of the old house, which Brian liked to call his 'music room'. The conversation was apparently amicable. Keith Richards says they explained to Brian that they were going to tour again and they needed a functional second guitarist. 'We offered him the chance to stay, but it was an offer we knew was going to be refused.' So it was decided that Brian would leave the Stones. He wouldn't do so empty-handed. He would receive a pay-off of £100,000 ($159,000), a considerable sum equal to three times the purchase price of Cotchford Farm, plus further annual payments.

Following the meeting, a statement was issued to the press in which Brian gave the impression he had quit for artistic reasons. He and the Stones no longer 'communicate musically. The only solution is to go our separate ways ...' This wasn't completely disingenuous. Brian had ambitions to form a new group, possibly featuring Mitch Mitchell from the Jimi Hendrix Experience, which disbanded that summer. At times Brian seemed genuinely optimistic about his future, but it is hard to see how whatever he did could rival the success he'd enjoyed with the Stones. To some extent, Brian was putting on a brave face when he spoke about the projects he had in mind. Friends saw glimpses of depression, and little wonder. It was a defeat and a humiliation to be ejected from the band he had founded, on top of the other humiliations he had suffered: his experiences in court, where his drug history and mental state were laid bare, and losing Anita Pallenberg to Keith. Brian had loved Anita, even though he abused her, and now she was having Keith's baby. Meanwhile the word from London was that the new Stones album was sounding great, Mick Taylor was a brilliant musician and the band was planning a summer concert in Hyde Park. The Stones were moving ahead, leaving Brian behind. It is hard to believe that his death within four weeks of leaving the band was unrelated.

It should also be remembered that Brian had been living dangerously for years, flirting with Death on a daily basis through his reckless use of drink and drugs. We might imagine Death as a character in the second half of this history of the 27 Club, as it has been represented in art through the centuries, usually depicted as a wraith with a skull face, wearing a black cowl and holding an hour-glass to remind the living that their time is nigh, as in Dürer's *Knight, Death and the Devil*. In Ingmar Bergman's *The Seventh Seal*, Death has a white clown's face, an enigmatically solemn figure with a comedian's sense of timing and an ineluctable will. Brian had an appointment with this gloomy character.

2

Brian typically rose late at Cotchford Farm after staying up playing music, drinking and using drugs. Many friends swear that he was clean of drugs by the summer of 1969 – which was what he said – but it wasn't true. In addition to his asthma inhaler, Brian's prescription drugs alone included Valium to calm his nerves, Mandrax to put him to sleep, and Piriton for hay fever. Ten days before he died Brian asked his doctor additionally for Durophet, a powerful sedative widely abused in the music community where the black pills were known as 'black bombers'. The prescription was small, but it added to a significant drug intake. By the account of his girlfriend Anna Wohlin, Brian was not clean of illegal drugs either, getting high on a gift of cocaine left by Keith Richards. And he was drinking.

After he got up, Brian typically put a record on his hi-fi, often Creedence Clearwater Revival, which he would blast through the open windows and down the valley where Christopher Robin had played. As June turned to July he spent much of the rest of the day indoors watching the tennis on television. It was the year of Pancho Gonzales's marathon five-hour match against Charlie Pasarell at Wimbledon, with victory for Ann Haydon-Jones in the women's final. It wasn't always easy to concentrate on the tennis, however, with the builders in.

Brian was having renovations done to his house. The man in charge was a 44-year-old Londoner named Frank Thorogood. Although he came recommended by the Stones' chauffeur-turned-tour manager, Tom Keylock, having worked for Keith Richards, the consensus is that Thorogood was an incompetent builder who, with his workmen, took advantage of Brian. '[Thorogood] was a nasty piece of work ... a bit of a cowboy builder,' says Les Hallett, who did odd jobs around Cotchford Farm while his wife Mary cleaned for Brian. The couple lived opposite. Hallett shakes his head as he describes watching Thorogood strip paint from the Elizabethan panelling in the dining room with a blow lamp, and recalls that another bodged job was the installation of wooden beams in the breakfast room to match the old beams in the house. One of the new beams fell down and almost brained Anna Wohlin. Brian seemed ready to sack Thorogood for this, but the builder stayed on the job. Indeed, he lived in the stable block, and Brian evidently forgave him because he invited Thorogood to the house for drinks and supper.

On 1 July 1969 a nurse named Janet Lawson came to stay with Frank Thorogood in the stables. That night the couple were invited for dinner with Brian and Anna. Typically, Brian drank wine with dinner, and consumed more alcohol as well. Then he went for a late-night swim. There was a heated open-air pool on the terrace adjacent to the house, overlooking Eeyore's Gloomy Place. Installed by the previous owners, after the Milne residency, the pool was forty feet long and eight feet deep at the end nearest the house, where there were steps into the water and a diving board. Brian kept the water temperature high, and floodlit the pool at night. Going for a swim on a full stomach, having consumed alcohol and medication, not to mention any illegal drugs he may have obtained, was, of course, dangerous.

The weather continued fine the following day, Wednesday, 2 July. Brian rose at eleven a.m. and sat down to watch the men's quarter finals from Wimbledon. He and Anna ate a salad lunch and Brian spoke to people on the telephone, including the Stones' office and Amanda Lear, whom he invited to the house. 'He said, "I'm really together now. I've got myself together and I'm leaving the Stones and I've been to Morocco recording some sounds in the mountains ... amazing folk music, I'm really interested in all this." [He] was talking a lot. But I don't think he was very together. And he was very hurt that the Rolling Stones had turned [their] back to him.' Lear says

Brian sent a car to collect her, but she told the driver to take her to Heathrow, where she caught a flight to Spain. She'd had enough of Brian's crazy life. 'That remained always a [source] of guilt … If I had gone there, perhaps I could have helped, or something different would have happened.'

In the early evening Brian sent Frank Thorogood to the Dorset Arms in the village to buy wine, vodka, brandy and whisky. When Frank returned with the bottles, the men had a drink. Then the builder went back to the stables. That evening, after ten o'clock when Anna Wohlin was ready for bed, Brian became restless for company. He fetched a torch and walked over to the stables to rouse Thorogood and Janet Lawson, who told the police that Brian was already 'unsteady on his feet'. Nevertheless, they followed him back to his house where the men had more to drink. Brian was drinking brandy and his speech was garbled.

'I've had my sleepers,' he said, a term he sometimes used for his black bombers.

Anna had witnessed him swallowing several such pills. Having mixed alcohol with medication, Brian now wanted to swim. 'He seemed anxious to be occupied and invited us to swim,' Janet said, in her police statement. As a nurse, she warned Brian and the others not to swim in their condition, but they ignored her. She decided 'they were all being very stupid'.

Brian tottered onto the diving board. 'Brian was staggering,' Frank Thorogood told the police. 'He had some difficulty in balancing on the diving board, and I helped to steady him …' The water must have appeared inviting to Brian as he stood on the board: an undulating rectangle of aquamarine under the pool lights. Beyond the lights the trees of the '100 Aker Wood' would have been rustling in the dark. Anna got into the water first. It was very warm. Brian had turned the temperature up during the day. Then Brian flopped in from the board. 'His movements were sluggish, but I felt reasonably assured that they were all able to look after each other,' said Janet. So she went inside.

Brian asked Anna for his inhaler, which she gave him at the poolside. Then she went upstairs to their bedroom to change, leaving the men in the water. After twenty or thirty minutes Frank Thorogood came inside for a towel and a cigarette, leaving Brian alone. The telephone rang. Anna answered the extension in the bedroom almost at the same time as Frank picked up the phone downstairs. There was confusion as to who should replace the receiver. Meanwhile, Janet went back outside. 'I went out to the pool and on the bottom I saw Brian. He was face down in the deep end. He was motionless and I sensed the worst straight away.'

Janet shouted up to Anna in the bedroom, the windows of which overlooked the pool: 'Something has happened to Brian!'

Janet tried to get Brian out of the water, but she couldn't do so alone. Frank and Anna came to help. While they struggled with the body, Janet went inside to dial the emergency services, but the telephone was engaged. Seemingly Anna hadn't replaced her receiver when she'd rushed out. When Janet came back to the pool the others had Brian on the side. They turned him over and Janet tried to pump the water out of his lungs, while Frank went to the telephone. 'It was obvious to me that he was dead, but I turned the body back and I applied external cardiac massage,' Janet told the police. 'I carried on for at least fifteen minutes, but there was no pulse.'

An ambulance arrived around midnight, followed by a constable from Sussex Police. Brian was pronounced dead at the scene.

PC Albert Evans had a look round the house. He found a bottle of brandy, four fifths empty; a bottle of vodka, two thirds empty; and a bottle of Scotch, half empty. This was seemingly all that was left of the bottles Frank had brought back from the pub. The constable also recovered a handful of tablets – Valium, Mandrax and Piriton – and 'many empty bottles'.

Brian's corpse was taken to the Queen Victoria Hospital in East Grinstead where Dr Albert Sachs conducted a post-mortem. Dr Sachs looked into the possibility that Brian had drowned after an asthma attack, but the signs associated with asthma attacks were not present. More to the point was the amount of alcohol in Brian's blood: 140 milligrams per decilitre, a third of the amount it took to kill Amy Winehouse (by comparison), but sufficient to make a person slurred, confused and unsteady on their feet, which was how Janet Lawson and Frank Thorogood described Brian before he went swimming. The pathologist also found an unusually high level of an 'amphetamine-like substance' in Brian's urine, more than eight times what would be considered normal. It is unclear what this was; tests were not exhaustive. But Brian had evidently taken something. An examination of his liver showed evidence of years of abuse. Dr Sachs found that Brian had 'severe liver dysfunction due to fatty degeneration and the ingestion of alcohol and drugs'.

Janet Lawson, Frank Thorogood and Anna Wohlin all gave statements to the police the day after the drowning. Their statements were typed, read for accuracy, and signed by the witnesses as a true account of what happened, on pain of prosecution. Close attention should be paid to these statements, which are the best available evidence of what happened to Brian.

The three witnesses told the police the same basic story: Brian had gone swimming when he was drunk and he drowned. There are contradictions over times, within a limited range, and differences in the order of who had done what after the alarm was raised. Those people who dispute the official account of Brian's death point to these discrepancies as evidence that some of the witnesses were lying. A disinterested reading draws one to the conclusion that the differences are minor, and to be expected from people who had been drinking and suddenly found themselves in an emergency. It is also generally true that almost any group of people asked individually about an incident will give differing accounts of what happened, and each will swear that they are correct. The important point is that, broadly speaking, the witness statements are consistent, and the story is convincing.

The Rolling Stones were in the studio when they were informed that Brian had died. They went ahead with their work, recording an edition of the television show *Top of the Pops* later that day. Meanwhile, Brian's father had the woeful duty of identifying his son's body.

Lewis Jones told the police that he and his wife had stayed with Brian at Cotchford Farm in May, and he had last spoken to Brian by telephone three weeks ago – 'at that time he was full of beans'. In an interview with the *Daily Express*, Mr Jones reflected on his son's short life, admitting that Brian 'exasperated me beyond measure in his younger days', but adding that the family had been reconciled recently, and that Brian had telephoned frequently during his problems 'to seek our understanding and sympathy'.

Few of Brian's celebrity friends seemed shocked by his death. Pete Townshend said cynically that it was 'a pretty normal day' for Brian. 'He always seemed to be losing out one way or another.' In California, Jim Morrison wrote an elegy, 'Ode to LA While Thinking of Brian Jones, Deceased', recalling his 'porky satyr's leer', an evocative image of the dissipated and overweight guitarist of recent years. The Stones' concert in Hyde Park on Saturday took a poetic turn when Mick Jagger read from Shelley's elegy 'Adonais' in memory of Brian. The choice was apposite, not least because Shelley also drowned in his twenties.

In answer to questions from the coroner at the inquest, on 7 July, Anna Wohlin said she had seen Brian taking his black pills the day he died. Janet Lawson emphasised that she had warned Brian and Frank Thorogood not to swim in their inebriated condition. 'They disregarded my warning.' The pathologist said Brian's liver was twice normal size, his heart was larger than it should have been, and he had taken a fairly large quantity of a drug, though he didn't specify what. The coroner recorded a verdict of misadventure. Brian had drowned 'whilst under the influence of alcohol and drugs'.

The funeral took place three days later at St Mary's Parish Church in Cheltenham. Charlie Watts and Bill Wyman attended, as did the Stones' keyboard player Ian Stewart, but not Mick Jagger or Keith Richards. Of Brian's many lovers, the only identifiable attendees were Linda Lawrence and Suki Poitier. Anna Wohlin had already returned to Sweden. Pat Andrews says she would have come from London if the man from the *News of the World* had given her a lift, as he promised, but he didn't. 'So I had no way of going, did I?' Still, there was a large crowd of press and curious onlookers at what was one of the first big pop-star funerals, and the first major 27 Club funeral, not that anybody used that term yet. The crowd followed the hearse to Cheltenham Cemetery where they watched the coffin lowered into the earth.

3

The death of Brian Jones seems clear cut. The inquest evidence was simple and convincing. Brian drowned in his swimming pool under the influence of drink and drugs.

Death was ascribed to misadventure, a legal word for accident. And so it was. But some deaths are more accidental than others. Musicians on the 27 Club long-list who died in road accidents, such as Dennis Boon of the Minutemen, who broke his neck after being thrown from his band's tour van, or those who perished in plane crashes, like keyboardist Wally Yohn, clearly died through no fault of their own. Then there are others, including Brian Jones, whose death was the direct result of his behaviour. To mix alcohol and drugs, and then dive into a swimming-pool, was to swim into the arms of Death. Brian may not have meant to die at that moment, but he had been so careless for so long that it is not surprising he lost his life.

As clear as this seems, the death of Brian Jones has become one of the mysteries of rock 'n' roll, with many people questioning the official version of what happened at Cotchford Farm. Even members of the Rolling Stones are doubtful. 'And still the mystery of his death hasn't been solved,' Keith Richards has said. 'I don't know what happened, but there was some nasty business going on.'

He was referring to the widespread belief that Brian was murdered. The prime suspect is Frank Thorogood. It was well-known that Jones and Thorogood clashed over the building work at Cotchford Farm. The commonly suggested motive is that Brian wanted to fire Thorogood. This is unconvincing, not least because Thorogood was still on the job when Brian died, still friendly enough with his boss to socialise with him. Why would Brian ask Thorogood to his home for drinks and dinner if he meant to fire him? And why would Thorogood want to kill the man who paid his wages?

That is not to say that Thorogood was a nice person. There were incidents after Brian's death that showed the builder in a poor light. Friends and neighbours were surprised when Thorogood and Tom

Keylock made a bonfire of Brian's possessions in the garden of the house shortly after the musician died. Why they did so is unclear. '[Frank] said they was told to do it,' says handyman Les Hallett. 'I went down there that evening after he died and on the bloomin' bonfire was a sitar, half burned away. They chucked out a lot of stuff, burned it.' Items went missing from the house during this clear-out, possibly stolen. Thorogood also took part in a drunken wake at the house that seemed like an excuse to have a party at Brian's expense rather than honouring his memory. Then a local taxi driver who'd worked for Brian, Joan Fitzsimons, was beaten up and admitted to hospital with a fractured skull. The police looked into a suggestion that Thorogood may have been behind the assault, because of Fitzsimons's supposed knowledge of what had happened to Brian. This led to a story in the *Daily Express* in August 1969, the first to question the official account of Brian's death: 'Brian Jones Death: New Probe'. But there was nothing to this. Fitzsimons had been assaulted by her boyfriend. He was later convicted of the crime.

For every question about Brian's death, there is a simple and convincing explanation. Yet theorists tend to turn a blind eye to the facts, focusing instead on discrepancies in the story, or introducing new 'evidence', which is actually speculation or make-belief.

Those who claim that Brian was unlawfully killed typically argue that he was too good a swimmer to drown, pointing out that he had been a lifeguard in his youth. They forget that Brian was in poor health by 1969. He was also doped and drunk, though theorists dispute this. Linda Lawrence, mother of Brian's son Julian (the second), is typical of the theorists in stating in an interview for this book that Brian consumed only 'a couple of beers' the night he died, which was not what the witnesses said or what the post-mortem found. Brian was drunk, having consumed the equivalent of seven shots of whisky, or three and a half pints of beer, according to blood analysis. The post-mortem also revealed that he had ingested drugs, the potency of which would have been enhanced by alcohol.

Nicholas Fitzgerald, who claimed to be a friend of Brian, was an early theorist. He said he actually witnessed Brian's 'murder'. His sensational story is undermined by the fact that he waited seventeen years to go public, finally telling his tale in a 1986 book, *Brian Jones: The Inside Story of the Original Rolling Stone*. On the night in question, Fitzgerald claimed he tried and failed to reach Brian on the telephone, so he and a friend went to Cotchford Farm. They were walking through the grounds in the dark when they saw Brian climbing out of his pool. Three men came forward, pushed Brian into the water and drowned him. Fitzgerald couldn't identify the men because the lights 'blotted out their features and made their faces look like blobs'. He claimed he had kept quiet for years for fear of his life. Sussex Police interviewed Fitzgerald and concluded that he was not a credible witness. 'All we have here are unsubstantiated allegations from a man who will not make a statement, and whose memory, temperament and motives are questionable,' the police informed HM Coroner.

The willingness of the media to report such stories, however wild, has encouraged theorists, especially around anniversaries in the case, which provide an excuse to revisit the story. In advance of the 25th anniversary of Brian's death, Terry Rawlings began work on a book in conjunction with Tom Keylock, who now had an extraordinary story to tell. Keylock said that he had visited Frank Thorogood in hospital in the autumn of 1993, shortly before the builder's death, and during the visit Thorogood had made a startling confession. 'We started talking and he told me he wanted to put his house in order,' Keylock is quoted as saying in Rawlings's book, *Who Killed Christopher Robin?*

'There's something I have to tell you,' said Thorogood. 'It was me that did Brian.'

Keylock asked why.

'Well, I just finally snapped, it just happened. That's all there is to it.'

This confession is unconvincing, not least because it lacks detail. There is just the bald statement 'It was me that did Brian', which reads like a line from pulp fiction. And there is only Keylock's word for it. Frank Thorogood's daughter has disputed that her late father said any such thing, pointing out that he didn't know he was about to die, so he was unlikely to incriminate himself. Nevertheless, the 'deathbed confession' became the centrepiece of Rawlings's 1994 book. The 'murder' as described was apparently preceded by an argument between Brian and Thorogood over money, and Brian's decision to fire his builder. The author concluded that the men argued again in the pool. 'Frank became enraged [and] began plunging Brian repeatedly under' until he drowned.

Another, even less impressive, book was published to coincide with the 25th anniversary of Brian's death. In *Paint it Black*, Geoffrey Giuliano presented his readers with a transcript of an interview he claimed to have recorded with a man who approached him in a hotel in 1991 saying that he had been a labourer at Cotchford Farm in 1969, and had been in the pool with Brian and another workman the night Brian died. In fact, he and his mate had killed Brian. They had drowned him at the behest of Frank Thorogood. Giuliano referred to the confessor as Joe, an invented name, he admitted, adding that he didn't know his real name. The confession is as absurd as it is unconvincing. Indeed, I air this and other theories not because they have merit but as examples of the fantastical stories typically told about the 27s after death.

Anna Wohlin chipped in with a book of her own, *The Murder of Brian Jones*. She disputes that Brian had a drink problem at the time of his death, or that he was abusing drugs, legal or illegal, as many theorists do. Yet she contradicts herself with stories of Brian doing exactly that. Wohlin was using prescription drugs at the time to get high, as she writes, keeping her drugs hidden from Brian. The couple had a fight when Brian discovered her stash. 'My drugs are my business,' she retorted. In the hours after Brian died, when the police were at Cotchford Farm, one of Wohlin's priorities was to hide her pills. She also admitted to popping pills on the day she gave evidence at the inquest. Her book is most valuable for the insight it gives into the personality and behaviour of the woman Brian lived with at the end of his life.

As for how Brian died, the title of Wohlin's book implies murder, but she doesn't make a compelling case. Wohlin writes that Brian and Frank Thorogood were horsing around in the water, Brian pulling Frank under, the builder dunking Brian in return. Then she had gone indoors so she didn't see what happened next. She drew her conclusions from the way Frank behaved afterwards – head bowed, hands shaking – and from a comment he made the next day, warning her to think about what she told the police. As a result she wrote that she had 'concealed the truth' from the authorities. If anything her vague allegations would point to manslaughter, not murder, but there is no hard evidence for either scenario.

Poor though these three books are, they served as the basis for a 2005 feature film, *Stoned*, which dramatised Brian's life and death. In the movie Frank Thorogood is shown drowning Brian accidentally during horseplay in the pool. Partly as a result of the film this is the story that has gained popular acceptance. In fact, there is no strong evidence that Thorogood drowned Brian either accidentally or on purpose.

Coinciding with the release of *Stoned* the Brian Jones Fan Club issued a request for the police investigation to be reopened. Trevor Hobley, who runs the club, and Brian's former lover Pat Andrews were of the opinion that Brian had been murdered, and believed that the best way to settle the matter was for his body to be exhumed and a new post-mortem conducted. That the musician had been buried in a metal casket offered hope that his remains were preserved. Despite their efforts, Brian continued to rest in peace.

Having kept silent for years, the nurse Janet Lawson re-entered the story, apparently telling a journalist that her 1969 police statement had been 'a pack of lies … a load of rubbish'. She was quoted in the *Mail on Sunday* in 2008 saying the police put words into her mouth, which is hard to accept, considering her oral evidence to the coroner matched her sworn statement. She now believed Frank Thorogood drowned Brian accidentally during horseplay. Janet didn't see Frank do it, any more than anyone else had. Like Anna Wohlin, she inferred guilt from the way the builder behaved: apparently he was slow to react when the alarm was raised, and he was shaking afterwards. Still, Sussex Police found no reason to reopen the case.

One by one the people involved in the story of Brian's life and death were themselves dying. Frank Thorogood died in 1993. Janet Lawson died in 2008. Tom Keylock died in 2009. So did Allen Klein, the American accountant who had taken over management of the Stones in the 1960s, also getting involved in the management of the Beatles. Both bands fell out with Klein, who is often characterised as a crooked, even sinister figure. The most serious proven indictment against him was for tax evasion, for which he served a short prison sentence. Posthumously, he is named by theorists as the Mr Big behind Brian's assassination.

'Brian was murdered,' asserts Brian's ex, Linda Lawrence. 'We've got evidence now.' She is referring to herself and Trevor Hobley, of the fan club, whose research underpins her beliefs. Hobley is of the view that Brian was attacked by a gang of three workmen at Cotchford Farm on 2 July 1969 (though no such people were mentioned in the police statements). Hobley says that two of the three killers are still alive. He claims to know who they are, but doesn't have sufficient evidence to name them, adding that neither has been spoken to by police. He says Brian was 'rendered unconscious' by these men and then drowned, while Tom Keylock and Frank Thorogood watched, Keylock apparently directing the murder (thought he wasn't at the house, according to the inquest).

'It was a horse trough that he'd been drowned in,' says Linda Lawrence. This stems from a statement made years ago by the discredited Nicholas Fitzgerald, who said he had seen Brian being held upside down in a trough at the farm (though he wrote contradictorily in his book that Brian was drowned in the pool). The fact that the post-mortem states that Brian drowned in fresh water is used by theorists as corroboration that it was a horse trough. If he had drowned in the swimming-pool, Hobley and Lawrence presume tests would show the water in his lungs to be chlorinated. 'He'd been pushed down into a horse trough,' says Linda Lawrence, firmly. She is sure, having spoken to a mysterious figure – whom she and Hobley don't name – who was apparently an assistant to the pathologist who carried out the post-mortem. What this person had to say convinced the theorists that officials in the case falsified evidence at the time – Lawrence says they were paid off – all of which is part of a conspiracy.

Linda Lawrence isn't shy about using the c-word. 'There's been conspiracies all over the world about many, many things, and that's just one of them,' she says, further alleging that it was Allen Klein who ordered the assassination of Brian to gain control of the Rolling Stones, not wanting to deal with the band's founder, who may have had a claim to ownership of the name and was due a substantial pay-off. 'The Stones were broke at the time and Allen Klein, who I knew very well, and Don* and I knew very well, [he was] Mafia,' she says. Pat Andrews also believes Klein was behind Brian's death. By this argument not only Klein, but the pathologist, HM Coroner, Sussex Police, the three witnesses, and goodness knows who else, would all have been involved in one of the greatest crimes in show-business history and would have had to lie for decades to cover up the truth. This is not credible. And people are only free to talk in this way about Klein, without fear of being sued, because he is dead. 'I would have said it to his face,' asserts Lawrence. She had opportunities to do so. 'I don't know why I didn't, but again I have a life of my own.'

Linda Lawrence and Pat Andrews are passionate on the subject of the 'murder' of Brian Jones partly because of their sons, Brian's children, the two Julians, now middle-aged men, and the millions they feel their boys are owed. Brian died broke. Although he founded the Rolling Stones, he had fallen behind Mick Jagger and Keith Richards in earnings because they wrote the songs. He also wasted money, as young people do, the 27s being typical in that respect. His estate was valued at only £33,787 ($53,721), most of which was the value of Cotchford Farm. His liabilities were much larger, £191,707 ($304,814). Because Brian didn't make a will, his estate passed to his hapless parents. Lewis Jones said at the time that royalties and other money due would probably cancel his son's debts. It is not known what if any agreement the family subsequently came to with the Rolling Stones over Brian's share in the band, but a financial settlement was seemingly reached. Brian's parents moved to a slightly bigger house in Cheltenham where they lived out their lives in modest comfort. In contrast, the surviving Stones became fabulously wealthy.

---

* Her husband, singer Donovan Leitch.

Sir Mick Jagger was worth an estimated £200 million by 2013 ($318 million). But money has not percolated down to Brian's sons, to the irritation of their mothers.

Pat Andrews maintains that her boy, Julian Mark (Julian I), should have inherited the Rolling Stones name, which she considers his birthright. Instead, she and Julian received nothing, and have had to put up with Jagger and Richards downplaying Brian's role in the band, sometimes denigrating Brian personally. 'And my life's ambition has been to get justice for Brian,' says Pat. 'Yeah, he was a swine. He wasn't the best of people. He didn't always do what was right. He didn't always treat people – particularly women – [well]. I'm not saying he was perfect, because he wasn't.' Nevertheless she loved him, and she believes he was murdered for money, a crime orchestrated by Allen Klein. 'I think that deep down inside that's what I believe,' she says. Then she adds, with less conviction: 'Maybe I watch too many detective [shows].'

It is a shock when someone dies young, even if they were heading for trouble. It is disturbing to think that such a death came about because the deceased was a fool, or suicidal. When famous people die, the circumstances are often embellished and complicated until mysteries arise. This is borne out repeatedly with the 27s, and it goes back a long way. After Robert Johnson died in 1938, his life was turned into a supernatural legend involving a pact with the Devil, as a result of which he was gifted with extraordinary musical powers. This fanciful story has been told so often that it has become part of his biography, almost as if it might be true. The fact that Robert Johnson and Brian Jones died at the same age as a series of other performers has encouraged mythologising. Theories entwine around these unhappy lives, like the ivy that smothers tombstones, until it becomes difficult to make out what actually happened.

Nine

NODDING OUT

I'm here to have a party, man, as best as I can
while I'm on this Earth.
Janis Joplin

1

Causes of death recur on the 27 long-list. Road-accident fatalities are surprisingly common; there are several murders and fully realised suicides; but most striking is the number of deaths, like Brian Jones's, that are related to the abuse of drink and drugs.* A third of the fifty deaths can be attributed to drink or drugs. The word 'overdose' occurs repeatedly, mostly in connection with self-administered injections of heroin. In addition there are fatalities where drugs were a significant contributory factor to death, if not the primary cause. This chapter deals with two of the most notable drug-related deaths in the 27 Club, those of Jimi Hendrix and Janis Joplin, friends and peers at the apex of the music business, who died within a month of each other in 1970.

Death did not come out of the blue. There had been symptoms of trouble for years, and in the last months the warning signs flashed repeatedly.

On his way to a show in Canada on 3 May 1969, Jimi Hendrix was arrested at Toronto International Airport for possession of hashish

* See the Appendix, page 303, for the 27 long-list.

and heroin, both of which were found in his flight bag with his toiletries. He denied that the drugs were his and was acquitted at trial, the Canadian jury accepting his assertion that the drugs had been planted by fans. Fans did give Jimi drugs, as they gave them to other rock stars as a tribute, typically slipping them into their pockets as they made their way through a crowd. It would seem unlikely, though, that fans would want, or be able, to smuggle drugs into an artist's luggage. In truth, the drugs were probably his. Jimi dabbled with heroin, as many friends did at a time of experimentation. In the code of the hippies it was cool to use smack, though not to be a junkie, more cool to smoke heroin than shoot up, which was what junkies did. Jimi and his friends were also squeamish about needles. 'We all were,' says Deering Howe. 'We always said, "We're never sticking a needle in our bodies for any drug. If we take it, we'll snort it." We both had a tremendous aversion to needles.'

That summer Jimi disbanded the Experience and took a vacation in Morocco with Deering Howe and two women. The availability of drugs in Morocco has long been part of the attraction of the North African kingdom for Westerners. It is no coincidence that Brian Jones and Jim Morrison also chose Morocco as a holiday destination towards the end of their lives. 'It was really his [Jimi's] first vacation ever, because Michael Jeffrey had his nose to the grindstone and was trying to reap every penny he could from Jimi by constantly having him on tour,' says Howe, who recalls that Jimi had to ask his manager for holiday money before they went away – a striking example of how little control he had over his finances at a time when he was one of the highest-earning acts in show business. 'He had no money,' adds Howe. 'I think he got two or three thousand dollars … I mean, a ridiculous situation.'

Jimi returned from Morocco in the late summer of 1969 to perform at the Woodstock Festival where he topped the bill. Because the festival ran behind schedule, he didn't appear until the morning of Monday, 18 August, by which time many people had gone home. Playing before what looked like a deserted battlefield in the cold light of day, at the end of the sixties, his set had a sombre quality. He performed with a new five-piece band, featuring Mitch Mitchell on drums and his old army buddy Billy Cox on bass. Although not entirely happy with the band, Jimi delivered one of the outstanding performances of his career. His interpretation of 'The Star-Spangled Banner' alone showed him to be one of the most original artists in music and remains a touchstone moment in the 1960s.

Less celebrated was Janis Joplin's set at Woodstock in the early hours of Sunday morning. Janis was working with a slick new band complete with a horn section. Sam Andrew had come across from Big Brother to play with the Kozmic Blues Band, but the rest of the musicians were session men. The other big difference between this band and Big Brother was that Janis was the boss, rather than a member of a group. Some critics thought that her new band lacked soul, though soul was what the musicians were trying to achieve. 'When they were putting the band together they wanted to assemble like a Stax-Volt/R&B kind of band of studio musicians, so at that point it was not very organic, and we got labelled as being, for lack of a better word, colder,' says drummer Maury Baker. '[But] some people liked us. "Finally, she's got some really good players." That's what they said.' Generally speaking, however, the Kozmic Blues Band was not well received, which added to Janis's anxieties.

She was drinking more than ever, lining up cups of tequila on stage each night. Unlike Jimi Hendrix, Janis had also become a full-blown injecting heroin addict. All addicts run the risk of overdose, because they are greedy, or inadvertently buy a stronger batch than they are used to. There was a dramatic and frightening incident with Sam Andrew in London when Janis brought the Kozmic Blues Band to the city. They did better in the UK than at home, and Janis and the boys celebrated their success with a party at which there was 'some really good heroin', as Sam recalls. He used too much and overdosed, 'nodding out', in drug parlance. Fortunately, Janis and other friends were there to save him, putting Sam into a cold bath to revive him while a girl gave him the kiss of life. After a while he started to kiss her back. 'So she said, "He's OK."' Janis wasn't chastened by this. She overdosed six times in 1969. Any one of those incidents could have proved fatal. It was just luck that she and Sam had survived thus far. Luck, or lack of it, plays a significant part in the 27 Club.

As for why Janis carried on in this way, she was an insecure, somewhat unhappy person who used drink and drugs as an anaesthetic, like other 27s. She was also a hedonist. Janis was warned many times – by friends, doctors and acquaintances – not to push herself so hard, but she shrugged off such advice. Journalist David Dalton captured a fascinating conversation between Janis and a member of the public in San Francisco, during which Janis was warned that she might end up like the late Billie Holiday if she didn't curb her behaviour. Janis observed that Holiday's self-destructive lifestyle may 'contribute to the romantic mystique. It's intriguing.' But when pressed, she became defensive: 'I'm here to have a party, man, as best as I can while I'm on this Earth. I think it's your duty to,' she said. 'When I'm ready to retire I'll tell you about it. If I start worrying about everything I'm doing, you know – like this'll give you cholesterol or cirrhosis or some other dumb, unaware trip – I'd just as soon quit now. If that's what I gotta do to stick around another forty years, you can have it.' This attitude has a logic of its own, one that is echoed by great minds through the centuries. 'Live while you live: tomorrow, perhaps, you may die,' Pierre says, in Tolstoy's *War and Peace*. It is the same sentiment. But there isn't necessarily a clean break between living life to the full and dying. A life of excess often leads to a period of impairment first, and this is true of several 27s.

The toll taken by drink and drugs was apparent by the autumn of 1969 when Janis toured with her new band in support of their album, *I Got Dem Ol' Kozmic Blues Again Mama!* 'She [always] liked to drink before her performance, but it was sort of a measured approach [before],' says her road manager, John Byrne Cooke. 'She wanted a particular kind of boost for the start of a performance, and she'd drink more after. Then she doesn't have to measure it, she doesn't have to watch herself afterwards. But in '69 I was feeling maybe she was drinking more before performances. It just seemed to me the whole thing of drinking and drugs was affecting the performances, whereas it hadn't before.' Byrne Cooke became so unhappy with the situation that he quit, and when Janis came off the road in December, Albert Grossman persuaded her to seek professional help. 'One of her problems was that intellectually she was so advanced, [but] her emotions were childlike and uncontrollable,' said Dr Ed Rothchild, who treated Janis for addiction. His words would be just as applicable to Amy Winehouse.

As Janis limped offstage at the end of 1969, Jimi Hendrix was also working towards the end of his hedonistic decade. He didn't have such acute problems as Janis, though. Jimi didn't drink as much. He tended to stick to wine, his favourite tipple being Mateus rosé. As for drugs, Jimi and his friends indulged freely, but he seemed able to handle it. 'Drugs were always there, the booze was always there, the women were always there. It was just open season to have fun,' says Deering Howe. 'We were [in our twenties]. We didn't give a shit. "Let's party as hard as we can for as long as we can."' Another friend, record producer Alan Douglas, agrees that drugs weren't a problem. Using drugs was 'part of living. It was part of the life, being in that scene.' Douglas insists that Jimi was never an addict. 'He could always overcome the dope. He could always overcome the travelling. He could always overcome the business problems. When he started to play the guitar, he played the guitar, and there was nothing else in his way.' Still, drugs would kill Jimi.

The guitarist turned 27 in November, celebrating his birthday by watching the Rolling Stones performing at Madison Square Garden in New York, with Mick Taylor in place of Jimi's recently departed friend, Brian Jones. Jimi stayed on in New York for Christmas, which he spent with Deering Howe, who notes that Jimi, who 'didn't give a shit about politics', was starting to come under pressure from the black-power movement to show solidarity with African-Americans. This pressure may have influenced the formation of the Band of Gypsys, in which Jimi played with Billy Cox and drummer Buddy Miles. The Band of Gypsys gave four shows at Bill Graham's Fillmore East over New Year's Eve and New Year's Day 1969/70. The shows were recorded and the tapes given to producer Ed Chalpin in part-settlement of a legal claim against Jimi, stemming from their 1965 contract. The resulting live album, containing new songs such as 'Machine Gun', is an important addition to the Hendrix canon.

Another pressure came from audiences, who expected Jimi to play his hits in concert and perform his now famous stage tricks, something he was increasingly reluctant to do. Jimi gave the Fillmore audience the full show, up to the point on New Year's Day 1970 that Bill Graham told him he didn't have to pluck his guitar with his teeth and all that shit. Fillmore patrons just wanted to hear the music he wanted to play. That was not true of most audiences. In the last months of his life Jimi was booed in concert when he eschewed his tricks and hits and tried to introduce new music to audiences. 'The general public didn't want to hear his new music. They wanted to hear "Purple Haze" and "Hey Joe". That drove him nuts,' says Deering Howe. 'He did not want to be trapped in the past by his own success, but he found himself totally trapped musically in the past.'

2

Janis Joplin turned 27 on 19 January 1970. She seemed surprised to have made it. She wrote home: 'I managed to pass my – gasp – 27th birthday without really feeling it.'

She was taking some time off work, staying home in Larkspur, an area of Marin County on the north side of the Golden Gate Bridge, where she had bought an A-frame house in the woods. Janis used the break to get her house fixed up and to get clean of heroin. She also took a trip to Rio de Janeiro for the carnival.

It was in Rio, in February 1970, that Janis met an American named David Niehaus. In comparison to the youths she picked up on the road, then discarded with her empty bottles, Niehaus was a mature man with whom she entertained the idea of a relationship. When he suggested they might travel the hippie trail together, even get married, Janis was delighted. Part of her craved family life, as was true of Amy Winehouse, and as the women moved into their latter twenties the urge became more pronounced. David Niehaus came to stay with Janis in California after the Rio carnival but, like so many holiday romances, theirs did not survive a dose of real life. 'I think she really liked David, and [marriage] was something she was thinking about, but he really wasn't into the fame-and-fortune thing. And it didn't go well,' says Lyndall Erb, who shared Janis's house in Larkspur and looked after the property when she was away. 'When he came back to California, he just didn't like her lifestyle here.' That lifestyle included sleeping with other people, women as well as men. Niehaus continued on his travels alone.

When Janis went back on the road in early 1970 she did so with the Full Tilt Boogie Band, led by a Canadian guitarist named John Till. This was a better fit for her than the Kozmic Blues Band, and Janis seemed in better shape for having had some time off. She had quit heroin and managed to stay clean. John Byrne Cooke returned as her road manager and Janis gave impressive concerts throughout the South, Midwest and in New York before joining the Festival Express tour of Canada. This unusual event saw Janis, the Grateful Dead and other acts touring Canada by train. Despite the debauchery of the tour – several of the musicians were notorious drug-users and/ or big drinkers, including Pigpen McKernan – Janis stayed away from heroin during the tour, writing proudly to David Niehaus that she was no longer a junkie.

Like many addicts, Janis was quick to announce that she was clean. But in her case this was for a relatively short time, perhaps five months of 1970, not so much an end to addiction as part of a stop-start pattern. 'You don't have to worry about the junk. I'll never do it again – not unless I do it deliberately to go out!' she told her publicist Myra Friedman, who reports the remark in her book, *Buried Alive*, as an example of Janis's ambivalent attitude to drugs and as one of several allusions the singer made to suicide during her last year.

Friedman also quotes Janis saying, in reply to being asked what she would be doing at thirty, that she didn't believe she would live that long. As we have seen, Kurt Cobain said the same thing. In fact, all of the principal 27s made similar remarks. Whether they believed what they were saying is unknowable. That none lived beyond 27 makes such comments seem prophetic, but many young people make similar prognostications only to live to old age. In Janis's case her comments should be seen in context. At the turn of the 1960s many contemporaries were dying young, famous names and everyday friends, often because of drugs. Nancy Gurley – the wife of Big Brother guitarist James Gurley – died of a heroin overdose in

1969. More deaths followed in 1970. 'I think twelve of our friends died that year,' recalls Lyndall Erb. 'The majority of it was related to drugs ... At that point we were all [thinking], "Will any of us make it to thirty?"'

Janis returned home to Texas in August to attend her tenth high-school reunion. She went on Dick Cavett's TV show beforehand to say that she had been laughed out of Port Arthur by her contemporaries, so now she was going back as a celebrity to laugh at them. It didn't turn out that way. 'That was an awful experience for her,' says Lyndall Erb. 'She thought that being a big star her classmates would like her now, [but] they were still the [same] Texas good ol' boys and, no, they didn't like her. She was too strange for them, and especially for her family.'

Bipolar Janis was on a high as she blew into Port Arthur from the West Coast, dressed in hippie regalia, with an entourage of hipster buddies, including her road manager John Byrne Cooke. Janis behaved as she typically did when she was high, talking loud and fast, cracking jokes, impersonating W. C. Fields, putting on a show for the people, including the local press, who met her at the airport and trailed her around town. They had so many questions that she held a press conference.

'What do you think about Port Arthur now?' she was asked.

'Well, it seems to have loosened up a little bit since I left,' Janis chuckled. 'There seems to be a lot of long hair and rock, which also means drug use, you know. It looks like it's doing just about what all the rest of the country is doing: getting loose, getting it together, getting down, having a good time.' Janis said she was having a good time, though between the wisecracks she didn't look entirely happy. She was sensitive to questions about her family, and thoughtful in answers to questions about her school days. She said she'd been a recluse at high school in Port Arthur and 'felt apart' from her fellow pupils. 'I didn't go to the high school prom.'

'You were asked, weren't you?' asked a reporter.

'No, I wasn't. I don't think they wanted to take me,' said Janis, as if it still bothered her. Then she cackled: 'And I've been suffering ever since!'

The actual reunion was a bore. 'There wasn't anything to do,' complains John Byrne Cooke. 'We went to the dinner. We went to one sort of get-acquainted thing where everybody was walking around a room with a drink in their hand, and they have a name tag on.' Janis and her buddies decided to find some better entertainment, driving to a roadhouse with Janis's sister, Laura, to see Jerry Lee Lewis perform. But this proved a drag. Janis was told that she had to pay to get into the club, like everyone else, and the meeting with Lewis was a disaster. When the man they called the Killer made a crack about Laura's appearance, Janis slapped him and Lewis slapped her back.

There was also tension at home. Janis's parents were not pleased when she rolled in late at night drunk with her buddies, one of whom crashed on the sofa. Still, Janis left Port Arthur with a kinder view of her family. Previously she'd made no secret of the fact that she didn't get on with her parents or Laura. As a result, she had made a will that bequeathed her estate in trust to her kid brother, Michael. She revised this will after the reunion.

'She had sort of a reconciliation with her family,' says Janis's lawyer, Bob Gordon. 'I don't know whether it was the parents or not, but when she came back [to California] she told me she felt a lot better about her family, and I suggested to her that she change her will. She shouldn't leave everything just to her brother, and she agreed. And so the will turned out to leave it to her family in equal shares.' Gordon drafted the change while Janis went to work on her new album.

3

The success of the 1967 Monterey Pop Festival led to a series of larger music festivals across the United States and abroad, most notably Woodstock in 1969. The biggest British festivals were held on the Isle of Wight, off the south coast of England, starting with a small event in 1968 and becoming a major festival in 1969 when Bob Dylan headlined. The following year a huge number of people travelled to the Isle of Wight – probably less than the 600,000 estimated, but still a vast number – to attend a five-day festival featuring the Doors, Jimi Hendrix and the Who.

This was a bad time for the Doors. The band seemed bereft of new musical ideas and Jim Morrison's lyrics were degenerating into self-parody. Yet they were contracted to deliver more albums to Elektra Records. In search of a fresh musical direction the band recorded their fourth studio album, *The Soft Parade*, with the accompaniment of strings and horns, which made them sound middle-of-the-road. There were disagreements about what they were doing. 'The members of the band were not getting along,' says Harvey Brooks, who played bass on *The Soft Parade*. 'The band was in chaos.' As ever Jim was part of the problem. He was drinking hard and using cocaine to get through the sessions. Then came Miami.

The Doors concert at the Dinner Key Auditorium in Miami, on 1 March 1969, was meant to launch a US tour. Instead it was a catastrophe that practically destroyed the band. Jim showed up drunk and seemed less interested in singing than in stirring up the audience. Tired of his pretty-boy image, he had altered his appearance dramatically by growing a full beard, which made him look much older. He was also intent on shocking people. Partly inspired by an experimental theatre troupe, he began a fake strip-tease on stage in Miami. 'There are no rules, there are no limits,' he told the audience, as he made to undo his fly and flash his cock at the crowd, as if that was what they really wanted to see. Road manager Vince Treanor had to hold Jim's trousers up so he didn't expose himself. The police also came onstage, which was when the concert degenerated into anarchy, with Jim at the epicentre of a near riot as his band mates put down their instruments and fled.

A few days later the sheriff of Dade County, Florida, issued an arrest warrant for Jim on charges of lewd and lascivious behaviour, indecent exposure, profanity and drunkenness. Although it is generally agreed that Jim Morrison didn't expose himself in Miami, the case proved serious. The tour was cancelled, because no promoter would risk putting the band on for fear of what Jim would do next. The Doors had also fallen out of fashion with the critics. *The Soft*

Parade received negative reviews upon release, and disappointing sales. Jim had still bigger problems. He faced prison if found guilty at his trial in Miami.

It was by arrangement with the judge that Jim was given leave to fly to Britain in August 1970 to perform with the Doors on the Isle of Wight. The band were joint headliners with the Who on Saturday, 29 August. Jim appeared onstage bearded and thicker-set than before, though he didn't yet look unhealthy. He gave a subdued performance, which his band mates thought lacked energy, but which comes across as refreshingly restrained and thoughtful on Murray Lerner's concert film, showing Jim to be a skilful frontman for a band that, despite its problems, was still distinctive, subtle and powerful. No doubt Jim was also trying to behave, with the court case hanging over him. He had to fly straight back to Miami after the show.

Jimi Hendrix closed the Isle of Wight Festival the following night, actually performing in the early hours of Monday because the festival ran over schedule, as such events usually did. This was his first appearance in Britain for eighteen months. Like the Doors, he crossed the Atlantic for the money, Michael Jeffrey having convinced him that they needed revenue to pay for Electric Lady Studios, Jimi's new recording facility in New York. He was performing as a trio again, with Mitch Mitchell on drums and Billy Cox on bass. This was not the last time Jimi would stand on a stage, but as he died three weeks later, and the Isle of Wight performance was filmed, the show retains special interest.

There were times during the last weeks of his life that Jimi was strung out on drugs, but that was not the case at the Isle of Wight. 'He had come to do a professional job,' says Ray Foulk, one of the promoters. 'He certainly didn't give the outward sign of being particularly depressed, or on drugs. He wasn't high or anything, as far as one could see.' Foulk's impression is borne out by Lerner's concert film, including backstage footage of Jimi in which he looks healthy and speaks coherently. Even though he performed very late at night, with an under-rehearsed band, and had sound problems, Jimi delivered a compelling show. The audience's lack of engagement with his new music was the biggest problem, as it was wherever he went these days. 'If you want the same old songs, we can do that,' he sighed during the show, before playing a crowd-pleasing 'Foxy Lady'.

After the Isle of Wight Jimi took his band to the continent for a short European tour. Once again, Gothenburg in Sweden proved unlucky. Jimi had freaked out there in 1968 when he was high, and he got high as a kite in 1970, giving a shambolic concert as a result. 'He was so wrecked he'd start a song, get into the solo section, and then he wouldn't even remember what song they were playing,' says his former manager Chas Chandler, who attended the concert. More bad fortune followed when Billy Cox fell ill the next day, having apparently had his drink spiked with drugs, which seriously disrupted the tour. Jimi's mood darkened. Before a show in Aarhus, Denmark, he gave an interview in which he said he sacrificed 'part of my soul' each night onstage, adding a comment that seems prophetic: 'I'm not sure I will live to be 28 years old. I mean, at the moment I feel I have got nothing more to give musically ...'

Jimi was wrecked onstage in Aarhus, so out of it that he staggered off after two numbers. He seemed better in Copenhagen. German shows followed: Berlin and the Isle of Fehmarn festival. Although it was billed as a festival of 'love and peace', the event was marred by poor weather and crowd trouble. Jimi was booed. 'I don't give a fuck if you boo, long as you boo in key, you mothers,' he told the audience angrily.

He returned to London where the decision was made to cancel the rest of the tour, primarily because Billy Cox was unwell. Jimi checked into the Cumberland Hotel at Marble Arch, his London address during the last ten days of his life. He spent relatively little time there, however, choosing instead to hang out with friends, including Alan Douglas, who happened to be in town, staying at a house in Kensington.

Over the next few days Jimi discussed his career and future plans with Douglas. 'He was getting older. He didn't want to go on the road. He wanted to write his music [and] he wanted to read and write [music],' says the producer. 'So when he got to London we made a plan.' The plan was that Jimi would play a cluster of shows four times a year, similar to the series he had given at the Fillmore over New Year, freeing up time for recording and taking music lessons. Jimi had decided that educated musicians like Miles Davis – a mutual friend of himself and Douglas – had a broader musical palette. There was a tentative plan for Hendrix and Davis to work together. 'Jimi absolutely fascinated Miles Davis,' says Douglas, 'that here was a guy who never took a lesson in his life and could play like this.' Plans to go back to school and make a jazz-rock album would have brought Jimi into conflict with Michael Jeffrey, but here is evidence that Jimi was thinking ahead. That is not to say he was entirely happy. His relationship with Jeffrey was increasingly difficult. His last few concerts had been uneven, partly due to problems with audiences and the band, while Jimi was unable to carry on at times because he was stoned. To some extent drugs were now getting the better of him and he seemed to have lost his sparkle. Mitch Mitchell: 'I have to say that Jimi was not too bright at this time, for whatever reason, and he did seem depressed.'

Jimi's female companion during these last days in London was a 25-year-old German named Monika Dannemann whom he had met on tour. Jimi and Monika were together on the evening of Tuesday, 15 September, when Jimi went to Ronnie Scott's club in Soho to jam with Eric Burdon's band, War, but he was unable to play. He was high, and he didn't have his guitar, which was uncharacteristic. 'Jimi was a mess – dirty, out of control like I'd never seen him and, for the first time, without his guitar,' Burdon wrote in his autobiography. 'He had a head full of something – heroin, [Quaa]ludes ...' Burdon asked him to come back the following night when he was straight, and to remember to bring his guitar.

Wandering through Soho, Jimi bumped into John Altman, a young saxophonist he'd jammed with when he'd first come to London, and who later came to know Amy Winehouse at the Ten Room club. 'We only talked for a couple of minutes, [because] he was sort of zoning out,' says Altman, but he remembers Jimi saying he'd been booed in Germany. 'Hendrix was absolutely mortified that he'd got booed ... People were throwing things at the stage.' As Altman points out, Amy was also booed offstage in Europe at the last. It is a melancholy coincidence that two great careers ended in the same shabby way.

Jimi spent Tuesday night with Monika Dannemann at the Samarkand Hotel, a self-catering establishment on Lansdowne Crescent in Notting Hill, just off Ladbroke Grove. The hotel was part of a handsome Victorian crescent of four-storey houses smothered in white stucco. Monika rented a little room in the basement. The entrance was via steps down from the street into the area at the front of the house, with access to a communal garden at the back. The Samarkand was anonymous and unprepossessing, one of countless small hotels in west London, named incongruously for a city on the ancient Silk Road. It was an unlikely place for Jimi Hendrix to end his days.

On Wednesday, Jimi returned to Ronnie Scott's. This time he sat in with Eric Burdon. Again he spent the night with Monika at the Samarkand Hotel.

The following day, Thursday, 17 September, Jimi and Monika rose late at the Samarkand. After they had dressed, Monika took photographs of Jimi in the garden. Jimi spoke to Mitch Mitchell on the telephone. Then he and Monika went out, calling at the Cumberland Hotel to collect his messages, and doing some shopping.

During the day the couple met a well-off young man named Philip Harvey, who invited them to dinner at his home. Monika became jealous of the women present at the dinner party. 'It was a lovely evening until nine thirty when the woman introduced as Monika got fed up with the other girls,' Harvey said. 'She stormed out and Jimi followed her. They had the most terrible row for about half an hour.' Nevertheless, the couple returned to the Samarkand where it seems they had more to eat and drink.

In the early hours of Friday, 18 September, Jimi left the hotel to attend a party at the apartment of a friend. After a while, Monika turned up at the address, ringing the door bell and honking her car horn to get Jimi's attention. Although Jimi seemed irritated by her presence, he returned to the Samarkand with her.

Monika Dannemann gave so many differing accounts of what happened during the remaining hours of that night, when she and Jimi were alone at her hotel, that it is hard to know what really happened. But at some point Jimi took some of her sleeping tablets and lay down on her bed. Nobody knows for sure how many pills he swallowed, or whether he understood what he was taking. The drug was a strong barbiturate called Vesparax. Half a tablet was enough to put a man to sleep for eight hours. Jimi may have swallowed as many as *nine*, the number Monika counted as missing the next day. He had also been drinking. This was as foolish and reckless as Brian Jones drinking and taking pills, then going for a swim. But it was in character. During his years on the road Jimi had got into the habit of using drugs indiscriminately and immoderately. 'Jimi would take a handful of shit, not even knowing what it was,' says his friend Deering Howe. 'It was not uncommon for him to do something like that.'

Jimi and Monika fell asleep. Monika woke sometime between nine and eleven a.m. She gave different times in her various statements and interviews. She said Jimi was sleeping when she woke. So she went out to buy cigarettes. When she returned a few minutes later she said she noticed he had been sick and raised the alarm. This was almost certainly a lie. Based on the evidence of the ambulance crew, and the doctor who examined Jimi's body, the more likely scenario is that Monika awoke to find Jimi dead, or dying, and panicked.

She rang friends to ask what to do, including Alvenia Bridges, who was spending the night with Eric Burdon. Monika spoke to Burdon, apparently telling him that she was having trouble waking Jimi. In his memoir, Burdon writes: '[I] told her to slap his face and give him some coffee.' After Burdon put the phone down he realised this could be serious and rang Monika back to tell her sharply to call an ambulance. 'She didn't want to, as there were drugs in the apartment.'

Burdon lost his temper. He screamed: 'Call a fucking ambulance.'

A call was made at eleven eighteen a.m. An ambulance arrived at the Samarkand within nine minutes. The emergency workers, Reginald Jones and John Sava, found the door to Monika's room open and Jimi alone on the bed, lying on his back, fully dressed and covered with vomit. 'There was tons of it all over the pillow, black and brown it was,' Jones told Tony Brown, author of the authoritative book *Hendrix: The Final Days*. 'His airway was completely blocked.' His bowels had also opened. Jones and Sava wrapped Jimi in bedding and carried him up the area steps to the ambulance where Sava used an aspirator to try to revive him while Jones drove them to St Mary Abbots Hospital in Kensington. The crew were obliged to attempt resuscitation even though Sava could not find a pulse and Jimi was not breathing.

Eric Burdon's part in what happened next is slightly mysterious. The singer writes in his book *Don't Let Me Be Misunderstood* that his girlfriend Alvenia went to the Samarkand Hotel after Monika's call, and Burdon followed her by cab. When he arrived at the address he saw the flashing blue lights of an ambulance and heard, from outside the flat, Monika and Alvenia weeping and wailing. But the ambulance men – who had seemingly just removed the body – didn't mention meeting the women, or Burdon, who goes on to describe in his book how he went into the hotel room and found a note in Jimi's hand-writing. 'Come on, let's clean this place up,' he told the women. 'Let's get rid of everything we don't want the cops to take. They'll be here any minute now.' Having removed items from the flat, including the note, Burdon and the women left.

At St Mary Abbots Hospital, Dr John Bannister attempted to resuscitate Jimi, even though he could not find a pulse. The doctor was struck by the condition of the body. Hendrix was covered with vomit, most of which seemed to be red wine. His clothes and hair were matted with it, and his throat and lungs were congested, leading the doctor to conclude that Jimi had 'drowned in red wine'. He certified him dead at twelve forty-five p.m., but he had been dead for hours. 'He was completely cold. I personally think he probably died a long time before. He was cold and he was blue.'

A pathologist told the inquest that Jimi Hendrix had died due to inhalation of his vomit, after taking an overdose of sleeping tablets – eighteen times the normal dose. His blood alcohol level was esti-mated at 100 milligrams per decilitre when he had swallowed the pills, enough to make a person uncoordinated. 'The question why he took so many sleeping tablets cannot be safely answered,' concluded HM Coroner Gavin Thurston, who said there was no evidence that he had intended to commit suicide and recorded an open verdict. Jimi's body was flown home to Seattle for the funeral.

4

When Janis Joplin's publicist telephoned her to say that Jimi Hendrix had died, and to ask if she had a comment for the press, Janis said: 'I wonder what they'll say about me when I die.'

Janis was staying at the Landmark Hotel on Franklin Avenue in Hollywood, at the foot of the Hollywood Hills, parallel with the tourist stretch of Hollywood Boulevard. John Byrne Cooke booked her and her band into the Landmark when they were in Los Angeles to record because it was near Sunset Sound Studios, the rates were reasonable and the rooms had kitchens so the musicians could cook for themselves if they wanted to. The Landmark was a typical Californian courtyard motel, built around a swimming-pool, with a distinctive double-height glass lobby. Janis checked into Room 105, a suite near the lobby comprised of a double bedroom, kitchen, a corridor-like dressing room and a bathroom. The front windows overlooked Franklin Avenue and, on the other side of the street, a small park with palm trees. If she was using drugs, Janis could stand at her window and watch for her connection coming across the park. She could also leave her Porsche – decorated with a psychedelic mural – conveniently under her window on the drive if she couldn't be bothered to put it in the underground garage.

Janis didn't attend Jimi Hendrix's funeral in Seattle on Thursday, 1 October 1970. She was in LA that day, signing her new will. By this document she left her estate in equal parts to her parents and two siblings, ordering that her body be cremated and that up to $2,500 (£1,572) set aside from her estate to pay for a 'gathering' for her friends. It is striking that Janis attended to her last will and testament three days before she died. People contemplating suicide often take the time to settle their affairs. Did Janis have suicide in mind? She had spoken of it. Yet friends do not believe she was suicidal. On the contrary, she seemed full of life. 'My God, I had never seen her happier,' says her lawyer Bob Gordon, who recalls that Janis had just been to the beauty parlour to have her hair tinted when she came to sign her will. 'She literally skipped into my office, being very joyous.'

Maybe Janis was pretending; she was forever putting on a show. 'I don't think I ever saw the real Janis,' says her friend Lyndall Erb. The main cause for Janis's excitement at this time, perhaps her *over-excitement*, was that she had a new lover, a handsome college boy named Seth Morgan, who claimed to be related to the J. P. Morgan banking dynasty, which seemed to be part of the attraction. Janis was tired of being the one with all the money. Apart from his wealth, Seth Morgan had the sort of bad-boy attraction Amy Winehouse found in Blake Fielder-Civil, and both men affected not to care that they were dating a star. Janis's friends distrusted Seth, as many of Amy's friends distrusted Blake. 'He was a nice guy, but not very nice to her,' says Lyndall Erb. 'Several of us tried to get her to see the real side of him. He was very insincere about what he was doing with her.'

Based on a brief relationship, Janis was engaged to marry Seth. He was staying at her house in Marin County and had been coming to LA at weekends while Janis was recording. He was due to fly down again on Saturday, 3 October. Janis had an idea that she and Seth might get married while he was in LA. When she spoke to Bob Gordon about this on the Thursday before the weekend, her lawyer suggested he draw up a prenuptial agreement, even though, like Brian Jones and Jimi Hendrix, Janis was not rich. '[Janis] didn't have a lot of money ... She had bought a house by the time she died, so that probably had some value. But in terms of having available money to live a carefree kind of existence, she wasn't there.' Janis told her lawyer to draw up the papers.

Recording was going well. Janis had decided to call her new album *Pearl*, a nickname she'd recently adopted. Songs on the album included a cover of Kris Kristofferson's 'Me and Bobby McGee', which showed that she could sing a ballad effectively without yelling. It is the song she became best known for posthumously, a tender number that turns melancholy when Janis sings, 'freedom's just another word for nothing left to lose'. Janis had a good working relationship with her producer, Paul Rothchild, who found her more *simpatico* than his other big client, Jim Morrison, and the Full Tilt Boogie Band was the best band Janis had worked with. The young Canadians were all good musicians, organic yet professional. They liked Janis and she liked them. 'We were near the end of the record. The record was going to be OK. She loved it,' says Ken Pearson, whose organ break at the end of 'Me and Bobby McGee' gives the song its final flourish.

Still, Janis was not entirely happy during the recording of *Pearl*. 'The feeling is that she started fooling around with heroin again because recording was boring,' says John Byrne Cooke. There was another user at the Landmark, a girlfriend of Janis's named Peggy Caserta. When Janis recognised a dealer visiting the hotel to supply Caserta with heroin, she decided she wanted some, too. 'She called the room and she said, "Bring me some." And I said "No." And she said, "Don't think that if you don't give me some, I can't get it, because I can get it the same way you got it,"' Caserta later said in a TV interview. 'And she said, "I'm coming up to your room, and I want some." And she did, and she came in, and [said] that she had gotten me high so many times, and how could I possibly not get her high? And, *um*, we did. And she started using again.'

Janis worked in the studio with her band on Saturday, 3 October. She had been expecting Seth to arrive to keep her company, maybe to make her his wife, but he hadn't left San Francisco yet. Janis called the house and spoke to Lyndall Erb. 'Seth was supposed to go down to LA that afternoon. He didn't want to drive to the airport. He wanted me to drive him to the airport, but the only car I had there was his, which was really hard to drive, and I said, "No, I don't want to drive your car." And so he didn't go. And he sort of blamed it on me. But he could have driven himself to the airport and parked his car. I think he just didn't want to go,' says Lyndall, adding that Seth was entertaining another woman at the house. Janis spoke to both her housemate and her lover on Saturday night. 'She was a little down that Seth wasn't coming down, and she was not really happy,' says Lyndall, recalling their last conversation. 'The recording session was going really well, but typical of recording sessions it was taking a long time, and I think she was feeling a little lonely.' 'Lonely' is the adjective Janis's friends use about her time and again. One of the last songs she recorded in LA was 'A Woman Left Lonely'.

After work on Saturday night, Janis accompanied members of her band to Barney's Beanery, a bar on Santa Monica Boulevard. They had something to eat and drink together and Janis told the boys she loved them. Suicidal people often make a point of telling friends and family they love them just before they end their lives. Around eleven thirty p.m. Janis gave organist Ken Pearson a lift back to the Landmark in her Porsche, which she parked on the drive. The park opposite was in darkness. Those of an imaginative nature might picture the sepulchral figure of Death loitering in the shadows beneath the palm trees, waiting for Janis to come home.

It is certainly easy to imagine Janis feeling intensely lonely as she returned to Room 105 that night. Seth had said he would be there, but he had let her down. As Janis sang in 'A Woman Left Lonely', she surely knew that her boyfriend was taking her for granted, and marriage would be a mistake.

It is not known what Janis did in her room for the next hour and a half, but at around one a.m. she got her heroin works out and injected a vein in her left arm, which bore the marks of previous injections. Then she put away her works and went to the hotel lobby – a few strides down the corridor – to get change from the night clerk for the cigarette machine, returning to 105 with the pack. She closed the door and went to her bed, which was in the corner facing the window. She started to undress, stripping down to her blouse and underwear, and reached to put her cigarette packet on the nightstand. As she did so she keeled over, hitting her face on the table as she fell to the floor.

Although the following day was Sunday, Janis and her band were due back at Sunset Sound in the evening to complete one of the last tracks on *Pearl*. As the day wore on Lyndall Erb became concerned that she couldn't raise Janis on the telephone, and made calls to find out where she was. Seth Morgan called John Byrne Cooke to say he was about to fly to LA, belatedly, but he couldn't reach Janis to arrange to be picked up. In the early evening, Byrne Cooke called

Paul Rothchild, who told him that Janis hadn't arrived at the studio. Where was she?

John Byrne Cooke gathered together three members of the band at the motel and took them down to his car in the underground car park to drive them to the studio. As he pulled out of the car park onto the drive he glanced across and saw Janis's Porsche parked under her window. 'I thought, Wait a minute!' he says, casting his mind back to that evening. 'I just pulled the car back into the garage, so I wouldn't block the entrance to the garage. I said, "Wait here. I'm just going to go check." And there was a light on in Janis's room. It was dusk. It was Los Angeles dusk, in early October, so you've passed the equinox, and it was just dark enough, I thought, that you might just turn on the lights ... Maybe she'd just come in.' Byrne Cooke went to the front desk to get a key for 105. He let himself in. Janis was on the floor, between the bed and the wall. She was dead to the touch, as she had been for hours, with the change from the cigarette machine still clasped in her cold hand.

The coroner asked members of the band about Janis's state of mind. 'I remember he said to me, "Did she ever feel down?"' says Ken Pearson. 'Now isn't that a naïve question to ask me? I said, "The title of her [third] album was I Got Them Ol' Kozmic Blues Again Mama!" "Oh," he said. "Well, what's Kozmic Blues?" I said, "I think it's more than you can't pay the rent." And so he said, "So, she was suicidal?" "No, I'm not saying that ..."' In fact, Janis had seemed fine to Pearson that last night in Barney's Beanery. Nobody knows for sure what was in her mind, but her death certificate records that she died by accident, caused by acute heroin-morphine intoxication – that is, an overdose. John Byrne Cooke and Laura Joplin believe Janis accidentally injected an unusually strong batch of heroin. Maybe. But the decision to shoot up was hers, and Janis knew the risk.

Janis's friends honoured her will by having a raucous party at her expense after the cremation. 'We really enjoyed it. It was kind of over the top, to tell you the truth,' says Sam Andrew. 'There was a lot of drugs, you know, a lot of very happy people.' Pearl was completed posthumously and released to acclaim. The album and the single 'Me and Bobby McGee' went to number one.

The members of the Full Tilt Boogie Band found themselves out of a job at the point of their greatest success. 'It's like the guy who pulls the tablecloth out, and everything is still standing ... Now what do we do?' says bass guitarist Brad Campbell. '[Janis] was great. She wasn't always wild, what people thought ... She was an intelligent person. A lot of intelligent people can get thrown off by something, and there is no path back. I think that's what happened to her ... I think that was probably [the case] with Amy [Winehouse], too.'

Ten

THE CRACK-UP

Die at the right time: thus teaches Zarathustra.
Nietzsche

1

'You're drinking with number three,' Jim Morrison supposedly told friends in Barney's Beanery after Janis Joplin died. The quote is apocryphal but irresistible, suggesting that, following the deaths of Jimi Hendrix and Janis Joplin, Jim foresaw his own end.

With hindsight we know that Jim had nine months to live. Unless he was clairvoyant, or determined to commit suicide, he cannot have known that death was so close. And, like Hendrix and Joplin, he had reasons to be optimistic about the future at this stage in his life. The Doors recorded some of their best work during these last months, and Jim fulfilled an ambition to set aside his pop career and go to France, where he pursued his interests in poetry and film. Some of his friends point to these factors as evidence that Jim was not in terminal decline in 1970–71, dismissing the image of a fat, drink-sodden, depressed and washed-up rock star as a misleading cliché. It is a simplification, but at the same time all was far from well.

Jim was a young man of 26, soon to turn 27, experiencing the nervous breakdown he'd warned his band mates about. Like F. Scott Fitzgerald, another American drunkard who enjoyed phenomenal success in his twenties and then went into self-destructive decline,

Jim had reached the point of crack-up, which Fitzgerald wrote about in an autobiographical story of that title. The crack-up broke both men, resulting in them dying young: Fitzgerald as a recovering alcoholic in Los Angeles in 1940, Morrison as a drunk and drug-abuser in Paris in 1971. Both seemed tired of life at the end, which was equally true of Jones, Hendrix, Joplin, Cobain and Winehouse.

A significant factor in Jim Morrison's decline was his conviction, in September 1970, for indecent exposure and profanity in Miami. He was acquitted on the other charges. The sentence was six months' hard labour, plus a fine. Jim was freed on bail, pending an appeal, which could go all the way to the Supreme Court and take a long time to resolve, but his lawyer, Max Fink, seemed to think that Jim might have to serve time. 'Max Fink was making it very clear that Jim could go to jail, and he was a very, very scared fellow at that point, and I firmly believe that a lot of his actions in Paris were the result of the pressure of the outcome of the trial,' says Vince Treanor, the Doors' road manager. 'That's going to weigh on anybody.'

In the meantime Jim returned to Hollywood where, despite his fame and money, he lived the life of a barfly. The nexus of this existence was the crossroads of Santa Monica Boulevard and La Cienega Boulevard. Barney's Beanery is on the north-east corner of the intersection. Diagonally opposite was the building the Doors used as their rehearsal space and office; they called it their workshop. On the other side of the street was a strip bar Jim frequented, next to which was the Alta Cienega Motel where he sometimes crashed when drunk. Unlike rock-star contemporaries who were buying big houses, and living expansively, Jim lived like a bum. When he got tired of the Alta Cienega Motel, which was a dump, he would check into the Chateau Marmont on Sunset Boulevard, which was more comfortable, but his was still a surprisingly low-rent lifestyle.

Jim also spent time with Pamela Courson at her new apartment on Norton Avenue, within stumbling distance of Barney's Beanery. It was remarkably modest, at 450 square feet with a bathroom the size of a closet and an ironing board that folded out of the wall.

Jim and Pamela had a curious relationship. He was generous with his girlfriend, bankrolling her boutique, Themis, and buying her a

Porsche. Pamela thought of Jim as her husband and sometimes referred to herself as his wife (though they never married), and Jim made her the sole beneficiary of his will. Yet the couple argued and were unfaithful to one another, and both were high for much of the time, which made the relationship chaotic. Something of Pamela's scatty character is conveyed in a story about her flying from LA to New York around this time to see the actor John Phillip Law, with whom she was having an affair. She carelessly left her Porsche in the short-term parking lot at Los Angeles International Airport with a bag of dope inside. 'So of course it got towed and then they opened it up and there was all this pot, so they arrested her when she came back,' says her friend Mirandi Babitz.

Physically Jim was now almost unrecognisable as the teen idol photographed in 1967. 'It was almost as though he forced himself to become the antithesis of what made him a star, and I don't think he was very comfortable as a star,' says poet friend Michael C. Ford. Jim let his hair and beard grow. He put on weight and took to wearing an army surplus jacket. The last time Mirandi Babitz ran into him he was shambling around Hollywood, his beard encrusted with vomit. 'A disgusting drunk kind of person ... He just let himself go.' Elektra executive Steve Harris hardly recognised Jim. 'He became paunchy. He got jowly ... He didn't want to be a sex symbol anymore.' Steve's wife, Nicole, sensed that something deep down was wrong, something that for all his intelligence Jim was unable to articulate or deal with. 'Something was bothering him from his youth, I think. I think he had a lot of secrets inside of him,' she says. 'Maybe he was abused or something. Nobody will ever know.'

This was the unhappy man who came to Sunset Sound in December 1970 to record the Doors' sixth studio album, which, with a live LP and a greatest-hits compilation, would complete their contract with Elektra Records. Producer Paul Rothchild had just finished Janis Joplin's *Pearl* in the same studio. In contrast to Janis, whom Rothchild had adored, Jim was difficult to work with, and the producer lost his temper with him and the band during the sessions. 'I worked my ass off for a week, but it was still just fucking awful,' Rothchild later complained. 'I'd go into them and tell them that, hoping that it would make them angry enough to do something good.' He told the Doors they were making 'cocktail-lounge music', hoping that the insult would spur them on to do better. 'But they just didn't have the heart anymore ...' So he quit.

The Doors decided to continue recording without Rothchild at their workshop on Santa Monica Boulevard. Their engineer produced the record. That was how they made the *LA Woman* album. Surprisingly, it turned out to be their strongest since their 1967 début, the band finding new focus in blues-based songs steeped in the sleazy atmosphere of night-time Los Angeles. 'Cars Hiss By My Window' and 'LA Woman' were especially evocative of the city of broken dreams, while the album concluded with an instant classic in 'Riders on the Storm'.

Jim celebrated his 27th birthday during the sessions by drinking with friends and recording poetry. Three nights later the Doors began a short concert tour with a show in Dallas where they performed 'Riders on the Storm' for the first time. It went well. The next night, 12 December 1970, they played New Orleans. Halfway through the show Jim suddenly stopped singing. Ray Manzarek said it was as if Jim's spirit had departed from his body. It is more helpful to think of this as a key moment in an ongoing nervous breakdown. Jim gave up on the show and sat down on John Densmore's drum riser. When Densmore asked him what was wrong – or shoved him with his foot, whichever version you believe – Jim picked up his microphone stand and smashed it repeatedly into the stage until he had broken through the wooden boards. Unable to continue, he walked off.

The tour was cancelled. Densmore, Krieger and Manzarek agreed that they couldn't perform live with Jim as he was and told him so. Back in LA, Vince Treanor sensed a new 'hostility' towards Jim from the others. Densmore in particular was starting to imagine the Doors without Jim Morrison, as Jim was thinking of a life after the Doors.

A couple of months later, when they were mixing *LA Woman*, Jim told the band that he was going to Paris. Pamela had flown ahead to find an apartment. He was going to have a sabbatical and write. He didn't say how long he would be away, or whether he would return to work with the group, but Elektra president Jac Holzman had little doubt that Jim had had enough not only of the Doors but of the rock 'n' roll business. 'I did not really think, especially after I said goodbye to Jim, that he would ever come back as a member of any band.'

Jim flew to Paris on 11 March 1971, when he was on bail pending an appeal in the Miami case. He may have had it in mind not to return to the USA until he knew the outcome of his appeal. He certainly didn't want to go to jail. 'When Jim left, he was in tremendous fear of jail,' says Vince Treanor. 'That was one of the reasons Jim wanted to get away.' As it turned out he never came back.

2

The contrast with Los Angeles was dramatic. Jim left a modern American city, where molten freeways run through dusty canyons of gimcrack architecture, and arrived in a cool, old-world city of stone. It was glorious to be in Paris in March, the sun bringing the trees into leaf and the flowers into bloom. The façades of the restaurants and bars gleamed invitingly; the museums were filled with treasure. Generations of visitors have fallen in love with Paris in the springtime. As a reader of French literature, Jim was coming to a city that had long been part of his intellectual life, a place where he might fulfil what he saw as his destiny as a poet.

Pamela had been in Paris for a month. Like many rich Americans she had checked into the George V hotel off the Champs-Élysées. Jim preferred a more Bohemian milieu so they moved into the apartment of an actress friend named Elizabeth Larivière who would be away filming most of the time, giving them the run of the place. The apartment was in an old building at 17 rue Beautreillis in the Marais. Double doors on the street opened onto a courtyard with a concierge. Up the winding stone stairs was Apartment 4, which had three bedrooms, a lounge, kitchen and dining room; spacious rooms with high ceilings, fireplaces, period furniture and tall, shuttered windows. Jim and Pamela slept in the second bedroom near the tiled bathroom.

Jim began to explore Paris on foot, often walking alone in the morning and at twilight. A short stroll north of the apartment brought him to place des Vosges, a famous old square surrounded by colonnaded buildings in which Victor Hugo had once lived. The park in the middle was popular with mothers and small children. Jim would sit and watch the children play while he tried to write in the 25 cent notebooks he'd brought from America. When he wanted a longer walk he went south to the river Seine, crossing pont de Sully to Île St-Louis. He then walked around the quay to the house where Baudelaire had lived, pausing to watch the boats pass. Typically, he would continue to Île de la Cité, past Notre Dame, crossing to the Left Bank and then strolling to St-Germain-des-Prés where he would stop at Deux Magots, which Jean-Paul Sartre had patronised, or Café de Flore on the next block.

'I saw him every day, for fifteen days, all the time at the Café de Flore,' says the actress Zouzou, who had last seen Jim backstage at the Roundhouse in London, with Brian Jones, when Jim was still 'so sexy'. Zouzou was shocked to see him bearded and bloated in Paris, 'so ugly … he had no neck anymore'. But he seemed happy. He told Zouzou that he was going to the galleries and he loved walking in the city, especially at dusk. Hardly anybody bothered him. The Doors had never toured France and were not particularly well known there. As Jim talked he drank Kronenbourg, tall glasses of beer and many of them. 'Then around six o'clock Pamela was coming and she was saying, "Come on, Jim. Let's go home." And he was saying, "Goodbye, see you tomorrow."'

Zouzou was one of several film contacts Jim had in Paris, helping form a connection with an industry he was ambitious to become more involved with. He had brought copies of his experimental films to France hoping to get them screened. He met the director François Truffaut. But nothing tangible resulted, which may have undermined his confidence. There is a sense that Jim's health and mood deteriorated as spring progressed and the days became longer and warmer. Although he enjoyed Paris, it wasn't enough to walk and drink and look at art. He tried to write, but the result was poor. His notebook jottings are disorganised, scatological and angry.

Jim and Pamela took a holiday in April, driving through France and Spain, then crossing the Strait of Gibraltar to Morocco, a country that had also drawn Brian Jones and Jimi Hendrix shortly before they died. The three 27s visited many of the same places, all spending time in Marrakesh. As noted, the availability of drugs in the kingdom was part of the attraction. Hashish is readily obtainable in Morocco, and Pamela could score heroin without difficulty. She was a heavy user, snorting rather than injecting the drug, and Jim was dabbling with it.

While he was in Marrakesh Jim shaved his beard. His once-chiselled face was revealed as puffy and deathly pale. In fact, holiday snaps taken during his European sojourn tell a story of their own. Sometimes he appears obviously inebriated, clowning and pulling faces for the camera. In other pictures he has the stunned countenance of the hung-over alcoholic, and the flatness of expression common to depressives.

On their return to Paris Jim and Pamela found that Elizabeth Larivière was using the apartment so they checked into L'Hôtel on rue des Beaux-Arts, where Oscar Wilde died (when the hotel had a different name). Jim almost did the same when he tumbled out of his second-floor window into the street, an extraordinary accident for most people, but not for Jim who had also recently fallen from a roof at the Chateau Marmont in LA. These incidents are usually dismissed as drunken high jinks, but they may have been suicidal gestures, unlikely to prove fatal yet gaining him the solace of attention.

A couple of nights later Jim went to the Rock 'n' Roll Circus nightclub on rue de Seine, which had a reputation as a place to score heroin. Jim was so drunk he was thrown out. A student named Gilles Yepremian, a rare French fan of the Doors, happened to recognise him and asked where he was staying. Jim was unable to answer coherently so Gilles decided to take the star with him. He hailed a cab and asked the driver to take them to a friend's apartment near L'Étoile.

Jim was very drunk. 'He was singing and he was crying,' says Gilles. When their cab crossed the Seine Jim tried to get out, saying he wanted to go for a swim. A late-night dip in the Seine in his condition would have been another suicidal gesture, which may have proved fatal. Gilles managed to restrain him. But Jim was in an obstreperous mood.

'Fucking pigs!' he shouted, as they passed some police.

They reached the apartment building of Gilles Yepremian's friend where their taxi driver asked for a big tip in compensation for Jim's behaviour. When Gilles explained to Jim, who didn't speak French, he took out a wad of francs and offered it all to the driver. 'The taxi man was afraid. He think maybe we are gangsters, or maybe we are mad,' says Gilles. '[He] gives back to Jim the money and he leaves. Funny.'

The evening was turning into a French farce. Gilles's next task was to get Jim up five flights of stairs, almost carrying the drunken American, who *shushed* the student not to wake the neighbours. Finally Gilles rapped on the door of his friend, a music journalist named Hervé Muller. It was late. The household was asleep. A student who was staying with Hervé and his girlfriend assumed it was a police raid and threw her marijuana out of the window.

'Who's that?' Hervé asked nervously.

'It's me, Gilles, with Jim Morrison.'

Hervé Muller opened his door to find, to his astonishment, that Gilles had indeed brought the lead singer of the Doors to his apartment – dead drunk. Jim stumbled forward, then crashed out on Hervé's bed, after which there was no waking him. Hervé and his girlfriend spent the rest of the night in a sleeping-bag.

The following day Jim had no idea where he was, or what had happened. When it was explained to him, he took Hervé Muller and his girlfriend for breakfast at a bar near the George V where he drank so much he started to weep.

Over the next few weeks Hervé Muller and Gilles Yepremian saw Jim several times. When he was sober, he was pleasant and subdued. When he was drunk, Gilles says that 'It was like speaking to the Devil.' The Frenchmen learned that Jim disliked talking about the Doors, though Hervé elicited that he had received a copy of *LA Woman* and was pleased with the album. The dominant impression was of a man with a serious drink problem that dramatically affected his mood. 'When he was drunk, he was really depressed. He cried,' says Gilles. 'But when he was [sober] he was OK.' He says that Jim seemed much older than 27.

One day Hervé hosted a luncheon for Jim, Pamela and Gilles at which he served Corsican wine. The Americans enjoyed the wine so much that they set off for an impromptu holiday in Corsica. It was the kind of impetuosity Jim was rich enough to indulge in. He also popped over to London briefly. Like any tourist, he wrote 'wish you were here' type postcards home from the places he visited and he made at least two telephone calls to Los Angeles. In one he spoke to a buddy named Frank Lisciandro. 'He sounded lonely and distant, as if it wasn't panning out for him ...' Jim also called the Doors' workshop where John Densmore picked up. The sound of Jim's voice put Densmore on edge; they'd never got along.

Jim asked how *LA Woman* was doing. John said the reviews were good, and the Doors were in the charts with the single 'Love Her Madly'.

Jim seemed pleased. 'Well, maybe we should do another one?' he said.

It is difficult to know whether Jim was serious about making another Doors album. John didn't tell him that he, Robby and Ray had already started to rehearse without him and that, personally, John didn't want him back. But he knew that if Jim decided to return they would probably have him, such was the power of a lead singer. He asked Jim nervously when he was thinking of returning. Jim said it would be a few months yet. Densmore was relieved when he rang off.

Jim may well have gained the impression from this conversation that he was not wanted in LA. If Ray Manzarek had answered the phone it would have been a very different conversation. As it was, he never spoke to the band again. 'I think that [call] was that in-famous straw that breaks a camel's back,' says Vince Treanor. 'He wanted to come back, to get back into [music], but John was very brutal ... there was a coldness there – unreceptive.'

It was now summer in Paris. Jim had made a reel-to-reel tape of himself singing drunkenly with two buskers he met on boulevard

St-Germain and wanted to have the tape transferred to cassette, which was then coming into use. He asked Elizabeth Larivière's boyfriend, Philippe Dalecky, if he would dub the tape. Philippe had met Jim a few times and found him unpredictable, depending on how much he had drunk. 'I think he was fed up with everything,' says Philippe, who noticed that one of the few things that lifted Jim's spirits was watching children play. Their *joie de vivre* took him out of himself. Interestingly, Amy Winehouse derived solace from the company of children when everything turned sour in her life.

Jim went to Philippe's apartment to have the tape dubbed. Just after he had departed, Philippe noticed that he had left his carrier bag behind, with one of his notebooks inside. He ran after him.

'Hey, Jim, you forgot this!'

'It's all right, keep it,' replied the American. 'See you. 'Bye!'

It is unusual for a writer to abandon his notebook, indicating that Jim may have been so far gone with drink that he didn't know what he was doing, or that he had given up on his ambitions to write and, by extension, possibly on himself. Much of the verse he had written in the notebook (which Philippe Dalecky kept and sold years later to a collector) was nonsensical. But it wasn't something a writer would simply discard. When Philippe looked through the book he found three words towards the end that struck him as significant.

Jim had written: 'I'm finally dead.'

In three weeks he would be.

3

In June a friend from UCLA, Alain Ronay, came to stay with Jim in Paris, and spent almost every day with him during the last weeks of his life. The men took long walks together through the city. During a stroll on Friday, 2 July, Jim turned the conversation to suicide, specifically to what Nietzsche had written about it. This was something he had discussed with other friends recently.

Nietzsche can be read as an advocate of suicide. 'The thought of suicide is a powerful comfort: it helps one through many a dreadful night,' is the philosopher's epigram on the subject. In *Thus Spake Zarathustra*, Nietzsche has his Dionysian prophet preach that it is important to choose the time of one's death:

Many die too late, and some die too early. The teaching sounds strange: '*Die at the right time!'*

Nietzsche also has Zarathustra address those who crave fame, into which category a rock star would fall. Such people had to learn to 'honour and practise the difficult art of – going at the right time'. That is, every performance ends as all lives end; the close of the stage curtain is a rehearsal for the final curtain. Know when to leave the stage.

Despite Jim's gloomy preoccupations, Alain Ronay insists that Jim was in better shape than is often supposed during his last weeks, arguing that his friend was not depressed, that he had lost weight and cut back on drinking. 'Jim was not fat,' he says, though photographs he took of Jim a week before he died show the singer with a distinctly fat face. '[He] was anything but despondent, and had stopped drinking – almost ...' There is a beer bottle in front of Jim in these last pictures. Still Alain is determined to look on the bright side. 'Truly he was not melancholy,' he insists. '[He] probably spent the happiest days of his life [in Paris] before his death. And, by the way, his career wasn't over at all. He had decided not to go back to rock, but his record was [selling well].'

Despite Alain Ronay's kindly words, Jim took a turn for the worse that Friday in July. Watching him shopping for a gift for Pamela, Alain gained the impression that his friend was trying to appear happy 'but really wasn't happy at all'. The men went for lunch and Jim had a violent attack of hiccups. Jim had been complaining of problems with his chest and breathing recently, including apparently coughing up blood. He had seen a doctor about it. Hiccups were the latest problem. The filmmaker Agnès Varda, a mutual friend of Jim and Alain from UCLA, who was also in Paris, describes Jim's hiccups as being 'like a motor car that rattles before breaking down'.

Around five thirty Alain said he had to go and meet Agnès Varda, with whom he was staying the night. Jim was loath to let Alain go, persuading him to have a drink first on place de la Bastille where the cafés face a column surmounted by a gilded figure of Liberty. Jim knocked back yet another Kronenbourg. Alain was sad to see him drinking heavily again. Suddenly Jim was racked by hiccups. Alain fancied for a moment that he was looking at a dead man. When Jim asked the waiter for another round of beers, Alain excused himself and left Jim sitting at his table.

4

In common with Jones, Hendrix, Joplin and Winehouse, Jim Morrison died overnight. As a result there were few witnesses to the stars' last hours, and in some cases none. Those witnesses who did exist were not always reliable, and many are themselves now dead. In Jim's case the only person who knew for sure what happened to him during the night of 2–3 July 1971 was Pamela Courson, and her testimony was coloured by an attempt to conceal her drug use from the French authorities. As a result Jim's death became unnecessarily mysterious, the mystery compounded by the fact that he died in a foreign land where his partner didn't speak the language.

What follows is the most likely account of what happened to Jim on the last night of his life based on the best evidence available, which includes Pamela Courson's police statement, in which she gave a selective account, and interviews Alain Ronay and Agnès Varda gave in 1991, which complete the story. Importantly, Alain Ronay belatedly went on the record saying that Pamela had confessed to him that she and Jim were snorting heroin on the night he died. She gave the impression that they were in the habit of using heroin. But she didn't tell the police that.

After Alain left Jim at the café on the evening of Friday, 2 July, Jim and Pamela went to the movies to see *Pursued*. They then returned to the apartment on rue Beautreillis. 'When we got there, we started snorting heroin,' Pamela told Alain. She said they also screened their holiday movies and Jim played all the Doors' records, which sounds like a suicidal ritual.

Jim took a lot of heroin that last night, by Pamela's account. 'Jim asked me for another sniff and eventually he took more than me,' she told Alain, saying that Jim had also taken some earlier that day, and they had both snorted the previous evening. He may even have meant to overdose. Like many of the 27s, elements of his behaviour indicate a suicidal mood. No one knows for sure. As with Jones, Hendrix, Joplin and Winehouse, there was no suicide note. But suicides don't always leave notes. Often they try to make death appear accidental. It is also true that Jim, in common with other 27s, was reckless and immoderate in his habits, introducing the element of accident or misadventure, while John Densmore concludes that Jim 'committed slow suicide' by abusing his body over a period of years. This is seen time and again in the 27s.

Around two thirty on the morning of Saturday, 3 July, Pamela nodded off on the bed. She was woken soon afterwards by Jim's stertorous breathing, as if he was struggling for breath. This was probably an overdose, and although Pamela panicked she knew what to do. She slapped him hard. Then she took him to the bathroom. A cold bath was a recognised method of reviving somebody who'd overdosed on heroin. It had worked for Janis Joplin's guitarist Sam Andrew. Crucially, however, Andrew was put into a cold bath, and his friends stayed with him until he regained consciousness. In her police statement Pamela said Jim 'told me he wanted to take a hot bath'. While a cold bath shocks the system, a hot bath is soporific. It seems that this bath was both hot and full. Jim spilled water over the side when he got in. He said he felt sick. So Pamela fetched an orange Le Creuset casserole dish from the kitchen and he was sick into it. Pamela emptied the pot three times and noticed blood in the vomit. Jim said he felt 'weird', but he didn't want a doctor. He told Pamela to go back to bed, where he would join her shortly.

When Pamela woke in the morning light she was alone in bed. Jim was still in the bath. In some accounts of his death, it is reported that the bathroom door was locked. Pamela made no mention of this in her police statement, and it would seem unlikely that Jim would lock himself in. It is doubtful that he ever got out of the bath once he had got into it, and Pamela wouldn't have locked him in.

She told the police that she simply returned to the bathroom in the morning where she found Jim unconscious in the tub, his head on one side, blood dribbling from his nose.

Pamela rang Agnès Varda's apartment and spoke to Alain Ronay. It was shortly after eight o'clock.

'Jim's unconscious and bleeding. Call an ambulance,' Pamela cried. She couldn't make the call herself because she didn't speak French. 'Quick, I think he's dying.'

Alain asked Agnès to make the call because she was more familiar with the emergency services in Paris. She decided to call the fire brigade because she thought they would get to Jim quickest. Alain asked her not to give them Jim's real name, just his address. For some reason, he felt they should conceal the fact that Jim was a famous rock star, which was the start of the confusion that ensued.

Having made the call, Agnès and Alain drove through the busy Saturday morning traffic to rue Beautreillis.

As she waited for help to arrive, Pamela Courson made another telephone call, to a French playboy friend named Count Jean de Breiteuil. Pamela had had a fling with the count, who supplied her and other users in the rock community with heroin. He was currently dating Mick Jagger's ex-girlfriend, Marianne Faithfull, who had become a heroin user. They were at L'Hôtel. Faithfull recalls in her memoirs that Pamela rang their room that morning and then the count left for Jim's apartment. He told Marianne that she couldn't come with him.

The emergency workers were on the scene by the time Alain Ronay and Agnès Varda arrived at rue Beautreillis. They were allowed upstairs. The apartment door was open. At the end of the corridor, surrounded by firemen and dressed in a white djellaba, stood Pamela.

'Jim is dead!' she cried. 'He left us.'

Agnès looked in the bathroom and saw Jim in the tub, an unforgettable sight. 'Jim's head was on the left, leaning on the edge of the white enamel bath, and the dark water covered his body like a cloth,' she told *Paris Match*. 'A trickle of blood had dried flowing from his nose, drawing a diagonal line to the corner of his mouth.' Agnès was struck by the similarity between the scene and David's portrait of Marat, who was assassinated in the bath.

The fire chief said Jim had been dead for at least an hour when they arrived. There was nothing they could do. They lifted the corpse out of the tub and laid it on a bed, leaving the door ajar so Jim's feet were visible.

A police inspector arrived. Alain Ronay told the officer that the deceased was an American poet named Douglas James Morrison (switching his first names around to conceal his identity). The policeman couldn't understand how a young poet could afford to live in such an expensive apartment. Alain said his friend had a private income.

When they had privacy, Alain asked Pamela what had happened. She readily confessed that she and Jim had been using heroin the night before. She said the first thing she had done when she found Jim dead was flush the evidence down the toilet.

As they spoke, a call came through from Count Jean de Breiteuil. Then he showed up in person. The count spoke to Pamela briefly, then hurried back to L'Hôtel. 'He was scared,' Marianne Faithfull wrote. 'Jim Morrison had OD'd and Jean had provided the smack that killed him.' The couple packed rapidly and left their hotel.

A police doctor arrived. He took a cursory look at Jim's corpse, asked how old the deceased was and whether he had used drugs. As Pamela had no French, Alain Ronay answered. 'He was 27 years old and never took drugs,' he told the doctor. He was trying to protect Pamela, and perhaps Jim's reputation. In his eagerness to portray Jim as drug-free, Alain went so far as to tell the doctor that even in America, where grass was almost as available as tobacco, Jim never touched dope. 'In fact, just yesterday—'

'That's enough!' cried the official, cutting short this cock-and-bull story.

Pamela went to the Arsenal police station where she gave a statement at three forty p.m. She maintained the subterfuge in her statement, saying that her boyfriend was 'a writer with a private income'. She described his recent breathing problems, and talked about Jim taking a late-night bath. She described how he had vomited, then told her he felt better and she should go back to bed. When she awoke, she had found Jim unconscious. She did not mention drugs.

The doctor and police seemed suspicious and not altogether sympathetic, no doubt seeing Pamela as the dissembling junkie she was. But later that day, when she had returned to the apartment, a second doctor arrived. He was friendlier. Dr Max Vassille observed that it was unusual for a young man of 27 to die suddenly of natural causes, but he thought it conceivable that someone who complained of chest pains and had also been drinking heavily in hot weather might suffer a cardiac arrest. This was the conclusion of his report, signed off at six p.m. 'I conclude that the death was caused by cardiac arrest (natural death).' Dr Vassille had given Pamela the death certificate she wanted, though it does not seem to tell us what really happened to Jim Morrison. Pamela had successfully covered up Jim's heroin use and, not insignificantly, her own. No post-mortem was conducted because death was deemed *naturelle*.

Still the police were reluctant to allow Jim's body to be removed from the apartment and Pamela, starting to show signs of being unbalanced, wanted to stay with it. A mortician who resembled Charlie Chaplin arrived. Alain Ronay told him that Pamela intended to sleep with the body. The mortician advised against it. He then packed Jim's corpse with ice and said he would return at intervals with more ice in an attempt to keep the cadaver as fresh as possible until the funeral could be arranged, but he warned that the warm weather was against them.

Jim was kept on ice at the apartment all weekend. Pamela slept near the corpse and, unsurprisingly, became increasingly *distrait*. Alain Ronay talked to her about funeral arrangements. Pamela wanted Jim cremated. Alain explained that burial was customary in France and suggested they try to get Jim into Père Lachaise, the famous necropolis on the east side of Paris. Established in 1804, Père Lachaise was almost full by 1971 with an exclusive cachet due to the fact that many great cultural figures rested there, including the composers Bizet and Chopin, the painters Ingres and Pissarro, and the writers Proust and Wilde, together with many more celebrities. Pamela said it sounded suitable and Alain went to the undertaker's to see if Jim might be admitted.

So far Pamela Courson had made no attempt to inform anybody

in the United States that Jim was dead. She had no intention of telling his estranged parents, and she didn't want to speak to the Doors, though she was anxious about how she was going to pay for the funeral without their help. Meanwhile, rumours of Jim's death began to reach journalists, who contacted Elektra Records for confirmation. The breaking story was impeded because Sunday was Independence Day in the USA, and Monday, 5 July, was also a public holiday. Finally, however, press enquiries reached the Doors' new manager, Bill Siddons, who called Paris to find out what was going on. Pamela told him that Jim was dead. Siddons told the band, who sent him to France by the first available flight. By the time Siddons arrived in Paris on Tuesday, Jim was in his coffin. The funeral was the next morning.

'I picked the gravesite,' says Alain Ronay, who told the undertakers that Jim was an American poet. In a land where writers are revered this made all the difference in getting him admitted to Père Lachaise.

'In that case, you are in luck,' replied the undertaker, offering a plot next to Oscar Wilde. Ronay turned down this prime site in favour of an obscure spot behind some old monuments in a less notable part of the cemetery. 'I made a point, actually, to make the grave almost inaccessible, and succeeded, I thought. So hard to find. And yet look! It didn't do any good.'

Only five people attended Jim Morrison's funeral on Wednesday, 6 July 1971. They were Pamela Courson, Alain Ronay, Bill Siddons, Agnès Varda and a young woman named Robin Wertle, who had being doing secretarial work for Jim. There was no priest. Everything was done as quickly and quietly as possible. Bill Siddons flew back to the USA the next day and the band released a press statement on Friday, explaining that they had kept everything quiet so far 'to avoid all the notoriety and circus-like atmosphere that surrounded the deaths of Janis Joplin and Jimi Hendrix'. *Rolling Stone* put the story on its front page, making the 27 link – between Brian Jones, Jimi Hendrix, Janis Joplin and Jim Morrison – for the first time. Others noted that the letter J kept recurring.

Jim's parents found out that their son was dead when they received a call from a reporter, which was an unfortunate end to an unhappy family story. 'The Doors had him in the ground before they even contacted my parents,' laments Andy Morrison. 'They didn't do a very good job by my parents.'

5

Jim Morrison's death has been the subject of endless debate. This was primarily the fault of Pamela Courson, and those who helped her conceal that she and Jim were heroin-users. Few people now accept that Jim died of natural causes, as the French record states. Andy Morrison points out that the family were unaware of Jim suffering from heart problems, or any significant health problems. It was only years later, when Alain Ronay revealed in *Paris Match* that Pamela had confessed to him that she and Jim had been snorting heroin the night he died, that it became apparent he had probably overdosed or had a heart attack while under the influence of heroin, which amounts to the same thing, losing his grip on life when Pamela left him alone in a hot bath. It is not unusual for heroin-users to die in the bath. There is another example on the 27 Club long-list, that of Kristen Pfaff (see p 306). Jim may have taken the overdose deliberately; he may have been greedy or careless. In any event it is unfortunate that his companion was someone as flaky as Pamela Susan Courson. As with some of the other 27s, notably Jimi Hendrix, the last witness to Jim Morrison's life was an unreliable and dishonest person, who was primarily concerned about herself. The fact that Jim's friends then helped Pamela bury him in what can only be described as furtive circumstances compounded the mystery, giving rise to wild stories about 'what really happened'.

After Jim's death, Pamela returned to Los Angeles where she continued to run her boutique and took to calling herself Pamela Morrison. This was another fantasy. Pamela had always wanted to marry Jim, but he had always refused. All the documents to do with Jim's life and death describe him as unmarried, including his will and death certificate, while Pamela described herself as Jim's girlfriend to the French police. Under the terms of Jim's will, Pamela inherited his estate, but it proved a poisoned chalice, spiked with legal bills and lawsuits. While Pamela fought these battles she received no income, and became an increasingly pathetic figure, dependent on drugs and obsessed with Jim's memory. One night she telephoned Jim's brother to suggest they have a Morrison baby – the baby Jim never gave her. 'This would be late at night when she was all fucked up,' says Andy Morrison. Eventually Pamela came into her inheritance, receiving $150,000 (£94,339) as part-payment of an estate then valued at around $400,000 (£251,572). One of the first things she did was buy a mink coat.

Within a year of getting her money, Pamela died of a heroin overdose at home in Los Angeles, on 25 April 1974. Her death certificate records her as a 'widow', and her overdose as 'accidental', though it is doubtful that either is true. She was 27 when she died. 'I think she seriously wasn't going to live any longer than Jim,' says Mirandi Babitz, who believes her friend took her life so she would die at the same age as Jim. 'She was going to be with him: suicide… I don't know if part of her death [was] guilt.' One of the wilder stories about Jim's death was that Pamela murdered him for his money. Those who knew her find this absurd. Pamela wanted to marry Jim, not murder him. And they were reunited in death when her ashes were interred with his remains at Père Lachaise.

The cult of Jim Morrison grew posthumously, taking off in 1979 when Francis Ford Coppola used 'The End' in the soundtrack for *Apocalypse Now*. Part of the cult of Jim was the coincidence of him dying at the same age as Brian, Jimi and Janis. The 27 link helped reinforce the idea that Jim had been special; that his death was fated; that there was something *weird* going on. The fact that Jim's girlfriend had died at the same age underlined the weirdness of the coincidence. This legend was familiar to everybody with an interest in popular music by 1994 when Kurt Cobain decided to join the club.

Eleven

THE SECRET HOUSE OF DEATH

Then is it sin
To rush into the secret house of death
Ere death dare come to us?
Antony and Cleopatra

1

None of the artists whose lives we have followed thus far left a suicide note. In the absence of clear evidence of intent, their death certificates record verdicts of accidental or natural death. Yet this doesn't tell the whole story. In prolonged abuse of themselves, Jones, Hendrix, Joplin and Morrison evinced a death wish as surely as if they had put a gun to their heads. 'Essentially, people who are heavily abusing substances – I don't care what the substance is, whether it's alcohol, or heroin, or whatever – it's a self-destructive, suicidal act. And when they continue to do that, they frequently end up very successful at it.' This is the view of David Burr, who staged the final intervention in the life of Kurt Cobain, the only one of the Big Six whose death is recorded as suicide.

It is widely recognised, however, that suicide statistics are artificially low. Where there is an element of doubt the authorities tend to ascribe death to accident or misadventure. There is the desire to give the deceased the benefit of the doubt, and to spare the feelings of family members, for suicide carries a stigma. Yet in many cases the

circumstantial evidence of suicide is strong. Of the 27 Club deaths
we have looked at so far, those of Al Wilson of Canned Heat and
Jim Morrison's partner Pamela Courson may well have been suicide,
though both are recorded as accidents.

Other 27 Club deaths that look very much like suicide, but are
not recorded as such, include that of the Russian singer-songwriter
Alexander 'Sasha' Bashlachev, who was obliged to work underground
during the Soviet era, performing his music for friends at private
gatherings and circulating his music on cassette tapes. It was a difficult life, and he suffered the additional problem of writer's block.
Bashlachev became depressed, apparently making several suicide
attempts before plunging from the ninth floor of his Leningrad
apartment building in 1988, aged 27.

After Kurt Cobain, the most notable confirmed suicide on the
long list is Peter Ham of Badfinger, one of the bands the Beatles
signed to their Apple label in the 1960s. Paul McCartney wrote
Badfinger's hit 'Come and Get it', while Ham and his partner Tom
Evans were talented songwriters in their own right, composing
'Without You', which was a smash for Harry Nilsson. Despite their
success Ham and Evans did not receive the royalties they expected
and became embroiled in disputes with management. As is the case
with suicides, Ham reached a point where death seemed to be the
only solution to his problems. He met Tom Evans in a pub on the
evening of 24 April 1975, three days before his 28th birthday, and
told him: 'Don't worry, I know a way out.' Fortified with drink,
Ham went back to his home in Woking, Surrey, wrote a note in
which he expressed his bitterness towards his manager, and hanged
himself in his garage. His girlfriend found his body. In a macabre
coda, Evans hanged himself seven years later.

The curious case of Richey Edwards of the Manic Street Preachers,
whose life we have touched upon, is a mystery that points towards
suicide. The Manic Street Preachers were a band closely associated
with suicide. Their 1989 début single was 'Suicide Alley'. Three years
later they returned to the subject when they released a cover of
'Theme from M*A*S*H', a.k.a. 'Suicide is Painless'. Edwards struggled with problems common to the 27s. He had mental-health issues,

including depression and eating disorders. He drank excessively and, as mentioned, he self-harmed, once cutting his arm with a razor during a discussion with a journalist. Edwards subsequently suffered a nervous breakdown and was admitted to the Priory Clinic, at branches of which Brian Jones and Amy Winehouse were also treated. He went missing in February 1995 after checking out of a London hotel to drive home to Cardiff. His car was found near the Severn Bridge, which is sometimes used for suicide leaps. Although Edwards' body was never found, he was declared 'presumed dead' by a court in 2008, when his family decided the time had come to wind up his estate. He was 27 when last seen alive. It is assumed that he jumped to his death and his body was washed away in the river.

Richey Edwards and Kurt Cobain had much in common. Both were born in 1967, dying within ten months of each other at the same age. Both were post-punk anti-heroes, complex, sensitive young men who attracted a following of similar people who empathised with them as outsiders. Furthermore, Edwards and Cobain flirted with suicide in both word and deed before committing the act.

In his last round of interviews in 1993, while promoting Nirvana's *In Utero* album, Kurt told Everett True of *Melody Maker*: 'I want to kill myself half the time.' In a contemporaneous interview with *Rolling Stone* he blamed his mental-health issues on his stomach pain, five years of which had made him, in his own splendid phrase, 'as schizophrenic as a wet cat that's been beaten'. There was dark humour here, but Kurt appeared to be serious when he said his stomach pain had been so bad that he wanted to kill himself 'every day' and 'came very close many times'. He said he had turned to heroin to dull the stomach pain. He claimed to be off smack now, and was feeling better, due to prescribed medication, an improved diet and that he had something to live for: his daughter Frances, whom he adored. 'I've never been happier in my life,' he told *Rolling Stone*, adding that he was only joking when he'd said he originally wanted to call the new album *I Hate Myself and I Want to Die*. 'Nothing more than a joke.' By his subsequent actions we know that this denial was the darkest joke of all.

Nirvana recorded *In Utero* in Minnesota in February 1993 with producer Steve Albini, who takes a purist view of the punk rock/ grunge subculture, arguing that it is uniquely different from other music genres, being made up of people such as Kurt who did not fit into tidy society. 'I'm not just saying that they were odd people with similar music tastes, I'm saying that these were street people, recent immigrants, petty criminals, *the insane*, the very people who are categorically lonely outsider weirdos. Those people were the people who turned up at punk shows, and the only thing that they had in common was that literally they couldn't get along in the straight world.' When Kurt called Albini to say Nirvana wanted to work with him he sounded wasted, barely coherent. But he was fit and focused at the studio, and he had strong songs, many of them auto-biographical, notably 'Serve the Servants' in which he commented with admirable concision in twenty lines on pop success, his feelings about his father, his parents' divorce and the public's perception of his wife, Courtney Love.

The band cut the album fast, in just two weeks, agreeing with their producer that they'd done good work. Then Steve Albini heard that Geffen Records thought the songs sounded too raw, which was when *In Utero* became as much of a hassle as Amy Winehouse's *Frank*. Albini was disgusted by the experience. 'All the shit they had to deal with, all of the people around them, like every single person that I interacted with that was not actually in the band, was a piece of shit,' he says. 'The three band members in Nirvana I admired, and I take my hat off to them for putting up with the bullshit they had to put up with. All of the other people around them, all of their management, all of their hangers-on, all of the people who were trying to profiteer through them, all the people who were trying to use them as a leg up on their own careers, all the dope-dealers who were exploiting them, all the asshole functionaries in the music busi-ness that were on a power trip by being involved with Nirvana – fuck all of those people one hundred per cent.'

Interestingly, Kurt bowed to record-company pressure, compro-mising on both the sound of *In Utero* – which was remixed to sound more mainstream – and the CD artwork, which was toned down for distribution in supermarkets. The fact that somebody who had always prided himself on his artistic integrity gave in to commercial pressure is open to interpretation. Steve Albini saw Kurt as a sell-out. 'I think that the record company told him what they would put up with, and then he complied. I wasn't involved in any of those decisions, but there's no such thing as a compromise in that situation. If you say, "This is my record," and the record company says, "We're not putting it out like that", that's not a compromise, that's a capitulation.' Others might see a maturing artist who had become pragmatic. Or maybe Kurt didn't care anymore. Having made an effort to stay clean long enough to record the album, he had already returned to heavy drug use. In those circumstances the mixing of *In Utero* was not his top priority.

Kurt and Courtney were renting a house on Lakeside Avenue NE in Seattle, overlooking Lake Washington, a vast body of water on the east side of the city. They had regained custody of their daughter, Frances, though they had help to look after her. Their choice of nanny was curious. They hired Courtney's teenage roadie and fellow drug-user Cali De Witt, who was surprised to get the job. 'Officially, all of a sudden, I'm the nanny. I don't realise what that means until [Frances] is put on my lap to see how she likes me,' he told Everett True, for his book about Nirvana. 'I felt like I needed taking care of, and I've got this baby.'

Kurt overdosed twice at Lakeside Avenue in 1993. The police were called to the property after an incident in May, and Kurt was taken to hospital. The following month Courtney, Kurt's mother, Krist Novoselic and others staged an intervention, during which Kurt was confronted with his drug problem and warned about the consequences of his behaviour if he continued to use heroin. Kurt brushed this intervention aside as he had the previous attempt. It was difficult to threaten him with consequences when he held all the power. In other bands, a musician with a heroin habit might be told he would be sacked unless he cleaned up. If Kurt was fired, Nirvana would cease to exist.

A few days after the failed intervention police were called to a domestic dispute at the Lakeside Avenue house that threatened to turn violent. Kurt and Courtney were arguing about Kurt's drug use and gun collection. Kurt was arrested for assaulting his wife, and officers confiscated hand guns and a semi-automatic rifle. Charges were later dropped. Kurt had become obsessed with guns. He said he bought the weapons for self-protection, which was surely nonsense. In truth, he knew that a bullet in the head was one of the surest ways of killing himself, if and when he made that fatal decision.

Death and violence were suddenly all around. In July 1993, Mia Zapata, singer with the Seattle band the Gits, was raped and murdered on her way home from a Seattle night club. She was 27, becoming the first of three 27 Club deaths in the Seattle music community in the space of eleven months. This is a striking coincidence. In Zapata's case, death was by homicide. The other two would be drug-related, reflecting the prevalence of drugs on the Seattle scene and bearing out one of the most common patterns in this history. Nirvana performed at a show to raise money to investigate Zapata's death.

Kurt's would, of course, be one of those three 27 Club deaths. Like Janis Joplin before him, he was flirting with death on a daily basis, increasingly careless of his life. He overdosed in New York in July while promoting *In Utero*, an incident that could easily have been fatal. He was unhappy with life in general, despite what he told journalists, at loggerheads with his record company and band, and dreading the prospect of touring to promote the new album. 'He said he was kind of getting tired of the contract requirements,' says his uncle, Chuck Fradenburg. 'They had him on some kind of schedule where he had to go from town to town, and he didn't get much sleep … He said he was not getting much rest, and he was getting tired of the pressure.'

Yet Kurt was still capable of good work. *In Utero* is a strong album, and he was still growing as an artist. The band's appearance on *MTV Unplugged* in November 1993 was a triumph. Kurt's performance of Leadbelly's 'Where Did You Sleep Last Night?' is riveting. Yet, like Brian Jones, Kurt was easily overwhelmed with self-doubt and indeed jealousy. He had started to suspect that Courtney was cheating on him. But drugs were by far the biggest problem. He and Courtney went to a rehab facility in Arizona at

Christmas. Kurt was warned that if he didn't quit heroin he would die. But he didn't believe he *could* quit, as he confessed to Uncle Chuck. 'He said [to me], "I know I can't get off. I'm stuck on that." I said, "That's too bad."'

2

The Seattle mansion Kurt and Courtney purchased for $1.4 million (£800,503) in January 1994, and where Kurt killed himself five months later, loomed above Lake Washington Boulevard East, like the house in *Psycho*. The property was nine miles south of their previous rental, four miles east of downtown, in one of the most affluent areas of Seattle, a place of big, beautiful homes with land-scaped gardens and mature trees. Until ten years or so ago Jimi Hendrix's father had worked for local residents, cutting their lawns and clipping their hedges as part of his landscaping business. The house Kurt and Courtney bought was built in 1902 in a commanding position above the lake. Its elevation, Gothic windows and tall chim-neys, gave it the look of a haunted house even before it became stained with Kurt's blood. 'That's probably why they were moving in,' chuckles friend Eric Erlandson.

The Cobains didn't own enough possessions to furnish a 7,000-square-foot mansion. They occupied parts of the house in the manner of squatters, moving in a beat-up sofa, setting up musical equipment in empty rooms, pinning bed sheets over windows where they wanted to sleep, trying to make a demarcation between the parts of the house in which drugs were used and the rooms where little Frances slept, ate, bathed and played. Kurt was proud of his house, which he showed off to family and friends, and he met his neighbours. 'I talked to him a couple of times,' says Dr Jim Pritchett, who lived opposite. He regarded his new neighbour with a profes-sional medical eye while they chatted. 'He was kind of a quiet, sickly guy … Even though he was young, he didn't look healthy.' Despite the phenomenal success of Nirvana, Kurt and Courtney didn't buy their house outright. It was purchased on a mortgage and Kurt soon became anxious that he might lose the property. This anxiety – not entirely rational – grew into a major concern.

There was another cause of worry in January when Kurt's grandmother, Iris Cobain, fell ill. Kurt visited her in hospital, with an armful of orchids. It is a curious coincidence that both Kurt and Amy Winehouse had such a close relationship with their paternal grandmothers, Grandma being the family member whose advice carried most weight with them. During this hospital visit Don Cobain telephoned to speak to his mother and Iris insisted that Kurt have a few words with his father. '[Iris] called Kurt over and said, "Here, now you take this. Now you get together with your dad." And they talked real friendly, at least to listen to Kurt,' recalls Leland Cobain. 'Kurt said he was going to get in touch with his dad, and they was gonna sort it all out and get friends again.' If Kurt had lived perhaps he and his father would have been reconciled. In his latter interviews Kurt showed a more mature attitude towards his parents. But, as it turned out, there wasn't time for a *rapprochement*.

Nirvana went into the studio again that month. One important new song emerged, 'You Know You're Right', in which Kurt wailed about his pain and sang with colossal irony that life had 'never been so swell'. This powerful song shows Kurt was still filled with the rage that had defined his career. But his recording career was now over. 'You Know You're Right' was his swansong.

A couple of days later Kurt flew to Europe with Nirvana. He didn't want to tour. He felt depressed and unwell and would have cancelled if the financial implications hadn't been onerous. At a photo call in Paris, he posed with a gun to his head, making a joke of an act he was contemplating for real. He turned 27 on 20 February 1994, on a day of travel between gigs, shortly after which came his second wedding anniversary. Although Krist Novoselic and Dave Grohl had their partners on tour with them, Courtney Love hadn't shown up yet and Kurt's suspicion and jealousy grew.

When the tour reached Germany, Kurt rowed with Courtney on the phone, after which he reportedly discussed the possibility of divorce with his lawyer. When Nirvana played Munich on 1 March they ended the show with 'Heart-Shaped Box', a song Kurt had written about Courtney. The next two dates were cancelled, allowing an overwrought and strung-out Kurt to take a break from the tour.

He flew to Rome and checked into the luxurious Excelsior Hotel where he planned a romantic reunion with Courtney. She was flying in with Frances from London, having done promotional work for the new Hole album. Kurt bought flowers and champagne for the hotel suite, and collected special gifts for his wife, including a stone he had stolen from the Colosseum because Courtney was interested in Roman history.

Kurt wanted to make love with Courtney when she arrived at the Excelsior, but she was tired and fell asleep. She woke in the night to find Kurt unconscious on the floor of their room having taken an overdose of Rohypnol. He had swallowed sixty tablets and left a suicide note in which he accused his wife of not loving him anymore, adding that he would rather die than go through a divorce like his parents. He was taken to hospital to have his stomach pumped, and was in a coma for several hours. The doctors couldn't say what state he would be in if and when he regained consciousness.

An overdose of prescription medication is a popular but uncertain suicide method. It is difficult to obtain lethal drugs. It is equally difficult for the layman to judge how many tablets constitute a lethal dose, which is affected by many factors including the potency of the drug (itself affected by its age and the conditions in which it has been stored), body size, personal tolerance, and whether or not one has been drinking or using other substances. People who toss back a random handful of pills hoping, in the words of Keats, to 'cease upon the midnight with no pain' are often disappointed. The body can reject the medicine, by vomiting. Even if the would-be suicide manages to keep the drug down, death is not necessarily quick, painless or sure. There may be violent and prolonged convulsions. Most alarming of all, perhaps, is when the victim is revived only to be left with brain or liver damage.

With many people who take an overdose, there is also a sense that they are not entirely serious. An overdose of pills can be a suicidal gesture, a dangerous way of seeking attention, but a gesture nonetheless. While Kurt had taken a large overdose of a fairly powerful sedative, he had done so in the hotel room in which his wife was sleeping, therefore hedging his bets that Courtney would wake up, find him and call for help, which was what happened.

The Rome suicide attempt was covered up as an accidental over-dose. Nirvana's European tour was cancelled. When Kurt felt well enough, he and Courtney flew home to Seattle.

3

The Emerald City was coming into bloom when the Cobains returned in March 1994, the cherry trees in blossom, the daffodils and blue-bells flowering along Lake Washington Boulevard. Yet spring does not bring joy to everybody. It is in springtime, when the world is bursting into new life, that suicide rates peak.

Kurt wasn't chastened by his experience in Rome. Rather, he remained bent on self-destruction, returning to his heroin habit with a vengeance and soon threatening suicide again. He and Courtney argued and, again, the police were called to intervene in their disputes. On one occasion Kurt locked himself in a room with a revolver, threatening to shoot himself. Again the police took away his guns. When Kurt couldn't stand the atmosphere at home, he checked into a motel on Aurora Avenue North, a soulless dual carriageway leading out of Seattle, lined with pawn-brokers, sex shops, car rentals and fast-food outlets. As the cars hissed by his window, Kurt shot up in peace.

There was now acute concern among Kurt's associates that he would do away with himself, one way or another, which would be sad, but it would also be the end of Nirvana, which would be bad for busi-ness. Another intervention was planned, this time a determined effort to make Kurt see sense. Danny Goldberg contacted David Burr, an older man who drew on his own experiences of substance abuse to persuade leading business figures, sports stars and entertainers to do as he had done and get clean. One of Burr's recent clients had been the Grateful Dead, whose members had called him in when they became concerned that their leader, Jerry Garcia, was destroying himself with drugs. The Dead were terrified that they would lose Garcia as they had lost Pigpen McKernan in 1973, and this time it might mean the end of the band. This is what happened in 1995, when Garcia died in rehab of a heart attack, aged 53.

Danny Goldberg called David Burr at home in New York on the evening of 24 March 1994. Burr flew into Seattle the following morning to meet Kurt's manager, Krist Novoselic and other key people in Kurt's life at a downtown hotel. The interventionist asked for a history of Kurt's life, and a timeline of his substance abuse. In his experience there was usually a familiar narrative. Famous people who became addicted to drink or drugs had often suffered a trauma in early life, which Kurt had, in common with the other principal 27s. This typically created low self-esteem, which didn't end with success. Rather, the artist tended to believe, deep down, that they were unworthy of success. 'It's almost as if they think, "Well, I've got the world fooled …" They don't believe it themselves.' The wealth that came with fame was destabilising, especially when it arrived suddenly. 'One day they were out there with $7.93 in their pocket, and the next day [they are] worth zillions, unheard of amounts. They don't know how to act, they don't know what to do. There's total chaos in their life, and they don't trust anybody.'

Drugs were a comfort. To remind ourselves of the words of Big Brother guitarist Sam Andrew, smack makes one feel that 'everything is beautiful and kind of warm and dreamy'. The user comes to believe they cannot function without getting high. This is common to creative people who drink or use drugs habitually. Singer-songwriters typically argue that they can't write or perform straight. That was part of Amy Winehouse's problem. In fact, users will seize on almost any excuse to get high. In Kurt's case, he blamed his stomach ache. David Burr considered this to be a bullshit excuse. Kurt was killing himself with drugs and his friends had to confront him with that fact, and the consequences. The only real leverage they had was his daughter. Kurt didn't want the authorities to take Frances away. But he had to realise that this was a possibility if he didn't clean up. 'That really was the most powerful consequence, as far as he was concerned.' As Burr discussed all of this with Goldberg and Novoselic – 'Krist was really pissed off [with Kurt]' – Courtney kept ringing to ask when they were coming over to the house. Things were getting out of hand.

So, the intervention party drove out to 171 Lake Washington Boulevard East, Kurt's haunted house by the lake. They found the place in chaos. 'It was a mad house. There probably were 25 people around there, most of whom were not *compos mentis*. And so the first thing I had to do was get rid of them,' says David Burr. '*Let's kick them out!*' Once the hangers-on had departed Danny Goldberg chased Kurt around the property to get him to sit down and talk to Burr, but Kurt was too stoned to do that. 'You can't have a rational conversation with an irrational person,' says Burr. So he waited for Kurt to come down from his high. As he did so, he looked around the house. 'Everything was a mess. Furniture was torn and soiled, and burned. Nothing had been cleaned. It was just horrible.'

When he was finally able to talk to Kurt, David Burr found the musician to be 'a kindly soul' but so far down the path of addiction he felt it would be a miracle if they could save him. Burr decided that Courtney – who had her own issues – was an aggravating problem. 'Her influence on him was very, very negative. The further away she was from him the better his chances.' So she flew to Los Angeles, checking into the Peninsula Hotel to detox. Tentative arrangements were made for Kurt to go into a nearby rehab facility in LA. It wasn't the place David Burr recommended, but it was as much as Kurt would agree to, having been there once before. Danny Goldberg also talked with Kurt during the intervention, trying to get him to see his problems in perspective. 'I remember saying to him, "Man, if you just make it to thirty things are gonna feel different." I do think there is something about the twenties that makes people more vulnerable.'

Everybody then left the house, save Kurt and the nanny, Cali De Witt. Kurt proceeded to go on a three-day heroin binge at the end of which he grudgingly agreed to go into rehab. On Tuesday, 29 March, Krist Novoselic drove his friend to Sea-Tac airport to catch a flight to LA. But Kurt really didn't want to go. They argued during the journey and, when they got to Sea-Tac, Kurt screamed abuse at

Krist and ran away. The following day Kurt went shopping in Seattle and bought a shotgun. He was clearly preparing for the end. But he wasn't quite ready. That evening he flew to Los Angeles where he checked into Exodus, a rehabilitation centre attached to Marina del Rey Hospital, which specialised in celebrity clients.

The following day, Thursday, 31 March, Kurt was interviewed by Exodus counsellor Nial Stimson, who recalls that Kurt was pleasant but in denial about the scale of his problem. 'He didn't see his heroin addiction as anything other than medicating his stomach problems,' says Stimson. 'And he was very opposed to the Twelve Steps organised rehab sort of thing. [He told me] "I don't want to go to any of the celebrity AA meetings, I don't want any of that…"' In this respect Kurt was the same as Amy Winehouse.

Stimson asked Kurt about Rome, knowing that he had tried to take his life. Kurt 'minimalised' what had happened at the Excelsior Hotel, saying, 'I just had a few too many of these pills, you know, and I went into a coma, and then I was OK.'

'Don't you realise you almost died?'

'Well, yeah, of course,' Kurt snapped. He denied that he was suicidal now.

Stimson suspected that Kurt was going through the motions of rehab to placate his wife, band members and business associates, while feeling under pressure to get back to work. 'Instead of the record company, and all his friends, saying, "We want him to get better, take as much time as you need", it was like, "You need to get better because we've got things we need you to do." And it sounded to me that he really hated having to go out on these tours. It was kind of over.' There are echoes here of other 27s.

Kurt was also agitated about a recent lawsuit brought against him by the director of a Nirvana video. 'He said, "If I lose this [case] I'm going to lose my house."' Together with losing custody of his daughter, this seemed to be his primary concern at the end of his life. 'I think he felt he was in sort of a trapped situation,' says Stimson, who suggested to Kurt that he take a break from his career, go away for a year, and reassess what he wanted to do. He tried to make Kurt understand that it was very unlikely he would lose his house. He was a rich man. But Kurt couldn't see it. He had developed the tunnel vision that suicides often have when they focus only on their problems.

Later in the day a child minder brought Frances to Exodus to see her father. Kurt saw his daughter again the next day, and spoke to Courtney on the telephone. 'No matter what happens, I want you to know that you made a really good album,' he told his wife. When Courtney asked what he meant by this, he told her he loved her and hung up. In retrospect it seems that Kurt had decided what he was going to do and was making his farewells on the first day of April, which T. S. Eliot called 'the cruellest month', for while it brings new life, spring stirs memory and emotion in the melancholy mind.

That evening Kurt climbed over the wall at the back of the Exodus wing, went to LAX and caught a plane to Seattle, arriving home in the early hours of Saturday, 2 April.

Cali De Witt and a girlfriend were at the house on Lake Washington Boulevard when Kurt arrived home. They spoke briefly. Then Kurt vanished. Cali came and went from the house over the next few days, but he didn't see Kurt again. It was a big house and he couldn't be sure whether Kurt was there or not. It seems that Kurt spent some of his time at the house and some of it doing drugs in a motel on Aurora Avenue. He also went shopping for shotgun shells. Now he had the gun and the ammunition. It was just a matter of choosing the time and place.

Courtney cancelled Kurt's credit cards to slow him down and stop him buying drugs. Kurt discovered what she had done when he tried to use them in a Seattle restaurant on Sunday. Meanwhile Courtney hired a private investigator named Tom Grant to find her husband.

On Monday, 4 April, Wendy O'Connor (or Courtney posing as Wendy) reported Kurt as a missing person, telling the Seattle police he had a gun and might be suicidal. Cali De Witt, Eric Erlandson and Tom Grant all visited the mansion on Lake Washington Boulevard looking for Kurt, calling his name in the spooky, empty rooms. The old house creaked in reply, giving the impression that Kurt might be hiding somewhere. Leaving the property one day, one of Cali's friends thought she glimpsed a pale face watching them from an attic window. Was it Kurt, or was it Death?

Nobody thought to check the garage at the back of the property where Kurt parked his car. Above it there was an attic room with glass roof panels and French windows at the gable ends. The room was small and peaceful, with views over Lake Washington. It was here that Kurt came at last with his shotgun, heroin works and suicide note.

The morality of suicide has exercised writers, philosophers and theologians through history, as it had occupied Kurt's mind, becoming his final obsession. To be or not to be, the fundamental question asked by Hamlet, was the dilemma Kurt faced. A couple of years previously a doctor had told Kurt that he must decide, like Hamlet, whether he wanted to live or die, and Kurt had pondered the analogy, referring to it in his Rome suicide note. 'Dr Baker [said] that, like Hamlet, I have to choose between life and death,' he wrote. 'I'm choosing death.' Several Shakespearean characters wrestle with suicide and, unlike Hamlet, some decide that they do not want to be, including the lovers Romeo and Juliet, and Antony and Cleopatra. In the final act of that second tragedy, after Mark Antony has been defeated and taken his life, the Queen of Egypt ponders whether she should follow his example or allow herself to be humiliated by victorious Caesar. 'Then is it sin/ To rush into the secret house of death/ Ere death dare come to us?' Cleopatra asks her maids, elegantly expressing the fundamental question most potential suicides wrestle with, for suicide seems sinful to most people. Cleopatra decided it was not a sin and clutched an asp to her breast.

In general, the people of the ancient world took a more liberal view of suicide than later civilisations. Seneca the Younger argued that suicide can be a noble end: for a sick old man, say, who does not wish to burden his family; and death is never to be feared because it is inevitable. Many leading figures of the ancient world shared his view and, like Seneca, committed suicide when their options narrowed. Antony, Boadicea, Brutus, Cleopatra, Hannibal, Socrates, Terence and Zeno are among those who chose suicide. Enlightenment philosophers, including David Hume, were influenced by the thinkers of antiquity, Hume arguing that a suicide 'bravely overcomes all the natural terrors of death [to escape] a hated life'. As we have seen, in the nineteenth century Nietzsche had Zarathustra declare that man must learn to 'die at the right time'.

Kurt Cobain's death would not be at the right time. He was a young man with a future he could not foretell and, crucially, he was father to a child not yet two years old, a little girl he said he adored. Seneca would not have approved of Kurt abandoning his wife and child. Friends feel the same. 'The thing that boggles the mind is that that wasn't enough,' comments Eric Erlandson. 'If that's not enough, what is?' Research shows that the children of suicides are more likely to kill themselves in adulthood, so Kurt's action was actually putting Frances in jeopardy. Of course, he would also be condemning his family, band mates, managers and friends to years of angst about what they might have done differently. He may have wanted to punish some of those people. But did he want to stain his daughter's life?

The disquiet people express when suicide is discussed is often related to religious beliefs. Most religions denounce suicide, including Christian leaders. Although the commandments given to Moses included 'Thou shalt not kill', nothing was said specifically about suicide, and it is not condemned anywhere in the Old or New Testament. Self-murder has nevertheless been treated as a crime in many Christian countries, the failed suicide facing the prospect of prison, the successful suicide denied burial rites, or having their property confiscated. Kurt had an interest in Buddhism, where more tolerance is shown. Some Buddhist texts can be read as an exoneration of suicide, suggesting that it might be a shortcut to nirvana. Others seem to warn against suicide as a cause of further suffering. As with most religions, the literature is ambiguous.

At some point Kurt was too weary to think further. He had reached his climacteric, and could not go on. 'On the whole, we shall find that, as soon as a point is reached where the terrors of life outweigh those of death, man puts an end to his life,' wrote Schopenhauer. Kurt had reached the *moment critique*, beyond philosophy and rational argument, for many would say that it is madness for a young man rich in advantages to take his life. And, in a sense, Kurt was mad. 'Addiction is part of mental illness, and he was definitely suffering some kind of mental illness,' says his counsellor, Nial Stimson. Kurt was now determined. He had made an attempt in Rome. This time there would be no mistake.

Kurt's suicide note is our best insight into his state of mind at the end, though suicide notes can be misleading. The writer wants to leave a statement and, often, make excuses for himself, rather than face problems that defeated him in life. Kurt addressed his note to Boddah, his imaginary childhood friend, writing in a wavering hand, with eccentric spelling and punctuation, perhaps showing the effects of drug use.

The first part of the note was verbose and solipsistic. 'Speaking from the tongue of an experienced simpleton who obviously would rather be an emasculated infantile complainee,' he began. 'This note should be pretty easy to understand ... I haven't felt the excitement of listening to as well as creating music along with reading and writing for too many years now. I feel guilty beyond words about these things.' He went on to compare his disinterest to the joy that a rock star like Freddie Mercury seemed to derive from performance. 'The fact is, I can't fool you,' he wrote in a note that was evidently meant for his public as well as his family. 'The worst crime I can think of would be to rip people off by faking it and pretending as if I'm having 100% fun.' He wrote that he 'must be one of those narcissists who only appreciate things when they're gone. I'm too sensitive. I need to be slightly numb in order to regain the enthusiasm I once had as a child ... There's good in all of us and I think I simply love* people too much. So much that it makes me feel too fucking sad.'

He mocked himself as a 'sensitive, unappreciated Pisces', before turning to his family.

---

* The writers of suicide notes often invoke love, in contrast to the violence and anger involved in the action they take, as if to plead that they were essentially good and pure of heart. Notice how frequently Kurt uses the word 'love' in his note.

I have a goddess of a wife who sweats ambition and empathy,
and a daughter who reminds me too much of what I used to be.
Full of love and joy, kissing every person she meets because
everyone is good and will do her no harm. And that terrifies me
to the point to where I can barely function. I can't stand the
thought of Frances becoming the miserable self destructive death
rocker that I've become. I have it good, very good, and I'm
grateful, but since the age of seven I've become hateful towards
all humans in general. Only because it seems so easy for people
to get along and have empathy. Empathy! Only because I love
and feel sorry for people too much I guess.

Thank you all from the pit of my burning nauseous stomach
for your letters and concern during the past years. I'm too much
of an erratic, moody, baby! I don't have the passion anymore and
so remember – it's better to burn out than to fade away.
peace love Empathy Kurt Cobain
Frances and Courtney, I'll be at your altar.
Please keep going Courtney.
For Frances
For her life which will be so much happier
Without me ... I LOVE YOU I LOVE YOU!

The final lines were written in large, wild letters, as if added at
the last minute, maybe after he had taken a massive overdose of
heroin. He didn't have time to hang around, though. In the minute
and a half before he passed out, he put the shotgun in his mouth
and pulled the trigger to make sure.

4

Kurt Cobain's body was discovered by an electrician installing security lights at the mansion on Friday, 8 April 1994. Kurt had been
dead for three or even four days; nobody knows for sure. The date
on his death certificate is 5 April.

Kurt's death was a shock, but not necessarily a surprise to those who knew him. Still, friends asked themselves if they could have done anything to avoid this outcome. Some of those involved in the recent intervention decided that it had been a mistake – 'a disaster … a huge mess', in the opinion of Eric Erlandson. Danny Goldberg, who organised the intervention, regrets it. 'I always torture myself. Could I have said something differently? Could I have done something differently? … Obviously, if I could do it again I would try something different, since what we did ended up with him dead a week later … I made a decision to be a very strong proponent of going to rehab, and stop taking drugs, to be the so-called grown-up, because I really was persuaded that, without that, any other thing he could do would be subsumed by this issue. If I could do it over again, what I would try is, "Look, man, why don't you come and stay with me for the weekend, just to get out of the house?" Maybe that would have put him in a different environment and a different head space … That would have been the other way to go. But to do that would have been against the dogma of the intervention, and that was a dogma I believed in, because so many people I know had been helped by that.'

The interventionist David Burr says the softly-softly approach Goldberg suggests would not have worked. 'Frankly, he [Goldberg] should have done that about three years before.' Personally, Burr was not surprised that Kurt killed himself.

Kurt's counsellor at Exodus remembered how worried the musician had been about losing his home in a lawsuit. 'Suicidal people tend to want to make a statement,' says Nial Stimson. 'I just kind of felt he killed himself in his house [as if to say], "You're not going to take my house, no matter what …"' Stimson also reflected on the fact that Kurt downplayed his heroin problem at Exodus. 'Who knows what went through his mind when he left? But certainly the first thing he did was score drugs. Maybe he got that shame and guilt. *No, I'm not a drug addict. But then why is [it that] the first thing I went and did is got heroin? Maybe I am a drug addict.* And all this mental-illness stuff starts. *I'm no good. I'm no good to anybody.* It's all part of the mental disease, the self-loathing.'

Chuck Fradenburg blamed heroin. 'I attribute his suicide directly to the use of heroin. He knew he couldn't get off. He didn't like that dependency.' But Kurt's heroin addiction, as with drinking and drug-taking in the other 27s, was a symptom rather than a cause, something he did to cope with life rather than his root problem. As with the others, that root problem seems to lie in childhood.

As we have seen, Kurt Cobain's mother coined the term '27 Club' in a doorstep interview as news of her son's death broke. The coincidence of a series of stars dying at that age was referenced heavily in coverage of the story as journalists tried to make sense of something that, to those with a casual knowledge of Kurt's history, seemed nonsensical.

Nirvana fans gathered in their thousands near the Space Needle at the Seattle Center on Sunday, 10 April, for a public memorial. The Reverend Stephen Towles said a few words and Courtney Love addressed the crowd via a pre-recorded audio message made with her husband's suicide note to hand. Like David Burr, Courtney wasn't surprised that Kurt had killed himself. 'I mean, it was gonna happen. But it could have happened when he was forty.' She nevertheless sounded distraught as she read from and commented on his strangely impersonal suicide note – 'it's more like a letter to the fuckin' editor' – telling Kurt with anger and fondness that he was 'such an asshole' and ordering the crowd to repeat the word after her. They did so in unison.

'ASSHOLE!'

Courtney went on to tell the audience, with her characteristic vulgarity and common sense, that they should remember his note was bullshit. If Kurt didn't want to be a rock star, he could have stopped. 'Just tell him he's a fucker, OK? Just say, "Fucker, you're a fucker …" [crying] And that you love him.'

The public memorial was organised partly to divert the crowd from a private service held almost simultaneously on the other side of Aurora Avenue at the Unity Church of Truth at which Stephen Towles also officiated. It was an unusual ceremony. Kurt had already been cremated, so there was no body, and some of the mourners brought alcohol to the church and had a drink beforehand. Instead of flowers, two small trees were carried into the sanctuary and photographs of Kurt as a child were distributed.

Courtney had chosen the Unity Church because it embraced all faiths, including Buddhism. 'All are welcomed,' is the church motto. Indeed, Towles and his co-minister Karen Lindvig were open to all sorts of ideas, including astrology. One of the more eccentric theories to have emerged in explanation of the 27 Club is that the entertainers were destroyed by the Saturn Return. This is the idea that the celestial movement of Saturn causes upheavals in human lives, the first occurring in our late twenties, sometimes with disastrous consequences. 'I've seen it over and over and over,' says Karen Lindvig, who believes the Saturn Return can be a positive force for change. '[But] if you are on the wrong path, you can get knocked off [course].' However, when one plots Kurt's Saturn Return from his date of birth the astrology shows that he, in common with all the main 27s, died *before* his Saturn Return, which in his case fell in 1996. And scientists say that astrology is bunk.

Copycat suicides are a real phenomenon, however, and there was a spate after Kurt's death, starting with that of a 28-year-old man who attended the Seattle Center memorial. He went home and shot himself. Over the next two years sixty suicides were linked to Kurt's. In such cases it seems that people who already have trouble in their lives associate so strongly with a celebrity that they want to emulate their death. It is a sort of madness.

One of the mourners at Kurt's memorial was Kristen Pfaff, a member of Courtney Love's band, Hole, and a former girlfriend of fellow member Eric Erlandson. Two months after Kurt's memorial, Pfaff died of a heroin overdose in the bath at her Seattle apartment, just like Jim Morrison. She was also 27, the third member of the Seattle music community to die at that age within a year. Although Eric and Kristen had broken up, they had remained friends, and in retrospect Erlandson says he wishes he had done more to help her deal with her drug problem, as he wishes he had taken a more active stance with Kurt. 'I should have been more aware what was happening with these people, and been more active. Now, if somebody starts talking that way to me, and they're drinking or having some substance problem, I [get] in their face. I'm not passive, you know. I was passive then …' he says, from the perspective of his forties, looking back on two friends who died before they had had time to mature. 'That's the part that I really regret, because that's not the right solution, and that's what everybody did. Everyone got [complacent].'

It would be difficult to find a clearer case of suicide than Kurt Cobain. He talked about suicide obsessively. He threatened suicide. He made an attempt. And when he determined to try again he wrote a note and chose a method that was unambiguous and sure. Furthermore, friends saw it coming. Kurt 'reeked of suicide', according to producer Jack Endino. Yet, as with so many 27s, there are those who refuse to believe the plain facts, with a number of theorists arguing that Kurt was murdered, as others argue of Brian Jones.

The chief theorist is Tom Grant, the private detective Courtney Love hired to find her husband. Grant failed in that task. When he visited the Lake Washington house he did not look in the room above the garage, where he would have found Kurt dead. Grant later became vociferous in his claim that Kurt hadn't killed himself, that this was a story fabricated to cover up a murder conspiracy, at the heart of which was Courtney, who had seemingly ordered her husband's assassination for fear he would divorce her and deprive her of his fortune. Grant's theory was based on discrepancies and anomalies he identified in the case: principally that someone apparently tried to use Kurt's credit card after he had died; the lack of legible fingerprints on the shotgun; and the contention that Kurt could not have operated his gun after having taken such a large overdose. Grant also interpreted the letter found in Kurt's pocket as having been addressed to fans, explaining why he was quitting the music business, rather than as a suicide note. There are satisfactory replies to all these points. Keeping flaky company as Kurt did, it would not be surprising if somebody had got hold of his credit-card details and tried to use them fraudulently after he had died; finger-prints are not always clear; if Kurt acted swiftly he would have had time to pull the trigger after shooting up; and the suicide note is self-evidently that. Yet theorists cling to the thinnest reeds.

Grant published his theories online, and aired them in interviews, including the 2002 documentary *Kurt & Courtney*, and an episode of the NBC show *Dateline*, broadcast to coincide with the tenth anniversary of Kurt's death. His theories also informed a book by two journalists titled *Who Killed Kurt Cobain?* Courtney's estranged father Hank Harrison agrees with the conspiracists, and implies that his daughter may have been involved in 'the assassination of Kurt Cobain', though he doesn't know for sure. 'She is a psychopath. She has a sociopathic personality like I do,' he told NBC in 2004, a wild statement he says he stands by. 'I don't know who killed him. I know who benefited from his death – my daughter being one.'

Kurt's grandfather is another conspiracist. 'I believe that Kurt was murdered; he didn't commit suicide,' Leland Cobain said, in an interview for this book at his trailer home in Washington state, where he lives surrounded by pictures and other reminders of his famous grandson. ('Kurt was here,' reads a sticker in the window.) Why does he believe Kurt was murdered?

'Shit, there's so many things. Like the shotgun was still on his chest, and there was no fingerprints on the shotgun whatsoever, not even on the bullet that killed him ...There was no fingerprints on it. I think they did find one fingerprint, but it was so smeared they couldn't tell what it was, and just all kinds of crap that way. And Courtney knew all of 'em – Courtney knew the detectives who were in charge, and she also knew the coroner. I couldn't figure out how in the hell they'd cremate him so fast. Usually damn near a week or so passes before they cremate 'em ... It was done [fast]. He was cremated just a couple of days afterwards, so somebody else couldn't come in and do an autopsy on him.'

'Who do you think killed him?'

'I don't know. I figure it was probably one of his best friends ...'

'And why?'

'For money, from Courtney. [Kurt] was going to file for divorce ... They had a prenuptial agreement. What was his, when they got married, was his. What was hers was hers. [But] if he died first she got all of his stuff. And by rights it should have gone to Frances.'

Courtney Love has always denied these allegations, which seem to be motivated by animosity rather than reason, revealing how dysfunctional the family is – father denouncing daughter, grandfather calling his grandson's widow a bitch – rather than providing evidence of a murder conspiracy. Indeed, there is no evidence that Courtney was involved in any such thing.

The answer to the question posed by the authors of *Who Killed Kurt Cobain?* is simple: Kurt Cobain killed himself. He did so with sudden, self-inflicted violence, leaving written evidence of his state of mind, factors that are missing from the other five main 27 Club deaths. But the downward trajectory of all these lives was remarkably similar.

Twelve

ONE LITTLE DRINK, THEN ANOTHER

Hasten to be drunk, the business of the day.
Dryden

1

After her spectral appearance at the Berkeley Square Ball in 2008, Amy Winehouse's friends feared for her life. Her condition worsened over the next couple of months. She went in and out of hospital, like a cuckoo, and when she wasn't in hospital she was often in the pub, not necessarily just to drink. 'You were talking to her and her eyes were all over the place,' says Sarah Hurley, landlady of the Good Mixer in Camden Town. 'And there was this geezer she'd come in with sometimes you *knew* was a dealer ... He was a scumbag just sitting there, like a *leech*, sucking all the life out of her, whilst taking her money.' Publican friends hoped that Amy would respect them enough not to score and get high on their premises, but she was caught doing drugs in the toilet of one Camden pub (not the Mixer). Still, she was forgiven. 'Because she was fun!' says Sarah Hurley.

The party continued after hours at Amy's townhouse in Prowse Place. 'I stepped into that madness,' says friend and publican Doug Charles-Ridler, landlord of the Hawley Arms. 'I used to go round the house, and used to go to the parties.' At some point in the night he would have to leave, along with others who had jobs in the morning. 'Whenever we left, we always left parties that were in full swing, then come home and get to sleep and then work, when I know [Amy and other friends] would just party all night, and then they would party all day, and then all night. And when you're getting to that [stage], where you're constantly either drinking to get pissed, or drinking coffee to stay awake, then you start searching for other things, don't you?'

Amy also liked having people around; she had a horror of being alone. If she found herself home alone she would reach out to friends in any way she could, becoming an early and frequent user of Skype, dialling up girlfriends online, people she had been to school with, or worked with years before, anybody to chat to. She sometimes sounded desperate, even paranoid, during these communications. 'Many times she was really scared, scared of all the people outside her house,' says her producer friend Stefan Skarbek, referring to the *paparazzi* who staked out Amy's home. 'She thought there were ghosts [in the house]. All sorts of things. I felt like I talked her off the ledge a couple of times, not off the ledge literally, but she was crying out for somebody ... In hindsight she probably was very, very tortured.'

When she was in the mood Amy would banter with the *paparazzi* who waited in the cobbled lane outside her house – young self-employed photographers hoping for a picture of crazy Amy to sell to the tabloids. Amy would joke with them, teasing them and sending them on errands to the shops, sometimes posing for pictures, even creating photo opportunities, such as the night when she came to the door dressed as a charlady. But the relationship was not always amicable. The *paparazzi* could appear aggressive and Amy could lose her temper. 'They are not good people. There's something odd about [them],' says neighbour Bryan Johnson, who lived next door to Amy. 'I hate to stereotype the whole profession, [but] they were scary ... They'd get right in her face, and they were really intimidating men. She was a small person. They would rush her in a taxi. It was scary [for her]. It would be terrifying, actually: ten big grown men with cameras.'

One afternoon in November 2008 Amy emerged from her house

'I am Death.' Death was memorably portrayed by Bengt Ekerot in *The Seventh Seal*.

By 1968 Brian Jones's debauched life had made him a mental and physical wreck, with the face of a much older man. He is seen here outside court, with Keith Richards and Mick Jagger.

Brian Jones drowned in his swimming pool in July 1969. This picture was taken the following day.

Brian Jones' funeral in Cheltenham was a major media event and a personal tragedy for his parents, who are in the middle of the picture.

Jimi Hendrix took a nap *en route* to his final concert in Germany, September 1970. The big sleep was two weeks away.

On tour with her Kozmic Blues Band in 1969, Janis Joplin was drinking and using heroin.

By 1969 Jim Morrison was a bearded and bloated alcoholic. He is seen here with his girlfriend, Pamela Courson. Both would die at 27.

Jim Morrison and Pamela Courson are pictured at a café in France five days before Jim died.

Kurt Cobain breaks down and weeps offstage, Seattle, 1990.

Kurt Cobain and Courtney Love are seen here with their daughter, Frances. Fatherhood was not enough to save him.

On tour in Europe in 1994, Kurt Cobain posed with a gun to his head, making a joke of an act he was soon to carry out for real.

Kurt Cobain committed suicide in the room above the garage (left of picture) at his Seattle mansion, April 1994

Amy Winehouse started dating filmmaker Reg Traviss in the spring of 2010. He was her last boyfriend.

Amy Winehouse's final concert, in Belgrade, 18 June 2011, was a disaster. Apparently drunk, she was unable to sing and was clearly distressed.

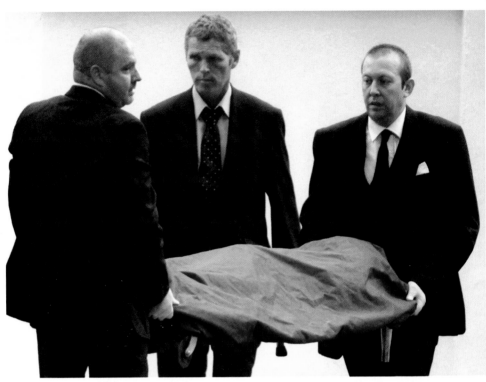

Two undertakers, watched by a police officer, removed Amy Winehouse's body from her home, 23 July 2011.

Two days after Amy died, her family came to look at the flowers left outside her house in Camden Square, which stands directly behind Mitch Winehouse. The windows are open in the room in which Amy died.

in a rage and attacked the photographers. 'Who's first? Who wants some?' she yelled, as she beat the men with her fists. This incident coincided with a development in the ongoing melodrama of Amy and Blake Fielder-Civil. Despite the initial intensity of her love for Blake, the couple's marriage had crumbled during his imprisonment for GBH and perverting the course of justice, with Amy seeing other men, and Blake talking about getting a divorce. When he was released briefly from prison to a private rehabilitation clinic in November, there was a row about whether Amy would pay his rehab bill, which, with the prospect of divorce, pushed her over the edge. The result was that she lashed out at the *paparazzi*.

Despite such problems it was at this time in her life that Amy found the resolve to quit hard drugs, starting this difficult process by checking into the London Clinic in November 2008. Although there were relapses in the months ahead, she ultimately succeeded in getting clean of heroin and crack cocaine, which was a considerable achievement. Unfortunately, like many addicts, she did so by substituting alcohol for drugs. The story of the last two and a half years of Amy's life is that of a woman battling alcoholism, to put the matter euphemistically, though it is more realistic to imagine a raging drunkard, a woman who gulped neat vodka until she was insensible. There were moments of self-realisation and disgust, when Amy stopped drinking briefly. But she always went back to the bottle.

Two weeks before Christmas Amy gathered together friends and minders and caught a flight to St Lucia where she spent the next few months on a drunken sunshine vacation. Family members and her *protégée* Dionne Bromfield joined her for Christmas at a resort hotel where Amy met a young actor with whom she dallied and was photographed. When Blake saw the pictures in the British newspapers, in his prison cell, he filed for divorce. Amy drank more than ever at her hotel. Fellow guests complained to the management, and the British tabloids published pictures of Amy crawling about the hotel restaurant on her hands and knees, giving their readers to understand that she was begging guests for drinks after bar staff refused to serve her.

For privacy Amy moved into a private villa on the beach, and for the next few months she lived the life of a beach bum in St Lucia. When she showed no sign of returning home, her management arranged for recording equipment to be shipped out. An adjacent villa was set up as a studio at considerable expense, and Amy's producer Salaam Remi and her band flew out to work with her in the hope that she would take this opportunity to record songs for her overdue third album. Amy had ideas for songs, even a tentative album title (*Kill You Wiv Kindness*), but she made little progress. She had become inhibited by the success of *Back to Black*, which had achieved the status of a modern classic – 'Rehab' and the other songs from the album were heard everywhere, on the radio, on TV, in bars and clubs the world over – and the fact that she was half drunk, or spaced out on medication, wasn't conducive to work. There were moments of clarity, as there were patches of sobriety, the two usually coinciding. Amy gave an impressive performance of 'Don't Look Back in Anger' at a rehearsal for the St Lucia Jazz Festival in May. '[A] couple of us were almost in tears, because it sounded so beautiful,' says her drummer, Troy Miller. But her appearance at the festival was a disappointment. She had been drinking, there were technical problems, and the audience booed.

Away from work, Amy continued to surf the Internet for company, finding her old stage-school pal Ricardo Canadinhas on Facebook, then dialling him up on Skype. 'Literally, within seconds I had a telephone call and there she is in the middle of St Lucia,' says Ricardo, who asked Amy how she was.

'Good. My life's changed quite a lot.'

'No shit, Sherlock, I read about you in the papers.'

'Oh, yeah,' said Amy, as if she didn't know her life was documented daily in the press. 'I got married.'

'I know! I read the papers,' laughed Ricardo, who decided that Amy was clueless, though she was perhaps being modest.

Amy talked about her new music, playing a snatch of a song seemingly titled 'You and Me' down the line. It was about Blake. 'I know what you're going to say,' she said defensively.

'You're a grown woman.'

'Yes, I am. I've grown my hair and everything.' Amy was always a joker.

Mitch Winehouse flew out to St Lucia to see his daughter, bringing documents for her to sign. He still had his black cab in London, but he didn't drive it much anymore. He devoted his time to Amy and her business, becoming a director of her company, Cherry Westfield, in November 2008 after his disqualification had ended. Indeed, he now gave his occupation as company director. Over the next few years he would be appointed director of a series of companies set up to channel Amy's money. In most cases Janis Winehouse was also a director, making Amy's career a family concern.

Along with documents, Mitch brought business people and journalists to St Lucia to see Amy, which didn't please her. One journalist, Daphne Barak, had an agreement with Mitch to make a film about Amy, but Amy wasn't co-operative. 'My daddy is always bringing people [here] for business,' she told Barak, when they met on the island, going on to complain about Mitch and Janis, 'saying horrible things about her parents', and moaning about people who got to her via her family. 'Why don't [these] people talk to *me*?' she asked. In a subsequent book, *Saving Amy*, Barak connected Amy's problems with what she saw as deep-seated family issues: 'Sometimes, I feel, Amy's problems are used as an excuse to mask other underlying and undealt-with issues in the family.' Barak also noted that, despite protesting how private the family was, Mitch gabbed to reporters constantly.

Barak thought she had an exclusive agreement with Mitch, but then he started to make a documentary with Channel 4, *My Daughter Amy*, bringing another camera crew to St Lucia. Amy avoided the Channel 4 crew, and seemed to avoid her father when he was with them. By the end of the project Mitch conceded that Amy was 'obviously uncomfortable with the camera being here' and asked himself why he'd brought a TV crew to the island when so much effort was made in normal circumstances to keep the media away from Amy. 'I'm starting to question my own motives.' Amy was dismayed by her father's film. 'WHY don't my dad WRITE a SONG when something bothers him instead of going on national TV? an you thought YOUR parents were embarrassing,' she tweeted, when the documentary was screened.*

Amy's relationship with her father was complicated. She loved him, despite his faults, or *wanted* to love him. One of her most perceptive friends, Stefan Skarbek, says that Amy 'seemed to love' her father. 'I mean, she seemed to *want* to love him badly.' Since Amy had become a star, a new element had been introduced to the relationship. Mitch was becoming well known by association with his daughter, and he seemed to like the attention.

On the back of Amy's success Mitch set out to become a professional singer in his own right, singing in clubs and recording a CD of saloon-bar standards, *Rush of Love*. He also conducted interviews with celebrities in the back of his (underused) cab for an online chat show. In these pursuits he was represented by the same management company as Amy, while also having a hand in her business affairs. Not everybody was impressed by the way he conducted himself. 'The only thing of which we can be sure is that Mitch Winehouse has managed to parlay his daughter's heroin addiction into a media career for himself,' wrote a critic in the *Guardian*.

Mitch decided that Amy might do better when she returned home from St Lucia if she stayed away from Camden Town. He rented a house in Hadley Wood, an outer suburb of north London, where Amy came to live in July 2009. She was in tears as she walked through Arrivals at Gatwick Airport, for in coming home she faced the end of her marriage. Blake was granted a divorce on 16 July. Blake says that when Amy asked her father how much he was getting in the settlement, Mitch told her, with satisfaction, 'Not a penny' (and she wrote a song of that title as a result). Blake insists that he was never interested in Amy's money, in contrast to Mitch, who took a sharp interest in his daughter's affairs. Blake referred to Mitch as the Fat Controller, after the rotund character in *Thomas the Tank Engine*. He says Amy grumbled about Mitch, but concedes that she loved him above all men, and concluded that

---

* Amy's capitalisation and spelling.

Mitch hadn't been such a bad father-in-law. At least he had visited Blake in prison.

After the divorce Amy had a breast enlargement and spoke about having rhinoplasty next, telling her father that she couldn't stand seeing herself in the mirror. The breast enlargement was too big for her physique, making her figure unbalanced, like that of a cartoon character. Her self-loathing was sad to behold. Shortly after the breast enlargement she hosted a thirtieth birthday party for her brother Alex at Hadley Wood, then ruined the party by getting drunk and telling everyone to leave. It was not the first or last time that Amy would upset Alex, and a family row ensued.

At the end of a difficult year Amy went to a Christmas pantomime. She drank five vodka and Cokes before a production of *Cinderella* in Milton Keynes in December 2009, entering into the spirit of the occasion with such gusto during the first half of the show that she was asked to quieten down. When she tried to order a double vodka at the interval the theatre manager suggested she might have had enough. Amy was infuriated. She pulled the man's hair and called him a 'fucking cunt'. This resulted in a court case in January 2010, at which Amy pleaded guilty to common assault and disorderly behaviour. She was fined and received a two-year conditional discharge. The judge noted that Amy already had two cautions for similar offences, but took into account a letter from her doctor saying that she was trying to curb her drinking.

2

Amy was soon bored of the suburbs and moved back to central London. She rented a penthouse above Bryanston Square, near Marble Arch. Going for a walk in the neighbourhood one day, she saw a young man sitting outside a pub on Devonshire Street.

'Amy walked past, and as she walked past she sort of looked at me, and sort of made eye contact, and then she just carried on walking ... I recognised who she was. Then she sort of looked over her shoulder,' says Reg Traviss, who finished his cigarette and went inside the pub, Inn 1888, which his parents owned. 'She came in and we both ended up at the bar at the same time and we got chatting.' This was the beginning of Amy's last significant relationship, spanning the final months of her life.

Reg Traviss was 33 in the spring of 2010, six and a half years older than Amy. Like Amy he was interested in 1950s style, dressing in the clothes of the era, usually in a suit and tie, with his dark hair cut short and slicked back. His pale face was typically set in an unsmiling expression that gave him a surly look, reminiscent of an old-time East End gangster. He had the voice to match. Again like Amy, Reg's family were from east London and, despite a successful career as a film director, he retained the accent and was, in fact, somewhat inarticulate. Yet he was polite, thoughtful and industrious. Reg had three pictures to his name: a Second World War drama, *Joy Division*, which came out in 2006; a 2010 horror film, *Psychosis*; and a prison drama, *Screwed*, which was due out in the spring of 2011. Reg lived for his work. He wasn't married, and eschewed drugs, which was a welcome change from Blake, as far as Amy's parents were concerned. In many ways Reg was an ideal prospective son-in-law.

'I thought she was really beautiful and always thought she was really gorgeous,' says Reg, of his first impression of Amy. As he got to know her he found that Ame (as he called her) was a paradox. Although she had stopped using drugs she looked back on her drug years with a degree of nostalgia, talking about the good times, and she was still wild, 'in a fun way'. Yet she was also a 'dreamy girl' with a domestic side, a woman who liked nothing better than spending nights at home, making snacks for her and Reg and intimating that she'd like to start a family. She was clever, with a facility for maths, yet she took little interest in her financial affairs. Indeed, money seemed to scare her. 'She had designated people who dealt with it, and that was it. And to a degree I would say she didn't like money, wasn't really interested in money, and large sums of it frightened her. The thought of a massive amount of money in any sort of context was something she didn't like thinking about.'

Reg did not find Amy depressive, but he believes that she had 'an issue with self-belief'. He was surprised to learn that she had released only two albums, the last four years ago. She was writing new songs, working at home on a keyboard borrowed from a member of her band. She sometimes sang to herself as she worked. There were recording sessions where she tried out her ideas. But she didn't seem close to making a third album. The truth was that she had suffered a fundamental loss of confidence. 'She always felt she wasn't a front-line performer,' says Reg. 'She always felt she was more of, like, a kind of backing singer …'

Amy told her friends that she liked Reg because he treated her well. 'She said, "He treats me like a lady,"' recalls Sarah Hurley. Yet Reg wasn't by her side all the time, and as a result some old friends wondered how serious the relationship was. 'Who is Reg? Does he exist?' asks Doug Charles-Ridler, facetiously.

Although Amy and Blake were divorced, she remained in contact with her ex, who was now out of jail and living in Sheffield with a girlfriend. Amy visited Blake in Yorkshire and saw him in London. They were photographed kissing in Camden in March 2010, shortly after which Amy tweeted: 'I love my husband Blake an it aint wrong! Marry for life.' The following month they were photographed walking hand in hand on a night out in the capital, during which they visited Jazz after Dark, a Soho club Amy frequented.

Reg refused to be jealous of Blake, accepting him as part of Amy's past. He took the view that she was over the relationship and was trying to deal with Blake in a civilised way. Sometimes it became too much, though. Amy changed her phone number to stop Blake calling. Then he wrote letters to her, sometimes asking for money. She sent him small amounts by return. Her new boyfriend kept his cool. 'I said to her at the beginning of our relationship, "Look, I don't feel threatened by this,"' says Reg, who believes that Amy never saw Blake again after he and Amy became a couple. 'At one point she asked me if I wanted to meet him. Because he was going to come to London. I said, "No, no, but you should go and see him." It never 'appened in the end … There was periods where she would hear from him quite a lot, and then he would bother her a little bit, which is all understandable. They were married. Then there were periods when she wouldn't hear from him, and she was quite 'appy with that ... There was no sort of feelings there. She had definitely grown out of that relationship. And she almost felt a bit more like a sort of mother figure. She felt sympathy for him, obviously, because of the sort of situations he was finding himself in, as did I ... We never once argued about Blake getting in touch, ever.'

For his part Blake seems envious of Reg, suggesting that Amy had traded him in for someone better. He noted that Reg's parents owned a pub, that he was a sharp dresser and, above all, a film director, whereas Blake had only ever been a teaboy for a video production company.

Meanwhile Amy continued to struggle with her alcoholism. It is often easier for people who drink to excess to stop altogether, rather than trying to moderate their drinking. Such people have an all-or-nothing disposition, commonly described as an 'addictive personality'. Boswell observed that Dr Johnson 'could practise abstinence, but not temperance'. The same was true of Amy. There were weeks when she was teetotal, banishing drink from her sight. Then she would fall off the wagon with a crash. There was no middle way, though Reg repeatedly refers to Amy having 'a little drink' with his blessing, because he thought she could handle it. This was a delusion. Amy's 'little drinks' were tributaries to rivers of booze in which she would drown.

That summer Amy went on a series of benders, which ended with her checking into the London Clinic. She was too drunk to attend a meeting with her record-company boss, Lucian Grainge, in May. She showed her father up in July when she arrived drunk at the Roundhouse to see their hero Tony Bennett perform in concert. And she performed drunk at her brother's engagement party in August, despite promising that she would stay sober.

After a midsummer spree, during which Amy drank all afternoon and all night, she was photographed splayed in the sunshine on a pub bench in central London early the following morning, the pub owned by Reg Traviss's parents. Reg says Amy was merely sunbathing, but it looked as if she had passed out drunk.

3

Amy turned 27 in September 2010. During the depths of her drug period she had predicted that she would join the 27 Club, according to friends Alex Foden and Alex Haines. She had, of course, grown up knowing about the Club. She was nearly eleven when Kurt Cobain died, her brother was a Nirvana fan, and though Amy disliked rock music she couldn't help but be aware of the series of deaths at 27 preceding Cobain's. Reg Traviss says that Amy made no reference to the 27 Club while they were together, but they discussed the problem of getting through one's twenties, Reg encouraging Amy to think about her future, as others had tried to make Kurt Cobain take a long view of his life. 'I did [say to her], "Amy, you've got so many possibilities, because of what you've already created ... Now I think you're at an age when you're going to start really developing as an individual."'

First, Amy had to stop drinking. In common with Mitch Winehouse, Reg was optimistic that Amy may have been on the verge of giving up the bottle completely at the end of her life, just as she had managed to kick drugs. 'I had a feeling that at that time the drinking was on the way out.' This seems optimistic. In truth, Amy was a very heavy binge-drinker until she died. That was what killed her. Her binges were so serious that they put her in hospital repeatedly. Her life became a pattern of binge-drinking followed by hospital visits, a short period of sobriety, then more drinking. Doctors struggled to help Amy, prescribing Librium when she was off the booze to help her cope with alcohol withdrawal (the drug had the side effect of making her dopy), patching her up after she fell off the wagon, and trying to get her to see the benefit of psychological therapy. She never did.

Amy typically turned to drink when she was due to perform, something she seemed less and less comfortable with. Stage fright had become a major problem. There was, however, financial pressure to give concerts. It is how music stars make their money, especially stars, like Amy, who aren't releasing new material. There was also a natural expectation from audiences that when Amy did appear in concert she would sing the songs from *Back to Black*. Unfortunately, Amy no longer felt comfortable singing about Blake and their drug use. 'She didn't want to sing anything she didn't mean,' says her drummer, Troy Miller. 'For instance we always used to open up with "Addicted". There was a point where she [said], "No, I don't want to sing 'Addicted'. It's about drugs, and that's not me anymore."'

Amy committed to a show in Russia at the end of 2010. The day before the show, Mitch visited Bryanston Square and found Amy drunk. They had a 'terrible row'. He came back later in the day and found her even worse, 'so drunk she couldn't speak'. Dr Cristina Romete was called to examine Amy, who was admitted to the London Clinic. Mitch writes that Amy nevertheless insisted on going to Moscow where she performed as scheduled, and her manager reported back that the show was 'fantastic'. This is one of a number of examples from Mitch's book where he paints a rosier picture of Amy than others do. In Troy Miller's memory, the Moscow show was 'slightly disappointing'. The band had got used to disappointments. 'There were points after gigs where we wouldn't [show] our faces at the after-show parties.'

Amy did a short tour of Brazil in the new year, starting with a festival appearance at Florianópolis on 8 January 2011. She was sober and focused for the first night. She sang properly, enunciating all the words, which was not always the case now, and she seemed to enjoy herself. Again, the band hoped she had turned a corner. 'It showed promise, and we all got excited,' says Troy Miller. But the tour was not without issues. Amy was drunk in Recife on 13 January. She larked around on stage, shouting lyrics and falling over while attempting a pirouette. Hearts sank. 'There was a lot of spectacle, and a lot of false hopes,' says trumpet player Henry Collins.

She rallied for the final show of the tour, in São Paulo, giving a performance imbued with the vulnerability of Judy Garland or Edith Piaf. When Amy sang 'You Know I'm No Good', her expression hovered between mischief and pathos, her personal story informing her act, as had been the case with Garland and Piaf. So long as Amy didn't drink too much this made for a riveting concert, indicating that she might have matured into one of the great torch singers.

When she came offstage Amy spoke to her father on the telephone, telling Dad that the Brazilian tour had gone well (which was true for the most part), and that she had stayed sober throughout (which wasn't). She was slightly more frank with her boyfriend, though she downplayed the state she had got into in Recife, the evidence of which is available for all to see online. 'We spoke about it,' said Reg Traviss. 'She just had a little drink, and I think that was probably just nerves.' Once again, there is a sense that people around Amy weren't facing up to the scale of her problem.

4

Camden Town drew Amy home like a magnet. Back in the spring of 2010 she had bought a three-storey house at 30 Camden Square, NW1, a handsome property built for the Victorian gentry in 1848, 42 years before Amy's Russian ancestors arrived in London. Camden Square was never particularly fashionable in the nineteenth century, however, and the area degenerated subsequently, with part of the square destroyed by enemy bombing in the Second World War. Many surviving properties were sub-divided into flats in the 1950s and 1960s, creating the low-rent Camden depicted in *Withnail & I*. Then the middle classes started to move back, renovating the old houses, which were fashionable and expensive by 2010 when Amy paid £1.8 million ($2.8 million) for hers.

As a result of this social history, Amy's neighbours in Camden Square were an eclectic mixture of people, including long-term residents, many of whom were working-class Irish, flat tenants, and wealthy single homeowners, several of whom were notable in public life. Amy's next-door neighbour on one side was the painter Tess Jaray, one of several artists living in and around Camden Square, and on the other the geneticist Professor Steve Jones and his film-maker wife Norma Percy. The sculptor Antony Gormley lived around the corner.

Amy moved into her new house in February 2011, after lengthy refurbishment. She loved the house, delighting in showing it off to friends, as Kurt Cobain had shown off his Seattle mansion. 'She seemed happiest at home,' says Troy Miller. 'I'd go round there [and] she'd always cook this meatball dish. That was her favourite. Very domestic. She was always making tea for people. Very welcoming ... very friendly.' Amy told her father she couldn't see herself ever leaving Camden Square. She didn't.

There were renewed concerns within the family that in returning to Camden Town Amy might be tempted into bad habits. It was always easy to score drugs in Camden and Amy could walk to the Hawley Arms or the Good Mixer from her house. But she seemed to have lost interest in drugs, and sympathetic landlords chose to stop serving her alcohol, in agreement with friends, like Amy's stylist Naomi Parry, who sometimes stayed with Amy at Camden Square. 'Naomi was in tears a lot, saying, "My friend's drinking herself to death. If she comes [in], just don't serve her booze,"' says Doug Charles-Ridler, landlord of the Hawley Arms.

Amy didn't stop drinking, though. 'It was very rare I'd see her sober,' says John Hurley, who helped his wife run the Good Mixer. As a reformed drinker, John saw the damage Amy had done to herself during the years she'd frequented their pub. 'She went from rosy cheeks – she looked great – to gaunt ... Although she went the way that she did via drugs, and the alcohol and that, it didn't change her personality. She was always still, right up until the end, a real sweet woman ... She was like a lot of us: she got lost with all the drinking.'

Amy was accompanied by minders everywhere she went – huge men, like Andrew Morris, who kept the *paparazzi* and drug-dealers at bay, and just as importantly kept Amy from going to dealers during her drug period. 'Part of the agreement was that [if the minders saw] her enter any premises which was known to sell drugs [they] would go back to the record company, and they would give her a big fine,' says John Hurley, but he notes that the heavies didn't stop Amy drinking if she was in the mood. Sometimes all they could do was help her home. One evening a couple of months before she died local people saw Amy in just such a state. 'You could see she was drunk,' says Rozh, a Kurdish worker in the dry-cleaner's on Murray Street at the bottom of Camden Square. He watched Amy being helped past the shop by two of her minders, on their way back to the house. 'They carried her home.'

When she was on the wagon Amy would impose rules on herself, including no booze in the house, but she broke her rules. 'There was never booze in the 'ouse, unless she wanted to have a drink,' explains Reg, 'and then she would nip out and get it.' As with many hardened alcoholics, Amy now favoured vodka, which she drank neat, and it wasn't always clear whether she was telling the truth about her drinking. Alcoholics drink vodka in preference to other spirits because it is colourless and virtually odourless and therefore easy to conceal. There is evidence that she lied on occasion about her drinking, such as when she told her father she hadn't had a drink in Brazil. Reg says that Amy would typically get up before him, when he stayed over, and go downstairs to make breakfast. It is possible that she used this opportunity to have a furtive nip of vodka to settle her stomach. It is what alcoholics do.

Amy's drinking made her prone to seizures. She had a seizure in front of her doctor in January 2011 and was admitted to the London Clinic as a result. She went back to the bottle almost as soon as she got home. In February she went to Dubai to perform and this time she stayed sober. But the show was bad. Amy looked bored. Her performance was flat, and the crowd became restive. She responded to catcalls by yawning and studying her nails during a lacklustre 'Rehab', which concluded with boos from those members of the audience who hadn't already left. 'Amy Winehouse was a disgrace!' wrote one patron online. Amy glowered at her audience, as if she wanted to curse them, but she held her tongue. In Dubai, swearing in public is a criminal offence.

Amy stayed on in Dubai with Reg Traviss for a week after the show. They spent most of their time in their hotel suite. They watched the revolutions in Egypt and Libya on television, and discussed their future. Reg told Amy that he had enjoyed her show, but Amy knew better and was despondent. 'She wasn't 'appy with it.' She talked about how uncomfortable she had felt singing the old songs. 'She had a real deep artistic integrity. And whilst you can get some people, pop stars and various other people, [who] can sing the same old songs for thirty years, some of them, sometimes with a similar amount of passion, Amy couldn't. Or at least she was going through a phase of her life where she was questioning that. Now, if everything that had happened in July [2011] didn't happen, who knows? Maybe in thirty years' time she could still be singing those songs. She was certainly going through a period where she was saying, you know, not that she didn't believe in those songs anymore, but she's expressed herself with those songs, and really now if she's going to carry on singing she needs to be singing new material. But that new material doesn't just come … She had to feel moved by something, essentially, to write this material.'

Reg encouraged Amy to look ahead, beyond her music, to what else she might do with her life. 'I said, "Look, you're [27]. You can do anything. You're a young gel. You can do anything you like."' Outside music, Amy had been offered opportunities to design clothing for the Fred Perry company, and to appear in the TV show *Mad Men*. Reg says a part had been written for her, which would seem to have been an ideal fit, though her lack of a US visa might have ruled the project out. He gave her a pep talk that sounds remarkably similar to the advice given to Kurt Cobain shortly before his death. 'I said, "Take a step back, have a look around and then maybe come up with something you haven't even thought about and do it … Even if you just do it for a year, six months, two weeks, whatever. The point is you can do anything. You haven't gotta just think, *I've gotta go out and sing these songs all the time.*" And she could. The world was her oyster, and she was very talented in a lot of other things that I don't think she gets credit for. I spent time discussing all that with her, and reminding her – not that she ever forgot, I don't think – just sort of reminding her that there was so many possibilities in life, particularly for someone so young who's in the fortunate position that [they] haven't got to go out and work every day.'

Amy had money in the bank, though less than if she had been more productive during the past five years. Every time she cancelled a show she was liable to reimburse promoters, and she insisted on paying her band even when they didn't play. As a result her touring company reported assets of just £8,000 ($12,720) that spring, while two of her other companies, Lioness Records and Goal Music Productions, recorded a loss. Meanwhile, she had frittered money on drugs and vacations, and had splurged £2 million on her new house. Still, she was far from broke. There was £2 million in her main company, Cherry Westfield, at the end of 2010, but that figure was diminishing fast and there was growing pressure on Amy to make her third album and return to touring on a business-like basis.

The relationship with Reg was also a cause of angst. 'She had issues with men, and every time there was a man in her life there was drama,' says Troy Miller. Amy wanted Reg to move into Camden Square, eager to develop their relationship, but he insisted on keeping his flat in Marylebone. 'She [first asked] me when she was living in Bryanston Square, but when she moved to Camden Square she asked a few times – "Look, you can move in,"' he says. 'But obviously the thing was that, quite honestly, as a bloke, I wouldn't have been comfortable living in such a grand place and not being able to say, "There's half of it." ... So I always felt that I should keep my own flat on until a time come that either we got married, or I had enough money to put something towards it. Otherwise, it would have always just felt wrong.' Mitch Winehouse writes in his book that this conflict, together with Reg's commitment to work, caused the couple to stop seeing each other for a time after Dubai, and there were press reports of them splitting up. Reg says this is untrue.

In the background was Amy's desire to have children. She went out of her way to talk to children wherever she went – friends' children, children she met on holiday, children on the streets of Camden. Because she was such a recognisable character, children would approach her and she would happily pose for photographs with them, while she might tell an adult to fuck off. She craved a family of her own. 'There was a moment when she said to me, "I think I might be pregnant,"' says Reg. 'I just said, "Fine. Great. Fine." We spoke about 'aving kids a lot, and there were periods when Amy talked about having kids and how she wanted to have kids a lot ... She had mentioned it to my mum and things like that. And it had all been freely talked about. Anyway, she wasn't pregnant.' Maybe she was testing her boyfriend to see how serious he was about the relationship. Some friends wonder whether she was unable to have children, and if that gnawed at her.

Although Amy was no longer seeing Blake, her ex was still capable of upsetting her. Blake was back on heroin, stealing to support his habit. In February 2011 he and another man were in a car that was stopped by police, who recovered stolen goods from a house burglary, during which personal items, including a child's ring, were taken. The police also found an imitation firearm in the vehicle. Blake was charged with burglary and possession of an imitation firearm, and remanded in custody. If convicted he faced another long prison sentence. Blake was about to turn 29, about to be a father, but far from establishing a stable, law-abiding life. Amy responded to the news by going on a binge of drinking and self-harming. Her brother's fiancée was so alarmed that she raised the old issue of whether Amy should be sectioned under the Mental Health Act. Mitch didn't think this viable or necessary.

It was days after this drama that Amy took part in her last significant recording session, singing 'Body and Soul' with Tony Bennett at Abbey Road Studios for his second album of duets. Although nervy, Amy gave a riveting performance of a classic song that is the outstanding track on *Duets II*, singing in a voice that has the ruined-life quality of Billie Holiday, making her sound more like a contemporary of Bennett rather than a girl of 27. It is noteworthy that, at the end, all of the principal 27s seemed much older than their years. 'It actually made me cry,' says Gordon Williams, noting how different Amy sounded from the girl with whom he had worked on *Frank*. 'I heard how tired she was. Like *everything* was in her voice. Oh, man, the honesty ... It sounds like she was reaching out for help, even though that's not what she's singing [about]. Her voice sounds like that. It's like, damn, man, how did you go from the voice I heard to that voice in such a short time?'

Amy suffered a relapse after the Tony Bennett session, culminating in an alcoholic binge at Camden Square that makes for one of the most shocking passages in *Amy, My Daughter*. Mitch describes how she got up at four a.m. on 15 April 2011 to drink a bottle of wine before going back to bed. She got up and drank a second bottle of wine at eight. When Mitch arrived at ten thirty he found Amy 'totally out of it'. When she had sobered up, they had a row. The following morning, Mitch returned to the house to find his daughter drunk on the kitchen floor. He bundled her upstairs to bed as she screamed abuse at him.

Over the next few weeks Amy alternated between drunkenness and periods of abstinence. She complained to her GP about stage fright, for which she was prescribed a small amount of diazepam. Her weight was down and Dr Romete suspected that she was bulimic. Amy denied it initially but then, on 16 May, confessed to her doctor that she 'made herself sick following food binges'. Amy then went on an all-night bender at Camden Square that put her in a coma. Her minders couldn't wake her. She was taken to the London Clinic. When she came round she left the clinic against medical advice. Dr Romete was informed that Amy had discharged herself 'and gone to the pub'. The woman was impossible.

Dr Romete sent Amy a 'strongly worded' letter, copied to her father and manager, explaining her medical problems, saying she would not be able to treat Amy further, and warning of the grave risk Amy was taking with her life. 'The letter said Amy was in immediate danger of death,' Mitch revealed in *Amy, My Daughter*. This came as a shock to the family, and to Reg Traviss, all of whom seemed to have been in denial about Amy and her 'little drinks'.

Dr Romete was persuaded to continue working with Amy, but things had to change. Amy needed specialist treatment for her alcoholism and psychological problems. Dr Romete believed she might benefit from dialectical behavioural therapy (DBT), recommended to people with personality disorders, notably those who have borderline personality disorder (BPD), a category of behaviour on the cusp of mental illness. Symptoms include a history of unstable relationships, fear of abandonment, self-image issues, impulsive behaviour (including substance abuse), self-harming and suicidal behaviour. BPD sufferers can also have feelings of emptiness, rage and paranoia.

Anybody who exhibits five or more of these characteristics over a period of time can be diagnosed as having BPD, and they may well have other problems, too. Amy seemed to fit the profile. The problem was that she resisted therapy, believing that she alone could sort herself out. Like many people with personality disorders, she had been like this for so long that she had got used to coping with her odd behaviour. But things were becoming desperate.

In a scene reminiscent of the final Kurt Cobain intervention, on the morning of 25 May 2011 family members, including Mitch Winehouse and Amy's aunt Melody (Mitch's sister), Reg Traviss and a doctor, assembled at Camden Square to confront Amy with her behaviour and tried to persuade her to go to the Priory Clinic for therapy. As with Kurt Cobain, this proved to be a difficult conversation. Amy was angry and abusive. The argument went on for hours, while a driver waited outside to take her away. Reg recalls a 'very, very long ... and very frank discussion', which made him late for work. Finally, around lunchtime, Amy capitulated.

'All right, fine,' she said. 'If you want me to go, I'll go.'

Amy was driven to the branch of the Priory in Southgate, the part of north London she came from. It is poignant to think of her returning, as a 27-year-old alcoholic, to the suburb where she had been born and raised, her limousine passing familiar shops and houses before turning through the gates of the clinic next to the park where she had played as a child.

Thirteen

THE GLASS IS RUN

The glasse is full, and nowe the glass is run
And nowe I live, and nowe my life is donn.
Chidiock Tichborne

1

Amy discharged herself from the Priory on 31 May 2011, angry with those people who had persuaded her to go into the clinic. Neither her brief stay nor her doctor's written warning altered her behaviour. 'She returned home and started drinking again,' notes her GP. Indeed, Amy joked about Dr Cristina Romete's warning that her drinking was putting her life in danger. 'She said, "Oh, the doctor doesn't think I'm going to last much longer …" You know, she won't last to the end of the year … She would constantly joke about it. And she would laugh about it,' says Amy's drummer, Troy Miller. '[And] we would all laugh – not in a sinister way – because she was genuinely joking about it. It's not that she knew it was going to happen, but … she was ill … She was sick.' By which he means that Amy had psychological problems. 'And she had a dark sense of humour.'

One might think that Amy was in no state to sing at a family bar mitzvah, let alone give a concert, yet there were plans afoot for a European tour starting in Belgrade, Serbia, on 18 June, continuing through another eleven equally out-of-the-way places, as if Amy's management was nervous about how she would perform. As well they might be. The wisdom of Amy touring at this time is questionable. Mitch Winehouse writes that Amy herself wanted to tour, despite the misgivings of her manager, and he describes a meeting with Raye Cosbert in June during which they concluded that the show should go on. 'Raye and I both felt she was showing signs of beating her alcoholism. Still, we agreed to proceed slowly before confirming the east-European tour,' Mitch writes in *Amy, My Daughter*, making it clear that he was effectively part of his daughter's management at this stage, while glossing over the fact that the tour had been planned for months, with thousands of tickets already sold. Proceeding slowly at this late date was not really an option.

Troy Miller agrees that Amy wanted to tour; at least, she said so initially. 'I remember her talking about the tour, and being excited about it. She really wanted to do it.' She ordered new stage suits for her band, and arranged to give a private warm-up show at the 100 Club in London on 12 June. It was at this club appearance that she betrayed warning signs of the disaster that was to follow.

Amy had been sober for several days – some say weeks – prior to the 100 Club gig. But on the day of the performance she was gripped with stage fright, craved a drink, and became very bad-tempered. She told her keyboard player that he was fired and she yelled at Troy Miller. 'She felt very tetchy. She was having withdrawal symptoms at that stage. She was very irritable with the band,' says Miller, whose misdemeanour was to introduce Amy to some people who took pictures of her backstage without permission. '[She] said, "Don't you ever do that again! You left me with these people. They were taking photos"... I went to hug her, you know. She said, "Don't touch me"... It was because she hadn't been drinking for several weeks, and we were all sort of very understanding of that, [but] she really went off on one.' Dr Romete arrived and gave Amy a small amount of diazepam to calm her down. Although Mitch Winehouse writes that Amy didn't drink at the 100 Club – as she shouldn't when taking diazepam, for alcohol would enhance its potency – her boyfriend says she *did* drink. 'She had a tipple,' says Reg Traviss. 'I think she had, like, one drink, one glass of wine or whatever.' Finally she was able to perform, and the show went tolerably well. But if Amy had got herself into this state at a club gig in front of family and friends, what would she be like on tour?

Five days later, on the eve of the east-European tour, Amy told her father that she didn't want to perform. Mitch asked her why, but he couldn't get a lucid explanation. The next day she apparently changed her mind again and boarded the private plane leased for the tour. Dr Romete had been asked for a prescription of Librium and diazepam to help Amy cope with the stress. Raye Cosbert was so nervous that he kept Mitch informed of virtually every step of their progress from London to their Belgrade hotel, where a floor had been made available for Amy and her entourage, all the rooms cleared of alcohol.

The first show of the tour, on the evening of Saturday, 18 June, was an open-air event in the grounds of the Kalmegdan Fortress in Belgrade, overlooking the river Danube. On a hot summer night Amy and a cast of support acts drew an audience of 20,000 from across Serbia and neighbouring east-European states. Once again Amy was gripped with stage fright. Mitch Winehouse (who wasn't present) writes that she became agitated before the concert and asked her manager for a drink, 'so Raye had allowed her one glass of wine to calm her down'. Unless this glass was as big as a bucket it would not account for the state Amy got into before going onstage. Either she drank a great deal more than one glass, or she mixed alcohol with medication, or both. She was out of her head by show time.

'People were coming into our dressing room [saying], "We need coffee … We need strong coffee,"' says Troy Miller, who reveals that by then Amy didn't want to perform. 'The management and friends were trying to encourage her to go on.' That was a grave mistake. But 20,000 people were yelling Amy's name, with eleven more dates to follow. 'She had taken on this tour. She then has an obligation to go on stage regardless of what state she was is [in]. She has a contract,' reasons Miller, 'there's a lot at stake. So you can understand it, from friends and especially management's point of view: "We need coffee."'

Finally the band was given the signal to begin the intro 'Shimmy, Shimmy, Ko-Ko-Bop'. Ade Omotayo and Zalon Thompson sang the song. Zalon caught Amy's eye as she lurched into the wings and announced her. Another artist on the bill, Ana Zoe Kida, was later quoted saying that Amy was 'pushed' on stage, which her management denied.

The audience roared as Amy appeared in a lime green mini dress. Her beehive was gone, replaced by a collapsed haystack of a wig, streaked like Cruella de Vil's hair. She scampered across the stage to embrace her musical director, Dale Davis, who stopped playing his guitar to welcome her. Then she sat down on a monitor, with her back to the audience, to fiddle with her shoes, which halted the show before it had begun. As with so much that Amy did during her final concert, as with much of her recent behaviour, she seemed to be doing everything possible to delay the moment when she had to sing, which she either didn't want to or wasn't able to do. She was so out of it in Belgrade that it wasn't entirely clear to her band that she even knew where she was. 'I don't know whether she didn't want to be there, or whether she didn't realise she was there,' says Troy Miller, who saw immediately that they were in deep trouble. 'The thing is we'd sort of know whether it was going to be a good or bad gig usually from the very first note. I seem to remember she just didn't come in [musically]. There was no clear entry point, [which] makes it very hard for a musician trying to play the song. You lose where you are in the song.'

The audience hollered encouragement as the band struck up 'Just Friends'. Amy slunk to the microphone, like a recalcitrant child, crossed her arms and began to mumble. The band quickened the tempo and Zalon gave Amy encouragement. 'Come on, baby!' Amy smirked as she slurred the lyrics about having a drink at the end of the day, words that seemed more apposite than ever, but she soon gave up. Instead she introduced her band to the audience as if they'd already reached the end of the show, shouting out their names and complimenting them on how handsome they looked in their new suits.

'What comes next?' she asked Zalon, when 'Just Friends' fizzled out.

'"Addicted".'

'What's it called?'

'"Addicted" ... "Addicted".'

Amy crossed her arms, steeling herself for the ordeal.

'I would say it was surreal. We had done a few shows like that, so it wasn't the first time, but you felt sort of helpless,' says Troy Miller. No show had been quite as bad as this. 'At one point I looked round to the side of the stage and Raye was just standing there with his arms folded. The expression on his face, I'll never forget – helplessness.'

Amy let the audience sing most of the first verse of 'Tears Dry on Their Own' while she danced with Zalon, shouting the occasional line. The song was about Blake, therefore one of the songs she found difficult. She roused herself to sing a couple of the most vivid lines about their doomed love, and the 'shadow' it cast over her life, then gave up.

The set list had been arranged to intersperse *Back to Black* material with less demanding songs. Yet perversely Amy asked Zalon if they could try 'Some Unholy War'. When Zalon assured her they could do this song about Blake and his drug addiction, Amy warned him that she might have problems with it. 'But you will have to catch me, though.' Latterly Amy had got into the habit of pretending to collapse on stage as part of her act, with the backing singers catching her in their arms. But when she was in this state she also needed Ade and Zalon to sing the words if she forgot them. 'OK. I'm just letting you know that I am going to fall.'

Amy assumed a pained look as the song began. The audience was becoming restive, with sections of the crowd barracking. She sang over the catcalls, delivering the words about how she would stand by Blake in his 'unholy war', as if he was a freedom fighter rather than a drug addict, in a shaky voice. True to her warning, she was unable to remember all the lyrics. Zalon prompted her. She repeated what he said, then turned away with a bereft expression, shivered, and closed her eyes. While the venue erupted with boos, Amy's most ardent fans sang the rest for her. Amy looked down at them as if to ask, *What are we doing here?*

The next moment she seemed to nod off, stumbled and grabbed

the microphone stand for support. People were laughing now. Amy made a desperate effort to rescue the song, looking like she might cry, vomit or collapse. She gathered enough energy to wail the histrionic line in which she asks Blake ('B' in the song) what he is 'dying for', adding that she would willingly trade places with him. Then she hid her face, turned and collapsed into Zalon's arms, smirking finally as if it was all a joke. Throughout the show Amy alternated between inebriation, pathos and schoolgirl cheek. 'Understand, Amy's an actress,' observes her friend Lauren Franklin. 'She loves the drama.'

The show dragged on. Indeed, it seemed to last longer than normal. 'It was such a strange [show]. It certainly felt like the longest gig,' says Troy Miller. When Amy failed to sing the next tune the band segued into 'Back to Black', which held her interest briefly. She sang the first line about Blake's infidelity with belligerence, then became tearful. The audience carried on, helping her describe the drugs she and Blake had preferred which lead to one of Amy's most original couplets in which she compared herself to a penny coin rolling around a pipe. In her prime Amy had delivered this unusual but compelling metaphor with confidence, evoking the image of someone who had no control over themselves. Now she was snivelling as she sang, wiping her nose with her hand.

It was hard to know whether she was acting or not when she sang 'You Know I'm No Good'. One minute she was grinning and fooling about. The next she was the picture of misery. She sang that she had warned everybody about herself, adding sorrowfully 'you know I'm no good.' Having apparently finished with the song, the show, and her career, she attempted to remove her wig.

The band launched into 'Valerie'. Amy made Zalon sing it. There was one more tune, an upbeat ska song, 'You're Wondering Now', which Amy sometimes used to close the show and lift the mood. It had a dance tempo, but the lyrics were dark, concerning the price paid for misbehaviour. The words seemed to describe the sad state Amy had got into during her short life.

The stage manager got Amy off as the crowd howled and booed, furious that they had paid to see a fiasco. There were no encores.

2

Amy's career ended in Belgrade. The concert was a catastrophic mistake that made everybody involved look bad, including her manager and father for letting the tour go ahead, while her band appeared foolish, though that wasn't their first concern. 'Probably the biggest emotion on stage for us musicians was disappointment, not embarrassment or anger,' says Troy Miller.

The tour party left that night for Istanbul where the next concert was due to take place. But the show was cancelled. Amy would never perform again. As with Jimi Hendrix, despite creating glorious music, and giving some extraordinary concerts, Amy was booed offstage at the last at an obscure open air gig in a foreign land.

Amy checked into the W Hotel in Istanbul, where she was joined by Reg Traviss, who flew in from London by prior arrangement. Amy had come offstage in Belgrade in a stroppy mood, and sulked on the flight to Turkey, but by the time Reg arrived his girlfriend was sober and contrite. 'She was taking it quite seriously. She was like, "Aw, fuck, what did I do?"' The band and entourage were sent home in Amy's private plane, rather than on the usual commercial flights, partly to compensate them for what had happened. They would be paid for the tour. Reg remained in Istanbul with Amy for a couple of days. Once again she asked him what she should do next, and he tried to explain that she was free to do whatever she liked with her life. Reg denies that Amy felt trapped, or that she was in conflict with her management: 'She had a *fantastic* relationship with her manager.'

Amy and Reg returned to London on 22 June. Dr Romete saw her at home in Camden Square that day, having been informed that Amy had become drunk in Belgrade. Amy told her doctor that she couldn't remember anything about it. Then she looked on YouTube to see amateur footage taken by fans in Belgrade with their phones. It was unusual for Amy to look at herself online, though she did so more than once during her final days. The footage was shocking and

Amy became increasingly contrite. She told her father that she was sick of drinking, and grew introspective, talking about her late grandmother, Cynthia, and asking for reassurance that she was talented and attractive.

Amy's surgeon cousin Jonathan Winehouse texted Mitch to express his concern, having seen the press reports of what had happened in Belgrade. 'I sent him a text to say something had to be done about it, and I wanted to discuss it with him.' Jonathan saw from the media coverage that Amy's alcoholism had reached a critical stage. 'The interesting part about alcoholism is that these people manage to hold it together. It's kind of a stepwise deterioration, where they just about hold themselves together and then they literally fall off a cliff.' Jonathan had a psychiatrist friend whom he felt could help Amy. But he didn't receive a reply to his message. 'I've never been able to get through to Mitch about it ... I don't know what the reasons are.'

Amy was sober for several days after Belgrade. Then she started drinking again, possibly triggered by news that Blake had been given 32 months for burglary and possession of an imitation firearm. He would serve his time in HMP Leeds, where he was given methadone to wean him off heroin. Blake remained in contact with Amy, speaking to her regularly by phone, and there is evidence that he retained a hold over her. There was a telling incident at Jazz after Dark in Soho when Amy sat at the bar to make a call on her mobile phone while Reg Traviss went outside to smoke a cigarette.

'Amy, I'm really happy for you,' the club owner Sam Shaker told Amy, whom he had known for some time. 'Reg is a very handsome, decent man ... He is better than Blake.'

'Shut up,' snapped Amy, covering her phone. 'I'm talking to Blake.'

Amy got back on the wagon around 5 July. 'It's what she periodically did and she had said she really had sort of had enough of being drunk around the 'ouse,' says Reg. 'So it was a combination of that, and it was getting into that middle part of the summer, and we were going to be doing things, and I think maybe that made her feel she wanted to give up, and she'd had enough of being drunk around the 'ouse for a few days here and a few days there, and then feeling shitty afterwards.'

Reg says that he and Amy felt there was 'a cloud' over them at this time, though he denies press reports that they split up. In Amy's case this uneasy feeling may have been to do with the fact she was making a concerted effort to remain sober, seeing her doctor again on Friday, 15 July, when she was prescribed medication to help with her withdrawal.

The dark mood lifted for Reg and Amy over the weekend of 16–17 July, which they spent at Camden Square. Both felt happier by Monday. Amy saw her doctor that day and Dr Romete noted that she was sober. '[The cloud] lifted for me. It lifted for her. And we were both really 'appy. It was really, really strange,' says Reg. 'The weekend before we'd stayed in watching films, having a laugh, just having a really, really nice time … On the Monday I was here in work and I was saying, "That thing has just lifted." She goes, "Yeah, it's just lifted, innit? Great." We were making plans for the week.'

Their plans included attending the wedding of Nick Shymansky the following Sunday. Beyond that Amy wanted to go to the Caribbean to celebrate her 28th birthday in September, and ultimately there was an understanding that she and Reg would marry, though the couple exhibited little of the customary excitement. 'I hadn't got down on one knee and produced a ring or anything like that, but we had talked about it and Amy said, "Well, let's get married," and I said, yeah, I would. And it was something that we were going to do. If what happened hadn't happened, I can only say that probably sometime around [2012] we would have probably been sorting that out. And I had resigned myself in my mind that we are going to get married.'

Reg spent Tuesday night at Camden Square, leaving for work on the morning of Wednesday, 20 July, around the time Amy's bodyguard, Andrew Morris, returned to work after a break. Reg says Amy was sober when he left the house, though she had got up early to go downstairs to make breakfast. 'So it's not impossible that she had had a drink and I didn't realise … It's not impossible. But I'm pretty sure she hadn't.' This is significant because Andrew Morris told the police that when he arrived at ten a.m. he realised that Amy *had* been drinking, 'because of the way she was speaking to me'. He wouldn't say she was 'drunk'. Andrew had seen Amy drunk too many times to use that word lightly. She was drinking moderately – for Amy.

Amy was going out that evening. She was going to hear Dionne Bromfield sing at the Roundhouse, the former train shed on Chalk Farm Road where Jim Morrison had performed with the Doors in 1968, with Brian Jones in the audience. This touchstone venue in the history of the 27 Club was less than a mile from Amy's house and turned out to be the scene of her last public appearance. Amy called Reg and asked him if he wanted to come to the show with her. 'I was going to go to that gig, [but I] got the times wrong, and it was starting quite early.' Reg could tell that Amy had been having a 'little drink' prior to going out. 'And the reason she'd had a little drink, I would say, is just purely because she was going out and she just needed that little lift.'

Dionne – still only fifteen, but a confident performer with a strong voice – introduced her 'godmother' to the audience at the Roundhouse. Amy bounded onstage wearing a Fred Perry top and jeans. She was chewing gum and looked edgy. Dionne gave the signal for the band to play 'Mama Said'. As she sang Dionne watched Amy carefully, as one regards a pet that is known to bite. She appeared to want Amy to join her in a duet, but Amy merely danced around the stage, looking evasive and high. When Dionne held the mike to her, Amy muttered a couple of words but clearly wasn't in the mood to sing. Still, she hugged Dionne at the end of the song and exhorted the crowd to cheer. Amy's exaggerated movements and shouty voice betrayed her inebriation. 'I heard she was backstage and she was drinking either vodkas, or gins, with Red Bull,' says Amy's publican friend Doug Charles-Ridler, who had last seen Amy when she'd come past the Hawley Arms a few weeks earlier. He had felt then that something was wrong. 'I held her and I was like, *Oh, my God*. She just didn't weigh anything. I thought, Oh, that's a bit weird.'

Mitch called by Amy's house the next day, Thursday, 21 July, and found his daughter looking at family photographs. He was flying to New York in the morning and didn't see Amy alive again. Amy spoke to Reg on the phone. He was busy at work and wouldn't be coming over that evening. As we have seen, Amy disliked being alone, but several people she would normally count on for company were unavailable. Her friend and occasional lodger Tyler James was visiting his mother. Naomi Parry wasn't around either. 'Naomi was living at the house, but Amy was getting more and more erratic and kept coming into Naomi's room, and Naomi was getting pissed off so she moved out,' says Doug Charles-Ridler.*

It was warming up to be a lovely summer weekend in London, with clear blue skies during the day and warm nights. It was later reported that Amy's neighbours heard screams and howling from Amy's house in the early hours of Friday, 22 July, one of several sinister stories that appeared in the press immediately after her death. All of Amy's close neighbours were spoken to for this book and none had heard a peep from her in the hours preceding her death, including next-door neighbour Steve Jones and his wife. 'We were here that weekend. We sleep in the front, so if there had been any noise we would know.' Indeed, neighbours had seen and heard little of Amy since she had moved to Camden Square. They saw her occasionally in the garden, or walking down to the Portuguese restaurant on Murray Street. Amy cut a distinctive figure, and her deep voice carried, but she was inconspicuous most of the time. 'That house was her retreat; it was not a party house,' notes neighbour Catherine Hays.

Janis Winehouse visited at lunchtime on Friday, with her partner Richard Collins, whom she would marry later in the year. Amy made tea and showed her mother the photos she'd been looking at. While this is evidence of reflection, perhaps an attempt to make sense of her life, Amy had plans for the future. Janis noticed that her daughter had dresses laid out to choose from for the wedding she and Reg were going to on Sunday. Then it was time for Janis to go. 'When we left, she hugged me and said, "I love you, Mummy." She was always calling me that and telling me she loved me. Amy never really grew up. She was like a little girl, permanently fixed in time as a kiddie. I said, "I love you, too."'

* Naomi Parry declined to be interviewed for this book, but says she 'never had a disagreement with Amy'.

Amy drank throughout the rest of the day. 'She was drinking vodka,' says Andrew Morris, who popped out between four and five in the afternoon to buy milk. When he came back Amy was in the kitchen having a snack of celery and a dip. Then she went up to her room, where she listened to music, watched TV and surfed the Internet.

In her eternal search for company Amy had been Skyping Ricardo Canadinhas recently. He was appearing in drag, as Miss Mince Meat, at the nightclub Heaven. 'When she was on Skype it was because no one was there,' says Ricardo, providing an insight into how lonely Amy had become. 'She was, like, "Talk to me, talk to me." I would be in between shows, the half-hour call, in intervals on Skype to her. I was, like, "I've got two minutes!" She was, like, "Get ready while you're on camera …"' The loneliness was almost palpable, reminiscent of Janis Joplin's.

Amy also spoke to a member of her band on that last day. During the conversation she referred to telling off Troy Miller at the 100 Club, something for which she hadn't apologised. 'Does Troy still love me?' she asked, which Miller cites as evidence that Amy considered the feelings of her musicians, 'and she did feel remorseful about things she had done or said, and she wanted to improve as a person. I believe that right to the end. I think she was just sort of a lost soul, really.'

Attempts to reach other friends failed. 'A lot of people had missed phone calls, because it was the Secret Garden [Party weekend],* so a lot of people were there. Basically everyone was out, so she was alone,' says Doug Charles-Ridler. 'I think Kelly [Osbourne] said she tried to Skype. Chantelle [Dusette] had missed calls.† Naomi [Parry] had missed calls. Everyone, like, had missed calls from her. No one picked up, and she was alone.'

To comfort herself Amy drank. She drank vodka more or less constantly during the last three days of her life. It is a mark of how dissipated she had become that drinking for days on end was

* An annual music festival in Cambridgeshire.
† Girlfriends of Amy.

considered normal within her entourage. 'She [was drinking] normally [*sic*], she didn't appear drunk,' Andrew Morris told the inquest. 'She was alert and she was calm.' It was another mark of how low Amy had fallen – and how strange her life had become – that her doctor called regularly at the house. At seven p.m. Amy received a final home visit from Dr Cristina Romete. 'She was tipsy, I would say, but she didn't slur her words, and she was able to hold a full conversation,' the doctor later said. Amy was vague as to when she had started drinking again, and when she might stop, telling Dr Romete she was drinking because she was bored. But the GP was satisfied that Amy wasn't suicidal. They discussed the matter in terms.

'She specifically said she did not want to die,' Dr Romete told the police, adding that Amy said there were still things she wanted to do.

After Dr Romete had left, Amy spoke to Reg on the phone. He suggested he might come over later with a takeaway. But Amy and Andrew ordered an Indian meal. When Reg rang again, later in the evening, he couldn't get an answer. 'Something told me it was a bit strange … I just left a long message. I said, "Look, I'm ready to come over. Call me back." Reg waited at his office for Amy to call. When she didn't, he walked into Soho where he had a drink, before getting a cab home where he sent Amy another long text message to which she didn't reply.

As we have seen, Amy spent much of the evening looking at YouTube with Andrew Morris. Although Dr Romete decided that Amy was not suicidal at their final meeting, such behaviour suggests that she was making an examination of herself. She may not have liked what she saw. Around two thirty a.m., Andrew went to his room where he watched a film. He could still hear Amy moving about upstairs.

Most of the principal 27s died at night. Like several others Amy was alone at the end. Andrew was in the house, but Amy was alone in her bedroom suite. As a result it is not known for certain what she did at the last, or what she consumed, other than that she probably drank more vodka, judging by the post-mortem evidence and the empty bottles found in her room.

What Amy's state of mind was when she took her last gulps of vodka is impossible to know. She didn't appear suicidal to Andrew Morris or Dr Romete, who stressed to the police that her patient 'did not appear depressed at any stage'. But it is hard to agree with Reg Traviss that 'there was nothing wrong' in Amy's life. Yes, she had plans for the weekend, and had talked of celebrating her birthday in the Caribbean. These are superficial matters that may not reflect her state of mind in the dark hours before dawn, a time when depression can come suddenly and overwhelmingly. She had said there were things she still wanted to do, but she seemed unable to take action. She may well have kept her deepest thoughts to herself. Despite being a remarkably honest and open person in many respects, she had always been cagey about her inner life. Observing Amy as we have, there is a strong sense that she was sick of her career by the summer of 2011. Like Jimi Hendrix and Kurt Cobain, she had become a prisoner of her image. She didn't want to sing the songs from *Back to Black* anymore. She didn't want to be that person. Amy's private life had become more important than her work. She badly wanted a family. But she had wanted that family with Blake. Reg remained a semi-detached boyfriend. And, as with Janis Joplin, her man was glaringly absent at the end. So were other people Amy had depended upon and, in many cases, exhausted.

So she drank to forget herself, and her problems, as drunkards do. She drank herself into a stupor in the early hours. Then she curled up to sleep as the sky lightened with the dawn. She may not have meant to die. But, like the other 27s, she had been living dangerously for a long time. Death had been shadowing her for years, sometimes coming close, sometimes retreating. Amy had imagined ghosts in the night. We can imagine Death materialising at the foot of her bed as the vodka bottle slipped from her grasp and the last grains of sand ran through the hour-glass.

3

'Who are you?' asks the knight in *The Seventh Seal*, as a sombre figure appears before him.

'I am Death.'

'Have you come for me?'

'I have been walking by your side for a long time.'

'That I know.'

'Are you ready?'

4

Andrew Morris checked on Amy at ten a.m. on Saturday. She was lying on her bed with the duvet back. He assumed she was asleep and so left her alone.

Reg Traviss rose late at his flat and went into Soho to pick up a suit and get his hair cut. When Andrew rang him around four o'clock, Reg didn't answer because he was in the barber's chair. Afterwards he went to the Groucho Club for a drink, then walked to his office in Holborn where he'd left a pair of shoes. He intended to return Andrew's call when he got upstairs. Then he was going over to Amy's. Before he had a chance to do so, friends were ringing his mobile phone to ask him about the news breaking on television and the Internet. They said Amy was dead.

Reg tried to hail a cab, but he couldn't find one. He panicked. 'I must have looked like a right state. It might have looked like I was drunk or something [because I was] completely frantic. No cabs were stopping for me and I thought, I've got to compose meself, otherwise no one's going to stop for me and I'm gonna fucking explode. And eventually I got a cab.'

By the time Reg reached Camden Square the police had sealed the house. Reporters, photographers and camera crews were gathering outside. Neighbours came to their windows to watch. After a while three men in suits emerged from the house, a police detective and two undertakers, the latter carrying a gurney on which lay Amy's corpse in a red body bag. The men carried it down the path and slid it into a private ambulance. As neighbour Steve Jones observes, it was a shocking sight to behold. 'It's very unpleasant to see a young lady in the garden one day, and then see her being carried out in a red plastic bag the next.'

Amy's death made front-page news around the world. Although she had long been heading for trouble, her death came as a shock to those who knew her personally and to the millions who knew of her, whether they liked her music or not. It crystallised a tragic life and gave new meaning to her songs, which were played relentlessly on radio and television from the moment her death was announced.

Media interest was intense at Amy's funeral on Tuesday, 26 July, an unusual two-part service on an overcast day in north London. First there was a public service at Edgwarebury Jewish Cemetery, followed by a private ceremony at Golders Green Crematorium. In practice, both were attended by hordes of people, including Amy's band and celebrity friends, as well as being thronged with journalists, camera crews and photographers, many of whom brought stepladders to get pictures over the wall.

Rabbi Frank Hellner was obliged to wear a microphone at Edgwarebury so his words could be broadcast to people who couldn't squeeze into the prayer hall. Although he had conducted countless funerals in his long career, including those of celebrities, the rabbi found Amy's funeral disconcerting. 'As far as I'm concerned a funeral is a private thing, and one doesn't expect or want the press to be there in a very conspicuous manner, and although they were kept at bay their presence was very much felt. It takes away from the decorum of the occasion.' The family didn't seem troubled by the attention, though, and, of course, the press had been part of Amy's life. 'Even those press people liked Amy, do you know what I mean?' says Reg Traviss.

In his eulogy Mitch Winehouse spoke of Amy's 'fantastic recovery' from drug addiction and gave the impression that she had been conquering her alcoholism. He said she was not depressed at the end. She was in good spirits when her mother had seen her, and he believed she had 'passed away happy, [which] makes us all feel better'. Mitch announced an idea that had come to him directly after Amy had died. He would be launching the Amy Winehouse Foundation, 'something to help the things she loved – children, horses – but also to help those struggling with substance abuse'. Some of Amy's friends took exception to Mitch's comments, and to the tone of the funeral.

'It was *The Mitch Winehouse Show*,' says Lauren Franklin. 'It was a media frenzy … so distasteful.'

In his remarks to the mourners, Rabbi Hellner observed that Amy's death put her in the same company as Brian Jones, Jimi Hendrix, Janis Joplin, Jim Morrison and Kurt Cobain. 'Not because I thought there was anything to read into it. More the tragedy of [lost] youth, the tragic circumstances in which youth is taken, and that ironically they happened to be the same age.' The emotion became too much for Amy's producer, Mark Ronson, who left the second service early, clearly upset.

Since Amy's death, fans had gathered outside her house in Camden Square. Opposite the house was a patch of grass where people left flowers, beer cans, miniature vodka bottles, cigarettes, cards and other tributes to Amy. They also wrote messages on the trees. 'RIP Amy', 'Oh Amy why?' Then, on the evening of Amy's funeral – a warm, dry night – the crowd swelled to a couple of hundred and took the form of a wake. A car was parked outside Amy's house with the windows wound down and *Back to Black* on repeat on the CD player, so loud it was distorted. A hardcore group of fans – several middle-aged women, a man in a wheelchair, local drunks – danced around the car to the music late into the night. As the evening wore on the dancers became increasingly wild and inebriated, joining together in raucous choruses of 'No! No! No!' An ambulance was summoned after one woman passed out. 'She was off her face,' explained reveller Michaela Van Es, who insisted that Amy would have appreciated this celebration of her life. Jim Morrison would have recognised the wake as a Dionysian rite.

Epilogue

THE DANCE OF DEATH

Jig, jig, jig, what a saraband!
Circles of the dead dance holding hands!
Henri Cazalis 'Danse Macabre'

1

Cynics say that death is a good career move, and so it has proved for the 27s. Amy Winehouse is at least as popular in death as she was in life. She is ubiquitous, sometimes in surprising forms. Amy Winehouse wigs, transfer tattoos and a 'Rehab babe' fancy-dress costume can be bought online for parties, while Amy's waxwork is one of the premier attractions at Madame Tussaud's in London. The other 27 Club stars are not forgotten. A billboard of Jimi Hendrix looms above Times Square in New York, while tourist shops on Broadway purvey Lizard King dolls, with nodding heads, modelled on Jim Morrison, as well as the ever-popular Jim Morrison T-shirts. Kurt Cobain T-shirts sell almost as strongly. Janis Joplin T-shirts are rarer, but plans are afoot to bring a musical about Janis's life to the stage. Meanwhile, the music of the 27s is heard everywhere, and endlessly repackaged. The 27s buck the decline of CD sales.

Least remembered is Brian Jones, whose part in the Rolling Stones story has been effaced by the success of the surviving members. Brian almost went without mention as the Stones celebrated their fiftieth anniversary in 2012. It was partly his own fault. He was the least likeable of the six principal 27s – neurotic, weepy and sometimes violent – and he was always going to be less iconic than Mick Jagger. Still, there are those who lament Brian's death. Cotchford Farm is a place of pilgrimage. Alastair Johns, who bought Brian's house from his estate, says Brian's fans are less troublesome than *Winnie-the-Pooh* readers, who trespass across his land, and he has had no qualms about using the swimming-pool in which Brian drowned. 'My children have enjoyed it enormously.'

Admirers also pay their respects at Brian's grave, particularly on his birthday and the anniversary of his death. Visitors to Cheltenham Cemetery leave small gifts and notes for their idol: flowers, homemade CDs, photographs. A book of remembrance is kept in a plastic lunch box to preserve it from the rain, the pages inscribed with fond messages. 'Thank you Mr Rollin Stone', 'Happy New Year, Brian … Never forgotten'.

Diehard fans aside, Brian is chiefly remembered for the circumstances of his death in 1969, which we have explored. The death of Jimi Hendrix the following year also proved rich material for theorists. Although no one knows what was in Jimi's mind when he swallowed those sleeping pills at the Samarkand Hotel, his death was adequately explained at his inquest. He inhaled his vomit while intoxicated. Yet theorists rushed forward at once to offer alternative explanations, including Eric Burdon, who went on television to suggest that his friend had committed suicide. 'He used drugs to phase himself out of this life,' Burdon told the BBC, basing his comments on the note he found next to Jimi's bed. He assumed initially that this was a suicide note. It turned out to be a song Jimi had been writing. Although Burdon got his facts muddled, the idea that Jimi Hendrix committed suicide is among the least incredible theories. In a sense he did kill himself. Other friends, including Noel Redding, went way over the top in suggesting that Jimi may have been murdered.

Putting aside the wilder stories, there was genuine confusion over Jimi's final hours, mostly because of the unreliable statements given by his girlfriend, Monika Dannemann. She claimed Jimi was alive when she woke up next to him on the morning of 18 September 1970, and still alive when she went with him in the ambulance to the hospital, blaming the emergency services for failing to save his life. This was a gross falsification. When the London Ambulance Service reviewed the case in 1992 it concluded that Jimi had been dead when the ambulance crew arrived at the scene, and he was alone. Monika Dannemann was nowhere to be seen, and she did not travel with Jimi in the ambulance. The truth is that if anybody let Jimi down, Monika did, and the guilt this surely created seems to have warped her mind.

Monika Dannemann gave numerous interviews about Jimi after his death, portraying herself as the woman he would have married had he lived, and turning her East Sussex cottage into a shrine to the star. When challenged about her reminiscences she went to law to defend her reputation, which proved to be a fatal mistake. In 1990 she unsuccessfully sued the publishers of Noel Redding's autobiography, in which he claimed that she had hesitated before calling an ambulance when Jimi died. Around the same time another of Jimi's former girlfriends, Kathy Etchingham, began to investigate what had happened at the Samarkand Hotel, speaking to the ambulance men and the police who had attended the scene. They told her Jimi was dead when they arrived. Kathy and Monika were now at loggerheads over the circumstances of Jimi's demise. When Monika described Kathy Etchingham as an inveterate liar, Etchingham sued for libel. The case was settled in her favour, with Dannemann promising not to repeat her allegations. When she did so in a 1995 book, Etchingham sued for contempt of court. Monika Dannemann was found guilty on 3 April 1996. Two days later she gassed herself to death in her car.

Jimi's financial and musical legacy is equally unedifying. When he died his estate was valued at £208,000 ($330,700), most of which was swallowed by debt. Because he died intestate, that is without a will, his estate passed to his father, to whom he had not been particularly close. After Jimi's manager, Michael Jeffrey, died in 1973, Al Hendrix entrusted the management of Jimi's music to a lawyer named Leo Branton in return for $50,000 (£31,446) a year, plus bonuses, which must have seemed like a lot to the aged gardener. To exploit Jimi's catalogue Branton went into business in 1975 with Jimi's producer friend Alan Douglas, who says that the estate had gone to seed by this time. Half of Jimi's publishing had been sold and the half the estate retained was only generating $400,000 a year (£251,572). Douglas bought back Jimi's publishing. 'And then I started to make records, and do merchandising, and do what one does with the music of Jimi Hendrix. Everything started to happen, and [by 1985] we were doing $15 *million* [(£9.4 million) a year].' Douglas achieved this turnaround partly by releasing new albums created from recordings Jimi had left behind, some overdubbed with session musicians. Many fans and critics considered this a misuse of Jimi's music.

Al Hendrix came to regret his deal with Leo Branton and sued for what he had signed away, 'not really understanding he was signing it away,' says Janie Hendrix, one of the daughters of Al's second wife. Al won the case and established a family company to handle Jimi's music, Experience Hendrix, managed by Janie. When Al died in 2002 the Hendrix estate was valued at $80 million (£50 million). Al left everything to Janie and other family members, but cut the children from his first marriage to Lucille, Jimi's mother, out of the will. For years he had denied paternity of most of these children, though it is likely that they were his. There was little doubt that Leon Hendrix was Jimi's blood brother. Jimi and Leon had also grown up together. If anybody should have benefited from the estate, it was Leon. But Leon had fallen out with his father and got nothing. He contested the will, but lost. Many of Jimi's friends were dismayed at this outcome, while also being surprised that Janie Hendrix, who was not a blood relative, had wound up running things.

As with the Branton-Douglas regime, under Janie Hendrix's leadership songs Jimi had not seen fit to release in life are being released posthumously. Janie takes the view that Jimi worked tirelessly in the studio to lay down a musical legacy, which she is sharing with the world, estimating his catalogue at 110 songs – twice as many as were released in his lifetime – 'and not just one version, but several versions'. This makes for a seemingly endless series of 'new' Hendrix releases. Meanwhile, legal wrangles over the estate continue, with Alan

Douglas, now in his eighties, still embroiled in disputes with Experience Hendrix. He cannot disguise his dislike of Janie Hendrix. 'She's nasty ... but she's smart.' And he does not think highly of Experience Hendrix, though his own custodianship of Jimi's music was criticised. The posthumous history of Jimi's affairs is frankly unpleasant. Naturally, it's all about money. 'It's always about money,' says Douglas. 'He still makes money now – today. People are fighting about it.'

As for Jimi's last resting place, it was originally a modest grave in Greenwood Memorial Park, south of Seattle. After Al died the family had Jimi's remains moved to a more prominent location in the park, and commissioned a massive new granite memorial, decorated with images of the musician and quotations from his lyrics. It is an ugly but robust edifice built to withstand the attentions of the 120,000 people who come to pay their respects each year. For when all is said and done Jimi Hendrix was one of the most original and exciting musicians of the rock era.

2

Janis Joplin was cremated and her ashes scattered in the Pacific Ocean off Marin County where she lived latterly. Janis owned her home and had money in the bank when she died in 1970, but she did not die rich. After the funeral, Laura Joplin asked Janis's attorney Bob Gordon how much the estate was worth. 'I said, "Well, I think it'll be at least fifty thousand dollars." But that was before *Pearl* came out.' *Pearl* was, of course, the album Janis had been recording with the Full Tilt Boogie Band when she died. When the record became a posthumous hit the money gushed like oil. 'The *Pearl* album has sold ten million copies – it's a lot – and there have been innumerable repackagings of her recordings and a lot of use of her songs for licensing for one purpose or another, so I think the family have done quite well,' says Gordon. 'As I understand it, the mother and father [willed] their portion to the children, so that the monies are now divided between Laura and Michael.'

A greatest-hits compilation released in 1973 built upon the success of *Pearl*, selling seven million copies in the United States. If Janis had not been rich in life the Joplin family were rich now. This was a remarkable result for Laura Joplin in particular, considering that she had been excluded from Janis's will until the last days of her sister's life. 'I think it's very funny that her sister has become extremely wealthy because of Janis,' says the singer's former housemate, Lyndall Erb. 'She really didn't get along with her family at all.'

Some of the musicians who worked with Janis, especially those on *Pearl*, are unhappy about the way they have been treated by the estate. 'My particular band has not had a happy relationship with her record company or her estate. It's very tiresome. Greed seems to have motivated both of them. It hasn't changed our feelings for Janis. The odd thing is that the way they've behaved is the absolute anti-thesis of how Janis felt about her last band,' says organist Ken Pearson. The band was paid union scale for recording *Pearl*, but not rewarded further. There is no contractual reason why the musicians should get any more money, but that doesn't stop them feeling hard done by. Pearson says that they only hear from the record company when new editions of *Pearl* are released and they are asked to do interviews to promote the CD. 'The history of pop music is littered with this sort of thing. Janis, she was fair and loved us, and we loved her, and it was an equal thing. The memory is fine. It's just how business gets done after that ... I guess the ten million records at ten dollars a record – which would be a hundred million (£62 million) – just wasn't enough. Do you know what I mean? It's obscene.'

Sam Andrew, who played with Janis in Big Brother, then the Kozmic Blues Band, and was a close friend, has a more personal regret. Having survived the 1960s and 1970s, which he terms 'a poisonous period', he finds himself enjoying a drug-free old age and wishes that Janis had lived to enjoy the same. 'Now is the best time of my life. I'd hate to have missed this. I'm sorry Janis did, truly sorry. She would have really enjoyed this.' Sam can imagine Janis Joplin at seventy. 'I know she wouldn't look very good. I don't ... But, you know, it's a happy time, mainly because there aren't so many drugs. So it's rational and logical, and you have a partner who you stay with. I've been married to my wife for a long time. It's a rich relationship. [Janis] probably would have found that.'

With no grave to visit, Janis's admirers gravitate to the Landmark Hotel in Hollywood (now named the Highland Gardens Hotel) where Room 105 is booked in advance on her birthday and the anniversary of her death. The suite is much as it was when Janis died there and her fans have taken to writing their names in the closets where she hung her clothes. Some visitors and hotel staff swear that Janis's ghost inhabits the hotel, knocking pictures off the walls, making telephones jangle when no one is calling, and opening doors. 'And occasionally the john flushes, which is funny,' says Don Hoyt, who often checks into 105 in memory of Janis, whom he says he knew. 'I say, "Janis has been drinking Southern Comfort and has to pee."'

3

Jim Morrison willed his estate to Pamela Courson. After her death in 1974 her parents, Penny and Columbus Courson, inherited Jim's portion of the Doors' royalties. Jim's mother and father went to law for a share of the money, with the result that the Coursons and Morrisons split Jim's quarter-interest in the Doors. Considering the *froideur* that existed between Jim and his parents, this is a surprising outcome, though the history of the 27 Club demonstrates that money trumps family feeling, and the people who benefit financially from the deaths often seem the least deserving.

The Doors attempted to continue without Jim, releasing two more albums, but they could not sustain a career as a trio and split in 1973. The rest of their lives would be lived in the shadow of their charismatic singer. 'It was over, and we would all be something slightly less. We would always have a part of us missing. For the rest of our lives,' Ray Manzarek has written.* But it wasn't the end of the Doors as a commercial enterprise.

When Francis Ford Coppola used 'The End' in *Apocalypse Now*

---

* Ray Manzarek died in 2013 as this book was going to press.

in 1979 he started a revival of interest in the Doors that hasn't abated. There was an immediate, dramatic rise in sales of the band's back catalogue. A new greatest-hits compilation, in 1980, went platinum. That year also saw the publication of *No One Gets Out of Here Alive*, a bestselling biography of Jim that built up the legend of a Dionysian rock star. Former Elektra Records executive Steve Harris told the authors about Jim suggesting he stage a 'death hoax' for publicity, and they cited the story at the end of the book to tease readers with the notion that Jim might have faked his death in Paris. A surprisingly large number of people were persuaded by this improbable idea, with sightings of Jim reported across the world over the next few years. Steve Harris doesn't buy it for a moment. 'I think he's completely dead. No doubt about it.'

Another popular theory is that Jim overdosed in the toilets at the Rock 'n' Roll Circus in Paris hours before his 'official' death in the apartment where he and Pamela were staying. A former manager of the Rock 'n' Roll Circus, Sam Bernett, claims to have found Jim's body in the club toilets. '[As] I am the one who found Jim dead I know what I'm talking about.' Bernett's story is compromised by the fact that he kept quiet for 36 years, making his claim in a 2007 newspaper article and book. Meanwhile, others tell a slightly different version of the tale, saying Jim was found unconscious at the club, rather than dead. Either way the story of what happened next is essentially the same.

Unnamed men – drug-dealers in Bernett's account – apparently smuggled Jim's inert body out of the Rock 'n' Roll Circus and through the back of the club, via an adjacent building, into a parallel street. They loaded it into a vehicle and drove it to rue Beautreillis where they carried it upstairs to Apartment 4 and dumped it in the bath. All this was supposedly done to avoid trouble with the police.

It is hard to believe that anybody would have gone to such lengths to cover up an accidental death. The idea that such an operation may have been conducted without anybody noticing is far-fetched. When one imagines smuggling a dead weight across the centre of Paris, in and out of vehicles and buildings, without being seen, as large and heavy as Jim's corpse would have been, incredulity sets in. Like all such theories, this one would rely upon many people, including Pamela Courson, agreeing to a conspiracy of silence, which is not feasible. Yet all this and more has appeared in print. 'Jim, I think, would love all these fantasies,' says Alain Ronay, who was with Jim the day before he died. He believes that if Jim were alive today he wouldn't sue for defamation. He would laugh.

It was Ronay who chose Jim's grave at Père Lachaise, believing he had found a plot that fans would not easily locate. When he returned to the cemetery a year later the grave had already become a popular tourist attraction. 'What I saw, which was really distressing, was the signs on the graves, saying, "Jim, this way," and so on, which I thought was terrible, that they had no respect whatsoever for the fact that it's a cemetery.' The surviving Doors were likewise shocked by the graffiti when they visited Père Lachaise in 1975, and surprised that nobody had erected a monument to Jim. Pamela had been given the money to do so, but hadn't got around to it. Jim's parents were also slow to give their son a headstone, though they did so eventually. Neither did they hurry to France to pay their respects. 'I guess my parents finally went one time, but it wasn't like they ran over [there] the first year – there was no purpose,' says Andy Morrison, noting that the admiral and his wife were not 'real religious', and the family didn't consider the circumstances of Jim's death particularly important. 'We didn't care whether it was drugs, or alcohol, or what [killed Jim]. He died in the bath tub, and he's dead. So what difference does it make – all the exact little details? The thing is he partied too hard and he's gone.'

Andy says his parents started to receive substantial income from Jim's estate – regular six-figure cheques – ten years after his death when the Doors revival got under way. The money has kept coming ever since. 'I guess it's never going to stop.'

The cult of Jim was fuelled by Oliver Stone's 1991 feature film *The Doors*. By this time merchandising as well as CD sales had become a significant source of income for the estate. People who were not born in 1971 took to wearing Jim Morrison T-shirts, wanting to associate themselves with a handsome and transgressive rock star. The image printed on the T-shirts is usually the iconic Joel Brodsky photograph of Jim in his beefcake prime. 'They think that's how he looked when he died. You know, live fast, die young, and leave a good-looking corpse,' observes Jim's friend Dickie Davis. 'I don't believe Jim had a good-looking corpse.'

Jim's grave is now listed in all the guide books to Paris, drawing millions of visitors to Père Lachaise, many of whom ignore the graves of Chopin, Piaf, Wilde and other luminaries, making straight for the Lizard King. Some say he is no longer in the grave, the family having repatriated his remains, but this is denied by the cemetery and the estate.

Although most visitors to Père Lachaise behave responsibly, a proportion of those who traipse up the cobbled lanes each year damage Jim's grave and those of his neighbours. Parts of Jim's memorial have been stolen. The very earth has been scooped up and taken away. At night fans climb over the walls to have sex on the grave or shoot up. One fan overdosed and died. More commonly, they scribble messages on Jim's grave, also marking the adjacent stones and the nearest tree, such inanities as 'Thank You, Jim', 'Light My Fire' and 'This isn't the End'. The unfortunate tree is also smothered in gobs of chewing gum inscribed with hearts. When the custodians of Père Lachaise complained to the Morrison family, Jim's parents paid for a steam-cleaning machine and a robust new memorial, but this has not solved the problem. There are currently crowd barriers around Jim's grave, uniquely in the cemetery, and a security guard stands on duty during opening hours.

Visitors to Jim Morrison's grave are a mixed bunch, of all ages from all over the world, not necessarily fans of the Doors. Rather, the grave has become one of the sights to see in Paris. 'It's an iconic life – live hard, die young,' observes Kyle Fisher, a middle-aged man from Ohio, visiting with his daughter in 2012. 'I think he was in the 27 Club.' Peter Niedner from Germany believes that the number 27 is important. 'The two and the seven is a nine, and nine is a special number,' he says enigmatically, at the graveside. 'What I think is amazing is that he is more than forty years dead and you can come whenever you want and you see fresh flowers.'

'Plastic.'

'Yeah, but someone put them there.'

Andy Morrison, who has visited Père Lachaise several times, has found it a mixed blessing being Jim's brother. People always want to talk to him about Jim, though some refuse to believe he is related. Once a sailor challenged him in a bar: 'If you're really Jim's brother, what was his nickname?'

'He didn't have a nickname.'

The sailor looked at his friends as if he had found Andy out. 'He doesn't know Jim's nickname was the Lizard King!'

'Excuse me. That's right,' replied Andy sarcastically. 'I remember my mother yelling up the stairs, "Come on down, Lizard King! Your eggs are getting cold."'

After his parents died Andy and his sister inherited the family share in the Doors, enough money for Andy to quit his job in construction and buy a 154-acre property in California. He enjoys his good fortune, but he believes that his brother is misunderstood and misrepresented, especially as portrayed by the actor Val Kilmer in Oliver Stone's film. 'He was a lot more human and down-to-earth [than people think]. Very friendly. Would get along with anybody ... he could be a very personable person [and] he had a wonderful sense of humour ... Val Kilmer, he never smiled.'

Andy is not keen on Jim's former band mates, especially keyboard player Ray Manzarek, whom he considers 'a stuck-up stupid asshole'. There is also a rift within the band, with John Densmore vetoing deals to use Doors music in advertising, and going to law to stop Ray Manzarek and Robby Krieger touring under the Doors name. As a result Manzarek and Krieger are obliged to tour under their own names if they want to perform Doors material, which makes the difference between playing clubs and giving concerts in arenas. In his memoir Manzarek describes Densmore as 'a pissant'.

Even though the Doors are inactive as a band – and riven by disagreements – they still put out product, such as a recent reissue of *LA Woman* with two previously unheard tracks. Doors projects are co-ordinated by a former record-company executive, Jeff Jampol, who has developed a niche career by representing 'legacy artists' – that is, dead rock stars. Apart from the Doors, he manages the estates of Jim Morrison and Janis Joplin from his office in Beverly Hills. He knew neither in life, being twelve years old when Jim died.

It must be less hassle representing Jim and Janis dead than alive, as difficult as they could be. 'You know, a lot of people tell me that,' says Jampol, 'but you have the beneficiaries, and lawyers and litigators and business managers and other reps ... I think I'd almost rather have one musician than fifteen reps and family members.' The Doors, for example, comprise numerous interested parties: not just the surviving band members, but also Jim's siblings, Anne and Andy, Pamela Courson's elderly mother, Penny, and her granddaughter, Emily. Everybody has to be consulted.

The enduring success of the Doors – only active for 54 months but still selling two million units a year – is in no small part due to the iconic status of Jim Morrison. When young men pull on a Jim Morrison T-shirt they buy into what Jeff Jampol calls 'the brand'. 'What does Jim Morrison stand for? He stands for questioning authority; he's a sexy rock god; he's an outsider; he's an iconoclast; he's a poet, that gentle soul with wit and wisdom and humour; he also stands for – the whole *raison d'être* of the Doors – it was about breaking on through,' Jampol explains. 'When you brand yourself with Jim Morrison that says something. Jim Morrison is like James Dean.'

Kurt Cobain was also a bit like James Dean, a depressed version in tatty clothes. Kurt's suicide at 27 made him a tragic hero for a generation, and as that generation ages, they cling to their love of Nirvana as older people listen nostalgically to the Beatles or Frank Sinatra. It is the music of their lives.

Thousands gathered at the Seattle Center to mourn Kurt's death in 1994. Today artefacts from his life are displayed in the EMP Museum in the park. Financed by Microsoft billionaire Paul Allen and designed by Frank Gehry, it was originally envisaged as a Jimi Hendrix museum. Over time EMP developed into a more general exhibition of pop culture, including a collection of Hendrix and Nirvana artefacts. Displayed along with Jimi's stage suits and guitars are such ephemera as Kurt Cobain's cardigans, spot-lit on mannequins in glass cabinets as if they are as priceless as Abraham Lincoln's hats. Jimi and Kurt would surely have laughed to see their lives commemorated in this solemn way.

Kurt's death put paid to Nirvana as a working band but, as with the Doors, there was still business to attend to. The surviving members, Dave Grohl and Krist Novoselic, formed a company with Kurt's widow, Courtney Love, which gave them equal shares in Nirvana LLC. The threesome soon fell out, however, suing and countersuing in 2002 over the use of unreleased material. Family relations also became strained. Courtney temporarily lost custody of her daughter Frances to Kurt's mother and sister, after Courtney reportedly suffered an accidental overdose, and she gave up custody again in 2009 for unspecified reasons. A year later, when Frances turned eighteen, she came into a trust fund that made her financially independent. Her relationship with her mother does not seem good. They had a public falling-out in 2012 over Twitter messages Courtney posted, suggesting that David Grohl had tried to seduce Frances, which both denied. Frances issued a rebuke to her mother: 'While I'm generally silent on the affairs of my biological mother, her recent tirade has taken a gross turn.' 'Biological mother' is not a term of endearment.

In happier times Kurt's mother and sister lived in an old monastery Courtney bought on the edge of the Capitol State Forest in Washington, between Aberdeen and Olympia. This is a beautiful area that Kurt visited in childhood, a remote and peaceful place largely devoid of the noise of mankind, a striking contrast to the racket Kurt made in Nirvana. The family built a Buddhist shrine in the garden, adjacent to McLane Creek in which Frances scattered some of her father's ashes in 1999. The creek would carry them into local rivers that flow ultimately into the Pacific Ocean, where we might imagine particles of Kurt dancing in the deep with the microscopic remains of Janis Joplin.

4

Sales of Amy Winehouse's music enjoyed a boom after her death. She went to number one in the UK charts, as well as in fifteen other countries around the world. Her US album sales increased more than tenfold, and there were 1.5 million posthumous downloads. This was to be expected. What was more remarkable was how her family rushed into action in her name.

Mitch Winehouse was in New York when he was told that Amy had died. He originally said that he had the idea for the Amy Winehouse Foundation on the flight home. Later he told a story about how Amy's voice miraculously came into his head while he was still in New York. 'I got the news [when] I was in my cousin's apartment in New York City. I got the terrible news that Amy had passed away. And almost immediately her voice came into my head and said, "Foundation ... kids ... Dad ... foundation, foundation,"' he told the BBC in 2013. 'I do believe in life after death. Some people might think I'm deluded, but it happened. Her voice.' In any event Mitch announced the foundation at his daughter's funeral in London, on 26 July 2011, registering the name three weeks later.

The foundation would be a charitable organisation to benefit young people, including those with addiction issues. While this might seem laudable, the Charity Commission recommends that people consider giving money to established charities before starting new ones, which dilute the charity sector and may duplicate work already being done. There has been a trend in recent years for bereaved people to start micro-charities and foundations in the name of the deceased as a memorial, or to cheer themselves up, even as a vanity project, although they might do better to make a donation to organisations that have experience. Mitch Winehouse has been quoted as saying that setting up the foundation saved *his* life, and that doing good in Amy's name 'makes me feel good'. It also gives him a reason to remain in the public eye.

Just as Mitch had rushed to launch the foundation, he charged ahead with publicity. He appeared on two American talk shows in September 2011 to discuss the foundation, speculating to the hosts, Anderson Cooper and Piers Morgan, that Amy had not died of drugs, or because she drank too much, but because she was in the habit of stopping drinking abruptly, which could cause seizures that might have accounted for her death. Mitch's peculiar suggestion that Amy died because she *stopped* drinking proved incorrect. He was reportedly paid $50,000 (£31,446) for appearing on Anderson Cooper's show, the money going to the foundation.

Between interviews Mitch found time to sing in concert and sell a book about his daughter. A deal with HarperCollins was announced on 10 October 2011, his proceeds going to the foundation. With Janis and Mitch already the directors of a number of companies handling Amy's affairs, they now set up more, including Bird and Butterfly Ltd, which became Amy Winehouse Foundation Trading Ltd. Mitch did all this before the inquest into his daughter's death had even been held.

The first inquest into Amy's death, at St Pancras Coroner's Court in London, on 26 October 2011, was a badly organised circus. A large number of press attended, kept outside the building by court staff while the Winehouse family, Amy's managers and friends were ushered inside, escorted by a phalanx of surly private bodyguards most of whom had no part in the proceedings. Others with a legitimate interest were denied admission. The blame for this shambles must lie with the court staff and police. Meanwhile, the coroner Suzanne Greenaway resigned a month later when it was revealed that she was under-qualified for her job. As a result a second inquest was held before a new coroner at the same court in 2013. These unfortunate circumstances aside, the evidence of the two inquests was consistent and clear.

Contrary to what Mitch Winehouse had said on American television, the court heard that Amy drank herself to death. Pathologist Professor Suhail Baithun explained that he found 416 milligrams of alcohol per decilitre in Amy's blood, over five times the UK drink-drive limit, and more than enough to stop her breathing. A police officer also told the court about the three empty vodka bottles found in her bedroom suite.

Dr Cristina Romete made clear in her evidence that she had warned Amy of the grave risk of binge-drinking. 'The advice I had given to Amy over a long period of time, in verbal and in written form, was about the effects alcohol can have on the system, including respiratory depression and death ...'

In her closing remarks at the second inquest, which rehearsed the evidence of the first, HM Coroner Dr Shirley Radcliffe said that Amy was not depressed or suicidal, and that a thorough police investigation had revealed no suspicious circumstances. But the singer had a history of heavy drinking, and blood tests showed that she had drunk to a level associated with fatalities. 'It was a deliberate act which took an unexpected turn in that it led to her death [and] I record a verdict of misadventure.' This concurred with the 2011 inquest.

The day before she died, Amy had told her doctor that there were still things she wanted to achieve in life, which was partly why Dr Romete concluded that her patient was not suicidal. One thing Amy had failed to achieve was the completion and release of a third album. She'd agonised over it for years. After her death her record company resolved the matter, with the family, in a flash. *Lioness: Hidden Treasures* was rushed out in time for Christmas. The album (titled after one of Amy's nicknames) received generous reviews on a wave of media sympathy, though this scrappy collection of odds and ends was surely not a CD Amy would have chosen to put out. Most of the twelve tracks were covers or out-takes of songs already released. 'Between the Cheats' is the only original song of note on the CD, and the fact that this recording dated from 2008 demonstrated that Amy's creativity had long since dried up. There were a few more songs in the can, arguably better ones, but the family vetoed their release on the basis that Amy hadn't wanted them to be heard. 'We've had to qualify [the album choice] in front of Amy's family. Her mum, her dad, her brother – that's her very vocal, protective brother – plus fiancés, stepfathers and more,' said record-company executive Darcus Beese, revealing that Universal faced the same headache as Jeff Jampol with his dead rock stars. Instead of dealing with one artist he had to handle a committee. Marketed with the spin that one pound ($1.59) from the sale of each CD would go to the Amy Winehouse Foundation, *Lioness: Hidden Treasures* went to number one in the UK.

Mitch maintained his high public profile in the months ahead, appearing with Janis and Tony Bennett at the Grammys in February 2012 to accept an award for the duet Bennett had recorded with Amy.

Back home the probate settlement of Amy's estate was announced.

Because Amy had died intestate, without a spouse or children, her fortune was divided equally between her parents. Net of taxes this amounted to £2.9 million ($4.6 million). In death Amy made her dad a millionaire. While Mitch is tireless in raising funds for his foundation, neither he nor his representatives made any reply when asked for this book how much, if any, of his share of the estate he intended to give to charity.

Along with Mitch and Janis, their spouses became directors of the Amy Winehouse Foundation in April 2012, sharing in doing good work in Amy's name. Interestingly, Amy's brother, Alex, who had been a director, chose to resign.

Blake received no money from Amy's estate, of course, though Amy may well have wanted him looked after before others. For all his faults, he was the love of her life and a needy case. Blake remained for the time being in HMP Leeds, struggling to deal with addiction issues, trying to work out what to do with his life when he got out. He thought about Amy a lot, and dreamed about her. In his dreams Amy had died falling off a cliff, a classic anxiety dream, which may betray his feelings of guilt.

In *Amy, My Daughter*, written in haste for publication in advance of the first anniversary of Amy's death, Mitch made clear that Blake had been a nightmare son-in-law. In chronicling his daughter's life, Mitch left Janis and Alex in the background, concentrating on his own dealings with his daughter during the years of her fame. The reader gained the impression that neither he nor Janis had managed to be a figure of authority in Amy's life, and as a result they could not curb her behaviour. Mitch did not identify, let alone address, what was fundamentally wrong with his daughter, perhaps because he was part of the problem. He admitted that he felt guilty about leaving home when Alex and Amy were children. Amy's waywardness might be interpreted as retribution for that misdemeanour, punishing her father endlessly, as if he were a soul in Purgatory. It was clear, however, that Mitch loved Amy. If setting up the foundation helped him feel better now that she was dead, she would probably approve. 'She always wanted her dad to be 'appy,' says Reg Traviss. 'If he was 'appy, she was 'appy. It was as simple as that.'

5

Amy Winehouse made a big impact on popular music in a short career without doing very much or going very far. As we have seen she lived her whole life in London, her homes within a few miles of each other, mostly connected by the Northern Line. Edgware is the last stop on the western fork of that line, nine stops from Camden Town. A short distance from the station is Edgwarebury Cemetery.

After Amy's body was cremated her ashes were passed around family and friends for a year while it was decided what to do with them. The family were mindful of the attention that other 27 graves had attracted, not least the worrying example of Jim Morrison in Paris. Ultimately Amy's wishes prevailed. She once said she wanted to be buried with her grandmother, Cynthia, who had been cremated in 2006.

Two days after what would have been Amy's 29th birthday, the family interred the ashes of Amy and Cynthia together at Edgwarebury Cemetery. They chose a plot near to the cemetery office so staff could keep an eye on the grave. A substantial black memorial was erected to mark the spot, standing out among the other stones because it is inscribed uniquely in sugar-pink lettering. There is a quote from the Bible, in Hebrew, expressing the hope that the souls of the deceased will be bound with God in eternity, a Star of David, the Amy Winehouse Foundation logo, and a list of Cynthia's and Amy's friends and relations. Mitch gets top billing.

Golden lads and girls all must,
As chimney sweepers, come to dust.
Cymbeline

Appendix

27 LONG-LIST

Dave Alexander played bass with the Stooges. He was born on 3 June 1947, dying in Ann Arbor, Michigan, on 10 February 1975. Fired by Iggy Pop for being unreliable, Alexander drank himself to death.

Elizabeth 'Bipsy' Amirian was an American singer. Born on 20 January 1982, she was stabbed to death by her fiancé in Temecula, California, 12 February 2009.

Alexander 'Sasha' Bashlachev was a Russian singer-songwriter. Born in Cherepovets, on 27 May 1960, he died in a fall from his Leningrad apartment, 17 February 1988.

Chris Bell was co-founder of the 1970s rock band Big Star. Born in Memphis, Tennessee, on 12 January 1951, he died in a car crash in Memphis, 27 December 1978. Leaving a rehearsal, his car hit a telegraph pole.

Jesse Belvin was an American singer-songwriter known as 'Mr Easy'. Born in San Antonio, Texas, on 15 December 1932, he died with his wife after a car crash in Arkansas, 6 February 1960.

Dennis Boon was singer and guitarist with the Minutemen. Born in Napa, California, on 1 April 1958, he died after being thrown from the band's tour van in an interstate accident near Phoenix, Arizona, 23 December 1985.

Louis Chauvin was a ragtime jazz pianist. Born in St Louis, Missouri, on 13 March 1881, a dissipated life ended in Chicago on 26 March 1908.

Arlester 'Dyke' Christian fronted Dyke and the Blazers. Born in Buffalo, New York, on 13 June 1943, he was shot dead outside a bar in Phoenix, Arizona, 13 March 1971.

Kurt Cobain was the leader of Nirvana. Born in Aberdeen, Washington, on 20 February 1967, he committed suicide in Seattle, 5 April 1994.

Pamela Courson was Jim Morrison's girlfriend and companion at the time of his death. Born in Weed, California, on 22 December 1946, Courson died of a heroin overdose in Los Angeles, 25 April 1974.

Zenon De Fleur was the stage name of Zenon Hierowski. Born in London on 9 September 1951, he played guitar with the Count Bishops. He died in London, 18 March 1979, following a car accident.

Peter de Freitas was the drummer with Echo and the Bunnymen. Born on 2 August 1961, he died on 14 June 1989 of head injuries suffered in a motorcycle accident on the A51 in Staffordshire, England.

Roger Lee Durham was a member of American R&B band Bloodstone. Born in Kansas City, on 14 February 1946, he was killed in a horse-riding accident, 27 July 1973.

Richey Edwards played guitar with the Manic Street Preachers, whose songs included 'Suicide Alley'. Born in Wales, on 22 December 1967, he went missing on 1 February 1995, possibly falling to his death from the Severn Bridge. Although his body was never found, he was declared presumed dead in 2008.

Valentín Elizalde, known as the 'Golden Rooster', sang songs glorifying Mexico's drug lords. Born in Navojoa, Mexico, on 1 February 1979, he was shot dead along with his driver and assistant after a concert in Reynosa, 25 November 2006.

Malcolm Hale was a member of Spanky and Our Gang. Born in Butte, Montana, on 17 May 1941, he died of carbon-monoxide poisoning in Chicago, 30 October 1968. He had slept in a room with a faulty heater.

Pete Ham was the leader of Badfinger. Born in Swansea, Wales, on 27 April 1947, he hanged himself at home in Surrey, 24 April 1975. His band mate Tommy Evans died in the same way seven years later.

Patrick 'Fat Pat' Hawkins was an American hip-hop artist. Born in Houston, Texas, on 4 December 1970, he was shot dead in Houston, 3 February 1998, while trying to collect a debt.

Joe Henderson sang the 1962 hit 'Snap Your Fingers'. Born on 24 April 1937, he died of a heart attack in Nashville, Tennessee, 24 October 1964.

Jimi Hendrix was born in Seattle on 27 November 1942. He died in London, 18 September 1970, after inhaling his vomit while intoxicated.

Nat Jaffe was an American jazz pianist. Born in New York on 1 January 1918, he died in New York of kidney failure, 5 August 1945.

Robert Johnson was perhaps the most influential of all blues guitarists. Born in Hazlehurst, Mississippi, on 8 May 1911, he died in Greenwood, Mississippi, on or around 16 August 1938. The cause of death remains mysterious, variously attributed to syphilis or murder by poison.

Brian Jones founded the Rolling Stones. Born in Cheltenham, on 28 February 1942, he drowned in his swimming-pool in East Sussex, 2 July 1969, while under the influence of drink and drugs.

Janis Joplin was born in Texas on 19 January 1943. She died of a heroin overdose in Hollywood, 4 October 1970.

Moses 'Moss' Khumalo was a South African jazz saxophonist. He was born in Soweto, on 30 January 1979. He hanged himself at home in Honeydew, near Johannesburg, 4 September 2006.

Helmut Köllen was a member of German rock band Triumvirat. He was born in Cologne, on 2 March 1950, and died there on 3 May 1977, having gassed himself in his car.

Aimee Leonard was a singer-songwriter born in Sudbury, Ontario, on 22 May 1983. She died of congenital heart failure at home in Ottawa, 29 January 2011. In common with many 27s, Leonard suffered with bipolar disorder, and spoke of suicide when depressed, but she died of natural causes. She was pregnant at the time.

Rudy Lewis sang with the Drifters. Born in Philadelphia, on 23 August 1936, he died in New York, 20 May 1964, the day he was due to record 'Under the Boardwalk'. Various causes of death have been cited, but most sources agree that his death was drug-related.

Sean McCabe sang with Ink & Dagger. Born in Pennsylvania, on 13 November 1972, he died in a motel in Indiana, 28 August 2000. A heavy drinker, he choked on his vomit.

Ronald 'Pigpen' McKernan was a founding member of the Grateful Dead, and the band's keyboardist. He was born in California on 8 September 1945. After years of heavy drinking he died of a gastrointestinal haemorrhage at home in Corte Madera, California, 8 March 1973.

Jacob Miller was a reggae artist. Born in Mandeville, Jamaica, on 4 May 1952, he died in a car accident in Kingston, 23 March 1980.

Damien 'Damo' Morris sang with the Australian band the Red Shore. Born on 22 May 1980, he died in a road accident near Coffs Harbour, New South Wales, 19 December 2007, after the band's van hit a tree. The driver was also killed.

Jim Morrison was lead singer with the Doors. Born in Melbourne, Florida, on 8 December 1943, he died in Paris, 3 July 1971. Officially, Morrison died of heart failure, but it is likely that heroin was a factor.

Nate Niec played bass in various US punk bands including No Holds Barred. Born on 3 March 1982, he died in a road accident in the state of Georgia, 6 October 2009.

Bryan Ottoson played guitar with American Head Charge. Born on 18 March 1978, he was found dead on the band's tour bus in South Carolina, 19 April 2005. He had died overnight, having consumed alcohol and prescription pills.

Kristen Pfaff played bass with Hole. Born in New York State on 26 May 1967, she died of a drug overdose in Seattle, 16 June 1994, shortly after the death of her friend Kurt Cobain. Her body was found in the bath.

Dickie Pride was the stage name of British pop singer Richard Kneller, also known as the 'Sheik of Shake'. Born in Croydon, on 21 October 1941, he was a heavy drinker and drug-user with mental health problems. At the end of his life he was living at the family home in Croydon where his mother found him dead of a drug overdose on 26 March 1969.

Raymond 'Freaky Tah' Rodgers was an American rapper. Born on 14 May 1971, he was shot dead leaving a party in New York, 28 March 1999.

Michael Rudetsky was an American keyboard player. Born in New York on 23 January 1959, he died at the London home of the singer Boy George on 6 August 1986. Rudetsky suffered a pulmonary oedema caused by heroin overdose.

Maria Serrano Serrano was a member of the European dance band Passion Fruit. Born in Holland, on 26 November 1973, she perished along with 23 others, including a fellow band member, in a plane crash near Zürich, 24 November 2001.

Abdillah Murad Md. Shari, known as 'Achik Spin', was a member of the Malaysian pop group Spin. Born on 1 July 1982, he died in a car accident on his way home from a show in Malaysia, 17 April 2010.

George 'Smitty' Smith was a founding member of American soul group the Manhattans. Born on 16 November 1943, he died of a brain tumour, 16 December 1970.

Gary Thain was a member of Uriah Heep. Born in Christchurch, New Zealand, 15 May 1948, he was found dead in the bath at home in London, 8 December 1975, having overdosed on sleeping pills.

Richard Turner was a British jazz trumpeter. Born in Leeds, 30 July 1984, he died on 11 August 2011 after suffering an aortic aneurysm while swimming.

Randy 'Stretch' Walker was a member of the rap group Live Squad, whose songs included 'Murderah'. Born on 8 April 1968, he was shot dead in New York, 30 November 1995.

Jeremy Michael Ward was a sound technician for the Mars Volta. Born in Texas, 5 May 1976, he died of a heroin overdose in Los Angeles, 25 May 2003.

Alan Wilson was a founder member of Canned Heat. Born in Massachusetts, 4 July 1943, he was found dead at the Los Angeles home of fellow band member Bob Hite on 3 September 1970, having taken an overdose of barbiturates.

Amy Winehouse was born in London on 14 September 1983. She died at home in London, 23 July 2011, of alcohol poisoning.

Wally Yohn played organ with the jazz-rock band Chase. Born on 12 January 1947, he was killed along with three fellow band members and their pilot when their aircraft crashed *en route* to a show in Minnesota, 9 August 1974.

Mia Zapata sang with the punk band the Gits. Born in Louisville, Kentucky, on 25 August 1965, she was raped and murdered in Seattle, 7 July 1993.

ACKNOWLEDGEMENTS

This book is the story of a number of lives that have become bundled together as the 27 Club. In order to see what, if anything, the 27 Club amounts to apart from a series of coincidental and tragic deaths, I needed to establish, first, how many musicians have died at 27. I researched the lives of more than three thousand people whose involvement in popular music since the start of the twentieth century was sufficiently notable for their careers to be recorded, compiling what I hope is the most complete and reliable long-list of 27s to be published. Most are musicians, indeed stars, but not all. I include Jim Morrison's girlfriend, for example, because she was a significant character on the music scene by association.

Having drawn up my long-list – comprising fifty individuals – I wanted to know whether or not these deaths were statistically significant. How I did this and what I discovered is described in the Prologue. I then focused on what I considered to be the six most prominent and interesting lives, to tell their individual stories and to identify common themes that may help explain why so many talented people died so young. This is the substance of the book.

For several reasons Amy Winehouse was always going to be my primary interest. First, I admired her as a singer and songwriter, and I thought she warranted a well-researched, independent biography, as opposed to some of the books published during her lifetime, many of which are shoddy works, and her father's partial account. This would not be a straightforward biography, however. The brevity of Winehouse's life and the relative paucity of her work (she only made two albums) is thin material for a full-length book. Rather, I decided to contrast her life with what I considered to be the other five principal 27s. In order of demise they are Brian Jones, Jimi Hendrix, Janis Joplin, Jim Morrison and Kurt Cobain. I deal with them in that order, book-ending with Winehouse.

I approached the family of Amy Winehouse at the outset of my work, meeting Mitch and Janis Winehouse on an evening in London when Mr Winehouse was performing his nightclub act. He told me he could not speak to me because he was under contract to write his own book (*Amy, My Daughter*). As a result, I have been obliged to investigate Amy's life without the assistance of her immediate family, and without the co-operation of associates who take their lead from the family. I was able to interview widely, nonetheless, both in regard to Amy Winehouse and the other principals. As with my previous books, I travelled extensively for research and sought out documentary evidence to bring these lives into focus.

I am grateful to the following people for answering my questions: Ryan and Liane Aigner, Patrick Alan, Steve Albini, Pernell Alexander, Jeff Allen, Nathan Allen, John Altman, Sam Andrew, Pat Andrews, Bill Ashton, the late Anthony Atherton, Teo Avery, Mirandi Babitz, Siobhan Bailey, Maury Baker, Professor Adrian Barnett, Maurice Bernstein, Dave Bishop, Ed Bogas, Angela Brew, David Brigati, Harvey Brooks, David Burr, John Byrne Cooke, Phil Cameron, Brad Campbell, Ricardo Canadinhas, Mo Cansick, Lonnie Castille, Ted Chandler, Doug Charles-Ridler, Leland Cobain, Marlene Cole, Henry Collins, Declan Connolly, Robert Crumb, Philippe Dalecky, Asher Dann, Richard 'Dickie' Davis, Glen Day, Pete 'Rok' Donaghy, Alan Douglas, Sammy Drain, Susi Earnshaw, Michael Eavis, Lyndall Erb, Eric Erlandson, Jason Everman, Peggy Fahey (*née* Lloyd), Victoria Fenton, Blake Fielder-Civil, Danny Fields, Snooky Flowers, Clem Floyd, Michael C. Ford, Ray Foulk, Chuck Fradenburg, Lauren Franklin, Melissa Gillespie, Danny Goldberg, Robert E. Gordon, Enid Graddis (*née* Stulberger), Les Hallett, John Hammond Jr, Ronnie Haran (and her husband Chase Mellen), Steve and Nicole Harris, Hank Harrison, Keith and Hazel Harrison, Henry Hate, Richard Hattrell, Catherine Hays (and her daughter Sofia), Rabbi Frank Hellner, Tommy Henderson, Janie Hendrix, Peter Hodgman, Mitch Holmquist, Deering Howe, Don Hoyt, Bob Hunter, John and Sarah Hurley, Jeff Jampol, Bob Jensen, Bryan Johnson, Inge Jones, Peter 'Buck' Jones, Professor Steve Jones, Prince Stanislas Klossowski 'Stash' De Rola, Britt Leach, Amanda Lear, Bradley Leckie, Linda Leitch (*née* Lawrence), Bob Leonard, Don

Letts, Aaron Liddard, Sir Michael Lindsay-Hogg, the Reverend Karen
Lindvig, Bonnie Lloyd, Andrew Loog Oldham, Edyta Lydon, Gered
Mankowitz, Michael Maska, Warren Mason, Sereg Mateke, Troy Miller,
Zoot Money, Jon Moon, Charles Moriarty, Andrew Morris, Andy
Morrison, Paul Murray, Breige Noonan, Sandra Olim, Adrian Packer,
Vidia Patel, Ken Pearson, Jay Phelps, Tibor Poor, Dr Jim Pritchett, Alex
Proud, Mischa Richter, Alain Ronay, Ron Schneider, Amie Schroeter (*née*
Wilson), Bob Seidemann, Sam Shaker, Lamont Shillinger, Steve Sidwell,
Stefan Skarbeck, Tomasz Skoczypiec, Nial Stimson, Dave Swallow, Jamie
Talbot, Stanley Targus, Andrea Todd (*née* Neathery), the Reverend Stephen
Towles, Reg Traviss, Vince Treanor, Paul Van der Hulks, Michaela Van
Es, Julia Vanellis, Mirek vel Stotker, Kim Warnick, Wavy Gravy,
'Commissioner' Gordon Williams, Beryl Winehouse, Carol Winehouse,
Etta 'Betty' Winehouse, Jonathan Winehouse, Lou Winwood, Gilles
Yepremian, Sylvia Young and Zouzou (a.k.a. Danièle Ciarlet).

Thank you additionally to Trevor Hobley of the Brian Jones Fan Club;
photographer Mike Charity, who showed me around Brian Jones's
Cheltenham; Alan R. Craze, HM Coroner for East Sussex; and Alastair
Johns of Cotchford Farm, East Sussex. Thank you also to Charles R.
Cross, who has written very good biographies of Jimi Hendrix and Kurt
Cobain, and gave me assistance when I visited Washington state. Mitch
Holmquist was my guide to Kurt Cobain's Aberdeen. Researching the
last days of Janis Joplin's life, I stayed in the room in which she died at
the Highland Gardens Hotel in Hollywood, formerly the Landmark.
Thank you to the manager, Jack Baklayan. Thank you also to Martine
Lecuyer at Père Lachaise in Paris, with other cemetery staff and the
following visitors to Jim Morrison's grave on a spring day in 2012: Kyle
and Courtney Fisher, Peter Niedner, Luke Sanders and Rachel Tyree. I
am also grateful to the residents, bar staff and shopkeepers in Camden
Town who spoke to me about Amy Winehouse, to Georgia Graham at
the *Camden New Journal*, and Edda Tasiemka at the Hans Tasiemka
Archives.

Thank you to my publishers: Fenella Bates at Hodder & Stoughton
in London, Ben Schafer at Da Capo Press in New York, and Diane
Turbide at Penguin Canada; and to my agents Kristyn Keene and Kate
Lee at ICM in New York, and Gordon Wise at Curtis Brown in London.

SOURCE NOTES

For shorthand the six principal 27s are referred to in the notes by initials: Brian Jones as BJ, Jimi Hendrix as JH, Janis Joplin as JJ, Jim Morrison as JM, Kurt Cobain as KC, and Amy Winehouse as AW.

The Wendy O'Connor epigraph is from the Aberdeen *Daily World*, reported in Charles R. Cross's biography of Kurt Cobain, *Heavier Than Heaven*. Full publication details of books referred to below will be found in the Bibliography (pages 342–346).

Part One 'Life'

Epigraph: Dante, *Divine Comedy*, first verse.

Prologue: **Exit, Gate 27**

Epigraph: Erlandson, *Letters to Kurt*.
Dr Romete's final house call to AW, dialogue and quoted remarks ('bored', etc.): second inquest into AW's death, held by HM Coroner Dr Shirley Radcliffe at St Pancras Coroner's Court in London, January 2013, where Dr Romete's sworn statement was read. The author also referred to the evidence of the first inquest, before Suzanne Greenaway at the same court in October 2011.
May 2011 incident and GP's warning letter: inquest evidence and Mitch Winehouse's book, *Amy, My Daughter* in which he writes that the letter warned AW was 'in immediate danger of death'.

AW did not want to die: second inquest evidence.

AW resistant to therapy: second inquest evidence.

Lyric quoted from 'Rehab' by Amy Winehouse © EMI Music Publishing Ltd.

AW joked about doctor's warning: see Chapter Thirteen, p. 267.

Layout of house/décor and furnishings: author's interviews, local enquiries and architectural plans.

Andrew Morris: his sworn statement at the second AW inquest, from which he is quoted throughout, save 'diamond person …' which is from discussions with the author.

Words with band members: author's interview with drummer Troy Miller.

Lauren Franklin: quoted from author's interview.

Charles-Ridler: quoted from author's interview.

Mitch Winehouse's last visit: Winehouse, *Amy, My Daughter*.

Janis Winehouse's appearance and character: author's meeting.

Janis Winehouse's last visit: *Hello!*, 16 July 2012 ('I love you, Mummy'); and *Daily Mail*, 25 July 2011 ('weary').

AW on medication: second inquest evidence.

Reg Traviss: quoted throughout from interviews with author.

Indian takeaway: Andrew Morris's sworn statement, second inquest.

Home secured by Morris: his evidence at second inquest.

Italian fan: author's interviews with Reg Traviss.

Behring Breivik outrage: *Observer*, 24 July 2011.

AW watches YouTube: Morris's statement, second inquest.

JM death: see Chapter Ten, pp. 221–22.

Texts Kristian Marr: his interview with the *Mail on Sunday*, 7 August 2011.

Didn't reply to Reg's texts: author's interviews with Reg Traviss.

Vomit in toilet: ibid.

Bulimic: Dr Romete's statement, second inquest.

AW kicked off her shoes: in Morris's statement, second inquest, she was found without her shoes on.

Position on bed: statement of paramedic Andrew Cable, second inquest, and author's interviews with Traviss.

Morris finds body: second inquest.

Ambulance response: statement of paramedic Andrew Cable, second inquest, quoted.

James arrives/calls made: Morris's sworn statement, second inquest.

Police involvement/bottles found: inquest evidence (first and second).

Blood alcohol levels: evidence at second inquest. Background on levels of intoxication: Peters (ed.), *BMA A–Z Family Medical Encyclopedia*.

Inquest verdict: HM Coroner Dr Radcliffe, quoted from second inquest.

Reg Traviss arrives at scene: author's interviews with Reg Traviss.

Wendy O'Connor: *Daily World*, 11 November 1991.

Coverage of AW death: newspaper reports, including the *Mail on Sunday* and *Washington Post*, 24 July 2011.

Survey of deaths: I drew on sources including Talevski, *Knocking on Heaven's Door*; Sadie (ed.), *The New Grove Dictionary of Music and Musicians*; Larkin (ed.), *The Encyclopedia of Popular Music*; Segalstad and Hunter, *The 27s*; www.thedeadrockstars.com; *Rolling Stone*, *Melody Maker*, numerous other publications and websites. All deaths were cross-referenced, certificates checked where available.

Professor Barnett and his colleagues: findings published in the *British Medical Journal*, Christmas 2011. I quote from the article, *Is 27 really a dangerous age for famous musicians? Retrospective cohort study*, and refer to my correspondence with Professor Barnett, who drew my attention to the Texas Sharpshooter Fallacy.

UK charts: I rely on Strong, *The Essential Rock Discography*.

Rock 'n' Roll Hall of Fame: see its website, www.rockhall.com.

Rock musicians are more likely to die young than general population: Bellis *et al.*,'Elvis to Eminem: quantifying the price of fame through early mortality of European and North American rock and pop stars', *Journal of Epidemiology and Community Health*, 2007, 61: 896–901 (www.jech.com).

Deaths of long-list stars: see Appendix, pp. 303–7.

Homicide and African-Americans: Bureau of Justice Statistics, 'Homicide Trends in the USA by age, gender and race, 1976–2005', www.bjs.gov.

Suicide illegal in Britain prior to 1961: Alvarez, *The Savage God*.

Quotations from Freud, *Beyond the Pleasure Principle*, and Durkheim, *On Suicide*.

WHO figures on suicide: Johnstone (ed.), *Companion to Psychiatric Studies*.

Al Wilson death: see Chapter Four, p. 94.

Pamela Courson death: see Chapter Ten, p. 222.

Bashlachev and Köllen: see Appendix, p. 303 and 305.

Eric Erlandson: quoted from his *Letters to Kurt*.

One: The Young Dionysians

Epigraph: Frazer, *The Golden Bough*.

William Wordsworth: 'My Heart Leaps Up'.

Philip Larkin: 'This Be The Verse'. *Collected Poems*. © The estate of Philip Larkin, 1983, 2003.

BJ background: author's interviews and background reading, including Jackson, *Brian Jones*; Wyman, *Stone Alone*; and Norman, *Symphony for the Devil*.

BJ described as 'an asshole': Richards, *Life*.

Pat Andrews, Marlene Cole, Declan Connolly, Richard Hattrell, Peter 'Buck' Jones and Linda Lawrence: quoted from author's interviews.

Lewis Jones: quoted from a 1971 BBC Radio interview, as reported by Jackson, *Brian Jones*.

JH background: author's interviews and background reading, including Cross, *Room Full of Mirrors*.

Pernell Alexander, Anthony Atherton and Sammy Drain: quoted from author's interviews. Thanks also to Tommy Henderson and Janie Hendrix. Other sources include JH's FBI file (1961 arrests) and exhibits at the EMP Museum in Seattle.

JJ's childhood: I consulted and quote from Laura Joplin's book, *Love, Janis*. Background reading: Echols, *Scars of Sweet Paradise*; Dalton, *Piece of My Heart*.

JJ laughed out of town: *Dick Cavett Show*, 25 June 1970.

Sam Andrew and John Byrne Cooke: quoted from author's interviews.

Kerouac: *On the Road*.

JJ on her trips to Houston and Los Angeles: letter dated 14 October 1965, reproduced in Joplin, *Love, Janis*.

JJ on leaving Texas: Dalton, *Piece of My Heart*.

JM's childhood and family background: I am indebted to his brother, Andy Morrison, whom I quote (save 'hard streak': Doors, with Fong-Torres, *The Doors*, from which I also quote his sister, Anne). Thanks also to Asher Dann and Vince Treanor (quoted). Background reading includes Hopkins with Sugerman, *No One Gets Out of Here Alive*; Riordan and Prochnicky, *Break on Through*.

JM on his parents and writing ambitions: *Rolling Stone*, 26 July 1969.

JM's interest in Nietzsche and the Dionysian archetype: Doors, *The Doors*; Hopkins with Sugerman, *No One Gets Out of Here Alive*;

Riordan and Prochnicky, *Break on Through*; Ray Manzarek, *Light My Fire*.

Nietzsche: *The Birth of Tragedy* (trans. Walter Kaufmann).

JM arrested in 1963: *Rolling Stone*, 8 July 2004.

I also referred, generally in this section about JM, to discussions with Danny Fields, the Doors' publicist at Elektra, Alain Ronay and Michael C. Ford (quoted on JM at UCLA).

JM's draft history: Selective Services record.

Beach meeting with Manzarek: Manzarek, *Light My Fire*.

Lyrics quoted from 'Moonlight Drive' © Doors Music Co.

KC's family history and early life: author's interviews, including KC's grandfather, Leland Cobain, and uncle, Chuck Fradenburg (both quoted); local enquiries in Aberdeen, Washington, and background reading, including the three principal Cobain biographies: Azerrad, *Come As You Are*; Cross, *Heavier Than Heaven*; True, *Nirvana*.

KC comment, 'redneck logger town': his *Journals*.

KC comment, 'suicide genes' and 'over the death of Jim Morrison': Cross, *Heavier Than Heaven*.

'I Hate Mom ...' and Wendy Cobain quote: Azerrad, *Come As You Are*.

KC comment, 'Every parent ...': ibid.

Divorce in America: my book, *Seventies* (Chapter One) and Frum, *How We Got Here: The 70s*.

'Something in the Way' by Kurt Cobain © EMI Virgin Songs, Inc.

KC, 'He got married ...': *About a Son* DVD (Sidetrack Films, 2008).

Penny Fahey (*née* Lloyd), Bob Hunter, Warren Mason and Lamont Shillinger: quoted from author's interviews. Thanks also to Phil Cameron, Victoria Fenton, Bonnie Lloyd, Stanley Targus and Andrea Todd (*née* Neathery).

Child of broken homes more likely to commit suicide: Grashoff, *Let Me Finish*.

Thanks to KC's friend Mitch Holmquist for showing me the Young Street Bridge, and discussing his friendship with Kurt.

KC, 'I've never taken sides ...': *Journals*.

Two: **Daddy's Girl**

Epigraph: Henry Wadsworth Longfellow

Winehouse family history: thanks to Beryl, Betty, Carol and Jonathan Winehouse (who made available family records and documents and is quoted from author's interviews).

Janis Winehouse on her similarity to AW: in conversion with the author, January 2012.

Mitch Winehouse on AW's childhood: Winehouse, *Amy, My Daughter*, including quotes, 'She was mischievous ...'

Beryl Winehouse: quoted from discussion with author.

Janis Winehouse, 'She was always very cheery ...': *Mail on Sunday*, 19 August 2007.

Juliette Ashby: quoted from the *Observer* magazine, 22 April 2007. The author spoke to the boy in the playground story.

Lauren Franklin: quoted throughout from author's interview.

Mitch Winehouse meets Jane (second wife): Winehouse, *Amy, My Daughter* (no affair 'for ages').

Janis Winehouse on affair: *Mail on Sunday*, 19 August 2007; and telling the children: *Mail on Sunday*, 23 March 2008.

AW on father leaving home, 'shady': *Guardian*, 28 October 2003.

Mitch Winehouse bankruptcy (case 11845 of 1993): the High Court (Bankruptcy); *London Gazette*, 26 January 1994; and the Insolvency Service.

Mitch Winehouse's changing addresses: company records and electoral registers.

Mitch Winehouse felt guilty: Winehouse, *Amy, My Daughter*.

Father sees song as a comment on him: ibid.

Lyrics from 'What is it About Men?' by Amy Winehouse, © EMI Music Publishing Ltd.

As Larkin wrote: 'This Be The Verse'.

Susi Earnshaw School: thanks to Susi Earnshaw, quoted from interview with author, also to teacher Siobhan Bailey, and contemporaries Melissa Gillespie and Julia Vanellis, both quoted from interviews with author.

Janis Winehouse's health: her interview with *Mail on Sunday*, 23 March 2008.

'Your daughter...': Winehouse, *Amy, My Daughter*. Also AW's birthday card.

Sylvia Young Theatre School: thanks to Susi Earnshaw, Sylvia Young, former students Ricardo Canadinhas and Amie Schroeter, all quoted from interviews with author.

Friendship with Tyler James and his background: thanks to Hamish Twist.

Piercings and tattoos: AW's interviews (*Rolling Stone*, 14 June 2007, quoted) and author's interviews with her tattooists: Henry Hate, Tomasz Skoczypiec and Mirek vel Stotker.

Moves to Guildown Avenue: thanks to neighbour, Mo Cansick.

Missing school: *Q* magazine, October 2011 (reproducing a 2007 interview in which AW also spoke about using anti-depressants).

Bill Ashton: quoted from interview with author.

BRIT School: thanks to Adrian Packer (quoted from interview).

Mitch Winehouse's directorship of double-glazing companies and his disqualification: I refer to documents filed at Companies House in London, the register of disqualified directors held and supplied by HM Courts & Tribunals Service (Case 853/2000), and my correspondence with David Rubin & Partners, who were the liquidators of City Savings & Loans Ltd, with thanks to David R. Stephenson. Thanks also to Glen Day, who served on the liquidation committee. I also refer to Winehouse, *Amy, My Daughter*.

Nick Shymansky described his introduction to AW in the BBC Radio 2 documentary *Amy Winehouse: Singer*, 25 July 2012 (quoted).

AW's ambition, to 'live like the bombshell I really am': from her 2001 notebook, reproduced in the *Sun*, 28 December 2010.

Three: **The Mad Ones**

Epigraph: Kerouac, *On the Road*.

Pat Andrews, Richard Hattrell, Linda Lawrence and Andrew Loog Oldham: quoted from interviews with the author.

Keith Richards and Bill Wyman: quoted from their memoirs (*Life* and *Stone Alone*).

JH letter (15 December 1961): EMP Museum.

Ruse to get out of army: Cross, *Room Full of Mirrors*.

Bobby Womack: quoted from Murray, *Crosstown Traffic*.

David Brigati and John Hammond Jr: quoted from author's interviews.

Linda Keith help: Richards, *Life*; Wyman, *Stone Alone*.

JJ letter to Peter De Blanc, on her 'gay period' and hopes for happiness: in Laura Joplin, *Love, Janis*. Also Linda Gottfried quote.

JJ, 'I wanted to smoke dope …' and on playing onstage with Big Brother: Dalton, *Piece of My Heart*.

Sam Andrew and Bob Seidemann: quoted from author's interviews.

Ray Manzarek's acid experiences and conversation with JM: Manzarek, *Light My Fire*.

John Densmore background and quotes: Densmore, *Riders on the Storm*.

Britt Leach: quoted from author's interview.

Admiral Morrison: quoted from a letter to the Florida Probation and Parole Commission, in documentary, *When You're Strange* (Wolf Films/ Strange Pictures, 2009). Thanks also to Andy Morrison.

Robby Krieger's defining event: Doors, *The Doors*.

JM gets out of draft: his Selective Service record, and Densmore, *Riders on the Storm*; report that JM posed as homosexual: Hopkins, with Sugerman, *No One Gets Out of Here Alive*.

Dickie Davis, Enid Graddis and Ronnie Haran: quoted from author's interviews. Thanks also to Mirandi Babitz.

'little girls in their Hollywood bungalows': 'LA Woman' by the Doors, © Doors Music Co. LLC.

Evening in New York: Densmore, *Riders on the Storm*.

KC and Aunt Mari: Nick Broomfield's documentary, *Kurt and Courtney* (Optimum Releasing, 2002).

KC's arrest for trespass: author's interview with Lamont Shillinger; also police records.

KC on first trying heroin: quoted in Azerrad, *Come As You Are*.

Ryan Aigner, Penny Fahey (*née* Lloyd) and Mitch Holmquist: quoted from author's interviews.

Krist Novoselic on KC: Novoselic, *Of Grunge and Government*.

KC's Christmas card: Cross, *Heavier Than Heaven*.

Mitch Winehouse on his daughter's new career: quoted from Winehouse, *Amy, My Daughter*.

'wedding singer': author's discussion with Tibor Poor.

Stefan Skarbek: quoted from author's interview.

Teo Avery and Gordon Williams: quoted from author's interviews.

Lyrics from 'Stronger than Me' by Amy Winehouse and Salaam Remi, © EMI Publishing Ltd.

Nick Godwyn: quoted from *The Times*, 30 July 2011.

Cherry Westfield Ltd: company records.

Mitch Winehouse's disqualification under the Company Directors Disqualification Act 1986, Section 7, meant he could act as company

secretary in 2002, but he was not allowed to take part in the management of a company until his disqualification expired in 2005.

Legislation: quoted from the 1986 Act; penalties described in the Act.

Examples of Mitch Winehouse advising his daughter: Winehouse, *Amy,
My Daughter.*

Lou Winwood: quoted from author's interview. Thanks also to Charles
Moriarty, who took the cover photo of *Frank.*

Break-up with boyfriend: AW, in *Blues & Soul*, 14–27 October 2003;
and *Sunday Times*, 5 October 2003.

Juliette Ashby: quoted from the *Observer* magazine, 22 April 2007.

Four: **Success**

Epigraph: F. Scott Fitzgerald's essay, 'Early Success', in *The Lost City:
Personal Essays 1920–40.*

Keith Richards on BJ and fame: Jagger *et al.*, *According to the Rolling
Stones.*

Gered Mankowitz: quoted throughout from author's interviews.

Wyman and Richards agreed on Jones's contribution to 'I Wanna Be Your
Man': Wyman, *Stone Alone.*

Linda Lawrence: quoted throughout from author's interviews.

Pat and Linda would go to law: author's interviews with Pat Andrews;
Wyman, *Stone Alone*; press coverage including *News of the World*, 16
January 1966.

Zouzou: quoted from author's interviews.

Keith Richards on BJ in the car: Richards, *Life.*

Andrew Loog Oldham on BJ: quoted from his memoirs, *Stoned* and *2
Stoned*; also author's interview.

Zoot Money: quoted throughout from a discussion with the author.

Richards, nasty to BJ: Richards, *Life.*

BJ's threats to commit suicide: described in biographies, including Jackson,
Brian Jones, and Davis, *Old Gods Almost Dead*, which documents him
cutting his wrist in 1964.

Seneca: quoted from Seneca, *On Anger*. Seneca's death is detailed by
Tacitus.

Alvarez: quoted from Alvarez, *The Savage God.*

Marianne Faithfull: quoted from her memoir, *Faithfull.*

BJ meets Pallenberg: author's interviews; Norman, *Symphony for the Devil*.

Ron Schneider: quoted from interview with author.

JH arrives in London: author's interviews; Etchingham, *Through Gypsy Eyes*; Mitchell, *The Hendrix Experience*; Redding, *Are You Experienced?*

Trip to Morocco: Richards, *Life* (quoted).

Prince Stash: quoted from author's interviews and correspondence.

Trip to New York: author's interviews with Deering Howe (quoted) and others. Also Cross, *Room Full of Mirrors*, and www.doorshistory.com.

The Doors' success: thanks to Steve Harris.

Monterey Pop Festival: the author referred to the DVD box set of D. A. Pennebaker's festival film, *The Complete Monterey Pop Festival* (Monterey International Pop Festival Foundation/Pennebaker Hegedus Films Inc., 2002), from which Townshend is quoted. Also author's interviews with performers and participants.

Al Wilson background and death: his death certificate; *Rolling Stone*, 1 October 1970; de la Parra, *Living the Blues* (quoted).

John Byrne Cooke: quoted from author's interviews.

Ron 'Pigpen' McKernan, background and death: death certificate; report of death in *Rolling Stone*, 12 April 1973; McNally, *A Long Strange Trip*; author's interviews.

Dr Johnson: Boswell, *The Life of Samuel Johnson*.

Danny Fields on JM: author's interview.

JM on photos: *Rolling Stone*, 26 July 1969.

JM's family find out about his celebrity: author's interview with Andy Morrison (quoted).

Admiral Morrison makes contact: quoted from his letter to the Florida Probation and Parole Commission, in documentary, *When You're Strange* (Wolf Films/Strange Pictures, 2009).

Clara Morrison tries to meet JM: author's interviews with Asher Dann, Steve Harris and Andy Morrison (all quoted).

Five: **Kurt and Courtney, Amy and Blake**

Epigraph: Song of Solomon 8:6.

Jason Everman: quoted from author's interview.

Everett True: *Nirvana*.

KC in Rome: Azerrad, *Come As You Are*.

KC on self-image and decision to use heroin: *Journals*.

KC consults doctors: Cross, *Heavier Than Heaven*, and *Journals*.

Mick Jagger on the rock-star life: Jagger *et al.*, *According to the Rolling Stones*.

Danny Goldberg on KC: quoted from author's interview.

Michael Maska: quoted from author's interview.

Sales of *Nevermind*: Recording Industry Association of America (RIAA).

Eric Erlandson: quoted from author's interview.

Courtney Love background: the principal Cobain/Nirvana biographies, profiles published in *Vanity Fair* (September 1992), *Rolling Stone* (15 December 1994), in which Love discusses her early life. I also corresponded with her father, Hank Harrison. Courtney Love didn't respond to requests for an interview. Additional background on Harrison's Grateful Dead connection: McNally, *A Long Strange Trip*.

Chuck Fradenburg and Leland Cobain on Courtney Love: quoted from author's interviews.

Stefan Skarbek: quoted from author's interview.

Jonathan Winehouse: quoted from author's interviews.

AW's comments about fellow artists: (London) *Evening Standard*, 18 August 2004, *Sunday Times* (5 October 2003), and *Observer Music Monthly* (January 2004).

One musician believed AW drew on her experience as a journalist: author's interview with band member Aaron Liddard.

Nick Godwyn: quoted from *The Times*, 30 July 2011.

Gordon Williams: quoted from author's interview.

Drinking at the Good Mixer: thanks to John and Sarah Hurley, and Bradley Leckie. Thanks also to local market stallholders and shop-keepers.

AW quoted from the liner notes of *Back to Black* on the book group.

First attempt to get AW into rehab: I take Mitch Winehouse's version in *Amy, My Daughter*, though it is contradicted by Godwyn, in *The Times*, 30 July 2011.

Lyric quoted from 'Rehab' by Amy Winehouse © EMI Music Publishing.

Blake's background: sources include author's meeting and correspondence with Blake Fielder-Civil (quoted); local enquiries, public records and previously published accounts including his mother's comments in the *Mail on Sunday* (1 Sept 2007 and 17 Aug 2012) and on the Jeremy Kyle television show.

AW tattoos: thanks to Henry Hate, who applied the 'Cynthia' and 'Daddy's Girl' tattoos.

Blake's friend told him he was 'too young and the wrong colour for [AW]': Blake Fielder-Civil to author.

Lyrics quoted from 'Back to Black' by Amy Winehouse © EMI Music Publishing.

Lyric quoted from 'Wake Up Alone' by Amy Winehouse © EMI Music Publishing.

Lyric quoted from 'You Know I'm No Good' by Amy Winehouse © EMI Music Publishing.

Thanks to Vidia Patel and other shopkeepers in Camden.

National Gallery meeting and nicknames: Blake Fielder-Civil to author.

Further tattoos: thanks to Eclipse in Camden Town, Edyta Lydon and Mirek vel Stotker. The author also discussed tattoos with Blake Fielder-Civil.

Six: **Excess**

Epigraph: Hill (ed.) *Johnsonian Miscellanies, Vol. II.*

JH and JJ have sex backstage: reported in Cross, *Room Full of Mirrors*, and elsewhere. JJ quoted in Friedman, *Buried Alive*, boasting of her conquests.

Anthony Atherton: quoted from author's interviews.

Noel Redding: Redding, *Are You Experienced?*

Amanda Lear: quoted from author's interview. Ms Lear's gender at birth has long been speculated upon (by Ian Gibson, for example, in *The Shameful Life of Salvador Dali*). She denies having been born male.

BJ's 1967 court case and appeal: author's interview with Prince Stash (quoted) and press reports including *The Times*, 13 December 1967.

AW gave few concerts: Nick Godwyn in *The Times*, 30 July 2011.

JH freaks out in Gothenburg: Redding, *Are You Experienced?*; Mitchell, *The Hendrix Experience.*

Redding, on drug use: Redding, *Are You Experienced?*

Contact with Al Hendrix and Seattle homecoming: author's interview with Janie Hendrix (quoted); Mitchell, *The Hendrix Experience*; Etchingham, *Through Gypsy Eyes.*

Anthony Atherton and Sammy Drain: quoted from author's interviews.

Steve Harris on death hoax: author's interview.

Robby Krieger on JM's suicidal depression: Doors, *The Doors*.

Dickie Davis: quoted from author's interview.

New Haven incident: author's interview with Vince Treanor (quoted); various published accounts.

Lines quoted from 'The Celebration of the Lizard' © 1968 Doors Music Company.

Mirandi Babitz and Clem Floyd: quoted from author's interviews.

JM on pressure to record: *Rolling Stone*, 26 July 1969.

Deering Howe on JM: author's interviews. The author also spoke to Bob Neuwirth.

JM at Steve Paul's Scene: author's interviews with Harvey Brooks, Asher Dann, Steve Harris and Danny Fields (quoted). I also referred to Friedman, *Buried Alive*; Davis, *Jim Morrison*; Doors, *The Doors*; interviews with Sam Andrew (quoted).

JM hit Bill Graham: Graham, *Bill Graham Presents*.

John Simon: quoted from *Buried Alive*.

Robert Crumb: quoted from correspondence with the author.

JM's nervous-breakdown conversation: Manzarek, *Light My Fire*.

BJ backstage at the Roundhouse: author's interview with Zouzou.

BJ's second bust and quote: *Daily Sketch*, 27 September 1968.

JM in Amsterdam: author's interview with Vince Treanor (quoted).

Jagger on BJ: Jagger *et al.*, *According to the Rolling Stones*.

Beggars Banquet food fight: Wyman, *Stone Alone*; Norman, *Symphony for the Devil*.

Rolling Stones Rock and Roll Circus: author's interview with Michael Lindsay-Hogg; Lindsay-Hogg, *Luck and Circumstance*; and DVD of the show.

Wendy O'Connor's letter: *Daily World*, 11 November 1991. She makes plain, in Azerrad, *Come As You Are*, that she ejected Kurt from the family home.

KC on using heroin with Courtney/ODs: Azerrad, *Come As You Are*.

JJ's doctor warned her: Friedman, *Buried Alive*.

Danny Goldberg and Michael Maska on KC at *Saturday Night Live*: quoted from author's interviews.

David Grohl: quoted from Azerrad, *Come As You Are*.

Kurt and Courtney marry: Cross, *Heavier Than Heaven*; True, *Nirvana: The True Story*.

KC intervention and Twelve Steps Programme: Cross, *Heavier Than Heaven*; author's interviews.

AA programme: Alcoholics Anonymous, www.aa.org.

KC contemplates suicide by gunshot: Cross, *Heavier Than Heaven*. Suicide background from Johnstone (ed.), *Companion to Psychiatric Studies*; Stone, *Suicide and Attempted Suicide*; gunshot suicide statistics are from Stone.

Vanity Fair episode: quotations from *Vanity Fair* (September 1992). Courtney Love's online denial: reprinted in Cross, *Heavier Than Heaven*.

Suicide pact argument: Courtney Love's interview with *Rolling Stone*, 15 December 1994.

KC threat to Hirschberg: Azerrad, *Come As You Are*.

KC tells Don (Cobain) to shut up: Cross, *Heavier Than Heaven*.

Lyric quoted from 'Serve the Servants' by Kurt Cobain © 1993 Virgin Songs/The End of Music BMI.

Seven: **Distress**

Epigraph: Kierkegaard, *Either/Or, A Fragment of Life*.

Patrick Alan and John Altman: quoted throughout from author's interviews.

Cobden Club: *Jewish Chronicle*, 24 November 2005; author's interview with Jonathan Winehouse (quoted).

Nick Godwyn: quoted from *The Times*, 30 July 2011.

Raye Cosbert becomes manager: Winehouse, *Amy, My Daughter*.

Don Letts: quoted throughout from author's interview.

Mark Ronson background: articles, including *Evening Standard*, 9 April 2010; *New York*, 22 April 2007. Ronson on 'Rehab': *Independent on Sunday*, 24 July 2011.

Jamie Talbot: quoted from author's interview.

Lyric quoted from 'Me and Mr Jones' by Amy Winehouse © EMI Music Publishing.

Blake Fielder-Civil on AW first using cocaine: July 2009 interview, in documentary, *Amy Winehouse: The Untold Story* (Channel 5, 2011).

Mischa Richter: quoted from author's interview.

Lou Winwood: quoted throughout from author's interview.

Aaron Liddard: quoted throughout from author's interview.

Nathan Allen: quoted from author's interview.

Eating disorder: inquest evidence (second).

Dave Swallow: quoted throughout from author's interview.

Jay Phelps: quoted from author's interview.

Heckles Bono: Johnstone, *Amy, Amy, Amy*.

Charlotte Church show and return to BRIT School: thanks to Lou Winwood.

Blake on AW's drinking, etc.: *Amy Winehouse: The Untold Story* (Channel 5, 2011).

Adrian Packer: quoted from author's interview.

Self-harming: Johnstone (ed.), *Companion to Psychiatric Studies*; Blake's self-harming: to author. Thanks also to Aaron Liddard and Dave Swallow (both quoted).

Richey Edwards: see Chapter Eleven, p. 224–5.

Maurice Bernstein: quoted from author's interview.

AW at Chateau Marmont: thanks to Stefan Skarbek.

AW on self-harming: *Rolling Stone*, 14 June 2007.

Spin photo shoot: video footage at www.spin.com.

AW and the Rolling Stones at the Isle of Wight: video film posted on YouTube.

AW meets Ray Manzarek: related to the author by the Doors' (current) manager, Jeff Jampol.

Seizure: Winehouse, *Amy, My Daughter*.

Jonathan Winehouse: quoted from author's interview.

At the Four Seasons: Winehouse, *Amy, My Daughter*; Janis Winehouse, *Mail on Sunday*, 19 August 2007; Georgette Civil, *Mail on Sunday*, 1 September 2007.

At the Sanderson: author's discussions with Blake, quoted from *Amy Winehouse: The Untold Story* (Channel 5, 2011), and widespread press coverage week ending 25 August 2007. AW to www.perezhilton.com, 24 August 2007.

Norway bust: *Independent on Sunday*, 20 October 2007; author's interview with members of the tour party.

Maurice Bernstein: quoted from author's interview.

Blake scored: *Amy Winehouse: The Untold Story* (Channel 5, 2011).

Zürich: author's discussions with Blake Fielder-Civil. Foden quoted in the *Daily Mirror*, 25–26 July 2011.

Troy Miller: quoted throughout from author's interview.

Blake arrested: *Daily Mirror*, 9 November 2007.

Birmingham show: video posted on YouTube.

US website: www.whenwillamywinehousedie.com.

AW considered Doherty an 'arsehole': author's interview with Sam Shaker.

Doherty to author: text messages, April 2012. In a subsequent interview with the *Daily Mail* (24 November 2012), he said he and AW had been lovers.

Blake angered when AW missed prison visits: in documentary, *Amy Winehouse: The Untold Story* (Channel 5, 2011) and in discussion with the author.

Alex Foden story: *Daily Mirror*, 25–26 July 2011.

Treated at Capio Nightingale: Winehouse, *Amy, My Daughter*; press coverage including the *Evening Standard*, 25 January 2008.

Alex Winehouse: quoted from *NOW*, July–August 2011.

US sales of *Back to Black*: RIAA.

Move to Prowse Place: thanks to neighbour Bryan Johnson.

Attempts at cure/condition at Dog House: Winehouse, *Amy, My Daughter*.

Records with Remi after row with Ronson: *NME*, 3 December 2011.

Alex Haines' account of affair: *News of the World*, 28 December 2008; Foden in *Daily Mirror*, 25–26 July 2011.

April 2008 assault case: *Sun*, 24 and 26 April 2008. Also *News of the World*, 27 April 2008.

Mitch Winehouse on AW breakdown at Dog House: Winehouse, *Amy, My Daughter*; Daphne Barak, *Saving Amy* (sectioning).

June seizure: Winehouse, *Amy, My Daughter*.

Emphysema: second inquest, St Pancras, 2013.

Nelson Mandela show: *Sun*, 28 June 2008.

Glastonbury 2008: author's interviews with Michael Eavis, Don Letts and Troy Miller.

Blake sentenced: *Daily Telegraph*, 21 July 2008.

'Heated' conversation with Lucian Grainge/persuaded to appear at V Festival: Winehouse, *Amy, My Daughter*.

Booed at V Festival: www.gigwise.com; footage of show posted on YouTube.

Doug Charles-Ridler: quoted from author's interviews.

Berkeley Square Ball: author's interviews with Patrick Alan and John Altman (both quoted).

Assault case: *The Times*, 25 July 2009.

Part Two 'Death'

Epigraph: Captain Ahab's last words, Melville, *Moby-Dick*.

Eight: **In Which Brian is Entirely Surrounded by Water**

Epigraph: Milne, *The House at Pooh Corner*.

Cotchford Farm: thanks to the owner, Alastair Johns.

A.A. Milne background: Thwaite, *A. A. Milne, His Life*.

BJ in the Priory: Wyman, *Stone Alone*.

Keith Richards recalls BJ's contribution to *Let it Bleed*: Richards, *Life*.

Zouzou: quoted from author's interviews.

BJ meets Anna Wohlin; she moves in: Wohlin, with Lindsjöö, *The Murder of Brian Jones*.

BJ 'quits' Stones: Richards, *Life* (quoted); *Daily Express*, 9 June 1969.

BJ pay-off: Norman, *Symphony for the Devil*; Davis, *Old Gods Almost Dead*.

BJ's prescription drugs: medical records collected for the inquest, supplied by HM Coroner; cocaine use: Wohlin, *The Murder of Brian Jones*.

Les Hallett: quoted throughout from author's interview.

Events leading up to and including BJ's death: based on the inquest bundle; quotations from Lawson, Thorogood and Wohlin: their sworn statements to police.

Amanda Lear: quoted from author's interview.

Lewis Jones: quoted from *Daily Express*, 7 July 1969.

Pete Townshend remark: *London Evening News*, 3 July 1969.

Lines quoted from 'Ode to LA While Thinking of Brian Jones, Deceased' © Jim Morrison 1969.

Evidence heard at the inquest into BJ's death: *The Times* and *Daily Express* (both 8 July 1969).

Pat Andrews: quoted throughout from author's interview.

Richards, on the 'mystery' of BJ's death: Jagger *et al.*, *According to the Rolling Stones*.

'Brian Jones Death: New Probe': *Daily Express*, 26 August 1969.

Linda Lawrence: quoted from author's interviews.

Fitzgerald story: press coverage, including *Weekend* magazine, 14 July 1986, and inquest bundle.

Thorogood's 'confession'/dialogue: Rawlings, *Who Killed Christopher Robin?*

Thorogood dies/daughter's denial: *Sunday Times* magazine, 21 August 2005.

Giuliano story: Giuliano, *Paint it Black: The Murder of Brian Jones*.

Anna Wohlin's story: Wohlin, with Lindsjöö, *The Murder of Brian Jones*.

Trevor Hobley/Pat Andrews theories: interviews with the author and *Independent on Sunday*, 6 November 2005.

Janet Lawson changes story: *Mail on Sunday*, 30 November 2008.

Klein background: author's research for *Fab: An Intimate Life of Paul McCartney*; Klein's obituary, *Independent on Sunday*, 6 July 2009.

Lawrence on Klein: author's interviews.

Pat Andrews: quoted from author's interview.

BJ's estate: *Daily Telegraph*, 15 May 1970.

Jagger's wealth: 2013 *Sunday Times* Rich List (21 April 2013).

Nine: **Nodding Out**

Epigraph: JJ, quoted from Dalton, *Piece of My Heart*.

JH busted: FBI file and *Rolling Stone* report, 26 July 1969.

JH and friends using heroin: author's interviews including with Deering Howe; Noel Redding, *Are You Experienced?*

Deering Howe: quoted throughout from author's interview.

Kozmic Blues Band: author's interviews with band members, including Sam Andrew (quoted), Maury Baker (quoted), Brad Campbell and Snooky Flowers.

Sam Andrew's London overdose: author's interview.

JJ overdoses: Myra Friedman writes in *Buried Alive* that JJ told her doctor she overdosed six times in 1969.

JJ conversation in San Francisco: Dalton, *Piece of My Heart*.

War and Peace: 1932 Everyman translation.

John Byrne Cooke leaves JJ's employ: author's interview (quoted).

Dr Rothchild: Friedman, *Buried Alive*.

Alan Douglas: quoted throughout from author's interview.

Conversation with Bill Graham: Graham, *Bill Graham Presents*.

JJ's 27th birthday letter: Laura Joplin, *Love, Janis*.

Holiday romance: Laura Joplin, *Love, Janis*; author's interview with Lyndall Erb (quoted).

JJ on death: Friedman, *Buried Alive*; *Rolling Stone*, 29 October 1970.

High-school reunion: video of JJ's Port Arthur press conference; author's interviews with John Byrne Cooke and Lyndall Erb (both quoted); Friedman, *Buried Alive*.

Slaps Jerry Lee Lewis: Laura Joplin, *Love, Janis*.

Bob Gordon: quoted throughout from author's interview.

Harvey Brooks: quoted from author's interview.

Miami: author's interview with Vince Treanor; Doors, *The Doors*; Hopkins, with Sugerman, *No One Gets Out of Here Alive*.

Isle of Wight Festival: I referred to an interview conducted with Ray Foulk for my book, *Seventies*, quoting him; also, concert films *Message to Love* (Sanctuary Records, 1995) and *Blue Wild Angel* (Experience Hendrix, 2003).

Chas Chandler: quoted on Gothenburg; Brown, *Hendrix: The Final Days*.

Alan Douglas: quoted from author's interview.

Mitch Mitchell: Mitchell and Platt, *The Hendrix Experience*.

Eric Burdon: quoted throughout from his book, *Don't Let Me Be Misunderstood*.

John Altman: quoted from author's interviews.

Philip Harvey: quoted from *Sunday Express*, 13 August 1995.

Monika Dannemann's version of events leading up to JH's death: her various interviews, including *Hello!*, 26 February 1994.

JH death: inquest evidence (the documents and press reports in the [London] *Evening Standard* [28 September 1970] and the next day's *Daily Telegraph*); death certificate; Brown, *Hendrix: The Final Days*.

Dr Bannister: quoted from *The Times*, 18 December 1993.

JJ on death of JH: Friedman, *Buried Alive*.

Landmark Hotel: author's visit to the hotel (now the Highland Gardens Hotel). Thanks to general manager Jack Baklayan, also to John Byrne Cooke, former members of the Full Tilt Boogie Band and JJ friends.

JJ meets lawyer: author's interview with Bob Gordon (quoted). The author also referred to JJ's will.

Lyndall Erb: quoted from author's interview.

Lyrics quoted from 'Me and Bobby McGee' by Kris Kristofferson and Fred Foster, Keith Prowse Music Pub. Co. Ltd.

Ken Pearson: quoted from author's interview.

Peggy Caserta: quoted from her interview with the Biography Channel (Fallen Legends, undated); Echols, *Scars of Sweet Paradise*.

John Byrne Cooke, Lyndall Erb and Ken Pearson: quoted from author's interviews on JJ's last hours and death. I also referred to *Rolling Stone*, 29 October 1970; the death certificate; Echols, *Scars of Sweet Paradise*; Laura Joplin, *Love, Janis*.

Sam Andrew on wake: author's interview.

Brad Campbell: quoted from author's interview.

Ten: **The Crack-up**

Epigraph: Nietzsche, *Thus Spake Zarathustra*.

JM on dying next: widely reported by biographers; for example, Davis, *Jim Morrison*.

JM sentenced in Miami: Doors, *The Doors*.

Vince Treanor: quoted throughout from author's interview.

Pamela Courson's LA apartment: the author visited the apartment which has been preserved much as it was when Courson lived there.

JM's will: copy, dated 12 February 1969.

Mirandi Babitz, Michael C. Ford and Steve and Nicole Harris: quoted from author's interviews.

Paul Rothchild: quoted from, Doors, *The Doors*.

New Orleans show: in his memoirs John Densmore says he merely spoke to JM when he sat down on his drum riser. It is reported elsewhere – in Davis, *Jim Morrison*, for example – that Densmore pushed JM off the riser.

Jac Holzman: quoted from documentary *Mr Mojo Risin': The Story of LA Woman* (Eagle Vision, 2011).

Apartment at rue Beautreillis: author's interviews and field notes in Paris; French TV documentary, *Jim Morrison: les derniers jours*.

JM's lifestyle in Paris: author's interviews and the major biographies of Morrison.

Zouzou: quoted from author's interviews.

Notebook jottings: copy of JM's last notebook.

Falls from hotel windows: Hopkins, with Sugerman, *No One Gets Out of Here Alive*.

Meeting Yepremian and Muller: author's interview with Gilles Yepremian.

Frank Lisciandro: quoted from the documentary *Mr Mojo Risin: The Story of LA Woman*.

JM's last conversation with John Densmore: Densmore, *Riders on the Storm*; also 'slow suicide'.

Vince Treanor: quoted from author's interview.

Philippe Dalecky: quoted from author's interview.

'I'm finally dead': JM's notebook, left behind: author consulted a copy.

JM spoke to Ronay of Nietzsche on suicide: *King*, July 1991. He had spoken to others on this subject: Davis, *Jim Morrison*.

Alain Ronay's dealings with JM, Pamela Courson and the Paris authorities: based on my discussions with Ronay and interviews he and Agnès Varda gave to *Paris Match*, 25 April 1991. I also refer to an interview with Ronay in *King*, 'Jim and I, Friends Until Death', July 1991. Ronay is quoted from discussions with the author, except 'but really wasn't happy at all', from *King*, and 'He was 27 years old and never took drugs ...', from *Paris Match*. JM's chest and breathing problems: Pamela Courson's police report; Davis, *Jim Morrison*.

Nietzsche's epigram: *The Basic Writings of Nietzsche*; *Thus Spake Zarathustra*.

Agnès Varda: quoted from *Paris Match*, 25 April 1991.

Pamela Courson on her and Jim using heroin: as quoted by Ronay in *Paris Match*, 25 April 1991.

Jim taken ill in the night: account of Pamela Courson to police, copy of the original police report.

Courson's call to Ronay/her friends respond: *Paris Match*, 25 April 1991; *King*, July 1991.

Marianne Faithfull and Jean de Breiteuil: Faithfull, *Faithfull*.

Agnès Varda on Jim in the bath: *Paris Match*, 25 April 1991.

Dr Vassille's report: copy of same.

Funeral arrangements: author's discussion with Alain Ronay and published sources including the major biographies of Morrison.

Press statement: *Rolling Stone*, 4 August 1971.

Andy Morrison: quoted from author's interview.

Pamela Courson's final years and death: her death certificate; *Rolling Stone* obituary, 6 June 1974; author's interviews with Mirandi Babitz and Andy Morrison (both quoted).

Eleven: The Secret House of Death

Epigraph: *Antony and Cleopatra*, Act IV, scene xv.

David Burr: quoted throughout from author's interviews.

Alexander Bashlachev's death: see Appendix: 27 Long-list, p. 303.

Peter Ham's death: ibid.

Richey Edwards's death: ibid; also *Daily Mail*, 2 March 1995; *Guardian*, 26 and 29 November 2008.

KC on suicide: *Melody Maker*, 2 January 1993; *Rolling Stone*, 27 January 1994.

Steve Albini: quoted from author's interview.

Cali De Witt: quoted from True, *Nirvana: The True Story*.

Events at Lakeside Avenue NE: copies of the original police reports; Cross, *Heavier than Heaven*; True, *Nirvana: The True Story*. Thanks to neighbour Bob Jensen.

Mia Zapata's death: see Appendix: 27 Long-list, p. 307.

Chuck Fradenburg: quoted throughout from author's interview.

Christmas rehab: Cross, *Heavier Than Heaven*.

New house: public domain real estate records; author's field notes; background reading in the major Cobain biographies. Thanks to neighbour Dr Pritchett (quoted).

Eric Erlandson: quoted throughout from author's interview.

Leland Cobain: quoted throughout from author's interview.

Lyrics quoted from 'You Know You're Right' by Kurt Cobain © EMI Music Publishing.

Cali De Witt says Kurt suspected his wife: True, *Nirvana: The True Story*.

Discusses divorce with lawyer: Cross, *Heavier Than Heaven*.

A piece of the Colosseum/Rome suicide attempt: Courtney Love, quoted in Cross, *Heavier Than Heaven*; *Rolling Stone*, 15 December 1994.

Suicide background: Alvarez, *The Savage God*; Durkheim; *On Suicide*, Johnstone (ed.), *Companion to Psychiatric Studies*; Stone, *Suicide and Attempted Suicide* were especially helpful.

Keats: 'Ode to a Nightingale'.

Suicide peaks in spring: one of the findings of Émile Durkheim; see *On Suicide*.

1994 intervention: author's interviews with David Burr, Eric Erlandson and Danny Goldberg (all quoted).

Sam Andrew: quoted from author's interview.

Exodus: author's interview with Nial Stimson (quoted throughout).

KC's last sees his daughter/last conversation with wife: Cross, *Heavier Than Heaven*.

Quotation from *The Waste Land* by T. S. Eliot. Collected Poems (London: Faber and Faber, 1963).

KC goes missing/search for: author's interviews with Eric Erlandson and others, background reading in the major Cobain biographies, and associated press coverage of his death, and copies of the original police reports.

KC and his Rome suicide note: Cross, *Heavier Than Heaven*.

Suicide in literature, philosophy and history: background reading includes Alvarez, *The Savage God* (a superb general study of suicide); Durkheim, *On Suicide*; Grashoff, *Let Me Finish* (a study of suicide notes); Hume, *On Suicide*; Nietzsche, *Basic Writings of Nietzsche*, and Seneca, *Dialogues and Essays*, *Epistles* and *Moral Essays*.

Schopenhauer: On Suicide (*The Essential Schopenhauer*).

Suicide note: the author consulted a copy of the note which is published in Halperin and Wallace, *Who Killed Kurt Cobain?*, and can be easily found online.

Finding the body: sources include *The Last 48 Hours of Kurt Cobain* (BBC, 2011).

Date of death: death certificate.

Reaction: author's interviews with Burr, Erlandson, Fradenburg, Goldberg and Stimson.

Courtney Love's message: recording of same.

Memorial services/Saturn Return: thanks to the Reverends Karen Lindvig and Stephen Towles.

Copycat suicides: *Rolling Stone*, 2 June 1994; *Guardian*, 1 June 1998.

Pfaff death: *Rolling Stone*, 11 August 1994; and Eric Erlandson: interview with author.

Jack Endino, quoted from *The Last 48 Hours of Kurt Cobain* (BBC, 2011).

Tom Grant theories: his website, www.cobaincase.com; his comments on

NBC *Dateline* (April 2004); Halperin and Wallace, *Who Killed Kurt Cobain?*

Hank Harrison: quoted from NBC's *Dateline* (April 2004); correspondence with the author.

Leland Cobain: quoted from author's interview.

Twelve: **One Little Drink, Then Another**

Epigraph: John Dryden, *Fables, Ancient and Modern*, quoted from Partington (ed.), *The Oxford Dictionary of Quotations*, Oxford, OUP, 1996.

Sarah Hurley: quoted throughout from author's interview.

Doug Charles-Ridler: quoted throughout from author's interview.

Stefan Skarbek: quoted throughout from author's interview.

Bryan Johnson: quoted from author's interview.

Attacks photographers: *Daily Mail*, 6 November 2008.

Blake wanted a divorce, and row about rehab bill: press coverage including *News of the World*, 9 November 2008; Winehouse, *Amy, My Daughter*.

AW in St Lucia: press coverage including *Sun*, 14 January 2009; Ricardo Canadinhas and Troy Miller: quoted from author's interviews. Thanks also to Jeff Allen.

Mitch Winehouse driving his cab less: Winehouse, *Amy, My Daughter*; *My Daughter Amy* (Channel 4, January 2010).

Mitch Winehouse directorships/companies established/gives occupation: Companies House records.

Daphne Barak's relationship with the Winehouses: Barak, *Saving Amy*, from which I quote.

Mitch Winehouse on his relationship with AW: *My Daughter Amy* (Channel 4, January 2010).

AW tweet: 8 January 2010, Twitter.

Criticised in *Guardian*: 6 November 2009.

'Not a penny', Blake on divorce settlement and view of Mitch Winehouse: Blake to author.

Pantomime fracas: *Guardian*, 20 January 2011.

Reg Traviss: quoted throughout from interviews with author.

AW photographed with Blake after the divorce: *Sun*, 1 March and 19 April 2010. Thanks also to Sam Shaker.

AW tweets re Blake: 25 March 2010, Twitter.

Reg on Blake/Blake on Reg: in discussions with the author.

Boswell on Dr Johnson: Boswell, *Life of Samuel Johnson*.

Drunken incidents in 2010: Winehouse, *Amy, My Daughter*.

AW on pub bench: *News of the World* video, September 2010. Traviss's explanation: author's interview.

AW told Haines and Foden she would join the 27 Club: Haines, *News of the World*, 28 December 2008; Foden, *Daily Mirror*, 25 July 2011.

AW's binge-drinking: evidence at the second inquest.

Russian show: Winehouse, *Amy, My Daughter*; author's interview with Troy Miller (quoted throughout).

Brazil shows: footage of concerts posted on YouTube; author's interviews with Miller and Traviss. Thanks also to Henry Collins.

Camden Square house: public domain and estate agent property records; author's interviews with AW's friends and neighbours, with thanks to Catherine Hays, Professor Jones and Reg Traviss.

Troy Miller: quoted throughout from author's interview.

AW tells father she never wants to move: *Amy, My Daughter*.

John Hurley: quoted from author's interview.

Rozh: quoted from author's interview.

Seizures: second inquest.

Dubai: author's interview with Reg Traviss; local reaction from concert-goers posted online at www.soulfood101.wordpress.com.

AW's money: company records.

Blake arrested for burglary, etc.: *Sun*, 4 March 2011.

AW goes on a binge: Winehouse; *Amy, My Daughter*.

Recording with Tony Bennett: *Daily Telegraph*, 28 July 2011.

Gordon Williams's reaction: author's interview.

Events of March, April and May 2011: second inquest. Dr Romete quoted from inquest evidence, including on bulimia, 'gone to the pub' and 'strongly worded' letter. Also Winehouse, *Amy, My Daughter*.

Trying to get AW to undergo DBT: evidence given by Dr Romete at the first inquest.

AW persuaded to go into Priory: thanks to Reg Traviss. Also Winehouse, *Amy, My Daughter*.

Thirteen: **The Glass is Run**

Epigraph: Chidiock Tichborne's elegy, written 1586, on the eve of his death in his early twenties, *The Oxford Book of English Verse*.

AW angry: Winehouse, *Amy, My Daughter*.

AW discharges herself from Priory and resumes drinking: Dr Romete, quoted from second inquest.

Jokes about doctor's warning: Troy Miller, quoted throughout from author's interview.

East-European tour: Winehouse, *Amy, My Daughter*. Raye Cosbert declined requests for an interview.

Belgrade ticket sales: *Blic*, 30 March and 10 June 2011 (by which date it was reported that 11,000 tickets had already been sold).

100 Club: Troy Miller and Reg Traviss, quoted throughout from author's interviews. Dr Romete gives medication: second inquest.

AW changes mind about tour: Winehouse, *Amy, My Daughter*.

Hotel arrangements: *Blic*, 10 June 2011.

Belgrade show: footage posted on YouTube and widespread press coverage in the UK and abroad (20 June 2011); author's interview with Troy Miller.

Claim AW pushed on stage: *Sun*, 22 June 2011.

Lyric quoted from 'Tears Dry on Their Own' by Amy Winehouse, Nickolas Ashford and Valerie Simpson © EMI Music Publishing, Jobete Music Inc. and Jobete Music (UK) Ltd.

Lyric quoted from 'Some Unholy War' by Amy Winehouse © EMI Music Publishing.

Lauren Franklin: quoted from author's interview.

Lyric quoted from 'You Know I'm No Good' by Amy Winehouse © EMI Music Publishing.

Reg Traviss: quoted throughout from author's interviews.

AW returns home/can't remember show: evidence at second inquest.

Looks at YouTube and becomes reflective: Winehouse, *Amy, My Daughter*.

Jonathan Winehouse: quoted from author's interviews.

Blake jailed: *Daily Mail*, 22 June 2011; author's prison visit and correspondence.

Sam Shaker conversation: quoted from author's interview with Shaker.

Final days: sources include inquest evidence (first and second, including statements of Andrew Morris and Dr Romete), and author's interviews with Reg Traviss.

Doug Charles-Ridler: quoted throughout from author's interview.

Tyler James away: his agent, Hamish Twist.

Naomi Parry footnote: author's correspondence.

Screams: anonymous neighbour quoted in the *Sunday Express*, 24 July 2011. The author spoke to all the neighbours and found no corroboration. Thanks to Catherine Hays and Professor Jones (both quoted).

Janis Winehouse's final visit and conversation with daughter: *Mail on Sunday*, 18 September 2011.

Ricardo Canadinhas and Doug Charles-Ridler: quoted from author's interviews.

Final hours: author's interviews with Reg Traviss and inquest evidence (Andrew Morris and Dr Romete quoted from both).

Dialogue with Death: Ingmar Bergman, *The Seventh Seal* (1957).

AW funeral: author's field notes at the funeral and interviews with Lauren Franklin, Rabbi Hellner and Reg Traviss; press coverage in the *Sun* and other papers, 27 July 2011.

Wake: author's field notes at the wake and interviews with fans on the night.

Epilogue: **The Dance of Death**

Epigraph: Henri Cazalis, 'Danse Macabre'

Merchandising: author's field notes during the researching of this book in the UK, USA and France.

Cotchford Farm: thanks to Alastair Johns (quoted).

Cheltenham Cemetery: author's field notes at the grave in 2012.

Eric Burdon on TV: *Daily Mirror*, 22 September 1970.

Noel Redding's murder theory: Redding, *Are You Experienced?*

Monika Dannemann interviews: *Hello!*, 26 February 1994, for example.

The Dannemann–Etchingham dispute is detailed in Etchingham, *Through Gypsy Eyes*.

Dannemann's court defeat and suicide: *Guardian* and *Daily Telegraph*, 6 April 1996.

JH estate: author's interviews with Alan Douglas and Janie Hendrix (both quoted). Background reading includes Murray, *Crosstown Traffic*; Cross, *Room Full of Mirrors*.

JH's grave: author's field notes at his grave in 2012. Thanks to staff at Greenwood Memorial Park, Renton, Washington.

JJ's remains scattered at sea: her will.

Bob Gordon, Lyndall Erb, Ken Pearson and Sam Andrew on JJ: quoted from author's interviews. Thanks also to Don Hoyt and the Highland Gardens Hotel (formerly the Landmark).

Record sales: RIAA.

Ray Manzarek on life after JM: Manzarek, *Light My Fire*.

Death hoax: author's interview with Steve Harris.

Rock 'n' Roll Circus theory: author's conversation with Sam Bernett (quoted); Bernett, interview with the *Mail on Sunday*, 7 July 2007.

Alain Ronay: quoted from author's interview.

JM's grave: author's field notes at the grave in 2012, interviews at gravesite and discussions with staff.

The Doors shocked: Densmore, *Riders on the Storm*.

Andy Morrison: quoted from author's interview.

Dickie Davis: quoted from author's interview.

Kyle Fisher and Peter Niedner: quoted from author's interviews.

Densmore lawsuit: *Rolling Stone*, 22 August 2008.

Manzarek on Densmore: Manzarek, *Light My Fire*.

Jeff Jampol: quoted from author's interview.

EMP: author's field notes at the museum in 2012.

Nirvana lawsuits: *People*, 20 May 2002.

Frances Bean Cobain custody: *Daily Mail*, 15 December 2009; *Sun*, 18 August 2010. Courtney Love did not respond to interview requests.

Twitter fracas: *Rolling Stone*, 12 April 2012.

KC's ashes scattered: thanks to neighbour Inge Jones.

AW posthumous sales: *The Times*, 1 August 2011; *Daily Mail*, 25 July 2011; Billboard.com.

Mitch Winehouse has idea for Amy Winehouse Foundation on plane: Winehouse, *Amy, My Daughter*. Her voice came to him in New York: BBC Breakfast, 19 February 2013.

The Amy Winehouse Foundation was registered with Companies House on 12 August 2011, later with the Charity Commission. Charity Commission advice on setting up new charities is at www.charitycommission.gov.uk. Mitch Winehouse on how the foundation made him feel: www.thirdsector.co.uk, 12 November 2012.

Mitch Winehouse speculates on cause of AW's death: *Anderson Live*, 12 September 2011; *Piers Morgan Tonight*, 13 September 2011.

$50,000 fee: *USA Today*, 10 September 2011.

Two inquests: author's court notes. Thanks also to Georgia Graham of the *Camden New Journal.*

Suzanne Greenaway resigns: *Sun,* 2 January 2011.

Darcus Beese: quoted from *Guardian,* 18 November 2012.

AW's estate valued and distributed: HM Courts and Tribunals Service.

Alex Winehouse resigns as a director of the Amy Winehouse Charitable Foundation: Companies House (Co. No. 7737209, 20 April 2012).

Blake Fielder-Civil: author's meeting at HMP Leeds.

Reg Travis: quoted from author's interview.

AW's grave: thanks to Rabbi Hellner, Reg Traviss and Paul Van der Hulks at Edgwarebury Cemetery.

The closing quotation is from Shakespeare's *Cymbeline,* Act IV, scene ii.

Appendix: 27 Long-list

Selected sources are provided for brevity.

Alexander: Talevski, *Knocking on Heaven's Door*; Ambrose, *Gimme Danger: The Story of Iggy Pop.*

Amirian: online obituary and news reports: for example, *Valley News,* 20 February 2009.

Bashlachev: www.thesilverwings.tumblr.com.

Bell: Larkin (ed.), *The Encyclopedia of Popular Music*; press reports.

Belvin: Larkin (ed.), *The Encyclopedia of Popular Music.*

Boon: *Rolling Stone* obituary, 27 February 1986; Talevski, *Knocking on Heaven's Door.*

Chauvin: Sadie (ed.), *New Grove Dictionary of Music and Musicians.*

Christian: Larkin (ed.), *The Encyclopedia of Popular Music*; Talevski, *Knocking on Heaven's Door.*

Cobain: death certificate.

Courson: death certificate.

De Fleur: Larkin (ed.), *The Encyclopedia of Popular Music*; Talevski, *Knocking on Heaven's Door.*

de Freitas: death certificate.

Durham: Larkin (ed.), *The Encyclopedia of Popular Music*; www.findagrave.com.

Edwards: *Guardian* obituary, 26 November 2008.

Elizalde: *Los Angeles Times,* 26 November 2006; *Washington Post,* 9 April 2007.

Hale: Talevski, *Knocking on Heaven's Door.*

Ham: death certificate; press coverage including *Guardian*, 22 October 1999.

Hawkins: www.examiner.com.

Henderson: Talevski, *Knocking on Heaven's Door.*

Hendrix: death certificate.

Jaffe: *Melody Maker* obituary, 20 October 1945; Sadie (ed.), *New Grove Dictionary of Music and Musicians.*

Johnson: Pearson and McCulloch, *Robert Johnson: Lost and Found.*

Jones: death certificate; inquest bundle.

Joplin: death certificate.

Khumalo: report of death in the South African *Mail and Guardian*, 5 September 2006.

Köllen: Triumvirat.net; Talevski, *Knocking on Heaven's Door.*

Leonard: author's interview with her father, Bob Leonard.

Lewis: Talevski, *Knocking on Heaven's Door.*

McCabe: www.slendermusic.com.

McKernan: death certificate and *Rolling Stone* obituary, 12 April 1973.

Miller: Larkin (ed.), *The Encyclopedia of Popular Music.*

Morris: www.mydeathspace.com.

Morrison: death certificate.

Niec: www.legacy.com.

Ottoson: Segalstad and Hunter, *The 27s.*

Pfaff: *Rolling Stone*, obituary, 11 August 1994.

Pride: death certificate; Larkin (ed.), *The Encyclopedia of Popular Music*; online fan sites.

Rodgers: Talevski, *Knocking on Heaven's Door.*

Rudetsky: death certificate; press coverage including *Daily Express*, 22 December 1986.

Serrano Serrano: Segalstad and Hunter, *The 27s.*

Shari: Malaysian news sites including www.murai.com.my.

Smith: Larkin (ed.), *The Encyclopedia of Popular Music*; Talevski, *Knocking on Heaven's Door.*

Thain: inquest report, *Daily Mirror*, 11 February 1976; www.garythain. com.

Turner: *Guardian* obituary, 11 September 2011.

Walker: *New York Times*, 1 December 1995.

Ward: myspace; Segalstad and Hunter, *The 27s*.

Wilson: death certificate; de la Parra, *Living the Blues*.

Winehouse: death certificate; inquests.

Yohn: profile in *International Trumpet Guild Journal*, September 1997.

Zapata: news report in *Rolling Stone*, 2 September 1993.

BIBLIOGRAPHY

Alvarez, Al, *The Savage God: A Study of Suicide*, London: Bloomsbury, 2002 (1st edn, 1971)

Ambrose, Joe, *Gimme Danger: The Story of Iggy Pop*, London: Omnibus, 2004

Augarde, Tony (ed.), *The Oxford Dictionary of Modern Quotations*. Oxford: OUP, 1991

Azerrad, Michael, *Come As You Are: The Story of Nirvana*. London: Virgin, 1993

Barak, Daphne, *Saving Amy*, London: New Holland, 2010

Boswell, James (John Canning, ed.), *The Life of Samuel Johnson*, London: Softback Preview, 1996

Brown, Tony, *Hendrix: The Final Days*, London: Rogan House, 1997

Burdon, Eric, with J. Marshall Craig, *Don't Let Me Be Misunderstood*, New York: Thunder's Mouth Press, 2001

Byrne Cooke, John, *Janis Joplin: A Performance Diary 1966–70*, Petaluma (USA): Acid Test Productions, 1997

Cobain, Kurt, *Journals*, London: Penguin, 2003 (1st edn, 2002)

Cross, Charles R., *Heavier Than Heaven: The Biography of Kurt Cobain*, London: Hodder & Stoughton, 2002

Cross, Charles R., *Room Full of Mirrors: A Biography of Jimi Hendrix*, London, Sceptre, 2005

Dalton, David, *Piece of My Heart: On the Road with Janis Joplin*, London: Marion Boyars, 2000 (1st edn, 1972)

Dante Alighieri (trans. Dorothy L. Sayers), *The Divine Comedy: 1. Hell*, Harmondsworth: Penguin, 1949

Davis, Stephen, *Old Gods Almost Dead: The 40-Year Odyssey of the Rolling Stones*, London: Aurum, 2002

Davis, Stephen, *Jim Morrison*, New York: Penguin, 2004

de la Parra, Fito, with T. W. and Marlene McGarry, *Living the Blues: Canned Heat's Story of Music, Drugs, Death, Sex and Survival*, privately published in USA, Canned Heat Music, 2010

Densmore, John, *Riders on the Storm: My Life with Jim Morrison and the Doors*, London: Arrow Books, 1991

Doors, The, with Ben Fong-Torres, *The Doors*, New York: Hyperion, 2006

Durkheim, Émile, *On Suicide*, London: Penguin, 2006 (1st edn, 1897)

Echols, Alice, *Scars of Sweet Paradise: The Life and Times of Janis Joplin*, London: Virago, 1999

Eliot, T. S., *Collected Poems 1909–1962*, London: Faber and Faber, 1963

Erlandson, Eric, *Letters to Kurt*, New York: Akashic Books, 2012

Etchingham, Kathy, *Through Gypsy Eyes*, London: Orion, 1999

Faithfull, Marianne, *Faithfull*, Harmondsworth: Penguin, 1995

Fitzgerald, F. Scott, *The Lost City: Personal Essays 1920–40*, Cambridge: Cambridge University Press, 2005

Frazer, Sir James George, *The Golden Bough*, New York: Collier Books, 1963 (1st edn, 1922)

Freud, Sigmund, *Beyond the Pleasure Principle*, London: Vintage, 2001 (1st edn, 1920)

Friedman, Myra, *Buried Alive: A Biography of Janis Joplin*, London: W. H. Allen, 1974

Frum, David, *How We Got Here: The '70s*, New York: Basic Books, 2000

Giuliano, Geoffrey, *Paint it Black: The Murder of Brian Jones*, London: Virgin, 1994

Graham, Bill, and Robert Greenfield, *Bill Graham Presents: My Life Inside Rock and Out*, New York: Doubleday, 1992

Grashoff, Udo, *Let Me Finish*, London: Headline Review, 2006

Halperin, Ian and Max Wallace, *Who Killed Kurt Cobain?*, London: Blake, 2002

Hill, George Birkbeck (ed.), *Johnsonian Miscellanies* (Vols I and II), London: Constable, 1966 (1st edn, 1897)

Hopkins, Jerry, with Danny Sugerman, *No One Gets Out of Here Alive*, London: Plexus, 1980

Hume, David, *On Suicide*, London: Penguin, 2005

Jackson, Laura, *Brian Jones: The Untold Life and Mysterious Death of a Rock Legend*, London: Piatkus, 2009 (1st edn, 1992)

Jagger, Mick, *et al.* (eds Dora Loewenstein and Philip Dodd), *According to the Rolling Stones*, London: Phoenix, 2004

Johnstone, Eve C. *et al.* (eds), *Companion to Psychiatric Studies*, Edinburgh: Churchill Livingstone, 2010

Johnstone, Nick, *Amy, Amy, Amy: The Amy Winehouse Story*, London: Omnibus, 2008

Joplin, Laura, *Love, Janis*, New York: HarperCollins, 2005 (1st edn, 1992)

Kierkegaard, Søren (eds Howard V. Hong and Edna H. Hong), *The Essential Kierkegaard*, Princeton: Princeton University Press, 1978

Larkin, Colin (ed.), *The Encyclopedia of Popular Music*, Oxford: OUP, 2006

Larkin, Philip, *Collected Poems*, London: Faber and Faber, 2003

Lindsay-Hogg, Michael, *Luck and Coincidence: A Coming of Age in Hollywood, New York and Points Beyond*, New York: Knopf, 2011

Loog Oldham, Andrew, *Stoned*, London: Secker & Warburg, 2000

Loog Oldham, Andrew, *2 Stoned*, London: Secker & Warburg, 2002

Manzarek, Ray, *Light My Fire: My Life with the Doors*, London: Arrow Books, 1999

McNally, Dennis, *A Long Strange Trip: The Inside History of the Grateful Dead and the Making of Modern America*, London: Corgi Books, 2009

Melville, Herman, *Moby-Dick*, New York: Penguin, 2001 (1st edn, 1851)

Milne, A. A., *The House at Pooh Corner*, London: Egmont, 2004 (1st edn, 1928)

Mitchell, Mitch, and John Platt, *The Hendrix Experience*, London: Hamlyn, 1990

Murray, Charles Shaar, *Crosstown Traffic: Jimi Hendrix and Post-War Pop*, London: Faber and Faber, 2001

Nietzsche, Friedrich (trans. Walter Kaufmann), *Basic Writings of Nietzsche*. New York: Modern Library, 1992

Nietzsche, Friedrich (trans. Graham Parkes), *Thus Spake Zarathustra*, Oxford: OUP, 2005

Norman, Philip, *Symphony for the Devil: The Rolling Stones Story*, London: Linden Press, 1984

Novoselic, Krist, *Of Grunge and Government*, New York: RDV Books, 2004

Pearson, Barry Lee, and Bill McCulloch, *Robert Johnson Lost and Found*, Chicago: University of Illinois Press, 2003

Peters, Dr Michael, *BMA A–Z Family Medical Encyclopedia*, London: Dorling Kindersley, 2008

Rawlings, Terry, *Who Killed Christopher Robin? The Murder of Brian Jones*, London: Helter Skelter, 2005 (1st edn, 1994)

Redding, Noel, and Carol Appleby, *Are You Experienced? The Inside Story of the Jimi Hendrix Experience*, London: Fourth Estate, 1990

Richards, Keith, with James Fox, *Life*, London: Weidenfeld & Nicolson, 2010

Ricks, Christopher (ed.), *The Oxford Book of English Verse*, Oxford: OUP, 1999

Riordan, James, and Jerry Prochnicky, *Break on Through: The Life and Death of Jim Morrison*, London: Plexus, 1991

Sadie, Stanley (ed.), *The New Grove Dictionary of Music and Musicians*, London: Macmillan, 2001

Schopenhauer, Arthur (ed. Wolfgang Schirmacher), *The Essential Schopenhauer*, New York: Harper Perennial, 2010

Segalstad, Eric, and Josh Hunter, *The 27s: The Greatest Myth of Rock 'n' Roll*, Berkeley Lake (USA): Samadhi Creations, 2008

Seneca (trans. John Davie), *Dialogues and Essays*, Oxford: OUP, 2007

Seneca (trans. Richard M. Gummere), *Epistles* and *Moral Essays*, Loeb Classical Library series, Cambridge, Mass.: Harvard University Press, 1917

Sounes, Howard, *Seventies*, London: Simon & Schuster, 2006

Sounes, Howard, *Fab: An Intimate Life of Paul McCartney*, London: HarperCollins, 2010

Spiegelman, Art, *The Complete Maus*, London: Penguin, 2003 (1st edn, 1996)

Stone, Geo, *Suicide and Attempted Suicide*, New York: Carroll & Graf, 1999

Strong, Martin C., *The Essential Rock Discography*, Edinburgh: Canongate, 2006

Talevski, Nick, *Knocking on Heaven's Door*, London: Omnibus, 2006

Thwaite, Ann, *A. A. Milne, His Life*. London: Faber and Faber, 1990

Tolstoy, Leo, *War and Peace*, London: J. M. Dent & Sons, 1932

True, Everett, *Nirvana: The True Story*, London: Omnibus, 2006

Whitburn, Joel, *Billboard Book of Top 40 Hits*, New York: Billboard, 1996

Winehouse, Mitch, *Amy, My Daughter*, London: HarperCollins, 2012

Wohlin, Anna, with Christine Lindsjöö, *The Murder of Brian Jones*, London: Blake, 2000

Wyman, Bill, with Ray Coleman, *Stone Alone: The Story of a Rock 'n' Roll Band*, London: Viking, 1990

INDEX

PICTURE ACKNOWLEDGEMENTS

© Corbis: 1 (bottom left)/photo Michael Ochs Archives, 4 (bottom)/ photo Ted Streshinsky, 12 (bottom)/photo Alain Ronay. © Getty Images: 1 (top)/photo Paul Popper & (bottom right)/photo Marjorie Alette, 5 (top)/photo Mark and Colleen Hayward, 6 (top right)/photo Michael Buckner, 7 (bottom)/photo Gareth Cattermole, 8/photo Jon Furniss, 11 (bottom)/photo Jan Persson, 12 (top)/photo Estate of Edmund Teske/ Michael Ochs Archives, 13 (bottom)/photo Jeff Kravitz, 15 (top)/photo Danny Martindale. © Youri Lenquette: 14 (top). © Gered Mankowitz/ Bowstir Ltd 2013/www.mankowitz.com: 4 (top). © Mirrorpix: 9 (bottom), 16 (bottom)/photo Jason Shillingford. © Photoshot: 5 (bottom right)/ photo Retna/Ian Tilton & (bottom left)/photo Starstock/David Wimsett, 9 (top)/photo LFI, 11 (top)/photo Retna/Vanit. © Press Association Images: 10 (bottom), 16 (top)/photo Dominic Lipinski. © Rex Features: 2 (top & bottom), 3 (top), 7 (top)/photo Richard Young, 10 (top)/photo Daily Mail, 14 (bottom)/photo Sipa Press, 15 (bottom)/photo Brian Rasic. © Ian Tilton/www.iantilton.net: 13 (top). © WENN: 3 (bottom). © Lou Winwood: 6 (top left). © Xposure: 6 (bottom).

Chapter headings: © AF Archive/Alamy. 'Dance of Death;' from Ingmar Bergman's film *The Seventh Seal* (1957)

Every reasonable effort has been made to contact the copyright holders, but if there are any errors or omissions, Hodder & Stoughton will be pleased to insert the appropriate acknowledgement in any subsequent printing of this publication.